ANGLO-AMERICAN LIFE INSURANCE, 1800–1914

CONTENTS OF THE EDITION

VOLUME 1
General Introduction
What is Life Insurance? Why Should You Insure?
Selling Life Insurance to the Public

VOLUME 2
Running a Life Insurance Company

VOLUME 3
Mortality and Risk
Index

ANGLO-AMERICAN LIFE INSURANCE, 1800–1914

Volume 1
What is Life Insurance? Why Should You Insure?
Selling Life Insurance to the Public

Edited by
Timothy Alborn and Sharon Ann Murphy

Routledge
Taylor & Francis Group

LONDON AND NEW YORK

First published 2013 by Pickering & Chatto (Publishers) Limited

Published 2016 by Routledge
2 Park Square, Milton Park, Abingdon, Oxfordshire OX14 4RN
711 Third Avenue, New York, NY 10017, USA

First issued in paperback 2015

Routledge is an imprint of the Taylor & Francis Group, an informa business

BRITISH LIBRARY CATALOGUING IN PUBLICATION DATA

Anglo-American life insurance, 1800–1914.
1. Life insurance – Great Britain – History – 19th century – Sources. 2. Life
insurance – United States – History – 19th century – Sources.
I. Alborn, Timothy L., 1964– editor of compilation. II. Murphy, Sharon Ann,
1974– editor of compilation.
368.3'2'00941'09034-dc23

ISBN-13: 978-1-138-66046-5 (pbk)
ISBN-13: 978-1-1387-5019-7 (hbk)
ISBN-13: 978-1-84893-352-1 (set)

Typeset by Pickering & Chatto (Publishers) Limited

CONTENTS

Acknowledgements   ix
General Introduction   xi

Introduction   xxv
Bibliography   xxxiii

I. Guides and Prospectuses
  British Life Insurance in the 1840s   1
    Richard Morgan, *Familiar Observations on Life Insurance* (1841),
      Chapter 4   3
    *Life Insurance Offices, New and Speculative, with a Table of the
      Inducements Held Out by Each of the Existing Offices* (1846),
      excerpt   13
  The Emergence of American Life Insurance   21
    'Securitas', 'Life Insurance', *Connecticut Courant* (1833)   23
    T. R. Jencks, 'Life Insurance in the United States, Number I',
      Hunt's Merchants' Magazine and Commercial Review (1843)   27
    T. R. Jencks, 'Life Insurance in the United States, Number II',
      Hunt's Merchants' Magazine and Commercial Review (1843)   53
  Early Prospectuses   69
    William Frend, *Rock Life Assurance Company* (1809)   71
    *An Address from the President and Directors of the Pennsylvania
      Company for Insurances on Lives and Granting Annuities to the
      Inhabitants of the United States, upon the Subject of the Beneficial
      Objects of that Institution* (1814)   79
  Proposals and Rates of the Standard Life Assurance Company (1833)   89
  New American Prospectuses   111
    William Bard, *A Letter to David E. Evans, Esquire, of Batavia,
      on Life Insurance* (1832)   113
    *Life Insurance: Its Principles, Operations and Benefits, as Presented
      by the North Carolina Mutual Life Insurance Company* (1849)   121
    John Freestone, *Where to Insure: An Impartial and Independent
      Guide* (1890), excerpt   137

II. Religion and Domesticity
   Religion and Life Insurance in America   147
      *Charter of the Corporation for the Relief of the Widows and Children
        of Clergymen* (1769), excerpt   149
      'Life Insurance', *Religious Intelligencer* (1835)   151
      'Life Insurance – Ministers', *Christian Secretary* (1847)   153
      'Life Insurance – A Scruple', *Christian Secretary* (1847)   157
      'Life Insurance of Ministers', *Christian Secretary* (1847)   161
   'Prospectus of the Dissenters' and General Life and Fire Assurance
      Company', *Eclectic Review* (1839), excerpt   165
   Life Insurance as a Domestic Duty   179
      'Life Insurance', *Macon Weekly Telegraph* (1838)   181
      John Neal, 'Life Assurance', *Columbian Lady's and Gentleman's
        Magazine* (1846)   183
      Arthur Scratchley, *Observations on Life Assurance Societies, and
        Savings Banks* (1851), excerpt   193
      Arthur Reade, 'Before the Wedding Ring', *Policy-holder:
        An Insurance Journal* (1885)   199

III. Varieties of Self-Help
   *Benefit Societies versus Saving Banks and Insurance Companies:
      An Address to the Members of Benefit Societies and the Public in
      General* (1822)   203
   Life Insurance and Savings Banks in America   213
      A. B. Johnson, 'The Relative Merits of Life Insurance and Savings
        Banks', *Hunt's Merchants' Magazine and Commercial Review*
        (1851)   215
      Joseph B. Collins, 'Life Insurance', *Hunt's Merchants' Magazine
        and Commercial Review* (1852)   225
   Insurance and Self-Help in Britain   229
      'Insurance amongst the Working Classes', *Economist* (1858)   231
      Frank Ives Scudamore, *Life Insurance by Small Payments: A Few
        Plain Words Concerning It* (1861)   235
   Insurance and Self-Help in America   241
      George D. Eldridge, 'Assessment Life Insurance', *North American
        Review* (1890)   243
      B. H. Meyer, 'Fraternal Beneficiary Societies in the United States',
        American Journal of Sociology (1901)   249

IV. New Markets

Josiah C. Nott, 'Statistics of Southern Slave Population, with Especial
    Reference to Life Insurance', *DeBow's Commercial Review* (1847)   261
W. E. Burghardt Du Bois (ed.), *Some Efforts of American Negroes for
    their Own Social Betterment* (1898), excerpt   281
Arthur Wyndham Tarn, 'Some Notes on Life Assurance in Greater
    Britain', *Journal of the Institute of Actuaries* (1899), excerpt   291
Industrial Insurance in Britain   307
    Joseph Burn, 'Industrial Life Assurance', *Journal of Federated
        Insurance Institutes* (1902)   311
    J. F. Williams, *Life Insurance of the Poor: An Illumination of
        Economic Disadvantage* (1912)   323
Industrial Insurance in America   331
    John F. Dryden, 'The Social Economy of Industrial Insurance:
        A Lecture Delivered before the Senior Class of Yale University,
        1904' (1909)   333
    Frederick Hoffman, *Life Insurance of Children* (1903)   345

V. Anglo-American Interlopers

[Pelican Life Insurance Company], 'Life Insurance. To Parents,
    Guardians, and Others, Desirous of Securing a Provision against
    Sudden Death', *New-York Evening Post* (1808)   365
The 'American Invasion'   369
    'The Equitable Life Assurance Society of the United States',
        advertisement, *Insurance Record* (1874)   373
    Joseph Allen, *There is Dust in John's Eyes; or, American and British
        Life Insurance Offices Contrasted* (1882)   375
    Book review of *There is Dust in John's Eyes*, *Post Magazine* (1882)   391
    'The Mutual's English Business', *Independent* (1906)   393

Editorial Notes   395
List of Sources   407

ACKNOWLEDGEMENTS

This collection emerged out of informal conversations we have been having since 2007, when we were both completing monographs on the history of life insurance: one on Britain in the long nineteenth century, and the other on antebellum America. Although we were aware at the time of the strong cross-currents between these two national cultures of life insurance, neither of us chose to pitch our books in an explicitly comparative framework. When Daire Carr from Pickering & Chatto approached each of us independently in the spring of 2011 about possible book projects, we decided that this would be a perfect opportunity to join forces and to begin considering some of the comparative questions that our books had left unexplored. Subsequent conversations with other Pickering & Chatto editors, including Ruth Ireland and Marina Pattenden, as well as valuable feedback from two anonymous referees, helped us refine our ideas regarding the selection of sources and aspects of the industry that would make it a truly Anglo-American collection. Janka Romero, who took over as our project editor in August 2012, has been extremely generous with her time and patience as we tied down the numerous loose ends that a collection of more than 150 documents inevitably engendered.

As we suggest in our General Introduction, historians of insurance comprise a very small community, and we have been fortunate to share many friends in this cohort. Tom Baker, formerly head of the University of Connecticut Insurance Law Center, was an invaluable facilitator of intellectual exchange during the period when we were both writing our monographs; we first met, in fact, at one of his workshops. Robin Pearson has worked just as hard to bring together insurance historians from around the world, and our many encounters with him have helped to shape our thinking about the subject. Geoffrey Clark, whose work on eighteenth-century life insurance both pre-dated and informed our own scholarship, has likewise been a strong supporter and good friend to both of us. Finally, we have both learned much from Dan Bouk, who finished his dissertation on late nineteenth-century American life insurance shortly after our own books appeared.

This was the first time either of us have ever co-edited or co-written anything, and not only did we value each other's frequent flexibility and patience, we also leaned heavily, at various times, on the patience and moral support of our loved ones. Tim's deepest thanks go out to Alix Cooper, whose warm companionship during his sabbatical brightened the tedium of tracking down footnotes and proofing primary sources. Sharon couldn't have completed this without the unwavering support of Ken Forziati, and of course, lots of smiles, giggles and hugs from Amalia and Cono.

GENERAL INTRODUCTION

The life insurance industry was one of the most important financial institutions of the long nineteenth century on both sides of the Atlantic. The British life insurance market grew steadily from a narrow aristocratic base in 1800, contributing over £500 million to the capital market by 1914 and extending its services throughout the British Empire. In the 1860s British companies also pioneered 'industrial insurance', which charged pennies per week to provide for burials in working-class families. Although appearing on the scene somewhat later in the nineteenth century, American life insurance had by the 1890s outstripped its British counterpart in overall volume of business, size of individual companies and per capita coverage: by 1912 it was the second largest financial intermediary in America (second only to commercial banks), and by the eve of the Great Depression there was roughly the equivalent of one life insurance policy for every man, woman and child living in the United States.[1]

Throughout the Anglo-American world, life insurance served a critical role in ameliorating many of the dislocations wrought by urbanization and industrialization. As an institution dedicated to publicizing the financial risks associated with premature death, life insurance also drew attention to death, domesticity and thrift in ways that alternately dovetailed with and departed from other nineteenth-century institutions that focused on these issues. The unique nature of life insurers' liabilities and the volume of business they generated posed new challenges to the emerging regulatory apparatus of the British and American states. And finally, life insurance contributed in significant ways to technical developments in statistics and medicine, as actuaries and medical advisers struggled to formulate prices and gatekeeping procedures that would preserve their companies' long-term financial fortunes.

Despite its central role in the Anglo-American economy and society, life insurance long remained one of the least-studied financial industries. This has started to change over the past few years, as scholarly interest in all aspects of the history of life insurance has grown rapidly across a wide variety of disciplines, including history, economics, business, sociology, literature and law. Recent monographs on the British industry include Geoffrey Clark's cultural history of eighteenth-century life insurance; Timothy Alborn's study of life insurance and British society in the long nineteenth century; and Robert L. Carter and Peter Falush's general survey of twentieth-century insurance.[2] On the American side there has been Sharon Ann Murphy's examination of the American industry from its origins through the 1860s; Eric Wertheimer's study of the 'poetics' of insurance from the 1720s through the 1870s; JoAnne Yates's account of life insurance and information technology in the twentieth century; and Daniel B. Bouk's recent dissertation which places life insurance in the context of the history of science and public health.[3] A few scholars have even begun examining the industry beyond the Anglo-American world, including Klasien Horstman on the Netherlands and Cheris Shun-ching Chan on China, while research into other regions such as Spain or Germany has appeared in edited volumes or as journal articles.[4]

This recent scholarship has substantially expanded our knowledge of the general contours of life insurance within different national contexts, and has at the same time rendered the significance of life insurance intelligible to scholars in a wide range of disciplines beyond business and economic history. This has marked a major advance over previous scholarship, which had either focused on individual companies, on a single aspect of the industry (typically marketing), or on relatively narrow questions of regulatory policy.[5] What has yet to be accomplished are comparative or synthetic approaches that build from these single-country studies; even on the few occasions when articles from a variety of locales are included in the same volume, they rarely engage in any comparative dialogue.[6]

This collection is the first major attempt at a truly comparative history of the British and American life insurance industries, which encompassed both the largest and most important life insurers in the world during the long nineteenth century. We have tried to accomplish this both through our running commentary on the varied primary sources, and by selecting sources that speak to one another across national boundaries. Given their common political, cultural, economic and linguistic roots, there was significant overlap in the histories of the industries in Britain and the United States. With its much older origins, the British industry served as a model for the development of American insurance at the beginning of the nineteenth century. And the free flow of periodicals and literature back and forth across the Atlantic meant that it was both easy to exchange ideas and hard to prevent negative news stories from becoming widespread. Into the mid-nineteenth century, for instance, American firms relied on mortality tables that had originally been generated for the British market, while a financial scandal that rocked American life insurance in 1905–6 led to sweeping reforms on both sides of the Atlantic.

Yet despite their numerous similarities, the industries that developed were distinct in a variety of ways. For example, the younger American firms were able to learn some valuable lessons from the mistakes of their British counterparts, creating an industry that avoided the most heinous associations with gambling that had plagued the British industry in the eighteenth century. The American industry also operated within a much more complicated legal environment, having to deal with disparate state laws rather than being regulated by a single office in London. Each industry also faced challenges distinct to their respective markets, such as the underwriting of slaves and Civil War soldiers in America or landed aristocrats in Britain. And as the American industry matured, the student at times became the teacher, taking the lead on a number of new innovations later adopted by its British counterpart. Variants of the 'tontine' policies that dominated American life insurance after 1870 appeared in Britain within a generation; and efforts to protect widows' benefits from creditors, which state legislatures initiated in the USA from the 1840s, eventually found footing in the UK as well.

Early Modern Origins and Nineteenth-Century Take-off

Life insurance was one of several forms of insurance that first emerged in seventeenth-century Europe, all of which responded to the contingencies accompanying large-scale commercial growth by tapping into the accompanying fund of social and financial capital that growth created. Throughout the eighteenth century two other forms of insurance, protecting against shipwreck and fire, predominated over life insurance as the most common forms of risk-pooling. All three types of insurance experienced rapid growth between 1690 and 1720, part of a more general boom in company formation that culminated in the so-called South Sea Bubble of 1720.[7] In the wake of the ensuing stock market crash, Parliament passed a law, the 'Bubble Act', that prohibited the formation of new companies. This law affected fire, marine and life insurance in very different ways: it encouraged a steady rise in fire coverage offered by companies that had survived the 1720 crash; it diverted marine coverage to private underwriters; and it stopped life insurance in its tracks for the next half-century.

As of 1720 the British fire insurance market was limited to a handful of chartered London companies, most notably the Sun and Hand in Hand, which took advantage of the Bubble Act to consolidate their control of the London market and expand outward from there. The Sun, in particular, used provincial agents to cover risks generated by industrialization in the northern counties, and London insurers continued to use their superior capitalization and risk-spreading capacity to thrive in provincial markets long after local competitors started to appear in the 1770s. In 1790 two dozen fire offices covered around a third of all insurable property in Britain; the number of offices rose to seventy by 1850, covering 56 per cent of the country's property – despite the fact that the government levied duties that doubled the average premium charged.[8] By this time several major Liverpool companies vied with the original London pace-setters in this market;

and these firms, along with more recently formed London companies like the Phoenix and Commercial Union, also excelled as exporters – hence contributing in no small measure to the substantial 'invisible exports' that helped balance Britain's trade deficit.[9]

This consistent growth in British fire insurance stood in sharp contrast to the American fire industry, which suffered a series of major failures during the nineteenth century. Initially hampered by strict regulations limiting out-of-state sales, most firms focused on a small geographic region until 1835, when a major conflagration in New York City demonstrated the danger of such concentrated coverage, bankrupting twenty-three of twenty-six companies. The industry that rose from these ashes was much more geographically diversified, yet intense competition during the 1850s and 1860s drove premiums well below safe levels; as a consequence the industry was again devastated by major fires in Chicago (1871) and Boston (1872).[10] As American fire underwriters reeled, the more stable British offices went from strength to strength. As of 1900 British firms earned two-fifths of their premium income in the United States, and the British share of the American market ranged between 20 and 30 per cent over the second half of the century.[11]

Two of the British fire offices that pre-dated the Bubble Act, the Royal Exchange and London Assurance, sold marine insurance as well; they in fact secured a clause in the Act preventing the formation of any partnerships (however small) to compete with that side of their business. This clause did not proscribe private underwriting, however, and the group of merchants that had long been congregating at Edward Lloyd's coffee house to arrange such transactions enjoyed a competitive advantage over the companies in terms of access to information and knowledge of the relevant risks. The result was that Lloyd's of London (the name stuck after Lloyd died in 1713) dominated British marine insurance well into the nineteenth century. Insurance against shipwreck developed along similar lines in the American colonies, with underwriters congregating in coffee houses in Philadelphia and New York. These individuals lacked both the capital and connections of their counterparts at Lloyd's, however, and when the Revolution ended the Bubble Act's sway in the United States, merchants pooled their wealth in joint-stock companies to cover marine risks. Starting with the Philadelphia-based Insurance Company of North America in 1792, marine insurance companies had the market to themselves throughout the nineteenth century.[12]

In contrast to fire and marine insurance, which grew steadily on both sides of the Atlantic from the late seventeenth into the nineteenth centuries, life insurance developed much more sporadically in Britain, and it had a minimal presence in America until 1830. Britain experienced a brief wave of interest in life insurance in the three decades after 1690, when associations like the Amicable Society for a Perpetual Assurance Office and the Society of Assurance for Widows and Orphans attracted thousands of middle-class Londoners with the promise of mutual protection against financial risk and mutual sharing in a growing investment fund. After 1720, however, this once-thriving market 'spent the next several decades adrift in the doldrums', to quote Geoffrey Clark. Only three of the companies that survived the South Sea crash sold life insurance (the Amicable, London Assurance and Royal Exchange), and all three saw sharp declines in new business. Moreover, many of the policies that were issued, both by these firms and by private individuals, were more in the nature of gambling transactions on third parties than protection against financial loss. As Clark has observed, this macabre form of gambling became a popular pastime among rakish Hanoverian aristocrats: a quarter of all bets in one gentleman's club in the 1770s were on the death of a third party, compared to only 2.5 per cent on horse races. Parliament finally intervened with the Gambling Act of 1774, which required all policyholders to state an 'insurable interest', or pre-existing financial stake, in the life of the party insured.[13]

It was not until 1762 that 'modern' life insurance, as we now think of it, began to appear on the scene, with the establishment of the Equitable Society in London. Formed under a deed of settlement, which circumvented the Bubble Act, the Equitable popularized the practice of charging level age-adjusted premiums throughout a policyholder's life, and it set these rates much lower than any that had been offered up to that time. The man behind the new premiums, Richard Price, based them on mortality statistics that had been collected in Northampton, which (he assumed) predicted death rates that were lower than those of the nation's insalubrious capital; he also assumed, correctly as it turned out, that the Equitable's selection of healthy lives would justify its lower rates. These 'Northampton Tables' remained the industry standard for more than fifty years, and set the Equitable on the road to market dominance for the rest of the century: as of 1800 it had issued nearly half of the roughly £10 million's worth of life insurance then in force.[14] That abruptly changed during the decade after 1800, which witnessed the formation of sixteen new life offices. By 1830, following another burst of company formation during the stock exchange boom of 1824–5, more than fifty companies sold life insurance in Great Britain – including several in Scotland and provincial England. Another company boom in the mid-1840s ushered in two decades' worth of volatile growth, culminating in the failure of two companies in 1869 and 1872, each of which had absorbed dozens of firms before going bankrupt. After this, the market stabilized and growth resumed at an accelerated pace, assisted by the appearance on the scene of 'industrial' insurance, which catered to a previously untapped working-class market. By the end of the century the London-based Prudential Life Assurance Company, which had pioneered industrial coverage in the 1860s, expanded into 'ordinary' business and became the leading British insurer, with a market share approaching 30 per cent.[15]

American life insurance lagged significantly behind Britain until 1830, when new companies in Philadelphia, Boston, New York and Baltimore – modelled on their British predecessors – lay the foundations of a stable industry and then began to grow the market. A new wave of American mutual life offices, which formed in the 1840s, overtook these firms by pairing the promise of institutional investment with that of financial security.[16] After relatively steady, sustained growth from the 1830s into the 1860s, followed by a major boom-and-bust cycle in the 1870s, three New York-based companies, the Mutual Life, Equitable Life Assurance Society and New York Life, emerged to dominate the American life insurance sector. These 'big three' firms also flexed their muscles overseas, with special strengths in continental Europe, Latin America and (to a lesser extent) Great Britain: as of 1905 they earned $47 million in foreign premium income – equivalent to one-eighth of the value of American manufactured exports – and at the turn of the century they controlled more than a third of the American life insurance market. They shared their leading position with two 'industrial' firms, Metropolitan Life and the Prudential Insurance Company of America, based in New York and Newark respectively. In one sense, American and British life insurance markets in 1900 were similarly oligopolistic, with the top five firms earning nearly half the overall premium income in each case. The 'other half' of the American market was much more diverse than was the case in Britain, however, since it included fraternal orders and 'assessment' offices (described below in the Introduction to Volume 1) as well as regional insurers from Maine to California.[17]

Especially in the United States, this collection of companies dramatically expanded the overall volume of life insurance sold and the number of customers served between 1850 and 1914. American life insurance in force (including industrial insurance) increased from less than $100 million (£20 million) to nearly $30 billion (£6 billion), while British coverage experienced a more modest increase from £150 million to £1.2 billion over the same period.[18] The primary engine of growth in both cases was the introduction of new products that combined the attraction of a mutual fund with the security of family provision. In Britain this took the form of endowment insurance, which combined a deferred annuity with a term life policy, the latter of which typically matured in twenty years – when most breadwinners started to worry more about retirement and less about the financial fate of their dependants. In the United States this took the form of 'tontine' or deferred dividend policies, which paid cash bonuses to customers who survived a predetermined period of time. The Prudential in Britain and the 'big three' in the United States pioneered and aggressively marketed these forms of insurance, which not only helped drive their financial success but also transformed the contours of the industry.[19]

On both sides of the Atlantic, life insurance was a largely unregulated affair during the first half of the nineteenth century. American offices often needed to conform to certain requirements in their state charters, and Scottish offices exercised surprisingly efficient self-regulation by means of an informal cartel starting in 1840; but by and large, policyholders were left up to their own devices. This first started to change in the United States in the 1850s and 1860s, with the establishment of state insurance departments that supervised company accounts with varying degrees of vigilance. Many of these regulators, however, lacked the resources or the integrity to prevent abuses, and a rush of new company formations after 1865 revealed cracks in this system: between 1868 and 1877 nearly a hundred American life insurers failed (about two-thirds of the industry). *Laissez faire*, which held sway in England through the 1860s, was no more effective at preventing system-wide failure, culminating in the insolvency between 1869 and 1872 of two companies, the Albert and European, which had absorbed a combined total of sixty-nine start-up companies over the previous decade, greatly magnifying the impact of their failures. Parliament intervened in the middle of this crisis with the Life Assurance Companies Act of 1870, drafted in close cooperation with commercial actuaries, which eventually restored stability to the industry.[20] The final significant regulatory moment for life insurance came in 1905–6, when a major scandal surrounding the investment practices of the leading American insurers led to a policy overhaul in most state insurance departments; a concurrent House of Lords investigation in Britain led to an updated Assurance Companies Act in 1909.[21]

By the end of the nineteenth century, several other forms of insurance had emerged to accompany marine, fire and life coverage. Among other varieties, companies formed to protect against financial losses caused by dishonest employees, diseased cattle, boiler explosions and broken plate glass. Accident insurance (known in the United States as casualty insurance) first appeared in the 1850s to cover railway passengers, then became a leading sector after the British Workman's Compensation Act (1906) and similar state-level American laws forced employers to seek coverage.[22] Many English insurers had long sold fire and life coverage under the same roof, or in linked companies, and for them it was an obvious move at the end of the century to add these new forms of insurance to their business, either by absorbing specialist offices or building from scratch; by 1938 these firms sold around two-thirds of all life insurance in Britain. In Scotland and the United States, in contrast, specialist life insurance offices remained the norm well into the twentieth century. Beginning with New York at mid-century and spreading to most other states in the aftermath of the Chicago and Boston fires, state laws in America banned multiline insurance companies until the mid-twentieth century.[23]

Developing on distinct yet intertwining paths, British and American life insurance enjoyed significant advantages over other national life insurance sectors throughout the nineteenth and into the twentieth century, both in terms of per capita coverage in their home markets and penetration into foreign markets. A study in 1887 (tracking data through 1883) revealed that British firms held 40 per cent of the world's £1.27 billion in life insurance coverage, with American firms close behind at 30 per cent; total coverage in the Anglo-American world (including Canada and Australia) was £939 million, or nearly three-fourths of the total. France and Germany lagged far behind, each with slightly less than 10 per cent of the world's market. Per capita, Britons in 1880 insured their lives for an average of £13.29, compared to £6.35 (or $31.76) in the United States and under £2.40 in France and Germany; and close to half of the world's 281 life offices in 1883 were British or American, down from nearly 70 per cent a decade earlier.[24] To the extent that French offices succeeded in developing an indigenous life insurance market, it was by means of linking insurance to pensions from an earlier date than had been the case in Britain; and Germany's strict protective laws after 1870 helped fuel rapid growth in the life insurance sector during the last quarter of the century. These two markets, at any rate, far outstripped the efforts of life insurance offices (as well as other forms of insurance) in Russia, Italy and Spain during the nineteenth century.[25]

Plan of the Collection

Our collection consists of three volumes that are arranged thematically, with a loose chronological trajectory within each volume. Since its main object is a comparative history of life insurance in Britain and America, we have grouped the documents so as to highlight most effectively the similarities, differences and reciprocal interactions of the two industries. Throughout, our choice of sources reflects the wider-angle view of life insurance that has emerged in recent scholarship on the industry (including our own). Although we have included much material that will be familiar to the business historian, such as company prospectuses, legal documents and articles from trade journals, we have also devoted ample space to short fiction, light verse, popular exposés, and technical books and articles on medicine and statistics. Taken together, the collection represents a huge array of largely ephemeral documents, which attests to the paradoxical sense in which life insurance in the nineteenth century (as is the case today) was a pervasive part of people's everyday lives, yet seldom thought of by most people most of the time. These documents reflect efforts of insurance salesmen to get customers to pay attention to them; efforts of company lawyers and directors to get the government to understand their point of view; and efforts by those outside the industry to figure out what made life insurance tick.

Volume 1, *What is Life Insurance?*, most directly addresses this issue of life insurance's public face, in documents that reveal how the industry sought to define and market life insurance to the public. The first set of texts samples mid-nineteenth-century prospectuses and guides to life insurance in Britain and the United States, indicating the sort of information that was accessible to people who wanted to know how the business worked and how to distinguish among the growing array of different offices. The second and third sets locate life insurance in the context of nineteenth-century attitudes towards religion, domesticity and self-help, showing how commercial insurance companies managed to defend themselves against charges of irreligion, cloak themselves in the Victorian cult of domesticity, and compete successfully with alternative self-help institutions such as savings banks and friendly societies. A fourth set traces the extension of life insurance from its middle-class roots into the British and American working classes through the rise of 'industrial insurance'; the antebellum insurance of slaves in the United States, and of African-Americans after the Civil War; and the spread of life insurance throughout the British Empire. Finally, we identify literal examples of Anglo-American life insurance, first with the early efforts of British firms to sell life insurance in the USA, then with the more successful 'invasion' of the British market by several American firms at the end of the nineteenth century.

Besides catering to customers who numbered in the millions by the 1850s, life insurance offices also employed a growing army of clerks, agents, investment analysts and lawyers; they also increasingly occupied the attention of government regulators. Volume 2, *Running a Life Insurance Company*, reveals similarities and contrasts between how this varied labour force came together on both sides of the Atlantic, and differences in timing and policy regarding life insurance regulation. Topics include how life insurance companies organized their office staff and sales force; the tools they used and the buildings in which they worked; what they did with their accumulated funds, and how they marketed these investment strategies to their customers; the recurring spectre of company failures; and the ongoing dialogue between life insurance executives and government regulators over questions of accountability and the protection of dependents' benefits from their creditors.

Finally, Volume 3 examines issues of *Mortality and Risk*, including the collection of data and the development of mortality tables; the evolution of the medical exam and the use of medical statistics in risk assessment; the evaluation of risk factors such as disease, personal habits, climate and occupation; and the conundrums of suicide cases, gambling, fraud and murder. This volume complements *The History of Actuarial Science*, a ten-volume primary source collection published by Pickering & Chatto in 1995.

The types of documents included in these three volumes vary widely: they include accounts of life insurance in popular newspapers and magazines, company publications that were distributed extensively to the public, internal publications on the operations of an insurance office, and dialogues among industry executives and professionals in specialized insurance publications. The majority of these documents are relatively rare and difficult to obtain. Most either shed new light on corners of the history of life insurance that have only recently been examined in any detail, or foreground comparative questions about the development of life insurance in its two largest nineteenth-century markets.[26] In our introductory notes, we have provided some partial (and often still speculative) explanations for the differences that emerged in the respective trajectories of British and American life insurance, and we have also indicated various lines of communication back and forth across the Atlantic. Above all, however, we intend this collection as fodder for a wider, and we hope long-lasting, conversation that will move the history of this important sector beyond its traditionally national boundaries.

Note on Textual Principles

Every effort has been made to reproduce these texts as closely to the originals as possible without actually replicating the original typography. Original spelling, capitalization and punctuation have been retained, and only the most significant typographical errors have been amended where they undermine the understanding of the text. Please note that there can be significant variances not only between different editions of texts but also between individual extant copies. We have proofed our texts against a single original source, and we give details of those sources at the end of each volume. Any variances between our printed text and other original texts have to be considered in this light. The original pagination of the text is indicated by the inclusion of / within the text at the point of the original page break. Any sections omitted from the text are indicated by [...]. Any other editorial interventions are also contained within square brackets.

Note on Currency

For most of the period covered in this collection, the pound sterling was worth approximately five United States dollars. In our introductory notes we have used pounds or dollars to refer to premiums and policy values, depending on which country we are discussing, and we have usually left it up to the reader to convert to the other currency. Americans have used a decimal currency throughout their history; the British, from 1816 until 1971, divided the pound into twenty shillings and divided the shilling into twelve pence. Although we sometimes express fractions of pounds in decimal form in our headnotes, we have preserved the original reference to shillings and pence in the documents we have selected. Britain switched from minting guineas, worth twenty-one shillings, to sovereigns, worth twenty shillings, in 1816. Although most of our documents were published after that date, many still refer to guineas, which continued to circulate in people's memory, and continued to be used to set many professional fees: British doctors, for instance, commonly charged a guinea (twenty-one shillings) for their consultations.[27]

Notes

1. H. E. Krooss and M. R. Blyn, *A History of Financial Intermediaries* (New York: Random House, 1971), p. 122.

2. G. Clark, *Betting on Lives: The Culture of Life Insurance in England, 1695–1775* (Manchester: Manchester University Press, 1999); T. Alborn, *Regulated Lives: Life Insurance and British Society, 1800–1914* (Toronto: University of Toronto Press, 2009); and R. L. Carter and P. Falush, *The British Insurance Industry since 1900: The Era of Transformation* (London: Palgrave Macmillan, 2009).

3. S. A. Murphy, *Investing in Life: Insurance in Antebellum America* (Baltimore, MD: Johns Hopkins University Press, 2010); E. Wertheimer, *Underwriting: The Poetics of Insurance in America, 1722–1872* (Stanford, CA: Stanford University Press, 2006); J. Yates, *Structuring the Information Age: Life Insurance and Technology in the Twentieth Century* (Baltimore, MD: Johns Hopkins University Press, 2005); D. B. Bouk, 'The Science of Difference: Developing Tools for Discrimination in the American Life Insurance Industry, 1830–1930' (PhD dissertation, Princeton University, 2009).

4. K. Horstman, *Public Bodies, Private Lives: The Historical Construction of Life Insurance, Health Risks, and Citizenship in the Netherlands, 1880–1920* (Rotterdam: Erasmus Publishing, 2001); C. S. Chan, *Marketing Death: Culture and the Making of a Life Insurance Market in China* (Oxford: Oxford University Press, 2012).

5. The best company studies have included: B. Supple, *The Royal Exchange Assurance: A History of British Insurance 1720–1970* (Cambridge: Cambridge University Press, 1970); C. Trebilcock, *Phoenix Assurance and the Development of British Insurance*, 2 vols (Cambridge: Cambridge University Press, 1985, 1999); A. Rapone, *The Guardian Life Insurance Company, 1860–1920: A History of a German-American Enterprise* (New York: New York University Press, 1987); and R. C. Buley, *The Equitable Life Assurance Society of the United States, 1859–1964* (New York: Appleton-Century-Crofts, 1967). On marketing, see J. O. Stalson, *Marketing Life Insurance: Its History in America* (Cambridge, MA: Harvard University Press, 1942), and V. A. R. Zelizer, *Morals and Markets: The Development of Life Insurance in the United States* (New Brunswick, NJ: Transaction Books, 1983). On life insurance regulation in the United States, see M. Keller, *The Life Insurance Enterprise, 1885–1910: A Study in the Limits of Corporate Power* (Cambridge, MA: Harvard University Press, 1963), and H. R. Grant, *Insurance Reform: Consumer Action in the Progressive Era* (Ames, IA: Iowa State University Press, 1979); and in Britain, see H. E. Raynes, *A History of British Insurance* (London: Pitman, 1950).

6. See e.g. G. Clark et al. (eds), *The Appeal of insurance* (Toronto: University of Toronto Press, 2010), which includes chapters on life insurance in Britain, Germany, Spain and the United States; and the Spring 2008 issue of the *Business History Review* (82:1), with articles on Britain, the United States and Spain. See also P. Borscheid and N. V. Haueter (eds), *World Insurance: The Evolution of a Global Risk Network* (Oxford: Oxford University Press, 2012). Although many of the contributions to this volume, which covers the rise of insurance in more than two dozen different countries, touch on life insurance, its

primary comparative focus is on globalization, which has historically been less prominent in life insurance than in other forms of insurance (e.g. fire, marine and reinsurance).

7. Supple, *Royal Exchange Assurance*, pp. 22–44.

8. R. Pearson, *Insuring the Industrial Revolution: Fire Insurance in Great Britain, 1700–1850* (Aldershot: Ashgate, 2004), chs 1, 3.

9. Trebilcock, *Phoenix Assurance*, vol. 1, pp. 244–331, and vol. 2, pp. 1–298; R. Pearson, 'United Kingdom: Pioneering Insurance Internationally', in Borscheid and Haueter (eds), *World Insurance*, pp. 67–97, on pp. 69–76.

10. D. Barinoff, 'Fire Insurance in the United States', in R. Whaples (ed.), *Online Encyclopedia of Economic and Business History* (2008), at http://eh.net/encyclopedia [accessed 28 March 2013].

11. Supple, *Royal Exchange Assurance*, p. 213; P. G. M. Dickson, *The Sun Fire Insurance Office 1710–1960: The History of Two and a Half Centuries of British Insurance* (London: Oxford University Press, 1960), p. 221.

12. C. Kingston, 'Marine Insurance in Britain and America, 1720–1844: A Comparative Institutional Analysis', *Journal of Economic History*, 67 (2007), pp. 379–409.

13. Clark, *Betting on Lives*, pp. 50, 54, 73–80, 187.

14. Supple, *Royal Exchange Assurance*, p. 111. On the Equitable, see M. E. Ogborn, *Equitable Assurances: The Story of Life Assurance in the Experience of the Equitable Life Assurance Society 1762–1962* (London: George Allen and Unwin, 1962). On Price, see P. Buck, 'People Who Counted: Political Arithmetic in the Eighteenth Century', *Isis*, 73 (1982), pp. 28–45.

15. Alborn, *Regulated Lives*, pp. 22–9; *Statements and Abstracts of Reports Deposited with Board of Trade under Life Assurance Companies Act* (London: HMSO, 1903), pp. 434, 436, 444.

16. Murphy, *Investing in Life*.

17. Keller, *The Life Insurance Enterprise*, pp. 81–2; *Bankers' Magazine*, 73 (1902), p. 149; A. D. Webb, *New Dictionary of Statistics* (London: George Routledge and Sons, 1911), p. 347; *Statements and Abstracts*, pp. 432–44.

18. S. A. Murphy, 'Life Insurance in the United States before World War I', in R. Whaples (ed.), *Online Encyclopedia of Economic and Business History* (2002), at http://eh.net/encyclopedia [accessed 28 March 2013]; Supple, *Royal Exchange Assurance*, pp. 112, 220; *Statements of Assurance Business under the First, Second and Third Schedules of the Assurance Companies Act, 1909, Deposited ... December, 1917* (London: HMSO, 1918), p. 792.

19. On endowment insurance, see Alborn, *Regulated Lives*, pp. 210–18; on tontine policies, see R. L. Ransom and R. Sutch, 'Tontine Insurance and the Armstrong Investigation: A Case of Stifled Innovation, 1868–1905', *Journal of Economic History*, 47 (1987), pp. 379–90.

20. Murphy, *Investing in Life*, pp. 97–121, 287–94; Alborn, *Regulated Lives*, pp. 53–70.

21. Keller, *The Life Insurance Enterprise*, pp. 245–84; Alborn, *Regulated Lives*, p. 72.

22. O. M. Westall, 'Entrepreneurship and Product Innovation in British General Insurance, 1840–1914', in J. Brown and M. B. Rose (eds), *Entrepreneurship, Networks and Modern Business* (Manchester: Manchester University Press, 1993), pp. 191–208; P. V. Fishback and S. E. Kantor, 'The Durable Experiment: State Insurance of Workers' Compensation Risk in the Early Twentieth Century', *Journal of Economic History*, 56 (1996), pp. 809–36.

23. Alborn, *Regulated Lives*, pp. 48–51; Supple, *Royal Exchange Assurance*, p. 441; S. A. Murphy, 'New York State Insurance Department', in P. Eisenstadt (ed.), *The Encyclopedia of New York State* (New York: Syracuse University Press, 2005), p. 778. Exceptions in Scotland included the North British & Mercantile and the Caledonian, both Edinburgh companies. The few American exceptions to this rule, like the National Union Life and

Limb Insurance Company organized during the midst of the Civil War, were only able to do so through the passage of special legislative statutes. See R. C. Buley, *The American Life Convention, 1906–1952: A Study on the History of Life Insurance* (New York: Appleton-Century-Crofts, 1953), pp. 74–5; and M. James, *The Metropolitan Life: A Study in Business Growth* (New York: Viking, 1947), p. 22.

24. M. Besso, 'Progress of Life Assurance throughout the World, from 1859 to 1883', *Journal of the Institute of Actuaries*, 26 (1887), pp. 426–37, on pp. 431–6.

25. A. Straus, 'France: Insurance and the French Financial Network', in Borscheid and Haueter (eds), *World Insurance*, pp. 118–42, on pp. 120–1; P. Borscheid, 'Germany: Insurance, Expansion, and Setbacks', in Borscheid and Haueter (eds), *World Insurance*, pp. 98–117, on pp. 99–105; and P. Borscheid, 'Europe: Overview', in Borscheid and Haueter (eds), *World Insurance*, pp. 37–66, on pp. 37–46.

26. We have also chosen documents that are not already available in three existing collections of primary sources related to life insurance, which have mostly focused on Britain and on the actuarial side of the business: D. Jenkins and T. Yoneyama (eds), *The History of Insurance* (London: Pickering & Chatto, 2000); R. Pearson and M. Freeman (eds), *The History of the Company* (London: Pickering & Chatto, 2006); and, as mentioned above, S. Haberman and T. A. Sibbett (eds), *The History of Actuarial Science* (London: Pickering & Chatto, 1995).

27. On this topic, see T. Alborn, 'Money's Worth: Morality, Class, Politics', in M. Hewitt (ed.), *The Victorian World* (London: Routledge, 2012), pp. 209–24, on p. 215.

INTRODUCTION: WHAT IS LIFE INSURANCE? WHY SHOULD YOU INSURE? SELLING LIFE INSURANCE TO THE PUBLIC

It is no accident that much of the focus in the history of life insurance has traditionally been on the marketing side of the business. This was the side that was (and still is) most generally available for public consumption, in contrast to the clerical, statistical and medical activity that went on behind closed office doors. Also, life insurance offices were notorious for pushing their various marketing envelopes more insistently and from an earlier period than many other industries – certainly in comparison to other providers of financial services. The conventional reason for this is that people needed to be convinced to buy life insurance more than other forms of insurance for which the risk was more tangible (fire or shipwreck, for instance), and certainly more than was the case with food, clothing or furniture. Life insurance marketers defined their task as the challenging one of persuading people that they might die at any moment, then reminding them of the financial devastation their premature death would produce. To make this case, they tapped into, but also helped to reshape, pervasive nineteenth-century attitudes about death, domesticity and investment – and about what happened when these three activities intersected.

In practice, this sales pitch varied a great deal depending on the life being insured. Among the landed aristocrats who comprised the bulk of the British market in the early nineteenth century, selling life insurance required little if any marketing at all, since most such policies protected creditors from the risk that premature death would deprive them of unpaid loan instalments. A conversation at the club between a lawyer and a lender was the usual means of selling these policies; and lenders were quite happy to pass this cost along to borrowers, who were generally in no position to refuse.[1] A different sort of marketing was also on display in the antebellum American South, where life insurance on slaves was, for all practical purposes, little different from other forms of property coverage. This was especially the case in cities like Baltimore and Richmond, where slave owners applied the same capitalist calculus to their human property as they did to their factories and warehouses. Slaves, in this case, had no more say than bales of cotton regarding the advisability of being insured.[2]

Starting in the 1830s in the United States, and by the 1860s in Britain, the primary focus of life insurance marketing was the middle class, broadly defined to include merchants, shopkeepers, professional men and (in America, at least) farmers. To win a share of this market, and to expand that market's overall size, companies appealed to two very different sides of human nature, which they presented as complementary but which often stood in tension with each other. The first of these, and the dominant sales pitch during the first half of the nineteenth century, appealed to the husband's duty to be a responsible breadwinner. The second, which emerged in the United States in the 1840s and gained primacy on both sides of the Atlantic after 1880, appealed to the opportunity to 'look out for number one' while still providing for one's family, by tapping into the investment potential of the insurance office's pooled capital. These two patterns (which we also explore in Volume 2 of this collection, when we examine different insurance products) formed the twin poles of life insurance marketing, which pamphlets, prospectuses and guides ceaselessly circumnavigated throughout the long nineteenth century.

A final set of customers, only appearing as a target of life insurance marketing after 1860, was the working poor, who comprised by far the largest share of the population in both Britain and the United States. Since most working families were unable to buy enough coverage to provide anything approaching long-term subsistence should the breadwinner die prematurely, so-called 'industrial' insurance companies focused instead on a contingency within their reach: a 'proper' burial for family members when they died. Although the handful of companies that figured out how to provide this service enjoyed phenomenal commercial success, their entry into this market accompanied a great deal of controversy. Insuring the lives of children, besides being of dubious legality, invited a barrage of criticism from child welfare advocates owing to the moral hazard of child neglect that this practice allegedly engendered. And moral reformers more generally faulted industrial insurance for encouraging working families to divert their hard-earned savings from food and shelter to what many in the middle classes saw as the unnecessary luxury of a fancy funeral.

Besides competing with one another, life insurance offices found themselves, at different points in time, in competition with other forms of self-help. These overlapping markets especially occurred among skilled workers, who had been clubbing together in friendly societies since the eighteenth century, and who became the beneficiaries of charitable savings banks soon after 1800. British life insurance offices tussled with both of these institutions in the middle third of the nineteenth century, in the course of making uncertain inroads into the working-class market, and American insurers waged a more strident war with savings banks during the same period.

Friendly societies (or fraternal benefit societies, as they were often called in the United States) largely complemented the efforts of life insurance offices into the 1860s, focusing on the contingencies of sickness and old age instead of premature death. Although this *détente* persisted in Britain into the twentieth century, American fraternal orders, together with some commercial assessment offices, began offering life insurance in the 1870s in an attempt to capitalize on the apparent weakness caused by the failure of many for-profit life insurers. Much to the consternation of the surviving insurance offices, these organizations thrived by selling what many viewed as actuarially questionable 'natural premium' policies, which charged members based on the number of policyholders dying each year rather than charging 'level' premiums for the entire term of the policy. Although most of these assessment offices faded quickly from the scene by 1900, many fraternal orders switched to level premiums and continued to play a major role in providing life insurance to their members. In Britain a different sort of competition abruptly emerged between friendly societies and industrial insurance offices in 1911, when the government invited both types of organizations to compete with each other in the administration of its new national health insurance programme.[3]

Besides convincing people to insure their lives, individual life offices also needed to convince them to insure with one office as opposed to another. In the first half of the nineteenth century, when life insurance was still poorly understood by large sections of the public, it was also necessary to teach people how it worked, why it worked, and what it was good for. The first section of this volume, 'Guides and Prospectuses', provides a small sample of the enormous parade of printed documents that these various objectives generated over the course of the nineteenth century. The first four documents, published between 1833 and 1846, provided prospective policyholders in Britain and the United States with overviews of the array of companies and available products on offer. Richard Morgan's *Familiar Observations on Life Insurance* and the anonymously authored *Life Insurance Offices, New and Speculative* were among several treatises produced in Britain during the 1840s that were intended to provide more or (often) less unbiased advice in a market that had grown to more than eighty companies. At that point in time no such full-length treatments of the topic existed in the United States, where a handful of companies handled around 1 per cent of the business that was being done in Britain. Instead occasional newspaper articles (such as that included here from the *Connecticut Courant*) and longer magazine articles (such as the two included here from *Hunt's Merchants' Magazine*) provided American consumers with information about what was, for them, a still-nascent financial service.[4]

The next five documents, published between 1809 and 1849, are prospectuses, circulated by life insurance offices to assist directors, shareholders and salesmen in the task of disseminating their own particular merits and the merits of life insurance more generally. Life offices continued to issue prospectuses throughout the rest of the nineteenth century (and into the twentieth), but by 1850 the standard format was in place; the only departures involved the addition of new products and schemes, many of which are discussed in Volumes 2 and 3 of this collection. Over the first half of the century, however, shifts in format and emphasis appeared, as can be seen by comparing early efforts by the Rock Life Assurance Company (London, 1809) and the Pennsylvania Company for Insurances on Lives (1814) with later prospectuses issued by the Edinburgh-based Standard Life (1833), the New York Life and Trust (1832) and the North Carolina Mutual Life Insurance Company (1849).

The final document in this section is also the only one published after 1850: John Freestone's *Where to Insure: An Impartial and Independent Guide* (London, 1890). This publication, and many guides like his, provided a similar service as that provided in the 1830s by Morgan and others, but drew from an important new source of data. In 1870 Parliament passed the Life Assurance Companies Act (discussed in more detail in Volume 2), which yielded a huge amount of difficult-to-decipher financial information concerning the dozens of companies in existence, and it was Freestone's self-appointed task to translate this information into language that prospective policyholders could use. Although few such guides were commercially published in the United States, state insurance commissioners provided a similar service by issuing clear statements of the financial position of life offices doing business in their states. In both cases, the newfound prominence of investment, alongside the older emphasis on financial security, was clear: Freestone spent much of his time comparing how much money the various offices were likely to add to the value of their customers' policies.

The second section of this volume, 'Religion and Domesticity', focuses on the appeal to domestic duty as an incentive to purchase life insurance. For the most part, this emphasis on moral responsibility rode a rising tide of religiosity in the nineteenth century, which has been well documented by historians of evangelical Christianity in Britain and of the Second Great Awakening in the United States.[5] Protestant churches recognized a financial as well as theological logic in encouraging their ministers to pool their resources while alive in order to prevent parishioners from caring for their widows and children if they died prematurely. As Geoffrey Clark has observed, this financial incentive to stamp life insurance with official religious approval was missing in France, where priests lacked dependants, and he has speculated that this may have inhibited growth of the industry there.[6] Whatever the reason, various Protestant religious groups in Britain and America heartily endorsed life insurance as a thoroughly Christian activity, and the first six documents in this section show that process at work. Two of them describe specific organizations: the Corporation for the Relief of the Widows and Children of Clergymen, founded in 1769 by American Anglicans, and the London-based Dissenters' and General Life and Fire Assurance Company, founded in 1837. Four other articles, from the *Religious Intelligencer* (a weekly published in New Haven, CT) and the *Christian Secretary* (a Baptist magazine based in Hartford, CT), illustrate supplementary efforts to bolster the religious rationale for life insurance and to fend off any potential doubts that insurance ran counter to God's will.

Closely linked with the claim that life insurance was a religious duty was the presentation of life insurance as a crucial aspect of domestic responsibility. Most company prospectuses from throughout the period made this claim, often dripping with melodramatic deathbed scenes and other scare stories about the fate of widows whose husbands had failed to insure their lives. But this facet of life insurance also echoed loudly in the widespread mid-nineteenth-century culture of domesticity that prevailed among the middle classes in the United States and Britain, and we have selected four documents that indicate some of these deeper resonances. A paragraph in a Georgia newspaper paired the untimely death of a local lawyer with a plea for breadwinners to insure their lives lest their own loved ones face a similar 'bitter hour of affliction'; an American novelist placed a wife's secret decision to insure her husband's life at the heart of a domestic set piece, the heroine of which is 'a young and fashionable, and up to a certain time, a frivolous and thoughtless woman'; a London barrister inserted a chapter on 'The Moral Urgency of Life Assurance' in the middle of a treatise otherwise concerned with company law and statistical tables; and a freelance writer published a short story in a Manchester insurance journal titled 'Before the Wedding Ring'. These examples, which could have been multiplied a hundredfold, appeared between 1838 and 1885 and encompassed a golden age of life insurance sentimentalism. All provide glimpses of the uniquely empowering status the insurance version of domesticity gave to women: not only were women often enlisted to help convince their husbands to insure their lives, they were also expected to be capable of managing the money that came with the policy should he die prematurely.

The third section in this volume locates life insurance in the wider nineteenth-century world of self-help. It opens with a pamphlet, *Benefit Societies versus Saving Banks and Insurance Companies*, which illustrates the three-way battle between these types of organization in Britain during the 1820s, a time when commercial insurance companies were starting to eye the working-class market. Crossing the Atlantic, a *Hunt's Merchant's Magazine* diatribe by the savings bank manager Alexander Bryan Johnson (1851) is paired with a response by Joseph Collins of the Mutual of New York that appeared in the same journal the following year; the vehemence of this exchange, which was typical of the interaction between American savings banks and life offices at mid-century, reached heights that were seldom seen in Britain. This difference reflected the wider reach of American savings banks, which attracted numerous middle-class customers, and the firmer establishment of life insurance offices in Britain as institutional investors at the time when savings banks first started to appear.

It was more common in Britain, after 1850, to see working-class thrift and life insurance as two sides of the same coin. An *Economist* editorial from 1858 described friendly societies as 'the Insurance Companies of the poorer classes' and combined a mildly scolding tone regarding the societies themselves with triumphalism concerning Britain's superior habits of thrift relative to other countries. A pamphlet by a British post office official, Frank Scudamore, similarly presented the state-operated savings bank as a natural ally of commercial life insurance, which could assist workers to buy insurance by channelling their savings into approved companies in the form of monthly premium payments.

A final pair of documents illustrates the continuing divergence between British and American patterns of interaction among life insurance and other forms of working-class self-help as the nineteenth century wound down. As mentioned above, so-called 'assessment companies', which barely existed in Britain, prospered in the United States from the 1880s into the 1890s. George Eldridge, the actuary of one of the leading assessment offices, praises their low premiums in an 1890 issue of the *North American Review*; and B. H. Meyer's account of 'Fraternal Beneficiary Societies', from the *American Journal of Sociology* in 1901, documents the rise in life insurance provision by American fraternal orders such as the Knights of Pythias and the Odd Fellows over the previous two decades. Although equivalent organizations were certainly not lacking in Britain – the Odd Fellows, in fact, originated there and had more than 700,000 British members in the 1890s – they almost entirely stayed out of the life insurance market.[7] The failure of either assessment offices or fraternal life insurance to catch on in Britain reflected higher levels of market saturation by British insurance companies, which prevented an opening for such new providers to appear, and the related factor of more rapid population growth in the United States, which produced new customers faster than existing companies could meet the demand.

Closely related to the issue of competing forms of self-help was the expansion of the life insurance market in Britain and the United States beyond its original focus on the middle classes (and, in Britain, beyond its earlier focus on the landed aristocracy). This expansion included new races, with the appearance in the United States first of slave insurance and then, after the Civil War, African-American life offices; new spaces, with the expansion into previously untapped markets across the British Empire; and new social classes, with the rise of industrial insurance. The many challenges and opportunities these new forms of insurance produced are the topic of the fourth section of this volume, 'New Markets'.

The first documents in this section discuss the insurance of African Americans before and after the Civil War. Although insuring the lives of slaves originated in Britain and France during the eighteenth century, this typically only covered their journey across the Atlantic Ocean and was included as a rider to marine policies.[8] This form of insurance disappeared when the British abolished the slave trade in 1808, and did not reappear in the Anglo-American world until American firms (like Baltimore Life beginning in the 1830s) started to sell insurance to slave owners. In its own way, this practice was as controversial as industrial insurance would later become: authors like the racial theorist Josiah Nott, whose 'Statistics of Southern Slave Population with Especial Reference to Life Insurance' (1847) is reprinted here, worried that premium rates on slaves – which were already significantly higher than those on whites – were still not adequate to cover their actual rates of mortality. After emancipation in 1865, white prejudice against insuring people of colour persisted, and African Americans responded by forming their own mutual societies; W. E. B. Dubois's inclusion of life insurance on a list of 'Efforts of American Negroes for their Own Social Betterment' (1898) charts the progress of this movement, as does an appended report on Virginia by the black educator James M. Colson.

Another new market for Anglo-American life insurance in the nineteenth century was the rest of the world, a large piece of which was the British Empire. The London actuary A. W. Tarn surveyed the colonial market in his article on 'Life Assurance in Greater Britain', published in 1899. Although relatively few British life insurers did much of their business abroad (in stark contrast to their counterparts in fire insurance), those that did were market leaders, including the Standard Life, Commercial Union and Norwich Union. All the 'big three' American companies traded even more aggressively on foreign soil, although they tended to focus more on Latin American and European business, leaving British colonies to British firms. For the most part, these latter firms played the role of pioneer, standing aside after a few decades when indigenous life insurance offices took over.

The final four documents in this section focus on industrial insurance. Joseph Burn of the Prudential, the company which pioneered that form of insurance in Britain and quickly grew into Britain's leading life insurance company in overall business, describes and defends the industry in a lecture from 1902; the barrister J. F. Williams provides a typical laundry list of middle-class qualms about companies like the Prudential in a pamphlet from 1912. On the American side, we offer two strident self-justifications of industrial insurance from John Dryden and Frederick Hoffman, a director and an actuary from the Prudential Insurance Company of America. Dryden lectured Yale students in 1904 regarding the history, scope, structure and positive social effects of the business, while Hoffman responded to critics who claimed that industrial insurance promoted child neglect.

The final section of this volume focuses on what happened when British life insurance companies sold their wares in the United States, and vice versa. Until American life insurance started to take off after 1830, British companies wrote a large (though difficult to document) share of the business, and an early advertisement by the London-based Pelican Life Assurance Company from 1808 announced this presence; the British share of the American market continued to hover around 5 per cent into the 1850s, then became negligible after the Civil War. American companies returned the favour in the 1870s, soon becoming the largest foreign life insurance presence in Britain, with around 5 per cent of the market; the closest contenders came from Canada and Australia. Although this was not a huge proportion in terms of overall market share, the American firms' new sales tactics and innovative products (both on display in an Equitable of New York advertisement from 1874) created significant levels of anxiety in Britain. *There is Dust in John's Eyes*, penned by the Halifax insurance broker Joseph Allen, illustrates an extreme form of this response; the *Post Magazine*'s equanimous review of his pamphlet was probably a more typical reaction. The relative success of American companies in Britain came to an abrupt end in 1906, when scandals surrounding the major New York firms created a backlash, and new American laws that capped their sales volumes led them to shed many of their foreign markets. The final article in this volume, from a Boston newspaper in 1906, reports on the efforts by a British office, the North British and Mercantile, to capitalize on the scandal and woo away customers from the Mutual of New York.

Notes

1. R. Pearson, 'Thrift or Dissipation? The Business of Life Assurance in the Early Nineteenth Century', *Economic History Review*, 43 (1990), pp. 236–54; Alborn, *Regulated Lives*, pp. 142–7.
2. S. A. Murphy, 'Securing Human Property: Slavery, Life Insurance, and Industrialization in the Upper South', *Journal of the Early Republic*, 25 (2005), pp. 615–52.
3. T. Alborn, 'Senses of Belonging: The Politics of Working-Class Insurance in Britain, 1880–1914', *Journal of Modern History*, 73 (2001), pp. 561–602.
4. The first full-length accounts of the American industry would not appear until the 1850s, the two most well known being H. G. Tuckett, *Practical Remarks on the Present State of Life Insurance in the United States. Showing the Evils which Exist, and Rules for Improvement* (Philadelphia, PA: Published by the Author, 1851); and M. L. Knapp, *Lectures on the Science of Life Insurance* (Philadelphia, PA: E. S. Jones & Co., 1853).
5. On Britain, see C. Brown, *The Death of Christian Britain: Understanding Secularisation 1800–2000* (London: Routledge, 2001); and B. Hilton, *The Age of Atonement: The Influence of Evangelicalism on Social and Economic Thought, 1795–1865* (Oxford: Oxford University Press, 1988). On the United States, see M. A. Noll (ed.), *God and Mammon: Protestants, Money, and the Market, 1790–1860* (Oxford: Oxford University Press, 2002); and S. Davenport, *Friends of the Unrighteous Mammon: Northern Christians and Market Capitalism, 1815–1860* (Chicago, IL: University of Chicago Press, 2008).
6. Clark, *Betting on Lives*, pp. 26–7.
7. P. H. J. H. Gosden, *Self-Help: Voluntary Associations in Nineteenth-Century Britain* (London: B. T. Batsford, 1973), p. 104. A major exception was the so-called 'collecting friendly society', which competed with industrial insurance companies in selling burial insurance. Although technically friendly societies, in practice they were mutual insurance companies, with none of the rituals or traditions of self-government possessed by older friendly societies.
8. G. Clark, 'The Slave's Appeal: Insurance and the Rise of Commercial Property', in G. Clark et al. (eds), *The Appeal of Insurance* (Toronto: University of Toronto Press, 2010), pp. 52–74, on p. 71.

BIBLIOGRAPHY

Alborn, T., *Conceiving Companies: Joint-Stock Politics in Victorian England* (London: Routledge, 1998).

—, 'Senses of Belonging: The Politics of Working-Class Insurance in Britain, 1880–1914', *Journal of Modern History*, 73 (2001), pp. 561–602.

—, *Regulated Lives: Life Insurance and British Society, 1800–1914* (Toronto: University of Toronto Press, 2009).

—, 'Money's Worth: Morality, Class, Politics', in M. Hewitt (ed.), *The Victorian World* (London: Routledge, 2012), pp. 209–24.

Barinoff, D., 'Fire Insurance in the United States', in R. Whaples (ed.), *Online Encyclopedia of Economic and Business History* (2008), at http://eh.net/encyclopedia.

Behlmer, G. K., *Child Abuse and Moral Reform in England, 1870–1908* (Stanford, CA: Stanford University Press, 1982).

Beito, D. T., '"This Enormous Army": The Mutual-Aid Tradition of American Fraternal Societies before the Twentieth Century', in D. T. Beito, P. Gordon and A. Tabarrok (eds), *The Voluntary City: Choice, Community, and Civil Society* (Ann Arbor, MI: University of Michigan Press, 2002), pp. 182–203.

Besso, M., 'Progress of Life Assurance throughout the World, from 1859 to 1883', *Journal of the Institute of Actuaries*, 26 (1887), pp. 426–37.

Borscheid, P., and N. V. Haueter (eds), *World Insurance: The Evolution of a Global Risk Network* (Oxford: Oxford University Press, 2012).

Bouk, D. B., 'The Science of Difference: Developing Tools for Discrimination in the American Life Insurance Industry, 1830–1930' (PhD dissertation, Princeton University, 2009).

Brown, C., *The Death of Christian Britain: Understanding Secularisation 1800–2000* (London: Routledge, 2001).

Buck, P., 'People Who Counted: Political Arithmetic in the Eighteenth Century', *Isis*, 73 (1982), pp. 28–45.

Buley, R. C., *The American Life Convention, 1906–1952: A Study on the History of Life Insurance* (New York: Appleton-Century-Crofts, 1953).

—, *The Equitable Life Assurance Society of the United States, 1859–1964* (New York: Appleton-Century-Crofts, 1967).

Carter, R. L., and P. Falush, *The British Insurance Industry since 1900: The Era of Transformation* (London: Palgrave Macmillan, 2009).

Chan, C. S., *Marketing Death: Culture and the Making of a Life Insurance Market in China* (Oxford: Oxford University Press, 2012).

Clark, G., *Betting on Lives: The Culture of Life Insurance in England, 1695–1775* (Manchester: Manchester University Press, 1999).

—, 'The Slave's Appeal: Insurance and the Rise of Commercial Property', in G. Clark et al. (eds), *The Appeal of Insurance* (Toronto: University of Toronto Press, 2010), pp. 52–74.

Clegg, C., *Friend in Deed: The History of ... the Refuge Assurance Company* (London: Stone and Cox, 1958).

Clough, S. B., *A Century of American Life Insurance: A History of the Mutual Life Insurance Company of New York 1843–1943* (New York: Columbia University Press, 1946).

Cordery, S., *British Friendly Societies, 1750–1914* (New York: Palgrave Macmillan, 2003).

Daunton, M., *Royal Mail: The Post Office since 1840* (London: Athlone, 1985).

Davenport, S., *Friends of the Unrighteous Mammon: Northern Christians and Market Capitalism, 1815–1860* (Chicago, IL: University of Chicago Press, 2008).

Dennett, L., *A Sense of Security: 150 Years of Prudential* (Cambridge: Granta Editions, 1998).

Dickson, P. G. M., *The Sun Fire Insurance Office 1710–1960: The History of Two and a Half Centuries of British Insurance* (London: Oxford University Press, 1960).

Dunlop, A. I., *The Scottish Ministers' Widows' Fund, 1743–1993* (Edinburgh: St Andrew Press, 1992).

Emminghaus, A. (ed.), *Poor Relief in Different Parts of Europe* (London: Edward Stanford, 1873).

Farrell, B., *Elite Families: Class and Power in Nineteenth-Century Boston* (Albany, NY: State University of New York Press, 1993).

Fishback, P. V., and S. E. Kantor, 'The Durable Experiment: State Insurance of Workers' Compensation Risk in the Early Twentieth Century', *Journal of Economic History*, 56 (1996), pp. 809–36.

Gilbert, B., *The Evolution of National Insurance in Great Britain: The Origins of the Welfare State* (London: Joseph, 1966).

Gosden, P. H. J. H., *Self-Help: Voluntary Associations in Nineteenth-Century Britain* (London: B. T. Batsford, 1973).

Grant, H. R., *Insurance Reform: Consumer Action in the Progressive Era* (Ames, IA: Iowa State University Press, 1979).

Haberman, S., and T. A. Sibbett (eds), *The History of Actuarial Science* (London: Pickering & Chatto, 1995).

Hilton, B., *The Age of Atonement: The Influence of Evangelicalism on Social and Economic Thought, 1795–1865* (Oxford: Oxford University Press, 1988).

Hoffman, F. L., *Handbook and Reference Guide to the Exhibits of the Prudential Insurance Company of America* (Newark, NJ: Prudential, 1904).

—, *The Mortality from Cancer throughout the World* (New York: Prudential Press, 1915).

Horstman, K., *Public Bodies, Private Lives: The Historical Construction of Life Insurance, Health Risks, and Citizenship in the Netherlands, 1880–1920* (Rotterdam: Erasmus Publishing, 2001).

Hunt, M. R., *The Middling Sort: Commerce, Gender and the Family in England, 1680–1780* (Berkeley, CA: University of California Press, 1996).

Hudnut, J. M., *Semi-Centennial History of the New-York Life Insurance Company 1845–1895* (New York: The Company, 1895).

Ingham, J. N., *Biographical Dictionary of American Business Leaders* (Westport, CT: Greenwood Press, 1983).

James, M., *The Metropolitan Life: A Study in Business Growth* (New York: Viking, 1947).

Jenkins, D., and T. Yoneyama (eds), *The History of Insurance* (London: Pickering & Chatto, 2000).

Keller, M., *The Life Insurance Enterprise, 1885–1910: A Study in the Limits of Corporate Power* (Cambridge, MA: Harvard University Press, 1963).

Kingston, C., 'Marine Insurance in Britain and America, 1720–1844: A Comparative Institutional Analysis', *Journal of Economic History*, 67 (2007), pp. 379–409.

Krooss, H. E., and M. R. Blyn, *A History of Financial Intermediaries* (New York: Random House, 1971).

Mackie, A., *Facile Princeps: The Story of the Beginning of Life Insurance in America* (Lancaster, PA: Lancaster Press, Inc., 1956).

Morrah, D., *A History of Industrial Life Assurance* (London: George Allen and Unwin, 1955).

Moss, M., *Standard Life 1825–2000: The Building of Europe's Largest Mutual Life Company* (Edinburgh: Mainstream Publishing, 2000).

Murphy, S. A., 'Life Insurance in the United States before World War I', in R. Whaples (ed.), *Online Encyclopedia of Economic and Business History* (2002), at http://eh.net/encyclopedia.

—, 'New York State Insurance Department', in P. Eisenstadt (ed.), *The Encyclopedia of New York State* (New York: Syracuse University Press, 2005), p. 778.

—, 'Securing Human Property: Slavery, Life Insurance, and Industrialization in the Upper South', *Journal of the Early Republic*, 25 (2005) pp. 615–52.

—, *Investing in Life: Insurance in Antebellum America* (Baltimore, MD: Johns Hopkins University Press, 2010).

Noll, M. A. (ed.), *God and Mammon: Protestants, Money, and the Market, 1790–1860* (Oxford: Oxford University Press, 2002).

Ogborn, M. E., *Equitable Assurances: The Story of Life Assurance in the Experience of the Equitable Life Assurance Society 1762–1962* (London: George Allen and Unwin, 1962).

Payne, P. L., 'The Savings Bank of Glasgow, 1836–1914', in P. L. Payne (ed.), *Studies in Scottish Business History* (New York: Kelley, 1967), pp. 152–86.

Pearl Assurance: An Illustrated History (Peterborough: Pearl Assurance Plc, 1990).

Pearson, R., 'Thrift or Dissipation? The Business of Life Assurance in the Early Nineteenth Century', *Economic History Review*, 43 (1990), pp. 236–54.

—, *Insuring the Industrial Revolution: Fire Insurance in Great Britain, 1700–1850* (Aldershot: Ashgate, 2004).

Pearson, R., and M. Freeman (eds), *The History of the Company* (London: Pickering & Chatto, 2006).

Perry, C. R., *The Victorian Post Office: The Growth of a Bureaucracy* (Woodbridge: Boydell Press, 1992).

Ransom, R. L., and R. Sutch, 'Tontine Insurance and the Armstrong Investigation: A Case of Stifled Innovation, 1868–1905', *Journal of Economic History*, 47 (1987), pp. 379–90.

Rapone, A., *The Guardian Life Insurance Company, 1860–1920: A History of a German-American Enterprise* (New York: New York University Press, 1987).

Raynes, H. E., *A History of British Insurance* (London: Pitman, 1950).

Report from the Select Committee of the House of Lords on Life Assurance Companies (London: HMSO, 1906).

Reports of the Chief Registrar of Friendly Societies, Workmen's Compensation Schemes, Industrial and Provident Societies, and Trades Unions, for 1900 (London: HMSO, 1901).

Ryan, R., 'A History of the Norwich Union Fire and Life Assurance Societies from 1797 to 1914' (PhD dissertation, University of East Anglia, 1983).

—, 'The Early Expansion of the Norwich Union Life Insurance Society, 1808–37', *Business History*, 28 (1985), pp. 166–96.

Schwartz, J., *Fighting Poverty with Virtue: Moral Reform and America's Urban Poor, 1825–2000* (Bloomington, IN: Indiana University Press, 2000).

Stalson, J. O., *Marketing Life Insurance: Its History in America* (Cambridge, MA: Harvard University Press, 1942).

Statements and Abstracts of Reports Deposited with Board of Trade under Life Assurance Companies Act (London: HMSO, 1881–2, 1903).

Statements of Assurance Business under the First, Second and Third Schedules of the Assurance Companies Act, 1909, Deposited ... December, 1917 (London: HMSO, 1918).

Supple, B., *The Royal Exchange Assurance: A History of British Insurance 1720–1970* (Cambridge: Cambridge University Press, 1970).

Todd, C. L., and R. Sonkin, *Alexander Bryan Johnson, Philosophical Banker* (Syracuse, NY: Syracuse University Press, 1977).

Toon, E., 'Managing the Conduct of the Individual Life: Public Health Education and American Public Health, 1910 to 1940' (PhD dissertation, University of Pennsylvania, 1998).

Trebilcock, C., *Phoenix Assurance and the Development of British Insurance*, 2 vols (Cambridge: Cambridge University Press, 1985, 1999).

Wadhwani, R. D., 'Citizen Savers: The Family Economy, Financial Institutions, and Social Policy in the Northeastern US from the Market Revolution to the Great Depression' (PhD dissertation, University of Pennsylvania, 2002).

Walford, C., *Insurance Cyclopaedia* (London: Layton, 1871–80).

Watson, J., *American Life Offices in Great Britain* (Edinburgh: Bell and Bradfute, 1884).

Watts, E., and D. J. Carlson (eds), *John Neal and Nineteenth-Century American Literature and Culture* (Lewisburg, PA: Bucknell University Press, 2012).

Weare, W. B., *Black Business in the New South: A Social History of the North Carolina Mutual Life Insurance Company* (Durham, NC: Duke University Press, 1993).

Webb, A. D., *New Dictionary of Statistics* (London: George Routledge and Sons, 1911).

Wertheimer, E., *Underwriting: The Poetics of Insurance in America, 1722–1872* (Stanford, CA: Stanford University Press, 2006).

Westall, O. M., 'Entrepreneurship and Product Innovation in British General Insurance, 1840–1914', in J. Brown and M. B. Rose (eds), *Entrepreneurship, Networks and Modern Business* (Manchester: Manchester University Press, 1993), pp. 191–208.

Yates, J., *Structuring the Information Age: Life Insurance and Technology in the Twentieth Century* (Baltimore, MD: Johns Hopkins University Press, 2005).

Zelizer, V. A. R., *Morals and Markets: The Development of Life Insurance in the United States* (New Brunswick, NJ: Transaction Books, 1983).

BRITISH LIFE INSURANCE IN THE 1840s

Richard Morgan,[1] *Familiar Observations on Life Insurance* (Norwich: Josiah Fletcher, 1841), Chapter 4: 'Short Notices of the Principal Offices Established for the Assurance of Lives', pp. 62–80.

Life Insurance Offices, New and Speculative, with a Table of the Inducements Held Out by Each of the Existing Offices (London: Effingham Wilson, 1846), pp. 19–28.

Richard Morgan's *Familiar Observations* was one of many guides published in the early 1840s to help potential British policyholders make sense of what was becoming a crowded life insurance market. These occupied a space between more scientific treatises on life insurance, most notably Charles Babbage's *Comparative View of the Various Institutions for the Assurance of Lives* (1826), and pamphlet-length prospectuses that touted specific offices (see samples later in this volume). Morgan preceded his comparison of difference offices (excerpted here) with a more general introduction to 'the science of Life Assurance [in] its connection with many parts of philosophy and political economy'; this included chapters on 'the state and progress of population', the history of mortality statistics, and a primer on different types of life insurance. Although *Familiar Observations* could be purchased in bookstores, Morgan's office, the Norwich Union, also handed out copies to its agents to distribute as they saw fit.[2]

Between 1800 and 1840 the number of British firms selling life insurance had increased from five (the Amicable, Equitable, Royal Exchange, Westminster and Pelican, all based in London) to more than eighty, and the total amount of life insurance in force rose from around £10 million to more than £100 million. Growth had taken place in waves, with twenty companies forming during the boom years of 1823–5, and twenty more during a second stock market bubble in 1836–9. With this rapid growth in new life insurance offices came geographical breadth as well: fourteen Scottish offices formed between 1815 and 1840, and twelve offices joined the Norwich Union (est. 1808) in provincial England. Finally, especially with the formation of the 'class' offices mentioned by Morgan, the British life insurance market ventured away from what had mainly been an aristocratic customer base in 1800 to take on an increasingly middle-class flavour. Most of these firms established solid foundations: over three-fourths of the 126 offices that formed between 1800 and 1840 lasted at least twenty years, and seventy survived at least through 1860. In stark contrast, only 10 per cent of the nearly 250 life offices that formed between 1840 and 1860 lasted until 1880. Although the Equitable, which dominated the market from its formation in 1762 into the 1810s, continued to be a significant measuring rod in surveys such as Morgan's (and remained the market leader in premium income in the 1830s), by 1841 its days of hegemony had long since passed.[3]

Notes

1. Richard Morgan (1780–1852) was the founding actuary of the Norwich Union Life Insurance Society from 1808 until his death. He joined the Norwich Union after clerking for several years at the Rock Life Assurance Company.
2. Morgan, *Familiar Observations*, p. iii, 1; Alborn, *Regulated Lives*, p. 128.
3. Alborn, *Regulated Lives*, pp. 20–9, 33–7, 55; R. Ryan, 'The Early Expansion of the Norwich Union Life Insurance Society, 1808–37', *Business History*, 28 (1985), pp. 166–96, on pp. 166–7.

Richard Morgan, *Familiar Observations on Life Insurance* (1841), Chapter 4

SHORT NOTICES OF THE PRINCIPAL OFFICES ESTABLISHED FOR THE ASSURANCE OF LIVES.

Two different MODES OF CONDUCTING AN ESTABLISHMENT FOR INSURANCE naturally present themselves to the mind. The one, that the risk should be taken by a *distinct body of individuals*, raising a capital for protection, and enjoying any surplus which might accrue from the premiums paid by the assured, after discharging the claims arising by death. The other, that the assured should be *mutual guarantees*, dividing the responsibility, and depending on the sufficiency of the premiums for covering it.

After experience had indicated that the rates ordinarily taken, considerably exceeded the value of the risk, a third mode would be practised – viz. of dividing the surplus between the assured, and a body of shareholders who should engage to bear the consequences of any excess of loss beyond the amount of the fund created by the premiums, on condition of participating in the expected surplus. /

Under whatever system an institution proceeds, it is obvious that such a scale of premiums must be taken, as will, in all human probability, more than discharge the claims arising from deaths among the assured.

From such rates, of course, under ordinary circumstances, a surplus *must* be formed; and now arises the question, in what mode shall the surplus be returned to the contributor?

Various plans for effecting this object have been acted upon – the more common of which, are, that adopted by the EQUITABLE, &c. of assigning a reversionary sum, *bearing a given ratio to the amount originally assured*, and that introduced by THE NORWICH UNION Office, of making the amount of the reversion dependent *not* upon the magnitude of the *sum assured*, but on that *of the total amount paid in as premium by the party.*

THE PRINCIPAL INSTITUTIONS ESTABLISHED PRIOR TO 1837, (THE NAME OF THE NEW ONES SINCE ARISEN IS "LEGION") ARE AS FOLLOWS: –

THE AMICABLE SOCIETY. – This very singular Institution is the oldest of our establishments for insurance, taking date from 1706! and assuredly does not present, in its history, any very brilliant picture of the *"wisdom of our ancestors!"* /

According to its original plan, the same premium was taken at all ages under 45,* that rate being, in most instances, considerably more than double the correct sum – and the amount paid to the representative of the deceased member, depended *upon the number of individuals who happened to die in the same year!* so that the family of one insurer might by possibility receive but half as much as had been paid in a preceding year to the representative of another!

This exquisite specimen of ingenuity, has received no less than four subsequent alterations in fresh Charters, granted by the 3rd of George II – the 30th of George III – the 40th of George III – and the 4th of George IV – gradually reducing the original mass of absurdity, but still leaving the system imperfect.

As the AMICABLE improved its system, the amount of its business increased, though as late as 1790, (84 years from its establishment,) its capital amounted but to about £64,000, 3 per cents.,[1] and a few houses.

After the grant of the last Charter, the number of insurances was considerably enlarged, and the amount payable to the families of the members upon their decease, much enhanced – the original vice of the system (and possibly other concurrent causes) producing, however, an unpleasant result to the representatives of the *present* members, who, / it is understood, will, in the event of the decease of those parties, between 1842 and 1852, receive *considerably less than if the deaths had occurred prior to the present date*, although the contributions made by the assured to the funds of the institution will have become very much greater.

THE EQUITABLE OFFICE.

This great Institution was established in the year 1762, in consequence of lectures delivered by the celebrated mathematician, MR. SIMPSON,[2] recommending such a measure. For the first twenty years it did not make any remarkable progress.

Its rates, originally extremely high, were reduced in 1786 to the present scale, which is computed from the NORTHAMPTON Table of mortality, and was acted upon by all the other offices, until the formation of the NORWICH UNION SOCIETY.

The rates of the EQUITABLE being still considerably beyond what was necessary to provide the sums assured, a very respectable surplus was accumulated,

---

* No member was admitted whose age exceeded 45.

and various bonuses made at irregular intervals, until in the year 1800 it was determined, in the words of Mr. Wm. Morgan, "that none" (speaking of the additions) "should thereafter be made, without a previous investigation of the affairs of the society – that such investigation should take place at the end of every ten years, and that the amount of the additions in present value, should never exceed *two-thirds* of the *surplus stock* of the society."[3] /

By this regulation, a large sum was always accumulating at interest, and forming the materials of another bonus. But the mere difference (considerable although it be) between the value of the premium taken and that of the sums assured, would not, alone, have enabled the society to make such great additions as it did, to the elder policies, had it not happened, that the large receipts of the Institution were almost wholly invested in government securities during the long war with France.

The prices of the funds being very low during that period, (at one epoch the three per cent. consols were down to 46,) the capital of the society was worked (as it is technically termed) at a high rate of interest, and when peace arrived, the value of the stock of the Equitable office received an enormous accession. These favourable circumstances enabled the members to declare immense bonuses, and business flowed in, in consequence, so fast, that the late Actuary persuaded the members in 1816 to adopt a measure which has very effectually accomplished his object of preventing the growth of the Institution to an unwieldy magnitude.

This remarkable measure was, to restrict the division of the bonus, as regarded all persons joining the Institution subsequently to 1816, to the 5000 policies of oldest standing on the Society's books!! – thus establishing a "*privileged class*" among persons paying equal premiums, into which class, new members were (according to their seniority) / to be admitted, as the "noblesse" of the 5000 dropped off.

As nearly fifteen years elapsed before the persons whose assurances commenced in 1816 entered the "charmed circle," and it was found that no new Insurers could expect to participate in a bonus until they had been members many years, the result has been, that the *new* business of the EQUITABLE, has gradually, but rapidly declined; until, instead of issuing five or six hundred policies *per annum*, the number, of late, has not exceeded two hundred.*

---

* Violent efforts have been made by those on the outside of the sacred circle, to break the "*Taboo*" – but, of course, in vain – those who benefit by it are "THE MAJORITY"! and to *all* majorities and minorities probably, may the observation be applied, which *M. Grimani* made upon the British people and government fifty years since; when the former were the "*minority*" IN POINT OF POWER: –

"*Ils leurs est permis de parler mal du Roi, du gouvernment – d'en marquer leurs fautes, critiquer leurs actions – mais aussi à leur tour, ils prennent la liberté de s'en moquer, et de continuer leur train!*"[4]

Meantime, the numbers who have been cut off by death has been very great, and the liabilities of the establishment further reduced by the purchase of bonuses – that is, by the society paying down a sum in hand, in lieu of the greater one payable by way of addition to the amount assured, upon the decease of the party.

From the united operation of these two causes, aided by the discontinuance of many insurances, the liabilities of the EQUITABLE were lower by four millions in 1839 than in 1832.

The bonus declared at the last investigation was / less than at the preceding; this magnificent Institution feeling, like all other offices, the change in the health of the community between 1828 and 1834.

The directors are very prudently shifting their capital, by degrees, from the government securities, to mortgages on land – a most judicious course – since a war would operate very injuriously on the funds, and the great gains of 1815 and 1816 might, by such an event, be abstracted from the capital of this noble establishment.

Notwithstanding the great advantages derived from the "EQUITABLE SOCIETY," no considerable number of offices were established until within the last thirty-six years – from 1805 to 1808 inclusive, the ALBION, PROVIDENT, ATLAS, EAGLE, ROCK, HOPE, LONDON LIFE, and NORWICH UNION Society came into existence.

To the success of the latter, probably, is mainly owing the great extension of Insurance offices – by the bold and novel measure of effecting assurances on a scale of rates lower than those taken by the EQUITABLE, the UNION rapidly acquired an immense business. The eminent success of this Institution induced the establishment of various offices – of those which were originated prior to 1836, several adopted rates closely approximating to those of the UNION – a few published tables upon a lower scale.

Since 1836 a crowd of companies have started up, some of which have already terminated their career – it is to be regretted that among those of / very recent formation, the reduction of rates has been carried in some instances to a very dangerous extent. A considerable number remain of undoubted respectability.

The success of an Insurance office depends mainly on the care exercised in the admission of lives. The rigid scrutiny exercised by the directors of the NORWICH UNION may be judged of by the fact, that during the first twenty-one years of its existence, the sums paid for claims, arising by deaths among the members, amounted to but £680,000; while the premium received in the same period was no less than £1,600,000!! In fact, since the establishment of the Institution in 1808, *above two thousand five hundred* proposals, for sums amounting in the aggregate to nearly TWO MILLIONS have been declined!

The rapid progress of the Union is evidenced by the fact, that in ten years from its establishment it had issued above 4500 policies – *twenty* elapsed in the early history of the EQUITABLE, before that Institution had granted two thousand one hundred!

The receipt of yearly premium by the NORWICH UNION SOCIETY increased according to the following ratio: –

	£	s.	d.
In the year ending March, 1815, it was	33,441	5	11
In that ending March, 1821,	96,650	6	9
In the year ending March, 1830,	155,273	19	1
It is now about	190,000		/

THE LONDON LIFE ASSOCIATION, (established in Dec. 1806,) is an institution which does a very considerable amount of business, on the very peculiar plan of taking a remarkably high rate of premium, and after a period of seven years, *reducing* it, according to the amount of profits made by the society. This reduction has been very great, but it must not be concealed, that the principle of the system is decidedly opposed to the opinion of the late venerable Actuary of the EQUITABLE; who always laboured to impress on the members of that establishment, the danger of adopting such a mode of distributing a surplus. His argument was, that in the event of an *increased* mortality, the funds of an institution proceeding on this system must necessarily prove inadequate – they having been kept down to that amount only, which would cover the *probable average* waste of life.

In the case of the LONDON LIFE ASSOCIATION, this reasoning might be met, by reference to the power of raising the rate of premium on those policies upon which a reduction had been made.

This, if it could be generally carried into execution, would overcome the difficulty; but it must be confessed, that the exercise of such a power would be extremely obnoxious, and in many cases, productive of very serious inconveniencies to the assured.

A yet greater evil is within the limits of possibility – it may happen, that the mortality of several consecutive years may be so extremely severe as / to render the necessary elevation in the rate of premiums *very considerable*. In this case, vast numbers of the assured might discontinue their policies, because they could open new insurances with other institutions, at a lower rate; and the class who would thus sever their connection with the establishment would be precisely that which it could worst spare, viz. of those persons who having entered at a comparatively recent date, would be still in the prime of life and health.

The whole burthen of the struggle might thus be left upon the elder members, among whom the ravages of mortality must necessarily be greatest.

It is fervently to be hoped, that this evil will never fall on so important and respectable an establishment – but it might be well for the members to consider the *possibility* of it, and to make a provision against such an occurrence.

The ATLAS has now existed thirty-three years, does a very respectable amount of business, and makes considerable bonuses – on a system so peculiar, that it would require more space than can be spared to make it intelligible to the general reader.

The ASYLUM[5] professes to grant policies on the lives of persons not deemed eligible risks at other offices – of course an *extra* premium is required – but it is understood, that insurances are not effected, if the infirmity of the party be of such nature as / to render it probable that existence will be *materially* shortened.

The ROCK office, established in 1806, is an extremely respectable institution of the *mixed* character, having a body of shareholders, but assigning a portion of the profits to the insurers. Its subscribed capital is very large; upon which ten per cent. has been actually paid up. Its mathematical department is conducted by W. S. LEWIS, Esq., a gentleman of learning and experience, having been connected with the Institution for five-and-thirty years.

The ROCK assigns two-thirds of its surplus to the assured, by way of bonus, septennially – it takes the same rate of premium as the EQUITABLE, and as in the latter institution one-third of the surplus is always reserved as a guarantee fund, many persons suppose the system of the Rock to be as productive of additions to the policies as that of the EQUITABLE. This, however, is an unfounded assumption – in the Rock, the reserved third becomes absolutely the property of the *shareholders*, and never forms again any portion of the general assets. In the EQUITABLE, the third reserved at one computation of liabilities, merges into the general mass of assets again, at the next calculation.

If we suppose the third reserved at any given date, to be a million, and imagine that for three subsequent decennial periods, *no* profits are realized, / it is clear, that at the next ensuing computation to that at which the million was reserved, that sum (with its interest) being the only surplus, £666,666 13s. 4d. (with two-thirds of the interest accumulated) would be divided among the assured, and £333,333 6s. 8d. (with due proportion of interest) would constitute the *then* reserved fund. At the following division £222,222 4s. 6d. would be divided, and £111,111 2s. 2d. reserved; at the third, this sum would be again reduced by two-thirds, &c. Thus, ultimately, a great proportion of any reserved third becomes distributed among the assured, on the EQUITABLE system – while on that of the ROCK, it is wholly abstracted from their side of the account. The *present* system of the EQUITABLE, however, by excluding those who may die in the first dozen (or more) years of their insurance, from any bonus, has, for persons past the middle of life, wholly destroyed any ground for preferring that Institution to the ROCK.

The latter establishment compels its shareholders to keep up an insurance of considerable magnitude, as compared with their amount of shares – this secures business, but depresses the price of its stock in the market.

The WEST OF ENGLAND[6] (1807) is an energetically conducted Institution, and doubtless owes much to its secretary CHARLES LEWIS, Esq. – it takes rank immediately after the NORWICH UNION, / as a *Country* office, as regards its *Fire* Insurance business; and as its rates vary little from those of the latter Institution, in the *Life* Assurance Branch, it may be naturally assumed, that its business in that department is considerable.

The system of Insurance has within a few years made great progress in SCOTLAND, where several respectable Institutions have arisen – among which, perhaps, the "SCOTTISH WIDOWS' FUND" and "SCOTTISH UNION" are the most remarkable.

The rates and systems of these two establishments have a marked similarity to their predecessor the NORWICH UNION – and the secretary of the London department of the SCOTTISH UNION, a gentleman of talent and spirit, was formerly connected with its NORWICH namesake.

The "SCOTTISH WIDOWS' FUND" is supported by very extensive connexions in North Britain – the late very able Actuary died in the prime of life, and the society has justly and liberally made a provision for his widow.

In 1820, the SUN *Life* Assurance office was established – its mathematical department is under the supervision of Mr. MILNE,[7] whose very able and elaborate work has been before noticed.

The scale of rates is low at the early stages of life, but very high at the later. The extent of business of the SUN is unknown to the author; but / from the immense connexion of the FIRE Insurance Institution, it may rationally be assumed, that it is of considerable magnitude.

The PELICAN* is an office of long standing, supported, by the same wealthy proprietory as the PHŒNIX FIRE OFFICE, to which it may be considered the partner, or sister Institution. It takes the same rate of premium as the EQUITABLE, but not offering until lately the same advantages, its business is probably, in a certain degree, limited to that derived from its respectable body of shareholders, and their connexions.†

The GLOBE, established in 1803, in like manner, depends (it may be presumed,) mainly on the support of its numerous and influential shareholders. This company (which, like the PELICAN, adopts the EQUITABLE Society's scale of premium) raised an enormous capital – (£1,000,000 actually paid up) a measure which rendered certain the security of the parties insuring with it, but the expediency of which (looking at it merely in a mercantile point of view) may admit of a doubt.

* The date of its establishment is 1797.
† It has now two systems and scales of premium; adjusted to the alternative of participation or nonparticipation in profits.

It is clear, that as a trading speculation, the larger the capital embarked in a concern, the smaller is the *ratio* of profit to the capitalists, on a given amount of transactions. If the mere deposit of a million would produce a business five times as great / as could be commanded by a capital of £200,000, it is obvious that nothing would be lost by subscribing the larger amount ; but this is not the case with insurance : the insurer requires a conviction of *security*, but *beyond* this, he is indifferent – if he be satisfied that he is *absolutely safe*, by the office he insures with, having a capital of £200,000, he will not be drawn from it by the statement, that *another* Institution possesses five times as much.

The ROYAL EXCHANGE office is of the same class as the PELICAN and GLOBE – a proprietory company, adopting the NORTHAMPTON table as the basis of its rates; we are not aware of any peculiarity in the plan of this Institution.

The ALBION is of about the same age as the Union, and differs little in rates, but not making additions by way of bonus, to sums assured, contends at a disadvantage with other Institutions who offer that benefit.

The GUARDIAN takes date from 1821, and is chiefly remarkable for enjoying the very great advantage of having Mr. G. DAVIES for its Actuary – it is, of course, a most respectable establishment.

The CROWN, under the able actuaryship of Mr. RAINBOW is steadily progressing.

WITHIN THE LAST THREE OR FOUR YEARS, A CROWD OF NEW OFFICES STARTED INTO EXISTENCE, / and their institutors deemed it necessary to put forth some NOVEL claim to public approbation – in consequence, all kinds of variations were attempted, and different scales of premium presented – ascending, descending, for limited terms of payment, &c.

As the constantly increasing competition soon exhausted *these* resources, the next step was to form *combinations* of two or more *modes* of insurance, under each of which a policy could have been effected, singly, before – and of course as the possible number of combinations of a few elements is enormous, we have now an abundance of such projects. Of these little exertions of imagination we may say, that they are very harmless flights of fancy – that they doubtless answer the purpose intended, of causing John Bull to talk; and that at the worst, they are only open to the observation launched against the unlucky sculptor of "the olden time," who had overloaded his Venus with ornament, that "as he could not make his goddess *beautiful* he was determined to make her *fine!*"

The LAW LIFE ASSOCIATION, and the CLERICAL and MEDICAL INSURANCE office, present the novelty of being established by, and resting principally upon, particular classes of society, as indicated by their titles.*

---

*   The LAW office, is so fortunate as to command the great talents of Mr. Kirkpatrick as its Actuary.

They both do a considerable extent of business, particularly the former, as might be expected from / the very powerful influence of the legal profession.

There is every reason to believe, that each establishment is well and prudently conducted; of course both being in the "bloom of youth,"* the demands on the respective funds *must* be small, and an amount of profit realized – which no possible care and skill can be expected to produce at a *later* stage of existence, when the (now recently selected) lives shall have approximated more closely to the character of the average mass of the community.

The rates of premium of the LAW are those of the EQUITABLE office, and it makes septennial divisions of profits by way of bonus.

The scale of the CLERICAL and MEDICAL approximates very closely to that of the NORWICH UNION – it assigns a bonus quinquennially.

There is a peculiar expression in the last annual report of the CLERICAL and MEDICAL, which it is to be hoped and presumed, originated only in carelessness of composition.

The sentence alluded to is, that in which it is stated, that a sum of £52,000 was carried to the surplus fund as *a clear gain* – now, the ratio which this sum bore to the *total receipts of premium* of the year was such, that it was very improbable the *clear gain* could be in that proportion, because, out / of every year's premium, a certain considerable proportion must always be set aside to counterbalance the increased age of the assured.

The probability is, that the Directors merely meant to state the sum which remained *undisbursed*, i.e. which had not been required for payment of expenses and claims by death.

The idea of addressing peculiar interests was no sooner started by these two institutions, than it was eagerly followed, and offices forthwith arose, bearing the titles of "CHURCH OF ENGLAND," "PROTESTANT DISSENTERS," "UNIVERSITY," "AGRICULTURAL," "FARMERS," "INDIAN," "AUSTRALIAN," "MERCANTILE," &c.; even the body of "LICENSED VICTUALLERS," had its office.

Here our notice must stop; for if we attempted to enumerate the host of offices which have arisen within the last two years, we should find the catalogue more tedious (and not a whit more edifying) than Homer's list of the Grecian bands who poured forth from their "black ships" to besiege Troy.

In truth, these companies have sprung up with as much facility as the neverexhausted tales of the Sultana Schezerade, in the "Thousand and one Nights" of oriental fiction.

One advantage has resulted from the establishment of so many offices for the assurance on lives, viz. that it has brought into action the talents of / many distinguished men. These institutions can now boast of possessing a MILNE, a

---

* The "LAW LIFE ASSOCIATION" dates from 1823. The "CLERICAL and MEDICAL," from 1825.

DAVIES, a GOMPERTZ, an ARTHUR MORGAN, a KIRKPATRICK, an AUGUS-
TUS DE MORGAN, a WOOLHOUSE, a RAINBOW,* and a host of others whose
names would fill the page.

---

*   A few months since, an alarming illness threatened to deprive the world of this eminently
acute and intelligent gentleman: we trust that his health is now entirely restored. /

Life Insurance Offices, New and Speculative, with a Table of the Inducements Held Out by Each of the Existing Offices (1846), excerpt

[...]

In overlooking the subjoined Table any person will be surprised at the small number of purely mutual insurance offices, and will discover that the mutual principle spoken of in so many prospectuses is the principle of mutual advantage between the proprietors and the assured. He will also observe how profitable a business life insurance must have been supposed to have been from the / gradual increase in the proportion of the profits guaranteed to the assured, each new-comer bidding higher than its predecessors: thus, beginning with the Guardian, which offers one-half, and going down to the Star, which promises nine-tenths of its profits to its policy-holders, until at last the proprietary bodies become so anxious to insure their fellow-citizens, that they offer to do so for nothing, and to return to them the whole of the profits accruing from their insurances.

While therefore, we repeat it, long-established credit is the only real guar-antee for the stability of an office, the prospective bonus that is held out as an inducement to insurers must in the long run prove delusive, except in as far as the prospect is founded upon sound principles in the management of its affairs; and even former bonuses, so far from being a guarantee for future profits, may possibly be the very cause by which the stability of an office may be shaken. That these strictures are not unfounded the coming mortality among the offices will, we doubt not, eventually testify, – a mortality for whose prediction no commer-cial Cassandra is required. /

INDUCEMENTS TO INSURERS.

1706	AMICABLE	Mutual	The division among them of the whole of the profits by a septennial apportionment.
1714	UNION	Proprietary	A septennial participation in the profits.
1720	LONDON ASSURANCE	Do.	A return of two-thirds of the profits quin-quennially.

1762	EQUITABLE	Mutual	A decennial division of the profits.
1783	NEWCASTLE-UPON-TYNE	Proprietary	Local influence.
1792	WESTMINSTER	Do.	An unstated proportion of the profits.
1797	PELICAN	Do.	An undefined proportion of the profits periodically.
1803	GLOBE	Do.	No inducements.
1805	ROYAL EXCHANGE	Do.	A return of two-thirds of profits quinquennially.
–	ALBION	Do.	A return of four-fifths of profits triennially.
1806	ROCK	Do.	A return of two-thirds of profits septennially.
–	LONDON LIFE	Mutual	The whole of the profits applied to the reduction of the premiums.
1807	PROVIDENT	Proprietary	An undefined proportion of the profits quinquennially.
–	EAGLE	Do.	Lower rates for female lives than in any other office. Four-fifths of the profits periodically returned.
–	WEST OF ENGLAND	Do.	An unstated proportion of the profits periodically promised.
1808	NORWICH UNION	Mutual	The whole of the profits returned quinquennially. /
1808	ATLAS	Proprietary	An undefined proportion of the profits.
1809	NORTH BRITISH	Do.	Four-fifths of the profits returned septennially.
1810	SUN	Do.	The division among the assured "of such proportion of the profits of the society as to the discretion of the managers for the time being may seem most to the advantage of the parties interested."
1815	SCOTTISH WIDOWS' FUND	Mutual	The whole of the profits septennially divided.
1816	NATIONAL ASSURANCE OF IRELAND	Proprietary	A majority of Irish and therefore bad lives.
1819	EUROPEAN	Do.	Two-thirds of the profits returned septennially.
1820	BRITISH COMMERCIAL	Do.	An unstated proportion of the profits promised.
–	GENERAL BENEFIT	Mutual	Benefit club.
–	IMPERIAL	Proprietary	A return of four-fifths of the profits quinquennially.
–	MUTUAL ASSURANCE	Mutual	Benefit institution.
1821	GUARDIAN	Proprietary	One-half of the profits returned septennially.
1823	ECONOMIC	Mutual	The return of the whole of the profits quinquennially.
–	EDINBURGH	Proprietary	"The whole of the profits to the extent of four-fifths."

–	LAW LIFE	Do.	Four-fifths of the profits returned quinquennially.
1824	ALLIANCE	Do.	A participation in the profits promised quinquennially.
–	ASYLUM	Do.	Lives uninsurable at other offices insured at proportionable premiums; also the option of allowing one-third of the premiums to remain as a loan at compound interest at 5 per cent.
–	CLERICAL, MEDICAL, AND GENERAL	Do.	A return of five-sixths of the profits quinquennially. /
1824	LEEDS & YORKSHIRE	Proprietary	A return of three-fifths of the profits septennially.
–	MANCHESTER	Do.	A return of two-thirds of the profits decennially.
–	PALLADIUM	Do.	A return of four-fifths of the profits septennially.
–	PATRIOTIC	Do.	A majority of Irish and therefore bad lives.
–	UNITED KENT	Do.	A return of one-half of the profits septennially.
–	YORKSHIRE	Do.	Low rates but no profits.
1825	CROWN	Do.	A return of two-thirds of the profits to policy-holders of a certain standing septennially.
–	STANDARD	Do.	An undefined proportion of the profits promised quinquennially.
–	UNIVERSITY	Do.	A return of nine-tenths of the profits quinquennially.
1826	PROMOTER	Do.	A return of three-fourths of the profits quinquennially.
–	SCOTTISH AMICABLE	Mutual	The whole of the profits quinquennially divided.
1828	LIFE ASSOCIATION OF SCOTLAND	Do.	Periodical division of the whole of the profits.
1829	CLERGY MUTUAL	Do.	The periodical division of the whole of the profits.
1830	NATIONAL LIFE ASSOCIATION SOCIETY	Proprietary	An annual return of four-fifths of the profits.
1831	SCOTTISH EQUITABLE	Mutual	The whole of the profits triennially returned.
1832	FRIENDS PROVIDENT	Do.	The whole of the profits quinquennially returned.
1833	ARGUS	Proprietary	Low rates and no profits.
1834	MUTUAL	Mutual	The whole of the profits returned quinquennially.

–	UNIVERSAL	Proprietary	Three-twentieths of the profits to the policy-holders, one-twentieth to the shareholders, and sixteen-twentieths or four-fifths to an accumulation fund. /
1834	UNITED KINGDOM	Proprietary	A periodical return of two-thirds of the profits.
1835	FAMILY ENDOWMENT	Do.	Endowments and special risks undertaken.
–	LICENSED VICTUAL-LERS	Do.	A return of a portion of the profits quinquennially and a peculiar class of lives.
–	METROPOLITAN	Mutual	The whole of the profits quennially.
–	NATIONAL PROVIDENT	Do.	The whole of the profits septennially divided.
–	NOTTINGHAMSHIRE AND DERBYSHIRE	Proprietary	One-half of the profits after the payment of 5 per cent. upon the advanced capital.
–	PROTECTOR	Do.	The return of the surplus profits after the payment of 10 per cent. upon the advanced capital.
1836	LEGAL & GENERAL	Do.	A return of four-fifths of the profits quinquennially.
–	LIVERPOOL	Do.	Low rates but no profits.
–	MINERVA	Do.	A return of four-fifths of the profits quinquennially.
–	NORTH OF SCOTLAND	Do.	An unstated proportion of the profits promised septennially.
–	WESTMINSTER AND GENERAL	Do.	A return of four-fifths of the profits quinquennially.
1837	BRITANNIA	Do.	Half-credit rates and a liberal commission to solicitors and agents.
–	BRITANNIA	Mutual	Mutual assurance branch, do. do.
–	DISSENTERS AND GENERAL	Do.	All dissenting ministers insuring are agents, and profits accordingly.
–	MUTUAL ACCUMULATION	Do.	The whole of the profits periodically divided.
–	MUTUAL LOAN FUND	Proprietary	The loan of two-thirds of the premiums paid, under certain restrictions.
–	NATIONAL MERCANTILE	Do.	A return of two-thirds of the profits periodically. /
1837	ROYAL NAVAL AND MILITARY	Proprietary	A return of four-fifths of the profits septennially, and especial facilities to military men going abroad.
–	SCOTTISH PROVIDENT	Mutual	The whole of the profits divided among insurers of a certain standing.
1838	CITY OF GLASGOW	Proprietary	The generous proprietary offer to return the whole of the profits to the assured.
–	FREEMASONS AND GENERAL	Do.	Do. do.

–	VICTORIA	Do.	An unstated proportion of the profits promised septennially; also loans of one-half the sum insured, upon the security of the policies and the bonds of two or more sureties.
1839	ALFRED	Do.	A periodical return of four-fifths of the profits quinquennially, and high scales of annuities.
–	AUSTRALASIAN	Do.	Colonial investments.
–	ENGLISH AND SCOTTISH LAW	Do.	A return of two-thirds of the profits periodically.
–	LONDON, EDINBURGH, AND DUBLIN	Do.	The liberal proprietary promise to return the whole of the profits to the assured.
–	ROYAL FARMERS	Do.	No inducement.
1840	CHURCH OF ENGLAND	Do.	A return of four-fifths of the profits periodically.
–	PROVIDENT CLUBS	Benefit Association	Two-thirds of the profits divided quinquennially.
–	RELIANCE MUTUAL	Proprietary	The liberal proprietary promise to return the whole of the profits to the assured triennially.
–	TEMPERANCE PROVIDENT	Mutual	Members of Temperance Societies exclusively eligible for insurance in this society.
–	COMMERCIAL	Proprietary	An undefined proportion of the profits promised quinquennially.
1811	MEDICAL, INVALID, AND GENERAL	Do.	Lives uninsurable at other offices insured at advanced rates. /
1841	COMMERCIAL AND GENERAL	Proprietary	A return of two-thirds of the profits septennially.
–	NATIONAL INSURANCE OF SCOTLAND	Do.	A return of four-fifths of the profits.
–	WESLEYAN PROVIDENT	Mutual	The whole of the profits divided among the assured; confined, it is believed, to the Wesleyan Methodist connection.
1842	AUCTION	Proprietary	An undefined proportion of the profits. Loans on personal security.
–	WESTERN OF LONDON	Do.	Five-sixths of the profits returned septennially.
1843	EXPERIENCE	Do.	Five-sixths of the profits to be returned quinquennially.
–	SOUTH OF ENGLAND	Do.	No profits.
–	MARINERS AND GENERAL	Do.	Do.
–	STAR	Do.	Nine-tenths of the profits quinquennially. Wesleyan Methodist connection.

1844	BRITISH MUTUAL	Mutual	The whole of the profits divided among those parties whose subscriptions have amounted, at compound interest, to the sums insured.
–	EQUITY & LAW LIFE	Proprietary	Four-fifths of the profits returned quinquennially.
–	GREAT BRITAIN	Mutual	Whole of the profits divided annually; also credit for the first five years on giving security for the amounts of the premiums.
–	MERCANTILE	Proprietary	An undefined proportion of the profits divided quinquennially.
–	MERCHANTS' AND TRADESMEN'S	Mutual	The whole of the profits divided quinquennially.
–	SCOTTISH FREEMASONS	Do.	Do. do.
–	NATIONAL INSURANCE AND INVESTMENT COMPANY	Do.	Do. do. /
1844	SCOTTISH LIFE	Proprietary	A return of four-fifths of the profits.
–	PRESERVER	Do.	No profits.
1845	BON ACCORD	Do.	A proportion of the profits returned.
–	CATHOLIC	Do.	Three-fourths of the profits returned.
–	CITY OF LONDON	Do.	"Plans of a peculiar nature."
–	EAST OF SCOTLAND	Do.	"A very large proportion of the profits" returned triennially to the assured. Loans on personal security.
–	CONSOLIDATED	Do.	Do. do.
–	ECONOMY	Mutual	A directory of only two French gentlemen, both residing at Paris.
–	ENGLAND	Proprietary	The lives of invalids insured.
–	GLASGOW	Do.	Four-fifths of the profits.
–	HALIFAX AND BRADFORD	Do.	No profits.
–	HALIFAX, BRADFORD, AND KEIGHLY	Do.	Do.
–	LEGAL AND COMMERCIAL	Do.	Four-fifths of the profits quinquennially returned.
–	LONDON AND PROVINCIAL LAW	Do.	Four-fifths of the profits returned septennially.
–	OPERATIVE MUTUAL	Mutual	Benefit society.
–	PRACTICABLE	Proprietary	Two-thirds of the profits annually, with "a new method of division."
–	PRESTON & NORTH LANCASHIRE	Do.	No profits.
–	ROYAL	Do.	Two-thirds of the profits.
–	SHEFFIELD AND ROTHERHAM	Do.	Four-fifths of the profits.

–	SOVEREIGN	Do.	The loan of the whole sum assured, upon collateral (personal?) security being given. /
1845	UNITED DEPOSIT	Proprietary	Banking united with life assurance
–	WESTERN	Do.	Three-fourths of the profits.
–	NATIONAL CHURCH INSURANCE COMPANY	Do.	Clergymen taken in and done for – their lives insured, sons sent to college, funeral expenses provided, tithes guaranteed and collected, on the payment of moderate premiums divided.
–	MERCHANT TRADES-MEN'S & GENERAL	Mutual	The whole of the profits quennially divided.
–	CAMBRIAN	Proprietary	
–	CANDIDATE	Do.	
–	MITRE	Do.	

The collector of this Table has endeavoured to give the inducements in the most impartial manner, having in every case consulted the prospectuses of the Companies. He must, however, apologize for any unintentional error which may have crept into the table. The twenty-five Offices under the date of 1845 are, moreover, the only Offices of the ninety-six started or projected in that year which he believes to be still in existence.

THE EMERGENCE OF AMERICAN LIFE
INSURANCE

'Securitas', 'Life Insurance', *Connecticut Courant*, 26 August 1833, p. 2.

T. R. Jencks, 'Life Insurance in the United States, Number I', *Hunt's Merchants' Magazine and Commercial Review* (February 1843), pp. 109–31.

T. R. Jencks, 'Life Insurance in the United States, Number II', *Hunt's Merchants' Magazine and Commercial Review* (March 1843), pp. 227–40.

Although the first American life insurance enterprises can be traced back to the mid-eighteenth century, the progress of life insurance in America trailed significantly behind Great Britain. In the half century from 1787 to 1837, twenty-six companies offering life insurance to the general public opened their doors, but they rarely survived more than a couple of years and sold few policies. The only early companies to experience much success in this line of business were the Pennsylvania Company for Insurances on Lives and Granting Annuities (chartered 1812), Massachusetts Hospital Life Insurance Company (1818), Baltimore Life Insurance Company (1830), New York Life Insurance and Trust Company (1830) and Girard Life Insurance, Annuity and Trust Company of Pennsylvania (1836). Life insurance in force (the total death benefit payable on all existing policies) grew steadily from about $600,000 in 1830 to just under $5 million a decade later – which still paled before the more than $500 million in force in Britain at that time. Despite this growth in business, however, the knowledge of this product was still limited to only the most commercially oriented people of urban America.[1] Thus as late as the 1830s, articles on life insurance (like the first document reproduced here) provided an educational overview of what life insurance was and who should be insuring, including comparisons with more familiar industries like fire and marine insurance and savings banks. The tone of these early articles was always one of concern and surprise that the benefits of life insurance were not better known and taken advantage of in the United States.

Despite this tentative start, the life insurance industry made significant strides beginning in the 1830s. As a result, in 1843 *Hunt's Merchants' Magazine and*

Commercial Review – the pre-eminent publication on American business during the nineteenth century – ran two extensive articles detailing the global history, progress and current status of life insurance in America (both reprinted here). Although the author, T. R. Jencks of Massachusetts (about whom little is known), still bemoaned the continued low popularity of insurance, the willingness of editor Freeman Hunt to devote substantial space for these articles is indicative of the changing fortunes of the industry. By 1850 life insurance in force would surge to $100 million, spread among forty-eight companies. The top three companies – Mutual Life Insurance Company of New York (1842), Mutual Benefit Life Insurance Company of New Jersey (1845) and Connecticut Mutual Life Insurance Company (1846) – accounted for more than half of this amount.[2]

Notes
1.   Murphy, *Investing in Life*, p. 4. See also Stalson, *Marketing Life Insurance*.
2.   Murphy, 'Life Insurance in the United States before World War I'.

'Securitas', 'Life Insurance', *Connecticut Courant* (1833)

From the New-York Journal of Commerce.

LIFE INSURANCE.

Fire and Marine Insurance Companies have now established themselves in this country as well as abroad, upon a sure basis. Their utility has gained and will preserve public favor and patronage.

Another kind of Insurance successfully practised in Europe, is little known among us; I refer to Life Insurance.

The merchant who will not insure his vessel in order to avoid paying a small premium, is hardly pitied when his ship is wrecked. He is deemed worthy of his loss. The world is an ocean; life, a ship; death, a wreck; and that poor man, who will not take advantage of Life Insurance, has no one to blame but himself, if he dies in the bitter consciousness of leaving his family unprovided for, when he might have blessed them with a comfortable legacy.

The rates of Life Insurance have been fixed according to the probability of the duration of human life; and they vary according to the ages of the individuals. A man of twenty-five years pays, for instance, $10 per annum; an older man more, according to the mathematical calculation of the chance of his living another year.

The advantages of these institutions appeal especially to those who depend upon their regular exertion for their daily bread. The rich man may smile at the thought of leaving his family unprovided for; but he who feeds, clothes, and educates his family by the sweat of his brow, or by his constant professional exertions, looks forward to the accident* of his death, with anxiety and fear.

---

* It may save the feelings of some readers to say that the words accident, chance &c. as applied in this communication to the termination or continuance of human life, are mere technical phraseology, and import nothing in opposition to the doctrine of a superintending Providence. *Editors.*

This anxiety has led to the establishment of private clubs, in which every member pays an annual stipend, for the support of the families of deceased members. Now public Life Insurance Institutions are preferable to these private clubs, not only because they do not hold out temptation for convivial meetings, but because, by serving a greater number, they are conducted with less expense of time, trouble, and money; and also because they extend their convenience to any individual who may desire to take advantage of them.

When a gentleman who has depended upon his scanty salary, has died, the friends, the acquaintance, perhaps utter strangers, are called upon to contribute something for the maintenance and education of his family. This we do not object to; those who have fallen from respectable life, which they have not disgraced, into indigence, are objects of sympathy and of charity. But how much better is it, that men of this condition, should, while in health, by paying an inconsiderable annual sum, secure their families after their death, from either absolute want, or, – what is, to independent minds, hardly less severe, the shame of living upon public bounty. Is not the man who leaves his family in this condition, responsible for all the misery which his negligence to insure his life has occasioned?

It often happens that worthy, enterprising young men are kept down in life by their inability to give security for a loan of capital to start with. By insuring their lives one obstacle to their personal advancement, and to their becoming public benefactors by a more extended sphere of action, may be removed. – Some may think that Life Insurance would increase too much the facility of borrowing upon mere adventure. This is over caution. No person will loan money to a young man of no property, upon the mere certainty of being repaid *in case of his death;* money is not so easily got. A man must be able to show good grounds for believing that he will repay in case of his life's continuance before he can procure funds.

Savings Banks are excellent institutions. But men generally will not avail themselves of them. They prefer to risk their money in adventures, which promises larger returns. Savings Banks repay only as much as has been deposited with interest; and the deposit may be withdrawn for purposes of speculation at a moment's warning. Life Insurance Companies receive the small annual contributions of the healthy and comfortable, to give to the distressed widows and orphans of the deceased much more than has been advanced. True, Life Insurance Cos. do not disburse more than they receive, and therefore may be thought not to contribute to the public advantage; but the question is not precisely, *how much* money is distributed, but *how* is it distributed. – The question is not, whether wealth is created alone, – it is full as important to know whether it is well applied. It should be the object of all, as it is the operation of good institutions, to equalize the conditions of men, to obviate the evils of accidental misfortune – of chance. And what can we find so suitable to bear against chance as itself? Every perfect machine governs itself. Our chance of life should, by a little extra exertion, enable us to provide against the chance of death.

It may be said, that Life Insurance tends to make men improvident, – reckless of the future. But remember how few accumulate against the accident of death. A man's death does not subject himself to the evils of poverty. Those who are so improvident as to anticipate their death, will not be made the contrary by Life Insurance. They will desire to accumulate for their remaining years of life; for their future comfort, advancement, reputation; for future sickness or misfortune. – Men desire wealth for many reasons, besides that of securing their families from distress after their deaths.

The additional expense of Life Insurance, while it does not materially abridge the comfort of the active, demands in order to meet it, additional industry and greater economy.

Let the public pay to this subject the atention which it deserves.

SECURITAS.

T. R. Jencks, 'Life Insurance in the United States, Number I', *Hunt's Merchants' Magazine and Commercial Review* (1843)

Art. I. – LIFE INSURANCE IN THE UNITED STATES.

Acquisition of property is our national characteristic. For this, we emulate the dawn, we exhaust the lamp; no weary toil, the unhealthfulness of no occupation, deters us; the distance of no voyage stays us; and no postponement of the result, limits our perseverance or diminishes our ardor. We calculate receipts among fractions, and watch outgoes to the verge of parsimony; we marry at an early age, in Scripture expectation of a helpmeet, to get a living; we estimate our children by a money standard, and bound our duty to a fortune for them.

But, if by their fruits ye shall know them, we cannot have set forth our characteristic in disparagement. Our astonishing ingenuity, our unspeakable activity, our transcendant enterprise, resolve themselves into this; by this, we have outrun time, subdued a wilderness, and matured a nation. Can it be supposed, then, that our people will be inattentive to hedging their various and hazardous operations with safety, or careless of securing the certainty of their good results, and placing those results beyond reach of the universal accident of death?

The practice of life insurance companies, including their correlate branches of annuities and trusts, offers that safety, certainty, and security. Strange to say, it has never been popular in the United States. He who knows the shrewd appropriation of means among our citizens, cannot hesitate to ascribe this neglect to an ignorance or a misunderstanding of the operations and advantages of such companies. As society is constituted in this country, the tone of popularity on such subjects must be taken from the reading and thinking; an understanding of an object is the element of success. We have, therefore, thought we could not occupy in a more useful, if more interesting manner, the pages of a public journal, than in explaining the operations and advantages of life insurance, and giving an historical list of the sources of information on this important and national subject.

With the principles of insurance in general, all are well acquainted – the division of the loss, when it happens, so that it is compensated by payment / of small sums on many contracts, to receive a greater, upon the happening of that specified risk. The disproportion of the aggregate of losses to the aggregate number of contracts and their premiums, makes the ability of the insurer, and that ability constitutes the security of the insured. So general is now the practice of marine fire insurance, against the partial accidents of flood and flame, that he who, without having so many or so much as to become his own underwriter, leaves his ships or property uninsured, suffers in credit for wisdom or honesty.

We are subject to losses from crime, against which government is bound to protect; and from casualties, for which provision is made by insurance only. It forms one of the luxuries of a comfortable and quiet home, and is one of the chief ingredients of the certainty and confidence of commerce. Without the aid that it affords, comparatively few individuals would be found disposed to expose their property to the risk of long and hazardous voyages; but by its means, insecurity is changed for security, and the capital of the merchant whose ships are dispersed over every sea, and exposed to all the perils of the ocean, is as secure as that of the agriculturalist. He can combine his measures and arrange his plans, as if they could no longer be affected by accident. The changes of shipwreck or of loss, by unforeseen occurrences, enter not into his calculations. He has purchased an exemption from the effects of such casualties, and applies himself to the prosecution of his business with that confidence and energy which nothing but a feeling of security can inspire. The French Counsellors of State, M. M. Corvetto, Bégouen, and Maret, in their report to the Legislative Chambers, 8th September, 1807, at the time of the adoption of the Code de Commèrce, say: "Les chances de la navigation entraraient le commerce. Le systême des assurances a paru; et il a dit au commercant habile, au navigateur intrépide: certes, il y a des dèsastres sur lesquels l'humanitè ne peut que gémir; mais quant à votre fortune, allez, franchissez les mers, déployez votre activitè et votre industrie, je me charge de vos risques" – "The perils of navigation were stumbling-blocks to commerce. The system of insurance stepped forth to say to the able merchant and the intrepid seaman: there are, indeed, disasters, which humanity can only mourn; but, as to your fortune, traverse the ocean, lay out your activity and your industry, I take upon myself your risks."

Notwithstanding these advantages, and the extent to which marine insurance has now reached, it has been practised but four centuries; and fire insurance, not more than one hundred and fifty years. They have their Magens, Emerigon, Valen, and Phillips, as their historians or illustrators.

In England, with fifty or sixty offices, several having declined fire-risks, there were insured in the year 1832, two billion four hundred and seventy-four million eight hundred and forty-five thousand dollars' worth of property. To this it had grown in about a century and a half. In the city of Boston alone, there were, in 1841, about fifty millions of dollars' worth of fire risks, and about thirty-nine millions of marine risks, making together eighty-nine millions.

We have not the means at hand of ascertaining the extent of fire-risks in the whole United States. Add that, however, and to the sum put the probable amount of marine insurance in both countries, all property that ever floats is in the hollow of its hand; and we see the astonishing amount of security against partial accidents, for which the common caution of man has induced him to pay. /

Let us now turn to the history of life insurance. Comparatively, very few have ever thought at all on the subject; and it must be well to excite the public curiosity, and to furnish, so far forth as we may, the means to satisfy it. Upon this matter, too, we must recur to the British isles; for, curious as it may appear, the civil law having long before said, "Liberum corpus æstimationem non recepit" – "A freeman's life cannot be valued," the Dutch statute, in the year 1612, forbade it. In the year 1681, the French law, ordinance of Louis XIV, on the above maxim of the civil law, did the same; and repeated it in their modern code of 1807, that is, if we follow the maxim, "Expressio unius est exclusio alterius," – "That direct affirmation prohibits what is omitted." Life insurance is certainly not mentioned among the objects of the contracts of assurance, recognised in article 334 of that code, as confirmed by Louis XVIII in 1814. Baron Locre, Laporte, Delancourt, and Estrangin, and Boulay Paty, excellent commentators, construe the omission as a prohibition. M. Pardessus, also an able jurist, is in favor of the legality, in France, of life insurances; and in 1820, the French government established a chartered office, and there is now one other or two. It was likewise prohibited by the ordinances of Amsterdam, Rotterdam, and Middleburg.

The cause of the earlier prohibitions is probably fortified by a superstition, similar to the common one against making a will, the absurd notion sometime prevalent; and we will not undertake to say that it does not exist in these days and among our people, that it is an impious attempt to prevent or control the will of Providence, and will hasten, by way of judgment, as it is phrased, the event about which it calculates. The best answer to this absurdity, if it deserves any, is found in the tables of mortality, which show that the actual average of life of the insured is greater than that of the uninsured; as a philosophical view of the subject would lead us to infer from the increased tranquillity of mind, and comfort, and ease. It has not, however, been really worth the while for common sense to disabuse the public mind of such nonsense, or for prudence to advocate the practice of life insurance, which necessarily extends so far in time, and rests upon permanency, on the continent of Europe; where all institutions have constantly been uncertain and shifting, in silent change or awful convulsions.

Like marine insurance, life insurance has been strongly argued, for and against. Emerigon termed the former a kind of game, that demanded the utmost caution in those who played it. But our people, who are to be insured in life companies, have to look, not to the details of organization, but only to their results, and to the skill, honesty, and ability of the directors to fulfil their contracts.

The French committee of 1807, still speaking of marine insurance, call it "Un beau contràt, noble produit du génie de l'homme, et le premier garant du commerce maratime;" – "An excellent contract, noble product of human genius, and best security of commerce." And our admirable jurist, Chancellor Kent, adopts from Valin, the sound and luminous commentator on the French ordinance of Louis XIV, relating to insurance – "That maratime commerce cannot well be sustained without it; under its patronage, and with the stable security it affords, commerce is conducted with immense means and unparalleled enterprise over every sea."

It has been suggested, that national character has something to do with the reception of the practice of life insurance; if so, then we may expect / it to flourish, as soon as it is understood, among the enterprise, intelligence, caution, and shrewdness of the United States. The practice in Europe, of life insurance, is, in a great degree, confined to England; elsewhere, the legislation on this subject, from Justinian to Louis le Grand, and Napoleon, inclusive, as we have seen, has been founded on the principle that it was unfit and improper to allow such insurances. Writers have been earnest on both sides. "Le Guidon," a treatise on mercantile law, written in the sixteenth century for the merchants of Rouen, condemns life insurance as "contrary to good morals, and as being the source of infinite abuse." We shall see, however, that the modern contract or policy of life insurance, can be, and is so worded, as to take away almost all the chances for such abuse. Boulay Paty, in his Commentaries on the French Code, above referred to, inveighs bitterly against policies on human life as being gambling transactions of the most pernicious kind; see Kent's Commentaries on American Law, when he also quotes – "Ista conditiones sunt plenæ tristissimi eventus, et possunt invitare ad delinquendum;" – "Such contracts are full of the worst consequences, and may possibly invite to fraud." And what human, we had almost said, divine institution, is there in the freedom of man's erring will, of which such a possibility cannot be predicated? Boulay Paty says, further, "they ought to be left to their English neighbors."

On the other hand, life insurance was tolerated in the famous commercial ordinances of Wisbug in the Baltic, in those of Naples, and of Florence; and in Lombardy, the practice of such insurances, called *vitaligio,* exists without the formality of chartered companies. M. Pardessus, a commentator, also of the highest merit, on the French code, is in favor of their legality; and so is the French government, as we have seen. In France, however, though the premiums are moderate, more so, in fact, than in England, and the companies in good credit, they have met with little encouragement to their strenuous exertions to spread the practice; nor have they been more successful in carrying those exertions into Italy or into Switzerland. As an offset to Boulay Paty's sneer on this subject at the English, Marshall suggests that the prohibitions and objections to life insurance, in France and Italy, proceed from motives of policy, founded on a startling sense of the great infirmity of their public morals, which would expose to hazard lives so insured.

In the Netherlands, three life insurance companies were established previous to 1827, with reasonable anticipation of success, though we are not aware how that has been fulfilled. They were granted a monopoly against foreign companies. The same exclusion exists in Denmark, where there are several offices; but it is stated that, up to 1827, the companies there had done very little. An able and well-informed writer in the Edinburgh Review, to whom, as well as to Professor Vethake's edition of McCulloch's Commercial Dictionary, we would, once for all, make our acknowledgements, seems to think that the Netherlands, Holland, and the states of the Germanic Union, have a strong disposition in favor of the practice of life insurance, and from recent (1827) appearances will, ere long, generally resort to it; "because," as he says, "it is more congenial to their frugality, industry, habits, and tastes, than to the character of their more lively neighbors." Yet he, at the same time, states, that one small society established at Elberfeld, in the Dutchy of Berg, was, in 1827, the only institution to be found in Germany, including Austria and Prussia. Denmark, / with the habits supposed to be so congenial, does nothing; and he gives, as a reason for the inhabitants of Germany resorting to the Alliance Assurance Society, in London, that they have confidence in it, partly on account of the large capital invested in the undertaking, (it is over twenty-two millions of dollars,) but chiefly, from the names of some of its supporters being universally known in the mercantile world. We find N. M. Rothschild and M. Montefiore, are among its presidents.

From this account of the different manner in which the subject has been received, in southern and northern nations, and among those of the same character and habits, it would seem that the notion of the effect of manners is rather fanciful than otherwise. Ignorance, misunderstanding, instability, and insecurity of financial condition, have most to do with the retardation of life insurance; but no one all-sufficient cause can be pointed out. Commercial activity, knowledge, good organization and conduct, experience, stability of institutions, and security of investment, in short, confidence, must be the elements of the prosperity of life insurance in any country; and will, wherever they exist, compel the appreciation and the use of such a benevolent and philanthropic instrument. The following table shows the corporate and literary history of our subject at a glance, and may serve as a useful reference to sources of information: –

1706,	England,	Amicable Life Assurance Society,		Mutual Co.
1720,	"	Royal Exchange Life and Fire Society,		Proprietary Co.
1762,		Equitable Life Assurance Society,		Mutual Co.
	"	About this time some four, five, or more fire and annuity companies were commenced, and abandoned for want of success, as predicted by Mr. Price, being founded on wrong principles and calculations.		
1803,	"	Globe Assurance Company		Proprietary So.
1792 to	„	Ten Life Assurance Societies,		Proprietary.
1807,		Two Life Assurance Societies,		Mixed.
1807 to		Five Societies,	{Twenty were estab-	Mutual.
1827,		Three co's,	lished between 1823	Proprietary.
	"	Twenty-six co's,	and 1828, and five discontinued ab't 1824, two being combined in one.}	Mixed.
1818	U. States,	Massachusetts Hospital Life Insurance Co.,		Proprietary.
1820	France,	La Compagnié D'Assurance Générale,		"
1820 to	"	La Compagnié Royale D'Assurance,		
1827	Nether-	Three companies,		"
	lands,	Four (?) companies,		"
	Denmark,			"
	Germany,	One, at Elberfeld, Dutchy of Berg,		
	Austria,			"
	Prussia,			
1832,	U. States,	Baltimore Life Insurance Co.,		"
"	"	Pennsylvania Life Insurance Co.,		"
"	"	New York Life Insurance and Trust Co.,		"
1836,	"	Girard Life Insurance and Trust Co.,		Mixed.
"	"	Union Assurance, New York,		"
"	"	Southern Life and Trust Co.,		"
"	"	Dutchess County Assurance, New York,		"
"	"	Ohio Life Insurance and Trust Co.,		"
"	"	Farmers' Loan and Trust Co., New York,		"
"	"	American Life Insurance and Trust Co.,		"
1842,	"	Mutual Life Assurance Co., New York,		Mutual.

In England, corporations are continually forming. We do not know the exact dates of the establishment of all. /

1612,	Amsterdam,	Statute prohibiting Life Insurance.
"	Holland,	Van Hudden – Value of Life Annuities.
1661,	"	Jean de Witt, De Vardye van der Lipreuten – Value of Life Annuities.
1681,	France,	French Ordinance of Louis XIV, liv. 3, art 10, tit. 6, prohibiting Life Insurance.
1693,	England,	Dr. Halley's Essay, in Philosophical Transactions of the Royal Society, London, containing the first accurate Tables of Mortality, and compiled from observations in Breslau, in Silesia, during five years.

1724,	France,	De Moivre – Annuities on Lives, with Tables.
1740,	Holland,	Struyck.
1742,	England,	Thomas Simpson – Annuities and Reversions, with Tables from the London Bills of Mortality, but when the rate of mortality there was much higher than now.
1746,	France,	M. Anthony Deparcieux, sen. – Essai sur les Probabilitès de la Durèe de la Vie Humaine – Essay on the Probable Duration of Human Lives; which procured him a seat in the Academy of Sciences. He compiled his Tables from the registers of deaths in several religious houses in France, and the lists of the nominees in several Tontines. He was the first who made separate tables for males and females, and thereby showed that the latter lived longer. His tables are compiled with great care, and their results are very similar to those of the Carlisle Tables, hereafter mentioned, and which are generally used in England and the United States.
1748,	Holland,	M. Keerseboom – Table of Life Annuities; from Lists of Life Annuitants.
"	England,	James Dodson.
"	France,	M. Deparcieux, jun.
"	"	M. De St. Cyran.
"	Germany,	Leonard Euler – Tables of Annuities.
"	"	Sussmilch – Tables from Mortality at Vienna and at Berlin.
"	Sweden,	Peter Wargentin – Tables, compiled from the Mortality throughout Sweden.
"	France,	M. Buffon – Tables of Mortality, from Part of the Population of France.
"	Switzerland,	M. Muret – Tables, from Observations in the Pays de Vaud.
1766,	England,	Mortimer's Commercial Dictionary.
1770,		Dr. Price on Annuities. He published in this work the celebrated Northampton Table, compiled from the Register of Deaths, &c., in
	"	the parish of All Saints, Northampton, one of the centre counties and towns in England. This is considered a standard work. He also published the rates of mortality at Norwich and Chester, in England, and also in the kingdom of Sweden.
1772,	"	William Dale's Calculations and Introduction to the Doctrine of Annuities, with Tables.
1786,	"	Park on Insurance.
1787,	Scotland,	Miller – Elements of the Law of Insurance.
1787,	France,	M. Duvillard – Tables, from Observations on the Deaths among the Whole Population of France.
1795,	England,	Mr. Morgan's, of the Equitable Life Insurance Co., England – Address, on the Subject of Life Assurance.
"	"	Dr. Hutton's Mathematical Dictionary – Art., Life Annuities.
1810,	"	F. Baily on Annuities.

		Mr. Milne's, of the Sun Life Assurance Co., England – Treatise on Life Annuities and Insurances. In this work he published the Carlisle Tables, which have been considered as the most applicable to the United States, and which were made from observations of Dr. Heysham of the Mortality at Carlisle, in the northwest of England. /
1810,	England,	Encyclopædia Britannica, new edition – Art., Annuities, prepared by Mr. Milne.
"	"	Bell's Commentaries on Insurance, &c.
1802,	"	Marshall's Treatise on the Law of Insurance.
"	U. States,	North American Review, art. 15, vol. 7, pp. 323, &c.
"	England,	Finlaison's, of the National Debt Office, England – Tables.
"	France,	M. Pardessus – Collection des Lois Maratimes, and Commentaries on the Code of France, of 1807, relating to Insurance.
1818,	U. States,	Charter of the Massachusetts Hospital Life Insurance and Trust Company.
1820,	France,	The Proposals of the two French Life Assurance Societies, which were scattered through that kingdom and through Italy and Switzerland.
1823,	England,	George Farren's, Resident Director of the Economic Life Assurance Co. – Observations on Life Assurance; explaining the system and practice of the leading life insurance institutions in England.
	U. States,	Phillips' Treatise on the Law of Life Insurance, Boston. This is a treatise which embraces and supersedes all the works on the general subject which preceded him.
1826,	England,	Babbage on Life Assurance. This is a very full account of the subject – the organization, premiums, profits, and progress, of the various life assurance societies up to that time.
1827,	Scotland,	Edinburgh Review, vol. 45, No. 99. This is founded on Mr. Babbage's work, and gives cursorily the principles and the history of life insurance up to that year, in England and on the continent, and is a most able and instructive examination of the subject as it existed in Great Britain.
1828,	England,	D. Hughes' Treatise on the Law relating to Insurance.
"	"	Morgan's Account of the Rise and Progress of the Equitable Life Insurance Company, London; which was established, as we have before stated, in 1762. This work is one giving great information on the principles and practice of life insurance.
"	U. States,	Chancellor Kent's Commentaries on American Law, sec. 48 and 50.
1829,	England,	Parliamentary (Eng.) Reports, session 1829, giving the average rate of interest in England.
"	"	First and Second Reports of the Committee of the English House of Commons, on Friendly Societies; and Act 10 of George IV.
1831,	"	Companion to the English Almanac for that year.
1832,	"	Litten on Life Assurance.
"	"	Tables of Annuities, compiled and published by the Commissioners for the Reduction of the English Public Debt.

„	U. States,	Letter of William Bard, President of the New York Life Insurance and Trust Co., to David E. Evans, Esq., with Tables.
„	„	Proposals of the Baltimore Life Insurance Co., including Tables and Principles.
1833,	England,	The Laws of Fire and Life Insurance, by George Beaumont, Esq.
1836,	U. States,	Proposals of the Girard Life Insurance and Trust Co., Phil., with Tables, in pamphlet.
„	England,	Prospectus and proposals of the different life insurance societies in England, purporting to be founded on the best and latest calculations.
„	U. States,	Revised Statutes of Massachusetts, tit. 13, chaps. 36 and 44, bk. 37, § 40.
1830 and 1839,	U. States,	Proposals of the Massachusetts Hospital Life Insurance Co., and Tables.
1840,	„	Act of the Legislature of New York for the benefit of widows and their children, in relation to life insurance.
„	„	New York state, exempting from taxation.
„	„	Return of life insurance companies in New York, agreeably to standing order of the chancellor of the state, of 1831. /
1841,	Eng. & U.S.	McCulloch's Commercial Dictionary, Professor Vethake's edition, which gives one of the most succinct and satisfactory accounts of our subject, under the articles Insurance, and Interest and Annuities.
"	U. States,	Prospectus of a Boston Equitable Life Insurance – pamphlet.

There are various other works on the subject of life insurance; but this list will, at least, save others a great deal of trouble we own ourselves have encountered from the scarcity of materials, and will point to the remainder. We have not at present by us all that are referred to, and we may have made some mistakes.

It is remarkable in this connexion, that while, on the European continent, the science and literature of life insurance outran that of England yet the practice, founded on that science, was established in the British dominions much earlier and much more extensively than in the rest of Europe. Principles were published first and frequently in those countries where the practice has not obtained; but we must bear in mind that, in those countries, few literary works, and of such scientific works in particular, go into general circulation among the mass of the people. Even by those above the lower classes, and confined to the academies and coteries of science, they are passed as something like the calculations of astronomy or the antiquarian labors of Champollion, exclusively belonging there, and not the subject of interest or inquiry among persons not devoted to scientific pursuits.

The certainty of investments of premiums and capital, and the security of commercial and financial institutions, has contributed much to increase life insurance in England, as fast as a right understanding of it is obtained; and the same causes ought to assist in producing corresponding results in the United

States. The increase of life assurance, as it is there generally termed, in England, where it has frequently been joined with fire insurance, has been truly wonderful and cheering. The "Amicable Society," the first one in England, and incorporated A. D. 1706, is a mutual society. It began with four insurances on the books; at the end of eight years there were but four hundred and ninety policies; now, they amount to hundreds of thousands.

So successful has been the "Rock," a mixed company, that besides the profits paid to the stockholders, they were enabled, in 1819, to add twenty per cent to whole life policies of ten years standing; since then, the profits are so divided every seven years, – two-thirds, which is the usual division in such companies, being appropriated to the whole life policy holders, and one-third to stockholders. One hundred pounds sterling insured for life in 1806, received if it fell in, in 1819, £124; in 1826, £143; in 1833, £176 16s. The "Norwich Union," also a mixed company, paid their stockholders, and in 1830 added twenty-five per cent to their life policies. Many have thus added. The "Equitable" society in London, incorporated 1762, and which is a mutual society, from 1800 to 1820 insured one hundred and fifty-one thousand seven hundred and fifty-four single lives, being more than seven thousand five hundred policies executed annually by that office only.

This office divides most of its profits every ten years; the rates of which division have been such as to give to £1,000, insured for a life in 1816, and falling due in 1830, £520 additional; so that the assured paid the premium for only £1,000, and received £1,520. And yet, besides / this, the office had, in 1840, an accumulated fund of eleven millions of pounds sterling, or forty-eight millions of dollars.

It should be remarked, however, that there are peculiar causes which went to give this enormous profit. The tables first used for fifteen years of its existence, gave an average of life upon which to calculate premiums below the actual average; and a second reduction of fifteen per cent was made in its premiums at the end of twenty-four years from its establishment. After the American war, it is ascertained the average of life was considerably increased by tranquillity, introduction of comforts, &c. The entrance money, now dispensed with, was very considerable. They paid no commission or brokerage on assurance procured, as is the general custom in England now. For the first twenty-five years of its existence, more than half the policies were abandoned without any equivalent, (as is now allowed,) after the premium had been paid for a number of years; and the securities in which their investments were made have risen, during that investment, from fifty and sixty, to eighty and ninety. This accounts for the enormous profits, but the number of policies insured shows the rapid appreciation and the increase of the practice of life insurance.

"The Scottish Life Assurance Society," originally called the Scottish Widows' Fund Society, and a mutual company, established in 1815, had, in 1840. –

Subsisting assurances,	£4,140,977
Annual revenue,	178,203
Accumulated fund,	1,019,239

though they divide among the policy holders their profits every seven years. £1000 insured in 1830, and falling due in 1842, would receive, without increase of premium, £1,268. This society has, besides this, paid, from 1815 to 1840, £400,000, or *one million seven hundred and seventy-six thousand dollars,* to the families of persons insured.

"The Scottish Equitable Life Insurance Company," established in 1831, also a mutual society, declares its dividends of profits every three years, adds to the whole life policies, and sets aside for accumulation. The following are the results of one annual and three triennial investigations: –

	Amount insured.	Annual revenue.	Accumulated fund.	Added to policies, – Total of all periods.
One year, 1832	£67,200	£2,032	£1,828	
Three years, 1835	325,611	11,364	21,661	
Three years, 1838	824,275	30,228	71,191	
Three years, 1841	1,494,331	55,536	153,329	£75,239.

It must be recollected, that this prosperity has risen under a rate of interest for investments at from three to four and a half per cent per annum, annually, while in the United States the rates would certainly be greater.

At this date, 1842, there are in England more than two hundred and fifty thousand existing life insurance policies, and they are rapidly increasing in number, and becoming popular just in proportion as it is understood. But it is now feared that too zealous competition will injure the security and excellence of these institutions, which afford no exception from the danger and evil of extremes; and though their practice is becoming more in favor of insurers, as to the amount of premiums paid, it is doubtful if they may not become less favorable in point of security. /

We now propose to give a cursory history of the practice of life insurance in the United States. The subject has been slowly but gradually gaining ground here. We have given heretofore the names of thirteen life insurance companies among us, – one only in Massachusetts, two in Pennsylvania, two in Maryland, and seven in New York; one having failed in Baltimore. "The Massachusetts Hospital Life Insurance and Trust Company," established in 1818, is a proprietary or joint stock company, with a capital of five hundred thousand dollars, divided into five thousand shares. No stockholder is liable beyond the amount of instalments remaining unpaid on his shares.

Its proposals state, as the groundwork of its establishment, the importance and necessity of an institution in which property may be secured for the support of aged persons, widows, and children. This company has never transacted much life insurance, and has not wished, but rather declined it; most of their business and profits accruing from trusts, &c. In their charter there was a provision that "the company should pay over annually on the 3d of January, to the Trustees of the Massachusetts General Hospital, one-third of the net profits which shall have arisen from the insurance on lives made during the preceding year, and after this deduction, shall declare and divide so much of the remaining profits as shall to the directors seem safe and advisable." There was also in the charter the following tax, monopoly, or prohibition. "Be it further enacted, that so long as this corporation shall well and truly pay to the General Hospital the aforesaid share of profit, it shall not be lawful for any persons or corporation within the commonwealth to make insurance on lives upon land, unless empowered so to do by any future legislation of this commonwealth."

Under that provision it would seem that the agents of foreign companies, besides being subject to the fortieth section of chapter thirty-seventh of the Revised Statutes of Massachusetts, which must be, if there is any permission granted them, the future legislation required, subject to the following further provision of the charter. If life insurance companies were included in this fortieth section, it is strange that there was not incorporated therein the condition of payment of one-third of their net profits to the Hospital. If life insurance companies are not so included, then the foreign agents of such companies have yet to wait for future legislation, and have no right to exercise their functions here, or the above mentioned tax on the Hospital Life Insurance Company is released. The further provision of the charter is this: "And whenever any persons or corporations shall hereafter be thus empowered, the obligation of this corporation to pay the trustees of the General Hospital for the said Hospital, the third part of the net profits which may thereafter arise on insurance on lives, shall cease, unless the same obligation shall be imposed on such persons or corporation thus hereafter empowered."

Under the above provisions of one-third of the net profits on life insurance, the Massachusetts General Hospital received nothing at all, or very little; and in the year 1824, an act was passed by the legislature, "That the agreement entered into between the trustees of the Massachusetts General Hospital, and the Massachusetts Hospital Life Insurance and Trust Company, in the words following, to wit: 'That the trustees of the Massachusetts General Hospital do agree to receive one-third part of the net profits accruing to said company from insurance on lives by sea / and on land, reversionary payments, and generally from all kinds of contracts in which the casualties and contingencies of life, and the interest of money are principally involved, after deducting for the use of said stockholders legal interest on the amount of capital actually paid in by them, and invested in pursuance of the provisions of their said act, said interest not being calculated on any part of the profits of said stock, provided that the said insurance company shall bind itself in writing to pay over annually to the trustees of the Massachusetts General Hospital, for the use of said Hospital, one-third part of their net profits, computed on the principal above stated, as well on the reversionary payments, and all other contracts made by said company, in which the casualties of life and the interest of money are principally concerned, as are insurances on lives, which alone are mentioned in the seventh section of the act to which this is an addition,' be, and the same is hereby confirmed." By which agreement the Hospital, in lieu of one-third of the net profits of life insurance merely, before payment of any dividends to the stockholders, agreed to accept one-third of the surplus of the general profits, after paying to the stockholders legal interest, which is six per cent per annum, on the amount of capital actually paid in by them.

Under this latter agreement, the Hospital is in an annual receipt of from twelve to fifteen thousand dollars. This insurance company must, therefore, be flourishing, though not in life policies; and have an annual income, besides expenses, of forty-five thousand dollars over and above six per cent on money paid in as capital.

There might, perhaps, be a question as to what bearing this compromise, though sanctioned by the legislature, would have upon subsequently granted charters for life insurance companies. As it stands now, the Massachusetts Hospital Life Insurance Company having virtually declined to insure lives, the very object, according to their name, for which their charter and its prohibitory provisions were given, and having placed the rates much higher than others, and still keeping them so, the payment of so large a proportion of the profits of a company which should insure lives as its main business, injures the profits of a stock company, the safety and cheapness of a mutual, and the profits, safety, and cheapness of a mixed company, and operates as a prohibition as unwise, nay, far more so, than the monopoly against foreigners granted to the life insurance offices of Denmark and the Netherlands, and which has been judged to retard the practice there.

That these legislative provisions, and the practice of the Massachusetts Hospital Life Insurance Company under them, have operated in Massachusetts as a prohibition to the establishment of life insurance companies, is not a matter of mere reasoning. No other office has been applied for there until 1838, when a charter was obtained by some public spirited gentlemen of Boston;[1] but upon endeavoring to carry it into effect, the above clauses were found so much in the way, that it could not be got into operation, and the charter still remains as a dead letter.

We have been informed that a willingness was expressed to waive the monopoly and prohibiting provisions, if the legislature should sanction it. If so, we may hope that life insurance will yet flourish in a soil as genial to it as to enterprise, and when caution is as rife as acquisitiveness. There are at this time many persons in New England and in Massachusetts itself, who resort to New York, Philadelphia, and Baltimore for their / calculations whether a chance will or will not happen at all, for death cometh to all men; but on a calculation whether death will happen at a particular time. Yet, as there is no inherent principle of death, but, like the plant, man dies of exhaustion consequent upon the aggregate of attacks of his vital powers, or the vital power of his progenitors, that must be added to by adding years; so age, and the attacks of disease on his own person or the persons of his ancestors, with their modified effects of care, and climate, and occupation, enter into the calculation of chances for life or death. Every one that is born, must die; but most that are born, live several years. Now, to make the annual premiums paid until death, equal the sum to be paid in gross at death, together with expenses and just profits – to adjust the terms of insurance so that the parties insuring may pay neither too much nor too little – it is necessary that the probability of their lives failing in any subsequent year be determined with at least proximate accuracy. If men have a certain number of years of life allotted them, by subtracting any given number as their age, one can ascertain how many years are left them. By observation of the proportion of persons born, that die at the age of one year, two years, three years, &c., respectively, we can tell the proportion of those that live, and the chances of any individual's life, under the same circumstances of climate and living, that surrounded those whom we have observed. From these chances we can deduce the value of an annuity or an insurance, on a life of any age. If, of one hundred of any given age, at any place, we find, by observing successive years, that sixty die in one year, then forty live; and the chances at that age, that any one will die within one year, will be 60/100. If, then, an office contract to pay $1 for every one of those hundred persons who should die within one year, as sixty die, it must pay $60. To save itself then, it must charge enough to each one to pay itself that loss, and also the expenses of watching, calculating, &c., which, say, are $5; and then its profit to induce it to make such a contract, say $5 more, making $70. The office must then receive from each of the one hundred persons, of the age supposed, 70/100 of a dollar, or 70 cents, amounting in all to the $70. But as the premiums for insurance, and the purchase money for the annuity, would be paid at the beginning of the year, the office would have it to invest at interest, and give an income. Thus, at six per cent per annum, the present worth of money in this country, about $66.04 must be received from the one hundred persons, or little more than 66 cents from each.

Take another practical case. In the table of mortality framed by Carlisle, which is believed to represent the average laws of mortality in England with very considerable accuracy, and also to approximate that of the northern United States, out of ten thousand persons born together, four thousand complete their fifty-sixth year. And it further appears, that the number of such persons who die in their sixty-sixth year, is one hundred and twenty-four. So that, the probability that a life of a person now fifty-six years of age, will terminate in the tenth year hence, is 124/4000. Now, reckoning interest at four per cent per annum, which rate must be averaged for the whole number of years through which the calculation runs, as an essential element of that calculation, it appears, that the present value of $100, to be received ten years hence, is $67,556; consequently, if its receipt be made to depend upon the probability that a life of a person, now fifty-six years of age, will fail in its sixty-sixth year, its present value will be 124/4000 of $67,556, or 124x67.556/4000 = $2.094. /

Again, the present value of $100, receivable upon the life of a party now 56 years of age, terminating in the 57th, or any subsequent year of his life, up to its extreme limit, (which, according to the Carlisle Table, is the 105th year,) being calculated in this way, the sum of the whole will be the present value of $100, receivable whenever the life may fail; that is, of $100 insured upon it, supposing no additions were made to it for the profits and expenses of the insurer, which also enter into consideration and are properly adjusted. Upon these principles rest all life insurances and annuities. Observations of mortality are made through successive years, showing the chances of life at different ages and in the different sexes; for they find female longer than male lives. The expenses of management and profit are settled. The average rate of interest at which can be made investment of their premiums and of their capital, if they have any, is estimated. And from these they can make out, and have at different times made out, a tariff of proportionate premiums for sums to be paid in gross at death, commencing at any age, for any number, of years or for a whole life. A contract can be made understandingly, the loss is properly divided, and the grand aim of insurance attained.

Accurate observations are the groundwork of all these calculations; and, as in every other case, the wider in space and time, the larger the sphere of observation, and the greater the number of occurrences observed, the more certain is the result, and the more precise the law of average. Large space enables to compensate for the sickly localities, by the wholesome ones; the unfavorable pursuits, by those favorable to longevity; many years, balance those of epidemics by those of health, and allow an equalization and compensation for the irregularities of seasons, wet or dry, cold or warm; and, of course, time connects itself with another ingredient of average, number of subjects; in which, if it be great, the deaths under a certain age may approximate a compensation for those who live beyond it.

It may readily be perceived, that an insurance company can always secure themselves in the contract; if, for instance, the table shows that 60 persons die of a certain number at a certain age, and they make their calculations upon the supposition that 65 or 70 die, they will be upon the safe side, and may make sure, and probably very great profits. Such has been the case; and one English life insurance company, as we before stated, found they had been calculating too high, and have reduced the proportion of deaths on which they first calculated their premiums, some twenty or twenty-five per cent, and the premiums, in some cases, nearly thirty-five per cent. The insurers may make themselves safe;

and the insured must remember that it is upon the office's so doing, and calculating their premiums so high as to render the payment of losses, when they occur, absolutely certain, that their own security depends. It is the interest of the insured, even more than of the insurers, that there shall be no loss by cheap and inadequate premiums; for, an insurer to insist upon reducing premiums, or patronizing a company who put them too low, is to cut away his own support, and subject himself to loss of premium, and his heirs to loss of the sum insured by the bankruptcy of the unwise office. Premiums must be calculated somewhat higher than the bare mathematical rates, in order to afford leeway for the extent of time through which a contract for life insurance runs. The duty of the office is, to regulate its premiums as near the line of safety as it can; and then, the representatives of those insured who die, will certainly receive what was contracted to be paid upon the happening of that event. But what becomes of the money paid by / those who did not die within the time for which the premiums were calculated? They have paid their premiums each; and what have they got, or what are they to get for them? We apprehend that a satisfactory answer to this question will do more than anything else towards the popularity of life insurance, and towards the extension of its practice in the United States, where every cent has an appreciable value, can be turned over in our American activity, and is expected to produce, in its expenditure, its visible return.

We daily insure our property against fire or other casualty for a certain period, no disaster happens; – we paid our money but for the satisfactory and strengthening feeling of security, and yet we renew our policies. Why not do the same in life insurance? Suppose the sum insured, that we had contracted to have paid on our death, was large; suppose it was ten thousand dollars, and it was to pay an anxious debt hanging over us, our property, and our family, for which our life and personal exertions for another year were necessary! Suppose upon our living another year, was to depend a provision for a loved parent, or an affectionate sister, wife, or child! is the certainty and security, that if we died, it would be paid, worth nothing? the comfortable feeling, that death itself could not beggar our trusting friend or our dependent relatives, not worth the little premium we paid? We can well conceive of situations where the certainty of such provision could hardly be calculated by money; it forms itself an ingredient of success.

But the contracts are themselves framed to meet such cases. One may continue his insurance for a whole life, which is the best kind of life insurance, much better than for years, at a little higher annual premium; and if at any time the payment of that should become onerous, or the end for which one wished security, answered, one can sell his interest, and transfer the policy to some one to whom the payment would be convenient, and who would gain by it, as being an old policy, the premium is less than if a new insurance was made. Or one can surrender it to the company for an equivalent calculated upon known, fixed, and equitable principles, depending on the time for which it was insured, the probability of the policy's falling in, and the amount of premium already paid; or, still again, one can pledge the policy and borrow money from it, either from the company itself, or from others. In some organization of companies, the mixed or mutual, as will appear hereafter, a life policy that has been running some time, may become of very great marketable value.

Annuities, and endowments, and trusts, must be contracted for upon the same principles as those we have previously explained, with reference to life insurances. The chances of life, and the probable average rate of interest for the time embraced in the contract, are the elements of calculation in each. In trusts, the chances of life could only enter into them as limiting the period for which the average rate of interest would have to be estimated. In annuities, the influence of the results of these calculations will be somewhat reversed, as between the office and the annuitant; because, as we before stated, if the duration of life is underrated in these tables, the office receives the premium longer before it has to pay a loss upon death. But if they underrate the duration of life in contracting to pay a certain annual sum or annuity as long as that life lasts, they will have to pay it so much longer than they calculated for. As has been the case in one English office, the Equitable, the deaths among certain annuitants, / in twelve years, were only 339, when, by the Northampton Table, formerly much used, the number of deaths should have been 545.

The present value of an annuity for any given period, is the sum of the present value of all the payments of that annuity, and, therefore, demands much calculation; which, however, is now generally tabular. Annuities are to the annuitant, also, somewhat the reverse of an insurance for life, as requiring a payment in gross for smaller annual payments for a specific number of years, called an annuity certain, or for life or lives, called an annuity contingent; and must, by the office, be calculated in the former case, by counting compound interest, and the average rate of annual interest for the time, together with expenses and profits; and in the latter case, by combining the principles of the former with the principles of the duration of life previously set forth. Take an actual calculation: if it were required to find the present value of $1, the receipt of which is dependent (reverting to the same example given in a previous page) on the contingency of a person, now 56 years of age, being alive 10 years hence, taking the Carlisle Table of mortality, and interest at 4 per cent per annum, as before. Now, according to that table, of 10,000 persons born together, 400 attain to 56, and 2,894 to 66 years of age. The probability that a person now 56 years will be alive 10 years hence, is, consequently, 2894/4000; and the present value of $1, to be received 10 years hence, being, by calculation, 0.675564, it follows that, if its receipt be made to depend on a life 56 years of age attaining to 66 years, its value will be reduced by that contingency to 2894x0.6755648/4000 = $0.48877. If, then, we had to find the present value of an annuity of $1 secured on the life of a person now 56, we should calculate in this way the present value of each of the 48 successive annual payments, reaching up to 105 years, the limit of human life according to the Carlisle Table, which he might receive, and their sum would, of course, be the present value of the annuity.

Such is the principle on which annuities are calculated, though the process is shortened, and the results now reduced to tabular form, whose accuracy can be incomplete only from defect in the premises of observations on bills of mortality. The very names of Morgan, Milne, and Gompertz, added to the safety and confidence of the Equitable, Sun, and Alliance Life Companies of England, respectively, as did the name of the illustrious Bowditch to the Massachusetts Hospital Life Insurance Company.

From what we have said it will be learned that there exists considerable discrepancies in the tables of the duration of human life, according to which life insurances must be effected; and that the contracts will differ not only from that, but from the different average rate at which interest is calculated; and then, again, from the different per centage the respective companies may think necessary for expenses and profits.

Suffice it to say, that the historical explanation we have given, shows that safety and security for payment of all contracts, and excellent profits, can be guaranteed by life insurance companies, because such has been the case through a series of years; and that the constantly increasing patronage they have received, shows that all the rates of premiums which have been fixed to give that stability and income, have not been considered as onerous or prohibitory by the people. Still, there is no doubt, that the lower the premiums can be put, consistent with the stability and the security of the offices, the more extensive will be the practice and the usefulness of life insurance. /

In order that our subject may be perfectly understood, we give several of the tables of the probability of life at different ages, from which tariffs of premiums and of annuity purchases are calculated; and also, the tabular tariffs of the premiums themselves in some of the life insurance offices in the United States. With these tables, after they have been adopted by any office, the common cases of business can be transacted by them at a glance: –

A Table, showing the Expectation of Life at Every Age,
according to the two most used Tables.

Age.	Northampton.	Carlisle.	Age.	Northampton.	Carlisle.
0	25.18	38.72	52	17.02	19.68
1	32.74	44.68	53	16.54	18.97
2	37.79	47.55	54	16.06	18.28
3	39.55	49.82	55	15.58	17.58
4	40.58	50.76	56	15.10	16.89

Age.	Northampton.	Carlisle.	Age.	Northampton.	Carlisle.
5	40.84	51.25	57	14.63	16.21
6	41.07	51.17	58	14.15	15.55
7	41.03	50.80	59	13.68	14.92
8	40.79	50.24	60	13.21	14.31
9	40.36	45.57	61	12.75	13.82
10	39.78	48.82	62	12.28	13.31
11	39.14	48.04	63	11.81	12.81
12	38.49	47.27	64	11.35	12.30
13	37.83	46.51	65	10.88	11.79
14	32.17	45.75	66	10.42	11.27
15	36.51	45.00	67	9.96	10.75
16	35.85	44.27	68	9.50	10.23
17	35.20	43.57	69	9.05	9.70
18	34.58	42.87	70	8.60	9.19
19	33.99	42.17	71	8.17	8.65
20	33.43	41.46	72	7.74	8.16
21	32.90	40.75	73	7.33	7.72
22	32.39	40.04	74	6.92	7.33
23	31.88	39.31	75	6.54	7.01
24	31.36	38.59	76	6.18	6.69
25	30.83	37.86	77	5.83	6.10
26	30.33	37.11	78	5.48	6.12
27	29.82	36.41	79	5.11	5.80
28	29.30	35.69	80	4.75	5.51
29	28.79	35.00	81	4.41	5.21
30	28.27	34.34	82	4.09	4.93
31	27.76	33.68	83	3.80	4.65
32	27.24	33.03	84	3.58	4.39
33	26.72	32.36	85	3.37	4.12
34	26.20	31.68	86	3.19	3.90
35	25.68	31.00	87	3.01	3.71
36	25.16	30.32	88	2.86	3.59
37	24.64	29.64	89	2.66	3.47
38	24.12	28.96	90	2.41	3.28
39	23.60	28.28	91	2.09	3.26
40	23.08	27.61	92	1.75	3.37
41	22.56	26.97	93	1.37	3.48
42	22.04	26.34	94	1.05	3.53
43	21.54	25.71	95	0.75	3.53
44	21.03	25.09	96	0.50	3.46
45	20.52	24.46	97		3.28
46	20.02	23.82	98		3.07
47	19.51	23.17	99		2.77
48	19.00	22.50	100		2.28
49	18.49	21.81	101		1.79
50	17.99	21.11	102		1.30
51	17.50	20.39	103		0.83 /

A Table of Premiums in the United States, for the Insurance of One Hundred Dollars, upon a single life, for One Year, for Seven Years, and for the Whole Life; payable, annually, in the undermentioned Life Insurance Offices.

[Generally, the Premiums of the Philadelphia and New York offices are less than those of the Massachusetts Hospital Insurance Company; but in the Insurance for one year, the Premiums of the former become greater than those of the latter after the age of 60 years; in the Insurances for seven years, the Premiums of the former become greater than the latter at the age of 57 years: and in the Insurances for the whole life, the same comparative increase appears after the age of 49 years.]

	New York Life Insurance and Trust Company, New York, and Girard Life Insura'e, Annuity, and Trust Company, Philadelphia.			Massachusetts Hosp. Life Insurance and Trust Co., Boston. See Ages in the column on the Left.			Average of Premiums on Insurance of $100 for a Whole Life, in Twenty offices in England whose List of Prem's we have before us. Twelve other offices have the same rates as one of these.			Diff. between the Prem. on Male and Fem. policies, according to the only office in England that makes a difference – the Eagle Life Ass. Soc.	
Age.	1 y'r.	7 y'rs.	For lfe.	1 year.	7 y'rs.	For lfe.	Aver'e	High't	Low'st	Male.	Fem.
14	.72	.86	1.53	.89	1.08	1.88					
15	.77	.88	1.56	.90	1.15	1.93					
16	.84	.90	1.62	.96	1.23	1.99					
17	.86	.91	1.65	1.06	1.30	2.04					
18	.89	.92	1.69	1.16	1.38	2.09					
19	.90	.94	1.73	1.25	1.43	2.14					
20	.91	.95	1.77	1.36	1.48	2.18	1.93.5	2.17.9	1.58.3	2.03	1.15
21	.92	.97	1.82	1.44	1.50	2.23					
22	.94	.99	1.88	1.46	1.53	2.26					
23	.97	1.03	1.93	1.49	1.55	2.31					
24	.99	1.07	1.98	1.51	1.58	2.35					
25	1.00	1.12	2.04	1.53	1.60	2.40					
26	1.07	1.17	2.11	1.55	1.63	2.45					
27	1.12	1.23	2.17	1.58	1.66	2.50					
28	1.20	1.28	2.24	1.60	1.69	2.55					
29	1.28	1.35	2.31	1.64	1.71	2.61					
30	1.31	1.36	2.36	1.66	1.75	2.66					
31	1.32	1.42	2.43	1.69	1.78	2.73					
32	1.33	1.46	2.50	1.71	1.81	2.79					
33	1.34	1.48	2.57	1.75	1.84	2.85					
34	1.35	1.50	2.64	1.79	1.89	2.93					
35	1.36	1.53	2.75	1.81	1.94	2.99					
36	1.39	1.57	2.81	1.85	1.98	3.06					
37	1.43	1.63	2.90	1.89	2.05	3.14					

New York Life Insurance and Trust Company, New York, and Girard Life Insura'e, Annuity, and Trust Company, Philadelphia.			Massachusetts Hosp. Life Insurance and Trust Co., Boston. See Ages in the column on the Left.			Average of Premiums on Insurance of $100 for a Whole Life, in Twenty offices in England whose List of Prem's we have before us. Twelve other offices have the same rates as one of these.			Diff. between the Prem. on Male and Fem. policies, according to the only office in England that makes a difference – the Eagle Life Ass. Soc.	
Age.	*1 y'r.*	*7 y'rs.*	*For lfe.*	*1 year.*	*7 y'rs.*	*For lfe.*	*Aver'e*	*High't*	*Low'st*	*Male.*	*Fem.*
38	1.48	1.70	3.05	1.93	2.09	3.23					
39	1.57	1.76	3.11	1.96	2.15	3.31					
40	1.69	1.83	3.20	2.04	2.20	3.40	3.17	3.06	2.07	3.06	2.12
41	1.78	1.88	3.31	2.10	2.26	3.49					
42	1.85	1.89	3.40	2.18	2.33	3.59					
43	1.89	1.92	3.51	2.23	2.39	3.69					
44	1.90	1.94	3.63	2.28	2.46	3.79					
45	1.91	1.96	3.73	2.34	2.54	3.90					
46	1.92	1.98	3.87	2.39	2.63	4.01					
47	1.93	1.99	4.01	2.45	2.71	4.13					
48	1.94	2.02	4.17	2.51	2.81	4.25					
49	1.95	2.04	4.49	2.61	2.93	4.39					
50	1.96	2.09	4.60	2.75	3.04	4.54					
51	1.97	2.20	4.75	2.86	3.14	4.68					
52	2.02	2.37	4.90	2.95	3.24	4.83					
53	2.10	2.59	5.24	3.05	3.35	4.98					
54	2.18	2.89	5.49	3.15	3.48	5.11					
55	2.32	3.21	5.78	3.25	3.60	5.31					
56	2.47	3.56	6.05	3.36	3.74	5.50					
57	2.70	4.20	6.27	3.49	3.88	5.70					
58	3.14	4.31	6.50	3.61	4.03	5.94					
59	3.67	4.63	6.75	3.75	4.19	6.11					
60	4.35	4.91	7.00	3.90	4.35	6.36	6.11	9.05	5.17	6.11	4.15 /

Table of Endowments, which is the same for the Massachusetts Hospital Life Insurance Co., and for the New York Life Insurance and Trust Co.

[This table shows the sum which the companies will pay to the party for whom an endowment is purchased, if he should attain the age of twenty-one, for one hundred dollars purchase money, received by the company at the ages mentioned in the table.]

Age.	*Sum to be paid at 21, if alive.*	*Age.*	*Sum to be paid at 21, if alive.*
Birth,	$376 84	9 Yrs.,	$171 91
3 months,	344 28	10 „	164 46

Age.	Sum to be paid at 21, if alive.	Age.	Sum to be paid at 21, if alive.
6 months,	331 46	11 „	157 43
9 months,	318 90	12 „	150 64
1 year,	306 58	13 „	144 12
2 „	271 03	14 „	137 86
3 „	243 69	15 „	131 83
4 „	225 42	16 „	125 97
5 „	210 53	17 „	120 31
6 „	198 83	18 „	114 89
7 „	188 83	19 „	109 70
8 „	179 97	20 „	104 71

Table of the Rates at which the Company will grant an immediate Annuity of One Hundred Dollars, on a single life, at the Ages specified in the Table; the Payments to be made Annually, commencing one year after making the grant.

[This is calculated on the Carlisle Table at 4 per cent per annum, average annual interest; is used in the English Annuity Companies, and likewise in the Massachusetts Hospital Life Insurance Co., and in the Girard Life Insurance, Annuity, and Trust Co., Philadelphia.]

Age.	Sum paid down for purchase of the Annuity.	Rate of Int. allowed.	Age.	Sum paid down for purchase of the Annuity.	Rate of Int. allowed.
20,	$1,836 30	$5 45	48,	$1,341 90	$7 45
21,	1,823 30	48	49,	1,315 30	7 60
22,	1,809 50	52	50,	1,300 00	7 69
23,	1,795 10	57	51,	1,280 00	7 81
24,	1,780 10	62	52,	1,260 00	7 91
25,	1,764 50	67	53,	1,240 00	8 06
26,	1,748 60	72	54,	1,220 00	8 20
27,	1,732 00	77	55,	1,200 00	8 33
28,	1,715 40	83	56,	1,175 00	8 51
29,	1,699 70	88	57,	1,150 00	8 70
30,	1,685 20	93	58,	1,125 00	8 89
31,	1,670 50	99	59,	1,100 00	9 09
32,	1,655 20	6 04	60,	1,070 00	9 35
33,	1,639 00	10	61,	1,045 00	9 57
34,	1,621 90	6 17	62,	1,020 00	9 80
35,	1,604 10	23	63,	995 00	10 05
36,	1,585 60	31	64,	970 00	10 31
37,	1,566 60	38	65,	940 00	10 61
38,	1,547 10	46	66,	910 00	10 99
39,	1,527 20	55	67,	880 00	11 36
40,	1,507 40	63	68,	850 00	11 76
41,	1,488 30	72	69,	820 00	12 20
42,	1,469 40	81	70,	790 00	12 66
43,	1,450 50	89	71,	780 00	12 82
44,	1,430 80	99	72,	770 00	12 99
45,	1,410 40	7 09	73,	760 00	13 16
46,	1,388 90	20	74,	750 00	13 33
47,	1,366 20	32			/

A Table, giving a Comparative View of the Results of the undermentioned Tables of Mortality, in Relation to the following Particulars. *

	By Dr. Price's Table, North-ampton, center of England.	First Swedish Tables for both Sexes, published by Dr. Price.	By Deparcieux's Table, founded on the Mortality in French Tontines before 1745.	By Mr. Milne's Table on the Mortality at Carlisle.	By Mr. Griffith Davies Table, on Experience of Equitable Life Ins. Company.	By Mr. Finlaison's Table, on Experience of Government (Eng.) Life Annuities. First Investigation in his Evidence, 1825.	Second Investigation in his Evidence, 1827.
Of 100,000 persons aged 25, there would be alive at the age of 65,	34,286	43,137	51,033	51,335	49,930	Mean of both sexes. 53,470	Mean of both sexes. 53,470
Of 100,000 persons aged 65, there would be alive at the age of 80,	28,738	23,704	29,837	31,577	37,267	38,655	37,355
Expectation of life at the age of 25 years,	30.85	34.58	37.17	37.86	37.45	38.35	38.52
Expectation of life at the age of 65 years,	10.88	10.10	11.25	11.79	12.35	12.81	12.50
Value of an annuity on a life aged 25, interest being at 4 per cent.,	£15.438	£16.839	£17.420	£17.645	£17.494	£17.534	£17.634
Value of an annuity on a life aged 65, interest being at 4 per cent.,	£7.761	£7.328	£8.039	£8.307	8.635	£8.896	£8.751
Value of a deferred annuity commenci'g at 65 to a life now aged 25, interest at 4 p. ct.,	£0.55424	£0.65812	£0.85452	£0.88823	£0.88723	£0.99078	£0.98334

*   From McCulloch's Commercial Dictionary.

In all the tables above mentioned, it is to be observed that the mortality is deduced from an equal, or nearly equal number of each sex, with the single exception of Mr. Davies' table, founded on the experience of the Equitable, mostly, of course, there, males. But as it is agreed that females outlive males, the results of Mr. Davies' table fall materially short of what they would have been, if the facts on which he has reasoned comprehended an equal number of each sex. The tables have not, in all cases, been computed at 4 1/2 per cent, the rate allowed by government.

The Northampton Table, given before, by underrating the duration of life, was a very advantageous one, as has been stated, for the insurance offices to go by in insuring lives; but to whatever it might be beneficial to them in this respect, it became equally injurious when they adopted it as a guide in selling annuities. And yet, singular as it may seem, some of the insurance offices in England granted annuities on the same terms on which they insured lives; not perceiving that, if they gained by the / latter transaction, they must invariably lose by the former. The English government also continued, for a lengthened period, to sell annuities according to the Northampton Tables, and without making any distinction between male and female lives. A glance at the tables of M. Deparcieux, ought to have satisfied them that they were proceeding on entirely false principles. But in despite even of the admonitions of some of the most skilful mathematicians, this system was persevered in until within a few years. We understand that the loss thence arising to that government, may be moderately estimated at 2,000,000 sterling, or $8,880,000. Nor will this appear a large sum to those who recollect that, supposing interest to be 4 per cent, there is a difference of no less than £91 1s. ($404 59) in the value of £50 ($222) annuity per life, to a person aged 45, between the Northampton and Carlisle Tables.

There have not been any sufficient observations, or tables of mortality, made in the United States; but, as before stated, the calculations of our life insurance and annuities are made from the above table of Carlisle observations.

In 1839, the New York Life Insurance and Trust Company were engaged in ascertaining data from which to compute the average duration of life in the United States; and, to this end, procured authentic information from different parts of the state of New York, as to the continuance and length of life in about two thousand families. The facts and statements so ascertained were submitted to Mr. J. Finlaison, (of the English national debt office,) of London, with the intention, on the part of the company, of reducing their rates of life insurance, provided it shall appear by the result of Mr. F.'s calculations that they can do so with reasonable safety.

There were, in England, none made by order of government, until Mr. Finlaison (of the national debt office) was employed, a few years since, to calculate tables of the value of annuities, from the ages of nominees in the public tontines, and of individuals on whose lives the English government had granted annuities, in the strange manner we have above mentioned. Other tables were, as we have seen, the work of private individuals.

The following calculations and notes, on the recent census of the United States, appeared originally in a Cincinnatti paper; and, as they are germain to our subject, we extract them here: –

In the United States there occurs, between the ages of 15 and 25, one death in 211 persons; between 25 and 35, one death in 43; between 35 and 45, one death in 76; between 45 and 55, one death in 54; between 55 and 65, one death in 34; between 65 and 75, one death in 19; between 75 and 85, one death in 125; between 85 and 95, one death in 112; between 95 and 105, one death in 116.

The above shows a less proportion of deaths between 15 and 25, in proportion to those between 5 and 15, than the bills of mortality generally show. From the age of 45, the proportional number of deaths continually increase, until at the age of 75; but few remaining, their sifted constitutions suddenly change the proportion. This census of 1840, shows that there are 759 persons above the age of 100 years – more than 200,000 white persons in the United States are past the age of 70 years.

The laws of life and mortality between the sexes appear very remarkable:

1. The number of females born per an., is about 12,000 less than the males.
2. At 20 years of age, the females exceed the males. This proves that between birth and 20, the mortality among the males has been much greater than among the females. /
3. From 20 to 40, the men again much exceed the women; which shows that this is the period of greatest mortality among women.
4. From 40 to 70 the difference rapidly diminishes; the females, as in the early part of life, gaining on the males. This shows that this is the period of greatest danger and exposure to men, and the least to women.
5. From 70 onwards, the women outnumber the men; showing that, relatively speaking, in comparison with man's, the healthiest period of female life, is towards the close of it.

T. R. Jencks, 'Life Insurance in the United States, Number II', *Hunt's Merchants' Magazine and Commercial Review* (1843)

Art. II. – LIFE INSURANCE IN THE UNITED STATES.

NUMBER II. ORGANIZATION AND PRACTICE OF EXISTING LIFE INSURANCE COMPANIES.

We next turn to the organization and practice of existing life insurance companies, so far as we have the means at hand to do it just at present. Mr. Babbage[1] gives a very full account of the societies in England, as they are set forth in their proposals; many of those proposals we have now by us. The reader will be struck at the ingenuity of means contrived by different offices to get at the same ends: security, profit, cheapness, and popularity.

Marine insurance in England has been generally carried on by private underwriters; there being only a few chartered offices in England, and the four oldest do a great proportion of the business. The fire and life insurance societies were joint stock companies; some of the fire are called contribution societies. The Milanese *Vitaligij*, are similar contracts for life insurance; and the mutual offices, of which kind was the first life office in the island, seem to be much in vogue, though less so than the mixed, a species combining the two others. Just such have been the phases of the matter in the United States.

We are not aware that there any longer exists in the United States the practice of private underwriting; while, within a few years, the practice of mutual insurance seems to threaten to drive all other methods out of the field. Life insurance companies are, in their organization, divided into three classes, having their characteristic differences in the manner in which they provide security for the payment of losses, and in the pecuniary advantages which they offer to those who are connected with them. The first class are common joint stock companies, who undertake to pay sums certain upon the death of individuals insuring with them; the profits made by such companies being wholly divided among the proprietors of the capital stock. These may be termed proprietary companies. The peculiar advantages of this class are, the security of the subscribed and actually paid capital, and the private wealth of the individual partners, who are known, and in England are, except in the chartered companies, personally liable for the contracts of the company. This personal liability depends, in the United States, upon its limitation by the respective state legislatures. But in these companies, either from a too zealous wish for individual gain, or to provide for the safety of the capital, the premiums are sometimes thought to be too high; the assured have no control over them, and no compensating advantage accruing from their original excess. These proprietary companies have been very popular in England, because the people thought them more secure, and were not aware of the peculiar constitution and practice of the other classes of societies. Safety is the grand desideratum, and that must depend on the accuracy of tabular observations and calculations: the science of the actuary to apply the principles to practice, and the prudence and care of directors in making investments from which the funds to meet the expenses and losses shall be forthcoming. Having settled the safety of any particular office – and without settling that first, one would be a fool to enter on a contract which takes from him a large present sum, or annual payments through probably thirty, perhaps / seventy years, and through all chances, civil, political, and physical, before its consummation in his favor – having settled the question of safety, it is time to look at other points of popularity and desert in other kinds, which seem to be so much greater in them than in proprietary offices that it is thought the latter will dwindle before the favor that has been received by the mixed and mutual companies.

The second class of societies, which may be termed the mixed, are also joint stock companies, with proprietary bodies; but, instead of contracting to pay fixed sums at the termination of the life insured, they, first paying the stockholders simple annual interest, and setting aside a contingent fund, divide the balance of their net profits among those who have taken out policies for life at their office. The subscribing shareholders supply a capital, and take upon themselves the risk of loss; and then divide a certain proportion, generally, as we stated before, two-thirds, among the assured. This interposition before the policy holders, so far as the capital goes, affords the same security and safety that is provided in the first class, or proprietary societies. In an examination of the comparative merits of this second class, it is obvious that the great question still is, its security. The direct interest of the stockholders, and their responsibility, extending in England, and it may be here, according to our state statutes, to each individual, even beyond the amount of his shares, will cause them to watch well after the management; and the assured cannot suffer loss except over the loss of the stockholder. The assured, however, with such a mixed company, becomes liable as a partner to all contracts, he having a share of the profits. On the other hand, there is the advantage of a participation of profits, without investment of capital; depending for its degree in this class, also, on security, or the ability and honesty of the management of the affairs of the society. Some of these companies have a clause in their policies, limiting the responsibility of the individual members to their respective shares; this has been doubted to be good in law, but of course could be adjusted by direct legislation.

With the third class of life insurance societies, called the mutual, our community may be said to be somewhat acquainted, by means of mutual fire and marine insurance companies. In this class, the whole of the profits, after deducting expenses and a proportion to accumulate a guarantee fund, are divided among those who are holders of policies for life. Every one insured is, during the existence of his policy, a partner in the concern, and is mutually the insurer as well as the insured. This makes every policy holder in such an office interested in its smallest results, and jealously careful of the administration of its affairs, as affecting, not only his security, but his liability.

In short, good conduct is the Shibboleth of choice in this, as in the other classes. "As it would be absolute folly to effect insurances with a mutual insurance company, unless there were a complete conviction that respectability, and scientific knowledge, and sound discretion, characterized the parties in whose hands the management was placed; so it would be equally ridiculous to effect insurances with a mixed proprietary company, which was not distinguished, to the fullest degree, by the same qualities."

Security being equal, then, it seems to us that the greatest advantages, and the fullest ingredients of popularity and of usefulness, are offered by mutual societies. /

The main inducements held out by the mixed and the mutual societies, are the division of the profits. The way in which this division is actually effected, is as various almost as the societies are numerous. There are two general methods that have been adopted, which are the following: – At stated periods an investigation takes place, a balance sheet is made, and the proportion of the profits to be divided among the holders of policies for life, are apportioned to the individuals, either by addition to the amount, which they insured originally and upon which they paid their premium, and which they are to receive when the policy falls in; or, their proportion is applied under known rules, to diminishing the annual premiums that they are to pay in future. The details of these two methods are, as we have said, very various. The societies differ very much in the periods at which the stated dividends are declared. After the first from their establishment, which is so ordered as to give time for the society to get under way, they vary from five to seven, and ten years. Five would be most advantageous, no doubt, if always consistent with safety; but, as it is generally a cycle of the old magic number of seven years, that includes the mercantile ups and downs of the United States, it would be better in this country, perhaps, to select that number. This would give the policies a better marketable value; for, as the matter is now understood, especially in England, they are commodities like bank or railroad stock, or any other articles of sale and traffic.

For a more full understanding of our subject, we give some of the rules of division in the English companies. The Alliance Office requires, that life policy holders shall have paid five successive annual premiums. It may be proper to remark, that the dividends are always confined to insurers for a whole life, which is an inducement for such policies, and such actually form by far the greatest proportion of the contracts made. The "Law Life," requires three annual payments to entitle to a dividend. One society limits dividends to holders of whole life policies, of £100 and upwards. Another requires that it shall be one of the five thousand policies of oldest date in the office, and shall have paid six successive annual premiums to be entitled to a dividend. The general proportion of the profits so divided, is two-thirds; but some divide three-fourths, others all, after a moderate deduction for guarantee and expenses of management. Another, after a deduction like the last, divides equally between stockholders and assured. Another, takes one-fifth for a guarantee before division. The "Rock," sets aside £5,000 first, then divides the remainder of the net profits into three parts: one to be added to the capital, as proprietor's fund, and the other two-thirds to be divided, as stated in the contract policy, when made. Another, divides two-sixths among the policy holders; and another, intending to return to the stockholders the sum subscribed, together with one hundred per cent additional, sets aside one-tenth of the profits for this purpose, and divides the remaining nine-tenths between the assured and the shareholder, in the proportion of eight to the former, and one to the latter. While another office makes a positive addition of ten per cent, every tenth year, to all sums insured for a single life; and still another, the Mutual Life Insurance Company, London, established in 1824, adds to each policy as it falls in, not waiting for any fixed periods of dividends, its full proportionate share of these accumulated profits; and is, therefore, equally advantageous to old and new members.

The advantage of reducing succeeding premiums, which is the other / mode of sharing the profits, may be sometimes greater than that of adding to the amount of the policy when it falls in. For instance, when an annual payment becomes onerous or inconvenient, or when a debtor insures another's life, and wishes, of course, to secure himself at as cheap a rate as possible, and with the least outlay. Some offices combine the advantages of both methods, by making the addition to the policy at the stated dividend year, and thereafter applying the interest of the amount so added, to reducing the succeeding annual premiums; while another office stipulates that the additions shall be payable, without interest, at the time the policy falls in. In some societies, it is optional with the insured, to have the dividends applied as an addition to the policy, or to reduce the future premiums. In some, this option is confined to those insuring for their own lives, and in some, it must be declared at the making of the policy; in others, within three calendar months after the declaration of the dividend.

This great variety, is a consequence of the struggle for popularity of competition; but, fortunately, it also embraces points of advantage to the insurers, adapted to their various circumstances and situations. He who would profit by such useful and philanthropical institutions, should remember that their very essence is caution; and the peculiarity of their use is, suffering a small actual payment, to avoid a greater contingent one. He should, therefore, look at what he will save from risk, not only at what he pays; and should not be misled to overlook safety, in the unwise wish to get a cheap premium.

Nor is there less variety in the conditions of the policies of the different societies, and in the risks that they take. The premiums have been generally much reduced, and sometimes they even receive them quarterly. The same spirit of competition has been at work here; and has excited, not without reason, some fears that it will, in its results, trench upon the grand principle itself of life insurance – security. Some of the English offices require entrance money, or a payment of some per centage at the time of taking out the first policy. They also require personal appearance before the officer of the society. Both these have been in some offices dispensed with; the latter, upon a commutation for a non-appearance fine. Almost all offices allow commissions to those who bring custom to the office, and even extra commission is allowed to country solicitors who do so. Some companies have a regulation which requires the stockholders to effect assurance at their respective offices, not only under the proviso that they are inclined to effect them anywhere, but absolutely in proportion to their respective shares, and this, either by themselves or others; which requisition also becomes active upon every successive transfer of shares, and thus ensures considerable accession of business.

The directors of some offices are authorized to advance money to the members, on the security of their policies. There has also been an increased laxity in the selection of lives. Formerly, it was under this category: "Those lives, only, of individuals who appear in full health and vigor." This has now been changed for the following: "That all lives shall be accepted, where no positive disease has been manifested;" and other offices almost advertise to ensure a whole hospital upon a consideration. The consequence is, that though a man's life insurance may be rejected at one office, he can find some other at which he can obtain a contract. They have also made a like extension of the latitudes, climates, and voyages, into which the insured may go without vitiating his contract, / and even of the deadly professions he may follow; and have actually adopted, with its comprehensive risks, the technical phrase "whole world policies." The extremes of these circumstances are, of course, still met by additional premiums and special contracts; but the general tendency has been, to increase the facilities of life insurance. The profits which are an inducement to stockholders, and which form a large ingredient in the security of all offices, vary very much from twelve to seventeen, and thirty-nine.

The able writer whom we last quoted, thus characterizes the state of life insurance in England, in 1827: "In regard to the different establishments, it is impossible not to see that there is the greatest difference; as to the ability displayed in their management, much diversity; as to their principles in the acceptance of risks, the utmost inconsistency; as to the rates of premium, some charging little more than one-half of what is charged by others; as to the proportion the expenses bear to the amount of business effected, an incalculable difference." But we have said sufficient for our purpose, to sketch the various aspects which our subject presents; to serve as hints for caution as well as selection, in the practice and organization of life insurances in the United States.

We proceed to mention some of the details of the organization and practice on the above points, adopted in the offices already existing with us; which will show how they have aimed to attain the ends of security and profit.

The usual organization is, a board of directors, a president, several vice presidents, an actuary, and a secretary. The Massachusetts Life Insurance and Trust Company, which is of the proprietary class, transacts its business under the following rules and regulations: "Every person desirous of making insurance on his own life, or upon the life of any other person, or who wishes to contract for reversionary payments on annuities, must sign a declaration by himself or agent, according to a printed form to be furnished by the company, setting forth the age, occupation, place of birth, state of health, and other circumstances attending the life or lives insured, or the life upon the failure of which the reversionary payment of the annuity is to commence. The company may also require a certificate of the health of a person, from a physician of established reputation. An application for an annuity on a life, must state the age of the party to whom it is granted. Any misrepresentation in these declarations, vitiates the contracts.

"Policies of insurance and reversionary contracts are void, if the person whose life is insured shall die upon the seas, or upon any of the great lakes, or shall, without the consent of the company, previously obtained and endorsed upon his policy, pass beyond the settled limits of the United States, excepting into the settled limits of the British provinces of the two Canadas, Nova Scotia, or New Brunswick; or shall, without such previous consent thus endorsed, visit those parts of the United States which lie south of the southern boundaries of the States of Virginia and Kentucky; or shall, without such previous consent thus endorsed, enter into any military or naval service whatsoever, the militia not in actual service excepted; or in case he shall die by his own hands in, or in consequence of, a duel, or by the hands of justice, or in the known violation of any law of these states, or of the United States, or of the said provinces." This last provision is rather vague. "A person must have an interest in the life / he insures, if it be not his own life. No policy takes effect until the first premium shall be paid, and the annual premiums must be paid the day they fall due, otherwise the policy expires; but it may be revived at any time within fifteen days, the person on whose life the assurance was made being then alive and in good health, by the payment of said premium, together with an additional sum of ten per cent upon such premium. All claims will be settled within sixty days after notice, and satisfactory proof of the claim shall be made. Annuities must be demanded by the annuitant in person, or satisfactory proof must be given that the annuitant is still alive. A charge of one dollar is made for each policy of a common form; but where a special contract is required, the expense of drafting it must be borne by the assured. The company reserves to itself the right of making any alterations, which the particular circumstances of applicants may, in their opinion, render expedient. Insurances for one year may, or may not, be renewed at the pleasure of the company." Their refusal may be obviated by insurance for seven years, or for life.

ANNUITIES.

"The company will grant annuities during the continuance of any given life or lives, and make the payments either quarterly, half yearly, or annually, as shall be agreed upon. The payments may commence immediately, or be deferred for any given time. There are two methods of making these contracts, upon principles which differ essentially from each other. In the one, a moderate rate of interest is allowed upon the capital paid (either in money or stocks) for the annuity, and, at the expiration of the life, the whole of that capital is paid back (within sixty days from its falling in, and in the stock or property at fair valuation that the company has then on hand; the same is done in an endowment in trust) to the heirs of the annuitant, or to any person legally authorized to receive it. This contract may, for the sake of distinction, be called an annuity in trust." (It is a sort of savings' bank; the smallest sum so received is $500, and for any sum less than $2,000, the interest is payable only annually; over that, they may purchase it in semi-annual or quarterly payments.) "In the other case, a large interest is allowed during the life of the party, and, at his death, the capital becomes the property of the company. A contract of this kind, is generally called an annuity on a life.

"In the preceding proposals, the company," say they, "have offered as favorable terms to the applicants as they could, consistently with the safety of the property entrusted to their care, which object has been constantly kept in view." (In trusts, they charge for management one-half of one per cent per annum, only.) "The annual return made to the governor and council, which, without expressing the particular sums deposited by individuals, will contain a schedule of the amount of the capital stock and all the property in possession of the company, with the manner of its investment, will always be open to the inspection of any person transacting business with the company." The legislature direct the kind of property, in general, in which investments shall be made by the company; which is to consist in United States funded debt, or Massachusetts State stock, the stocks of incorporated banks in that commonwealth, ground rents or mortgages, and notes secured by mortgages. The above are, generally, the regulations of all our American life offices.

The Girard Life Assurance, Annuity, and Trust Company of Philadelphia, / which is of the mixed class, has similar rules and regulations, and profess to make insurance on the life of "a healthy person not engaged in any hazardous occupation, and residing within the settled limits of the United States, north of the southern boundary of Virginia and Kentucky, or within the settled limits of the two Canadas, Nova Scotia, or New Brunswick." They state, in their printed proposals, that it is their object to offer to the public the following advantages: –

1. Assurers for life to participate in the income.
2. A moderate scale of premiums.
3. Increased facilities for effecting assurances.
4. An ample capital, this being a mixed company, and, in 1837, the only one in the United States of that kind, paid in for the security of the assured.
5. Prompt settlement of claims, without dispute or litigation.
6. Repurchase of policies, in certain cases.
7. Payments of premiums, received either in the whole sum, or in smaller weekly or monthly amounts.
8. The reception and management of trusts.

"The improvements which experience has introduced into the business of life insurance and trusts in England, will be adopted by the company. The income of the company will be apportioned between the stockholders and the assured for life." It does not mention the rates, but we presume the usual English apportionment of one-third to the former, and two-thirds of the net profits to the latter.

"The rates of insurance, annuities, and endowments, will be as low as the most modern experience will warrant, with a due regard to the safety of the insured."

In France, the insurance is about the same as in England, though lives are shorter in the former country. In the Netherlands and Denmark, the premiums are higher than in England. By the table it will be seen, at a few specified ages, how the premiums, both of the Girard Insurance Company and the Massachusetts Hospital Insurance Company, compare with the English.

The Legislature of Pennsylvania, with a provident foresight, required the whole capital of this company to be paid in within two years from the date of its incorporation, and has authorized investigations by the courts into the state of its affairs; affording, if properly carried out, the most ample security to all who do business with the office. The managers, for the still greater security of all interested, have, for the present, limited the amount of policies to be granted in each case. No person can be elected manager who is not himself assured to a specified amount; nor can a person be a manager, unless he be a holder, in his own right, of at least one hundred shares of stock. No manager can borrow money of the company; which, in these days of logrolling and money nepotism in this republic, will perhaps be considered a transcendent item of security and safety. The company pays one-fifth the amount insured immediately, on satisfactory proof of the death of the assured; and the remainder of the claim within the period of sixty days.

Their charter authorizes them to receive and manage estates and trusts of every description, that may be committed to their charge, whether by courts of justice, individuals, or corporate bodies. They are authorized to become guardians of the estates of minors and lunatics and / trustees, under wills. From the moment a trust is accepted, the company becomes responsible for the safety of it, and the whole capital of the company is pledged for its repayment, with the proceeds or interest that may have been stipulated; and the by-laws and regulations of the managers are framed with a view to enforce that security. They also receive money in small or large sums in deposit, to remain one, three, six, or twelve months, or for a longer period, and subject to withdrawal at a short notice, on which interest will be paid; thus becoming a savings bank, as well as a bank of deposit. In the reception and execution of these various trusts, the company, say they, having due regard to the security of the institution and the safe investment of its funds, will make the most liberal arrangements, as to the allowance of interest and charge of commissions, that the circumstances of each particular case may warrant.

Having given the organization of a Proprietary Life Insurance Company, in the Massachusetts Hospital Life Insurance Company, and of a mixed company, in the Girard Life Assurance and Trust Company, we give below the organization of a Mutual Life Insurance Company, under that name in New-York, incorporated 12th April, 1842, and expecting to go into operation by the 1st of January, 1843, when the amount of $1,000,000 will be applied to be insured, they having, at this period, the sum of between $700,000 and $800,000 already entered on their books in the short space of eight months. The act makes those asking for it, and all other persons who may hereafter associate with them, in the manner hereinafter prescribed, a body politic and corporate, by the name of the Mutual Life Insurance Company of New York. In addition to the general powers and privileges of corporations, as the same are declared by the third title of the eighteenth chapter of the first part of the Revised Statutes, the corporation hereby enacted shall have the power to insure their respective lives, and to make all and every insurance appertaining to, or connected with, life risks, and to grant and purchase annuities. All persons who shall hereafter insure with the said corporation, and also their heirs, executors, administrators, and assigns, continuing to be insured in said corporation, as hereinafter provided, shall thereby become members thereof during the period they shall remain insured by said corporation, and no longer. The board of trustees shall consist of thirty-six persons. They shall, at their first meeting, divide themselves by lot into four classes, of nine each; the terms of each expiring successively, in one, two, three, and four years, so as always to have experienced men. They are re-eligible. The seats of these classes shall be supplied by the members of this corporation by a plurality of votes; an insurance of $1,000, at least, entitling a member to a vote.

Every person who shall become a member of this corporation by effecting assurance therein, shall, the first time he effects insurance, and before he receives his policy, pay the rates that shall be fixed upon and determined by the trustees; and no premium, so paid, shall be withdrawn from said company, except as hereinafter provided, but shall be liable to all the losses and expenses incurred by this company during the continuance of its charter. The whole of the premiums received for insurance by said corporation, except as provided for in the following sections, shall be invested in bond and mortgages, or unincumbered real estate within the State of New York; the real property to secure such investment of capital shall, in every case, be worth twice the amount loaned thereon. In / order to avoid a great land monopoly, all real estate as shall not be necessary for the accommodation of the company in the convenient transaction of its business, shall be sold and disposed of within six years from the time they acquire a title to the same. A certain portion of the premiums, not to exceed one-half, may be invested in public stocks of the United States, or of this state, or of any incorporated city in this state – New York. Suits at law may be maintained by said corporation against any of its members, for any cause relating to the business of said corporation; also, suits at law may be prosecuted and maintained by any member against said corporation, for losses by death, if payment is withheld more than three months after the company is duly notified of such losses.

The officers of said company, at the expiration of five years from the time that the first policy shall have been issued and bear date, and within thirty days thereafter, and during the first thirty days of every subsequent period of five years, shall cause a balance to be struck of the affairs of the company, in which they shall charge each member with a proportionate share of the losses and expenses of said company, according to the original amount of premium paid by him, but in no case to exceed the amount of the premium. Each member shall be credited with the amount of said premium, and also with an equal share of the profits of the said company, derived from investments and earnings in proportion to said amount; and in case of the death of any member of said company, the amount standing to his credit at the last preceding striking of balance as aforesaid, together with the proportion which shall be found to belong to him at

the next subsequent striking of said balance, shall be paid over to his legal representatives or assigns, within three months after the said last mentioned balance
shall be struck. Any member of the company, who would be entitled to share
in the profits, who shall have omitted to pay any premium, or any periodical
payment due from him to the company, may be prohibited by the trustees from
sharing in the profits of the company; and all such previous payments made by
him, shall go to the benefit of the company. A provision is made for an ample
public statement of the details of business, losses, profits, investments, &c. No
policy shall be issued by said company until application shall be made for insurance, in the aggregate, for $500,000 at least; and the trustees shall have the right
to purchase, for the benefit of the company, all policies of insurance, or other
obligations issued by the company. This company has, as we stated, thought fit
to transcend the last requirements of the act of incorporation, and not to go into
operation until there be application for $1,000,000 of life insurance. That they
have so nearly filled it up in so short a time, shows a cheering appreciation of the
benefits of life insurance in the United States; and that this postponement of
operations until the amount is subscribed is an ample guarantee of safety, may be
readily and fully understood by an illustration from practice.

The Rock Life Insurance Company, England, paid in losses, in twenty-five
years, $1,790,000, or $71,000 dollars a year; it had, in 1840, existing policies to
the amount of $28,385,000, which would make the losses about 1/329 of the
existing policies in a year. On $1,000,000 worth of policies, the loss, then, would
be annually about $3,000. Now, the amount of income from $1,000,000 worth
of policies, if the ages of the lives insured averaged 40, would be $20,000 a year:
if the ages average 35, the sum would be $18,000, about six times the average
losses. Again, / the amount of annual income in 1840, of the Rock Company,
was $791,000, and the above average annual loss would be about 1/11 of that
sum; which would make the calculation of safety, upon the receipt of premiums
upon $1,000,000, still more favorable. Here we may see, at once, the practice of
mutual life insurance offices, their peculiarities, and how they fulfil the grand
requisites of security and advantage.

It will be seen by the above that it is as Chancellor Kent[2] states: "The terms
and conditions of the English policies are more relaxed now than formerly; but
this is not the case with the American policies on lives." Even the old law requirement of an interest in the life assured, which is in full force here, and fortified
by the English Act of 14 George III., is now hardly looked to in some offices in
England, as appears from their printed proposals. The statutes of Massachusetts
make no provisions for life insurance companies by title, unless in case there is
any want of provisions in their charter, which ought to set out especially their
powers and liabilities. The first section of chapter thirty-seven of Massachusetts
Revised Statutes, headed, like the Code of France, with the broad title "Insur-

ance Companies," has this enactment: "All insurance companies that have been, or that shall hereafter be incorporated in this commonwealth, may exercise the powers, and be subject to the duties and liabilities, contained in this chapter, so far as may be consistent with the provisions of their respective charters." Section fortieth, of this thirty-seventh chapter, contains provisions concerning the exercise of foreign agencies for insurances, still under that broad title; upon this we have cursorily remarked before. The above chapter refers to chapter forty-fourth, which contains general statutory provisions concerning corporations.

April 1st, A.D. 1840, The People of the State of New York, represented in Senate and Assembly, did enact as follows: – Section 1st. It shall be lawful for any married woman, by herself and in her name, or in the name of any third person, with his assent, as her trustee, to cause to be insured, for her sole use, the life of her husband for any definite period, or for the term of his natural life; and in case of her surviving her husband, the sum or net amount of the insurance becoming due and payable by the terms of the insurance, shall be payable to her, to and for her own use, free from the claims of the representatives of her husband, or of any of his creditors; but such exemption shall not apply where the amount of premium annually paid shall exceed $300.

Section 2d. In case of the death of the wife before the decease of her husband, the amount of the insurance may be made payable, after her death, to her children for their use, and to their guardian, if under age.

Having explained, somewhat at length, the history and the principles of life insurance and annuities, we proceed with pleasure to that application of those principles which so ameliorates the anxious and severe in man's destiny. Those applications, with their corresponding advantages, are as various and numerous as the fluctuations of unstable fortune – meet them at every turn, and baffle them in every shape. We would press this matter upon our people.

A hasty compilation, only, can be given of the proposals of some of the offices for life insurance in the United States. Most of the offices propose that they, in similar language to the Massachusetts Hospital Life Insurance Company, will enter into various contracts, so as to accommodate persons in almost every age and situation in life. An insurance may be made for / one year, for several years, or for the whole life. It may be made on one life, on two, or on more lives; to commence immediately, or at a future day. The company will grant annuities upon two or more lives, in all the various forms of which they are susceptible; as, for example, on the joint continuance of the lives, (that is, an annuity which is to cease when any one of the lives fails,) on the longest of the lives, on one life after the death of another; as, for a wife after the death of her husband, or a child after the death of his father. Comfort and security, and consequent prolongation of life, arise from annuities. We do not believe in the objection sometimes made to them, that they deaden enterprise, sink capital; it is only charging the person who uses it, and makes its owner a mere consumer; because annuities are either a resort where security is worth more than enterprise, or a refuge when enterprise has won a rest from his labors, and age and infirmity has made them too hazardous or unproductive.

For persons of moderate property, and for the rich, the annuities and endowments in trust afford the means of making provision for widows and children, and securing the capital in a manner which no other institution has done. The contracts for these annual future payments may be purchased by a large sum down, or by instalments, and will make provision for a period of life when physical exertion and energy are expected to cease; letting persons in youth or middle age, provide for old age. But, excepting for some purpose of family convenience, few young men will purchase an annuity, because a reasonable compensation to the office, and the security of all parties, require that the annuity should be calculated, taking into account the changes of life, at a much lower rate than legal interest, up to forty or fifty years of age. At sixty years of age, some offices allow an annuity of nine and thirty-five hundredth (9 35/100) per cent per annum; at seventy years of age, twelve and sixty-six hundredths (12.66); at seventy-four, thirteen and thirty-three hundredths (13.33) per cent per annum.

By annuities, a person advanced in age, who has a property not sufficient without his personal exertions, which have been or must soon be intermitted, to support him, may purchase with his property, of the office, a competent annual support. So, too, the income of a relative or dependant may be increased at a future period; or an estate may, by an immediate payment of a certain sum, be exonerated from a dower charge, or any other annual incumbrance. A wife can thus, also, gain an equivalent for the surrender of her dower. These annuities may be immediate – deferred, to commence after a fixed period – or reversionary, to commence after the death of some specified person.

The most general use of life insurance is, by persons living on an income – to secure to a family, by its means, a comfortable support after the death of its head or parent. This may be accomplished by the payment, annually, of such portion merely of that income as can be spared. How long time would it be before that little sum, laid by, would accumulate to anything like a moderate support for one's family at his death? One might well be discouraged when he thinks of its slowness; and should he die prematurely, he leaves them to want. To such a person a life insurance office becomes a savings bank, peculiarly adapted to his case; because he may deposit small sums with the company, and convert them into a life insurance. In this manner, an insurance that would cost but little economy in expenses, or retrenchment of some unnecessary luxuries, / would oftentimes place a family in comfortable circumstances, that would, without such prudent management, have been left in wretchedness; and while his industry is providing for the support of those he loves, his small surplus gains are effectually guarding them against poverty in the hour of distress.

What greater obligation can exist for a husband or parent, than to make provision for the comfortable support of a wife or children, who are dependant upon his earnings for subsistence, to take effect at the very time they may most need such assistance – namely, at the period of his death? If an individual has a debt hanging over him, and fears, should he die, his family may be injured by the forced payment of it, he can provide against such a calamity by insuring his life for an equal amount.

A person commencing business may, by an insurance, add to his credit among those with whom he deals, and would add to it, and could even borrow money upon it sometimes from the office itself; were it understood that, in case of his death, there were means provided for quickly settling his debts.

A man receives a comfortable maintenance from the estate of his wife; should he die, her estate would pass into other hands, and her support be gone. By insuring her life he saves the amount, and he is secure in any event.

In our enterprising country, where capital is wanting, and credit on endorsed security is among the means to supply the want; where purchases of land, as well as merchandise, are made on borrowed money; how anxious are they who, dependant on endorsers, perhaps themselves mutual endorsers, see the safety of their friends, their estates, and the support of their families, all at hazard, should death suddenly overtake them. A life insurance, to the amount of their borrowed money or endorsed credit, relieves them from uncertainty, their endorsers from peril, their estates from sacrifice, and their families from ruin.

A creditor anxious about the safety of his debt, in case his debtor should die, may relieve himself by insuring that debtor's life, to the necessary amount; or friends, who wish to lend to a man of skill, industry, and integrity, may defy the chances of fate, which alone they believe constitutes their risk, by insuring their loan upon his life.

The smallest sum may be secured by insurance, and at a trifling outlay. The able, the emulous, the ambitious, the cautious, are desirous of entering upon a hazardous enterprise: they see in it a fair prospect of improving their circumstances, but it requires their personal skill and attention. They fear, should they die, their families will not be able successfully to conclude it: by a life insurance they put themselves at ease, for a slight expense. He who has a wife, an aged parent, an infant child, an infirm friend, an old domestic, depending on him for support, may pay a little sum year by year for the insurance of his own life, and secure them from want after his hand shall no longer move to sustain them.

A public-spirited individual, or a charitable, would aid, by a legacy, a school, a college, a literary society, or a charitable institution. His present means do not enable him to do so, to the extent of his wishes. They may be accomplished by an annual sum paid for an insurance, to the amount he wishes to leave to the favored object. What better way than this to do good and find it fame, with or without a wish so to find it?

How many worthy, pious, but poor clergymen, might be relieved from / anxious care, relative to their families, would their congregations unite and raise a small annual sum for the insurance of their lives; unfelt, like the gentle rain, but in its results. This seems, indeed, to address itself to the religious of New England, imbued as they still are, not only with the atmosphere of churches, but also with much of that personal respect and kindness towards their respective pastors which descend from their ancestors, who founded these ecclesiastical colonies, took the Bible for their constitution – *christo et ecclesia*, for their motto in civil and worldly matters, as well as in literature and religion; and made their pastors their judges in the land, like the ancient people of God their umpires and their spiritual guardians. Really, upon reflection, we wonder that there is a congregation or church in the land, that has not its beloved pastor's life insured for his family: he is not in every case, surely, too far removed from the "scrip, and take no heed of what ye shall eat and what ye shall wear," of the primitive apostles. The preachers of eternity should be separated from the anxieties of time.

It may be assumed, then, that nearly every person, and all persons in general society, have an inducement to embrace the benefits of life insurance; as almost all have a wife, children, or friends, whose support depends chiefly on their own lives; or whose own future support, or some portion of their property or pecuniary interests, is dependant on the lives of others. It were sooner told where life insurance is not useful, than where it is. It concerns the poor as well as the rich; it enables men in the church, the law, or in office, farmers, mechanics, medical men, tradesmen, annuitants, landholders, tenants for life, tenants of mortgaged or portion encumbered estates, creditors, and all who have advanced capital for education, apprenticeship, or business, debtors, philanthropists, men in the navy or the army, to make, cheaply and certainly, ample provisions for the time when their personal exertions must cease, and death stop their industry, payments, and accumulation. It renders contingent property nearly equal, in point of security, with absolute property; and affords scope and means alike for justice, benevolence, and piety.

Remember, too, (we would that we could speak in tones loud enough to be heard by the active conviction of all, of every parent, son, husband, or friend, or man that has not money enough laid up for all the comfort or honesty he would leave behind him in death,) that these varied and vast advantages are offered for petty sums, and they even decrease by the profits of a mixed or mutual office, which would not be missed in a year's expenditure; for the very pocket-money of a hundred expenses, whose payments and purchases are alike forgotten in the moment. Remember, further, that should the continuance of this little annual payment become at any time burdensome or inconvenient, the policy can be sold to him who can pay it, and who wishes the advantage of an established contract with its accumulated profits; or the life insurance office itself will receive the surrender of the policy, and return what has been paid, deducting for care and trouble. The office fairly calculates what is the value of the risk it has run, and gives back to the insured all he has paid over this sum, which went to make up the consideration for the risk to be run in future; and he pays only for the credit, the comfort, and the feeling of security and ease, of previous years.

There are, too, contracts of survivorship; insurances made upon two or more lives, an amount to be paid upon the contingency of one dying / before the other; and insurances upon joint lives, the amounts to be paid at the death of either of the persons. Contracts for deposits, endowments, and trusts, whether for a marriage settlement, provision for children, or guardianship, at simple or compound interest, do not need any explanation; suffice it to say, that life insurance companies, in practice, will carry out their proposals of bargaining "wherein the contingency of life or death is concerned, and their payments are made fully and fairly upon legal proof of life or death, as the contract may be."

Setting out, then, after our exposition, with, we trust, the fair postulate that life insurance is advantageous, safe, and patriotic, may we not assert, that it is peculiarly suited to the United States? We boast our wisdom and caution, and vaunt our benevolence and philanthropy. Where is there a better field, and where can there be a better appreciation of the object of insurance – pecuniary independence from the risk of death – than where life is unremittingly devoted to that end? We have not so many salary men, as in England, to lay by out of their annual incomes; but we have a universal credit, used by youth and age, by every occupation and by every trade. We have scanty capital, statutes of distribution; early marriages and large families, whose only hope, we had almost said, among the exertions and exposures to which they give rise, can be had in the economical reservations from daily expenditures, that are hoarded in life insurances. These considerations, and the shrewd caution of our race, all seem to call upon every individual to avail himself of its advantages, to encourage the institution of offices, and to point to the United States as the very home of life insurance.

Its principles find genial elements of safety and success in the great variety of investing capital that is offered in our stirring communities, and in the higher rates of interest which obtain here. Also, the very times stretch out their hands for aid, amid the wild disruption of other corporations; the crashing of speculating money institutions; the failing of all the sources to which the widow, the orphan, the creditor, the endorser, looked for future payment and needful support: amid all the gloom of distrust in trade and finance, amid the depression and barrenness of all small means of fortune-making, this mode alone of saving a fortune, seems peculiarly to approve itself to our citizens and country, as the only ark of posthumous security.

EARLY PROSPECTUSES

William Frend,[1] *Rock Life Assurance Company* (London: Privately printed, 1809).

An Address from the President and Directors of the Pennsylvania Company for Insurances on Lives and Granting Annuities to the Inhabitants of the United States, upon the Subject of the Beneficial Objects of that Institution (Philadelphia, PA: J. Maxwell, 1814).

On both sides of the Atlantic, life insurance companies that formed in the early nineteenth century did so under the long shadow of the London-based Equitable Life Assurance Society, which dominated the field from its establishment in 1762 into the 1820s. By the time the Rock formed in 1806, several firms had appeared in London to compete with the Equitable, including the Pelican, Globe, London Life and Provident. Of these, the Rock's structure came to typify that of most English life insurers, in that it paid dividends on share capital but also divided part of its profits with policyholders – in recognition of the Equitable's success using the mutual formula.[2] In the United States, only Girard Life of Pennsylvania (1836) operated as a 'mixed' office (like the Rock) prior to the 1840s. The first wholly mutual firm, New England Mutual Life, received its charter in 1835 but would not beginning selling policies until 1844, when it would be competing with a number of other newly chartered American mutuals.

When it appeared on the scene in 1814, the Pennsylvania Company – the first for-profit American office dedicated exclusively to the sale of life policies – signalled its debt to the Equitable in other ways: most obviously in its rate structure, which closely followed the premium scale that Richard Price had constructed for the Equitable. For a firm seeking both share capital and a thriving customer base, the Pennsylvania Company's home of Philadelphia was an obvious location; the city already housed most of the new nation's fire and marine insurers, and out-vied New York and Boston as its early financial centre. In short, it was the closest thing the United States had to London, which was home to the only British life insurance companies through 1806.[3]

Unlike many life insurance prospectuses, the Rock circular reprinted here was directed to the company's shareholders, who (owing to rules described below) generated more than a third of its premium income through 1815, by insuring either their own or their friends' lives.[4] For this audience, who could be assumed to be familiar with the benefits of life insurance through the Equitable's activities, basic information about the insurance contract was less important than details concerning the allocation of profits. Since Frend expected his shareholders to sell or purchase insurance themselves, he also included the company's gatekeeping requirements, which were typical of most early nineteenth-century insurers. The Pennsylvania Company, in contrast, needed above all to educate policyholders and shareholders alike about life insurance, starting with the basic concept and moving on to various scenarios in which it might be useful. This formula would reappear in most prospectuses, both in Britain and the United States, for the rest of the century.[5]

Notes

1. William Frend (1757–1841) was the Rock's actuary between 1806 and 1827, when he retired owing to poor health. He was Second Wrangler at Cambridge in 1780, and until settling down at the Rock, he had trouble holding down a job due to his heterodox religious and political views.
2. The Pelican and Globe would remain wholly proprietary into the 1840s, whereas the London Life and Provident followed the Equitable's model of dividing all (or nearly all, in the Provident's case) of their surplus among policyholders.
3. Murphy, *Investing in Life*, pp. 2, 6–7, 17–21.
4. Alborn, *Regulated Loves*, p. 78.
5. Murphy, *Investing in Life*, pp. 3–4, 128.

William Frend, *Rock Life Assurance Company* (1809)

No. 14, New Bridge Street, Blackfriars.

SIR,

I TRANSMIT to you the Tables for Ordinary Assurances on Lives, for your guidance in making Assurances on your own life, or that of a nominee; according to the plan laid down for the establishment of the Company, and to enable you to assist others, who are desirous of assuring with this Company. At the same time I take the opportunity of making some remarks on the nature of the institution, which may perhaps be not unacceptable, as, from the frequent inquiries made to me personally or by letter upon this subject, I presume that similar applications may have been made to you as a Proprietor; and a written sketch put into the hands of the inquirer, will convey to him ample information.

THE ROCK LIFE ASSURANCE COMPANY is formed on a principle different from that of any Society hitherto established for the Assurance of a Sum to the Representatives of a person assured. The Company consists of a number of Proprietors, possessing a Capital Stock of One Million; and each Proprietor is under the necessity of assuring a sum on his own life, if accepted by the Directors; or on that of an approved nominee, to the amount of one quarter of the Stock in his name. Thus by assuring each others lives, the Proprietors have a mutual interest in the support of the Society, and are engaged to each other to take care that no improper life should, with their knowledge, be admitted into it. The union of such a number of persons, mutually interested in the support of an institution, is a security to the public, that the interests of those, who assure with this Company, and are not Proprietors, shall be consulted with equal regard: for there is no difference between a Proprietor and a Stranger of the same age, in the premium that either pays for assuring a certain sum, or in the sum that may be received by either, provided they have paid their annual premiums for the same length of time.

Two modes of assuring property, to be received by the representatives of the assured, have hitherto been acted upon. By the one, the payment of a certain sum, annually secures to the representatives of the assured a certain sum, at his decease; but, whether the assured lives one year or fifty years, his representatives receive only the sum specified in the contract. By the second mode, the representatives of the assured receive a certain sum at his decease, and whatever addition may have been assigned to that sum by the previous resolution of the Society, agreeably to its deed of settlement.

THE ROCK LIFE ASSURANCE COMPANY follows the latter mode, by which the Society may pay a greater sum than the sum assured;[1] and to this very material feature of its institution, the Proprietors are requested to pay particular attention. Every person, also, who makes an assurance, should weigh it in his mind, that he may be well acquainted with the nature and result of his annual payments; for on this subject many persons are liable to be deceived. They look to the premium paid in different societies, and naturally prefer that Society whose premium is the lowest; but the difference in the premiums of Societies can be but very small, and bears no proportion to the advantage accruing from the addition of a sum to the Policy depending on the profits of the Society. It is necessary, that the Proprietors should be very attentive to the great advantage which our Society holds out by thus making the assured persons gainers by its profits; and for this reason, after the most serious and mature deliberation, those calculations have been adopted by the Court of Directors, which the profoundest wisdom first suggested, and the propriety of which has been confirmed by long experience.

Societies, which add to the sum assured, may be divided into two kinds. In the one, all the assured persons are Partners; they assure mutually each others lives, and are all responsible for the payments of the sums assured to each Partner on his decease. The representatives of the deceased person lose at his death all interest in the Society; they receive the sum assured, with the addition made to it by the previous resolution of the Society; and whatever may have been the further profits of the institution, they cannot participate in them. The safety of a Society of this kind requires, that a considerable portion of the profits should be kept back to answer future contingencies.

THE ROCK LIFE ASSURANCE COMPANY is of the second kind. They who assure in it are not all partners: they are not all responsible for the payment of the sum assured / to each individual. The assured are either Proprietors or Non-proprietors. The Proprietors are answerable each to a certain amount: they lay down a certain sum, and form a determinate Capital to answer all contingencies, and by thus forming a Capital, they are enabled to make a due assignment of the sum to be added at different periods to various policies of Assurance. The assured Non-proprietors have no share in the risque: they pay down definite premiums, which assure to the representatives the sum assured, and who partake equally with Proprietors in the addition which may be made at different periods to each Policy. The security for the payment of that sum is the Capital Stock of the company, and the amount of all the premiums, with the interest upon them. Such a security may be well said to be firm as a Rock; for the transfer of Shares will produce a continual renovation of Policies, which, with the Capital of the Company, and the amount of annual payments from Assurances, will form an increasing fund, adequate to every purpose of profit and security.

The Proprietors of this institution will, from the above, see sufficient reason to pay particular attention to the three following circumstances.

1st. THE ROCK LIFE ASSURANCE COMPANY pays the sum assured on each Policy, with whatever addition may have been assigned to it by the previous resolution of the Society.

2d. THE ROCK LIFE ASSURANCE COMPANY has formed a determinate capital of a Million, for which its Proprietors are answerable; and this Capital is not only a security to all the assured, but it also enables the Company to make such arrangements as shall never leave a superfluous Capital to doubtful expectations.

3d. THE ROCK LIFE ASSURANCE COMPANY has secured the grand and essential point on which the continued existence of an Assurance Company depends, and this it does by the perpetual renovation of Policies. Every Proprietor is under the necessity of making an Assurance; and, when it drops, a new Assurance must be made by his successor.

A full investigation of all the advantages attending each of these circumstances, and the disadvantages resulting from the neglect of them, would require more time, and will be deferred to another occasion. They require a volume rather than a letter: but it is hoped, that the Proprietors will find from the above sufficient reason to value the Institution to which they belong.

It is necessary to add, that as a Proprietor may have reasons for not making the Assurance required, the Court of Directors has agreed, that upon his producing two Substitutes at least, each to the amount of the sum required from him, it shall be allowed to accept their Assurances for his; but, whenever either drops, he will be under the obligation to provide for its renewal.

As it is highly for the interest of the Society, that every Proprietor should be thoroughly informed of the nature of its plans, and it is equally so that he should be ready to contribute towards the improvement of them, any suggestions of this kind, either in person or by letter, will be thankfully received by,

SIR,

Your most obedient Servant,

WILLIAM FREND, *Actuary*.

N. B. A Board of Directors sits on the Wednesdays, Thursdays, and Fridays, at the House of the Company, from Twelve till Two o'Clock.

TABLE OF PREMIUMS

For Assuring the Sum of one hundred Pounds upon the
Life of any healthy Person, from the age of eight to sixty-seven.

Age.	One Year.	Seven Year at an annual Payment of	For the whole Life at an annual Payment of
8 to 14	0 17 9	1 1 5	1 17 7
15	0 17 11	1 2 11	1 18 7
16	0 19 2	1 4 7	1 19 8
17	1 1 2	1 6 1	2 0 8
18	1 3 3	1 7 5	2 1 8
19	1 5 0	1 8 6	2 2 8
20	1 7 3	1 9 5	2 3 7
21	1 8 10	1 10 1	2 4 6
22	1 9 3	1 10 6	2 5 4
23	1 9 8	1 11 0	2 6 3
24	1 10 2	1 11 6	2 7 1
25	1 10 7	1 12 1	2 8 1
26	1 11 1	1 12 7	2 9 1
27	1 11 7	1 13 2	2 10 1
28	1 12 1	1 13 9	2 11 1
29	1 12 8	1 14 4	2 12 3
30	1 13 3	1 14 11	2 13 5
31	1 13 9	1 15 7	2 14 7
32	1 14 4	1 16 3	2 15 9
33	1 15 0	1 16 10	2 17 1
34	1 15 8	1 17 8	2 18 5
35	1 16 4	1 18 10	2 19 10
36	1 17 0	1 19 7	3 1 4
37	1 17 9	2 0 8	3 2 10
38	1 18 6	2 1 9	3 4 6
39	1 19 3	2 2 11	3 6 2
40	2 0 8	2 4 1	3 7 11
41	2 2 0	2 5 4	3 9 9
42	2 3 6	2 6 6	3 11 8
43	2 4 6	2 7 9	3 13 8
44	2 5 6	2 9 2	3 15 9
45	2 6 8	2 10 10	3 17 11
46	2 7 10	2 12 6	4 0 2
47	2 9 0	2 14 4	4 2 7
48	2 10 3	2 16 4	4 5 1
49	2 12 3	2 18 6	4 7 10
50	2 15 1	3 0 8	4 10 8
51	2 17 4	3 2 8	4 13 6
52	2 19 1	3 4 9	4 16 5
53	3 1 0	3 7 0	4 19 7
54	3 3 0	3 9 5	5 2 10

Age.	One Year.	Seven Year at an annual Payment of	For the whole Life at an annual Payment of
55	3 5 0	3 12 0	5 6 4
56	3 7 3	3 14 8	5 10 1
57	3 9 8	3 17 6	5 14 0
58	3 12 3	4 0 6	5 18 2
59	3 15 1	4 3 8	6 2 8
60	3 18 1	4 7 1	6 7 4
61	4 1 5	4 10 11	6 12 4
62	4 3 11	4 15 0	6 17 9
63	4 7 8	4 19 8	7 3 7
64	4 10 9	5 4 10	7 9 10
65	4 15 2	5 10 10	7 16 9
66	5 0 1	5 17 7	8 4 1
67	5 5 6	6 5 2	8 12 1

A TABLE OF ANNUAL PREMIUMS

Payable during the joint continuance of two Lives for Assuring one hundred Pounds, on the Contingency of one Life's surviving the other.

Ages.		
Life to be assured.	Life against which the Assurance is to be made.	Premium.
10	10	1 8 6
	20	1 9 1
	30	1 8 3
	40	1 7 8
	50	1 6 11
	60	1 6 0
	70	1 4 11
	80	1 3 4
20	10	1 16 6
	20	1 17 0
	30	1 15 9
	40	1 14 8
	50	1 13 6
	60	1 12 1
	70	1 10 6
	80	1 8 3
30	10	2 5 5
	20	2 6 0
	30	2 4 6
	40	2 2 9
	50	2 0 11
	60	1 18 10
	70	1 16 7
	80	1 13 9
40	10	2 19 2

Ages.

Life to be assured.	Life against which the Assurance is to be made.	Premium.
	20	2 19 10
	30	2 18 2
	40	2 15 11
	50	2 12 10
	60	2 9 4
	70	2 5 11
	80	2 1 10
50	10	4 0 11
	20	4 1 10
	30	4 0 1
	40	3 17 10
	50	3 13 10
	60	3 7 7
	70	3 1 6
	80	2 15 0
60	10	5 16 9
	20	5 18 1
	30	5 16 3
	40	5 14 0
	50	5 10 7
	60	5 2 4
	70	4 9 10
	80	3 17 11
67	10	8 1 0
	20	8 2 9
	30	8 0 10
	40	7 18 7
	50	7 15 6
	60	7 8 8
	70	6 10 8
	80	5 8 9

A TABLE OF PREMIUMS

Payable during the continuance of two joint Lives for assuring one hundred Pounds, to be paid when either of the Lives shall drop.

Age.	Age.	£. s. d.	Age.	Age.	£. s. d.	Age.	Age.	£. s. d.	Age.	Age.	£. s. d.	Age.	Age.	£. s. d.
10	10	2 17 1	15	35	4 3 1	20	67	9 13 9	30	60	7 15 0	45	45	6 7 4
	15	3 1 1		40	4 10 4	25	25	4 0 10		67	9 18 1		50	6 17 9
	20	3 5 7		45	4 19 5		30	4 5 0	35	35	4 19 0		55	7 11 0
	25	3 9 3		50	5 11 3		35	4 10 3		40	5 5 6		60	8 9 6
	30	3 13 9		55	6 6 1		40	4 17 4		45	5 13 10		67	10 11 1
	35	3 19 6		60	7 6 0		45	5 6 2		50	6 5 0	50	50	7 7 8
	40	4 6 10		67	9 9 5		50	5 17 10		55	6 19 2		55	8 0 3
	45	4 15 11	20	20	3 13 11		55	6 12 6		60	7 18 6		60	8 18 2
	50	5 7 10		25	3 17 5		60	7 12 5		67	10 1 2		67	10 18 10

Age.	Age.	£. s. d.	Age.	Age.	£. s. d.	Age.	Age.	£. s. d.	Age.	Age.	£. s. d.	Age.	Age.	£. s. d.
	55	6 2 8		30	4 1 9		67	9 15 9	40	40	5 11 9	55	55	8 12 2
	60	7 2 9		35	4 7 3	30	30	4 8 11		45	5 19 9		60	9 9 0
	67	9 6 3		40	4 14 6		35	4 14 1		50	6 10 8		67	11 8 5
15	15	3 5 0		45	5 3 6		40	5 0 11		55	7 4 5		60	10 4 9
	20	3 9 6		50	5 15 4		45	5 9 6		60	8 3 4		67	12 2 1
	25	3 13 1		55	6 10 2		50	6 1 0		67	10 5 6	67	67	13 15 8
	30	3 17 6		60	7 10 2		55	6 15 5/						

AN addition of twenty-two per cent, *computed upon the premium,* is charged upon military persons; and an addition of *eleven per cent.* on officers on half pay; officers in the militia, fencibles, and the like levies; also on persons not having had the small-pox.

THE Court of Directors have a discretionary power of fixing the Premium, when any peculiar hazard attends the life upon which the Assurance is made.

EVERY person making any Assurance with the Society pays five shillings in the name of entrance-money; and, if the sum assured exceed one hundred pounds, the entrance-money is charged after the rate of five shillings for every hundred pounds. But if the person, upon whose life an Assurance is proposed, does not appear before the Directors, the entrance-money is charged after the rate of one pound for every hundred pounds.

ALSO every person proposing an Assurance is required to make a deposit of five shillings, if the sum do not exceed one hundred pounds; for a sum under five hundred pounds, a deposit of one half guinea is required; for one thousand, one guinea; and so on, at the rate of one guinea per thousand pounds assured; which deposit, if the party afterwards decline making the Assurance, or neglect to complete the same for the space of one lunar month, is forfeited to the use of the Society; but if the Court of Directors refuse or decline making such Assurance, the money deposited is returned. /

FORM *of a* PROPOSAL *to be submitted to a* BOARD OF DIRECTORS.

Name of the Person to be Assured

Profession or Occupation, Title or Addition

Place, and Date of Birth

Present Residence

Age　　　　　Term　　　　　Sum

Two References on the State of Health of the Person to be Assured

To a Medical Person　　　　　}

To a Medical or other Person　}

 Has the Person to be Assured had the Small Pox?

 Has he had the Cow Pox?

 Has he had the Gout?

 Has he had a Rupture?

 Has he suffered a Spitting of Blood?

An Address from the President and Directors of the Pennsylvania Company for Insurances on Lives and Granting Annuities to the Inhabitants of the United States, upon the Subject of the Beneficial Objects of that Institution (1814)

ADDRESS, &c.

FELLOW CITIZENS,

AMONG the various modes of alleviating the misfortunes and calamities of life, which have been adopted by the inhabitants of Europe, none has more deservedly engaged the attention of the enlightened and benevolent, than the establishment of institutions for *insurances on lives and granting annuities.* In Great Britain especially has this subject been amply studied and pursued, and *there* have the benefits resulting from the most laudable exertions, been most extensively displayed. Innumerable are the instances wherein families and individuals enjoy the comforts or the affluence of life, who, without the aid of such establishments, would have been reduced to want. In America too, instances are within our knowledge, in which widows and children have derived a respectable subsistence from the same source, owing to the wise and prudent precautions of their husbands or fathers, and have thus been rescued from poverty and distress. But in these cases resort has been had to the institutions of England, because, in our own country, no such associations existed.

The want of a company in the United States, for insurances on lives and granting annuities, has been long experienced, and it is therefore with no small degree of satisfaction, that the existence of such an institution is now announced. /

The object of this address is to disseminate throughout the Union, in as concise a manner as the subject will admit, some explanation of the objects and views of this institution, in order that that portion of our fellow citizens, whose opportunities or acquirements have not enabled them to become acquainted with the nature of life insurances and annuities, may have some knowledge of their beneficial effects. We do not wish to appear as attempting to instruct those who are already acquainted with these subjects, but we most respectfully invite all such to assist us in the circulation amongst their less informed neighbours, of that kind of intelligence, which may lead to the permanent benefit of themselves and of the institution.

"The Pennsylvania Company for insurances on lives and granting annuities"* was incorporated with a capital of *half a million of dollars*, by an act of the legislature of Pennsylvania, passed on the 10th day of March, 1812. At that period some untoward circumstances, amongst which was the expectation of a war, depressed, for the moment, the disposition of capitalists to embark in new enterprizes; and the subsequent declaration of hostilities against Great Britain, rendered it advisable to withhold, for a time, any extraordinary exertions. In the spring however of 1813, the subject was resumed; the general sentiment was in favour of the institution, and the *whole capital stock was in a few days subscribed*. It was not however deemed advisable to call in the whole capital, inasmuch as few modes for the productive employment of large sums of money presented themselves, and inasmuch as such a measure / could not be requisite until the company had entered into engagements which would call for additional security. *Twenty per cent.* was considered as amply sufficient to meet any extent of responsibilities which would probably be incurred within the first two or three years, and the sum of *one hundred thousand dollars*, was consequently collected. As the business of the company progresses in extent, the remaining instalments of the capital stock will be called for, and thus will additional security be afforded as fast as it is required. This measure, whilst it is doing justice to the stockholders, the directors are persuaded will prove equally satisfactory to those who may transact business with the company; particularly when it is recollected that the associations for similar objects in England, many of which were established *without capitals*, upon the principle of *mutual assurance*, have been generally prosperous.

Having thus shown, as we suppose, that the institution is founded upon a solid and responsible basis, possessing a capital adequate to meet all the engagements for the performance of which it may at any time hereafter be pledged, it may now be proper to specify the particular species of contracts, into which the company is now prepared to enter, accompanied by an explanation of the nature of each, for the information of those who are unacquainted therewith.

First, The company will make insurances on lives.

Seconly, Grant annuities; and,

Thirdly, Contract for reversionary payments; in which latter will be included endowments for children. /

---

*   For the charter of incorporation, which is perpetual, see appendix.

OF LIFE INSURANCES.

An insurance on a life is a contract whereby an individual or company, in consideration of a certain premium, undertakes to pay a stipulated sum of money, in case the person whose life is insured, should die within the time expressed in the policy. Now an insurance may be made for *one* or *two* or *any other determinate number of years*, or *for the whole continuance of life*, as the parties may agree; and the premium charged will bear a proper proportion to the risk. The premium may be made payable in annual instalments, or it may be paid in one gross sum, at the time of making the insurance. The sum insured too, instead of being paid in one gross sum at the death of the person, whose life is insured, may be made payable in *annual portions* during the life of the person for whose benefit the insurance is made.

The circumstances which have given rise to life insurances, are those accidents and misfortunes to which human nature is so generally exposed, and they have been instituted for the purpose of rescuing from the afflicting severities of poverty, families and individuals who depend for support upon some relative or friend, of whose protection they may by death be deprived. But perhaps the benefit of this kind of contract may best be illustrated by a few familiar examples.

1st. A. is a person, who in the pursuit of his business is obliged to leave home upon a distant journey or voyage. He has a family dependent upon his exertions for support, who, should he die before his return, would be without the means of subsistence. /

2d. B. is a merchant, a mechanic, or farmer, who maintains his family by the annual or daily produce of his industry. His expenses are numerous, and he is not able, with all his endeavours, to provide the means for the comfortable subsistence of his family in case of his early death. But he sees a reasonable prospect of being able, should his life be spared for three, five, seven or more years, to amass an estate that will render their situation comfortable after his decease.

3d. C. is a public officer or clerk in some permanent employment, who receives a salary sufficient for his support, but has no resources or expectation for his family after his death.

All these men perhaps are so circumstanced that by prudence or economy, they can save from their annual revenues, without feeling the privation, a sufficient sum to pay such a premium as would entitle their families to receive after their death, an amount sufficient, or an annuity adequate, to maintain them with comfort and perhaps independence, and all such men should embrace without hesitation the opportunity now offered them. Again,

4th. D. is a man who enjoys a liberal or competent income from the estate of his wife, and he is aware that at her death he will be deprived of his usual, perhaps *only* means of support. Prudence will dictate to this man to effect an insurance on the life of his wife, so that after her death he will have another resource from which he may derive his subsistence.

5th. E. is a man who enjoys an income from an estate *during his life*, and is desirous of borrowing money for some speculation or other purpose, but can find no / one who is willing to lend it upon the security of his estate, on account of the uncertainty of the continuation of his life. But he can accomplish his design by causing an insurance to be made upon his life, which will entitle the lender to recover from the insurers the amount of his debt, in case it shall not have been repaid before the death of the borrower.

Instances may sometimes occur wherein the continuance of a person's life is of serious importance to another, who is not, as in the case of a family, dependent on him for support. A copartner in trade is frequently interested to a large amount in the duration of his associate's life; and we recollect one instance in which a merchant had 30,000 dollars dependent upon the safe return of another from a distant voyage, whose life was in consequence thereof insured. But there are cases in which this species of contract will be likely to prove highly advantageous to our fellow citizens in the humble walks of life. Insurances may be made for small sums, even though they be only sufficient to defray the funeral expenses of a person who may perhaps die in such a state of poverty and distress, as not to leave a sufficiency for that necessary duty, or for the temporary relief of their families under an unexpected bereavement.

It must be evident that *life insurances*, like all other contracts of a similar nature, are founded upon calculations of *chances;* and that the premiums charged thereon, must depend upon the age, state of health, occupation and residence of the person insured. The life of a young man will be insured for less than that of an old man: a healthy person, for less than a sickly one: a man / pursuing a profession of a safe kind, for less than one exposed to dangers; and a person resident in a healthy country, for less than one who lives in a sickly climate or situation.

A long and studied attention to the bills of mortality in England, and elsewhere, have enabled writers and calculators upon the subject of life insurance, to form tables by which the chances of living to any certain period amongst a certain number of healthy persons of the same age, are so well ascertained, that any one may see at once, what premium would be considered as equivalent to the risk sustained by a company, who would insure his life for any given number of years. Some of these tables are to be found in the *appendix* to this pamphlet, to which we beg the serious attention of the reader, with a request, that should he not be able to comprehend them, he will inquire for an explanation from some of his neighbours who are better informed.

OF ANNUITIES.

An annuity is an allowance payable annually, half yearly or quarterly, as the case may be, by an individual or company *during the lifetime of a person*, in consideration of having received some gross sum from that person or some other. An annuity may be either *immediate* or *deferred*. An *immediate annuity* is where the payment commences immediately after the contract. A *deferred annuity* is where the payment does not commence until after a specified length of time, as 3, 5, or 7 years; or until after the occurrence of some particular event, as, for instance, the death of some other person. Annuities may be also contracted for, payable during the / continuance of two or more joint lives, as to a man, his wife and children, and to the survivers of them.

The object for which annuities were instituted, was to enable persons not having a sufficient income to maintain themselves, or not being able to pursue their usual occupations for support, to provide against the infirmities of old age, inability to labour, or some other mischance which might reduce them to want. But the utility thereof can, possibly, be best exemplified, as in the former case of life insurance, by stating a few of the instances which most frequently come within our notice.

1st. A. is a single man, who from age or infirmity is no longer capable of procuring a maintenance, but is possessed of some property, the income of which is not adequate to his support. Every year he consumes a portion of his principal, and he evidently perceives that should his life be prolonged for a number of years he will expend all his substance, and thus be reduced to absolute want. This man, by appropriating in time what he possesses to the purchase of an annuity, may perhaps find that his income may be increased to such an amount as will render his future days comfortable, and free him from all those anxieties to which, in his prior situation, he was exposed. Again,

2d. B. is a man who possesses a revenue sufficient to support him with economy, but as he has no relatives to provide for, is disposed to employ the whole of his estate in an annuity, in order that he may enjoy the superfluities of life, or devote a larger share of his income to purposes of charity. A reference to the tables annexed will show that this man may considerably increase, / perhaps do more than double his resources, and at the same time remove all his anxiety respecting the employment of his capital.

3d. C. and D. are a man and his wife in the decline of life, without children to whom they can look for assistance in their latter days, situated we will suppose in point of circumstances, like either of those described in the two former cases. By employing their property in the purchase of an annuity payable during the lives of both, and after the death of one, during the life of the surviver, they can perhaps render their situation independent or affluent.

4th. E. is a person having dependent upon him some relative or friend, who, from infirmity, old age, or intemperate habits, is incapable of supporting himself, and who after the death of his patron will be reduced to the most abject poverty. He is desirous of devoting a portion of his wealth to provide for the permanent subsistence of the object of his benevolence, and finds that he can effectually accomplish his design by procuring an annuity for him. All the preceding cases, it will be observed, are *immediate annuities*. We shall now exemplify a few that are *deferred*.

5th. F. is a man in the present possession of property, who sees before him a reasonable prospect, by his exertions and industry, of maintaining himself and family for some years to come: but he is desirous to guard against misfortunes or inability which might thereafter assail him, and deems the best mode of attaining his object to be, to purchase an annuity on his own life, or the lives of himself and wife, and the surviver, to commence at the distant day which he contemplated: or, he is persuaded that as long as he lives he can maintain / his family, but is desirous of providing for his wife after his death, which he is completely enabled to do by the purchase of an annuity to be paid to his wife during her life and to commence at his death, whenever that should occur.

These are amongst the principal instances in which the purchase of annuities may be beneficial to individuals and families; and we doubt not that many will take advantage of the opportunity now afforded them by the establishment of the Pennsylvania Company. It need scarcely be remarked that from the nature of this contract it is one which, like insurances, depends on calculations of chances. A certain number of annuitants will die before they have lived to the period of life upon which the calculation is founded, which affords to the company an average profit adequate to meet the losses which they will sustain by others living beyond the time contemplated.

We shall now proceed to an explanation of the third branch of business to which the institution extends its views.

OF REVERSIONS.

A *reversionary payment* is that sum which a person in consideration of a certain amount paid by him, or some other, to an individual or company, will be entitled to receive at a future day, *provided he should live so long*. This species of contract rests upon the principle of a *deferred annuity*, but differs from it in the circumstance of its being payable in a gross sum instead of periodical instalments. It is evident, therefore, that the same instances which were enumerated in speaking of deferred / annuities will apply to reversions, if, instead of annual payments, a gross sum, equivalent thereto, should be stipulated. But we will quote a few examples of what are called *endowments*.

A. is a man of moderate fortune, who has a number of young children, neither of whom, after his death, will have a sufficiency for support. He is, therefore, anxious to provide respectable marriage portions for his daughters, and capitals for his sons wherewith they may enter into business. If he be a merchant, he may unexpectedly, by the casualties of trade, be reduced to indigence; but he can, without inconvenience to his accustomed mode of living, annually devote a portion of his wealth to the purpose of securing to one or more of his children, should they live to the age of eighteen or twenty-one, a liberal establishment. This is to be effected by the purchase of a *reversion* dependant on their lives; and although he would be a loser should the children die before the age specified, yet it is a loss which he could reasonably afford, inasmuch as he would no longer have to incur the expenses of their education and support.

B. is a mechanic, a farmer, or other person, who maintains a numerous family of children by his industry, but who sees no prospect of assisting them in life when they arrive at full age. He would like to give his sons small stocks to enable them to begin their trades, and to his daughters a sufficiency to purchase furniture towards house-keeping. He can spare a small sum from his annual earnings, whilst his children are young, and by appropriating it to the purchase of a *reversion* on the life of each, completely effects his object. / Prudent wives too, who have prodigal and dissipated husbands, might, from the wreck of their property, by careful management, provide in this manner for their own and their children's future comfort.

Having now in a plain and concise manner, adapted, as we suppose, to the comprehension of most readers, explained the nature of life insurances, annuities and reversions, and the extensive advantages which may result from the establishment of this institution, it remains for us to say something concerning the *rates* which will be charged by the company upon the transaction of their business.

OF THE RATES.

As it is of the utmost importance to the permanent stability of the institution, as it respects the interest of the present and future stockholders, as well as that of present and future annuitants and persons assured, that those who now have the direction of its affairs should act with proper foresight and prudence in determining the rates to be demanded for premiums and annuities, it may be useful to hear what has been said in other countries on the subject by wise and experienced men, and especially to attend to the counsel which was given many years ago, by the Reverend Dr. Richard Price, on a similar occasion, to the society for equitable assurances on lives and surviverships in London, where he expresses himself as follows: viz.

"First. They should consider what distress would arise from the failure of such a scheme in any future time, and what dangers there are which ought to be carefully guarded against in order to secure success. I / have already more than once observed that those persons will be most for flying to these establishments for insurances who have feeble constitutions, or are subject to distempers which they know render their lives particularly precarious; and it is to be feared that no caution will be sufficient to prevent all danger from hence."

Again: "In matters of chance, it is impossible to say that an unfavourable run of events will not come, which may hurt the best contrived scheme. The calculations only determine *probabilities*, and agreeably to these it may be depended on, that events will happen *on the whole*. But at particular periods and in particular instances, great deviations will often happen, and those deviations, at the commencement of a scheme, must prove either very favourable or very unfavourable.

"But further. The calculations suppose that all the monies received are put out immediately to accumulate at compound interest. They make no allowance for losses or for any of the expenses attending management. On these accounts the payments to a society of this kind ought to be more than the calculations will warrant, and the interest money ought to be reckoned low. Mr. Dodson, I find, has paid due attention to all this by reckoning interest in his calculations for this society at three per cent. and taking the lowest of all the known probabilities of life, or those deduced from the London bills of mortality.

"Certainly a society that means to be a *permanent* advantage to the public, ought always to take *higher* rather than *lower* values, for the sake of rendering itself / more secure, and gaining some profits to balance losses and expenses." Price, vol. ii. sec. 7.

Before Dr. Price's time of writing these advices, several associations of this kind in London, by transacting business at too low rates, had involved themselves in embarrassments, so as to be obliged to discontinue their business; but the society above named, to whom they were addressed, by attending thereto, have progressed from that time to the present in uninterrupted prosperity.

Their business has been so extensive that in 33 years, from January 1768, to January 1801, they made 83,201 insurances on *single lives* alone, which is more upon an average than 2500 per annum.

The present Directors of *"The Pennsylvania Company"* have duly considered this wise and prudent counsel, advanced by a man eminently qualified therefor, and especially as a due regard for his equitable and cautious system has proved, by an experience of more than forty years, so highly beneficial to a similar institution.

Before the rates proper to be demanded can be determinately fixed, it is necessary to ascertain the rate of compound interest at which the Company will be able *permanently* to improve their monies for a course of fifty years to come, clear of all losses, by sums lying at intervals unproductive for a week, a month or more at a time, and also clear of all losses which might possibly occur from insufficient securities taken from mortgagers or others. By the nature of such an institution, its contracts made at the present day, extend their consequences and effects to distant times and to future / generations. An annuity now purchased for a child of ten years of age, might continue to be payable for seventy or eighty years to come, and it is therefore of the utmost importance, and to the interest of all concerned, that the strictest caution should be observed from the commencement, in order that annuitants and persons assured should ever be impressed with a firm conviction of the solid foundation of the institution, and of its entire capacity to comply with all its engagements.

Impressed with these and other similar considerations, the Directors are firmly of opinion that although the legal interest of Pennsylvania is six per cent. they will not be able to employ their capital and the money received by them, permanently during states of peace and war, as they may occur, at a higher rate *than five and an half per cent. compound interest.* Upon this *datum* then, are their calculations founded; and they doubt not that the reasonableness of their position will appear manifest to all, who are in any wise conversant with the employment of large sums of money.

With these remarks the Directors conclude their address, respectfully soliciting the attention of all persons into whose hands it may fall, and requesting them to make its contents known to those of their friends and neighbours, who are in a situation to be benefitted by the opportunities hereby afforded them. /

APPENDIX.
RULES OF THE COMPANY.

EVERY person desirous to make assurance with the Company must sign a declaration by himself or agent, setting forth the age, state of health, profession, occupation, residence, and other circumstances of the persons whose lives are proposed to be assured: and also, in case such assurance is made upon the life of another person, that the interest which he has in such life is equal to the sum assured. This declaration is the basis of the contract between the Company and the person desirous to make such assurance; and if any artful, false, or fraudulent representation shall be used therein, all claim on account of any policy so obtained, shall cease, determine, and be void; and the monies which shall have been paid upon account of such assurance shall be forfeited to the use of the Company.

In like manner a declaration will be required from all persons who apply for the purchase of an annuity or reversion. No policy takes effect until the first premium be paid, and if any subsequent premium remains unpaid after the time stipulated in the policy, such policy becomes void; but if the defaulter shall, within two calendar months after the time so stipulated (the person on whose life the assurance was made being then alive and in good health) pay the said premium, together with the additional sum of ten per cent. upon / such premium, then such policy is revived and continues in force.

All claimants upon the decease of any person whose life shall have been assured by the Company, must make proof thereof by affidavit or certificate, and give such further information respecting the same as the board of directors shall think satisfactory.

The time for payment of claims occurring by death, is within sixty days after proof of the death shall have been made as aforesaid.

In case the more immediate purpose of an assurance shall have ceased, and the owner of the policy shall be minded to dispose of the same; or any person assured by the Company, shall himself stand in need of that assistance which was intended for his family, the Company will, upon application, become the purchasers of such an interest at a fair price.

The policies of persons assured on their own lives become void, if the assured die by their own hands, by the consequences of a duel, or by the hands of justice.

The Company reserves to itself the right of making any alterations which the particular circumstances of applicants may in their opinion render expedient.

A charge of one dollar will be made for each policy of assurance or bond for annuity, besides the premium or computed purchase money.

The office of the Company is open daily between the hours of 9 and 3 o'clock, at No. 72, South Second-street, in the City of Philadelphia, where a committee of the directors sit three times a week to consider and decide upon the proposals which may be made to them. /

Letters directed to the President, *post-paid*, will be speedily attended to, and answers given to any inquiries which may be made, respecting the terms and rates upon which the Company will transact business.

THE PRESENT DIRECTORS ARE,

President – *Samuel Yorke*;

John Bohlen,	*Joshua Longstreth,*
Joseph Peace,	*Condy Raguet,*
John Claxton,	*Charles N. Bancker,*
Jacob Sperry,	*John Welsh,*
Cadwalader Evans,	*James Hemphill,*
Jeremiah Warder, jun.	*William Schlatter,*

Actuary – *Jacob Shoemaker.*

PROPOSALS AND RATES OF THE STANDARD LIFE ASSURANCE COMPANY (1833)

Proposals and Rates of the Standard Life Assurance Company, Established in 1825, and Constituted by Act of Parliament 2 & 3 Gul. IV. C. XXXII. For Assurance on Lives and Survivorships, Endowments for Children, Immediate, Deferred, and Survivorship Annuities, and for the Purchase of Reversions and Annuities (Edinburgh: Privately printed, 1833).

Like the Rock in the shadow of the Equitable, Standard Life needed to combine its obligation to shareholders with the need to satisfy policyholders who were accustomed to sharing in their office's surplus; and like the Rock, it presented its combination of share capital and profit-sharing as the best of both worlds. The looming presence in Standard Life's case was the Scottish Widows Fund, which had formed in 1815 in close imitation of the Equitable; additionally, professional men in Scotland had long pooled their resources to provide pensions. Although most other major Scottish life insurers would form as mutuals, Standard Life retained its share capital until 1925, but divided 80 per cent of its surplus with policyholders starting in 1836.

Into the 1880s Standard Life and the Scottish Widows Fund traded places as the top two life insurers in Great Britain. This dominance owed mainly to their innovative and aggressive marketing, some of which is on display in this prospectus. Also, like most of its fellow Scottish insurers, Standard Life catered to a much wider class of policyholders than was the norm in England, where market segmentation was the usual business strategy. Although Standard Life had not yet departed from basing its premiums on the Northampton table of mortality in 1833 (this would wait until 1841), it did reduce its rates by 5 per cent from what the Rock had charged in 1808, and it also offered an additional 5 per cent discount for customers who did not wish to share in its profits.[1]

Notes
1. Alborn, *Regulated Lives*, pp. 25–7, 33, 51, 131; M. Moss, *Standard Life 1825–2000: The Building of Europe's Largest Mutual Life Company* (Edinburgh: Mainstream Publishing, 2000), pp. 38, 45.

Proposals and Rates of the Standard Life Assurance Company (1833)

Governor,
His Grace the DUKE of BUCCLEUGH and QUEENSBERRY.

Deputy-Governor.
The Most Noble the MARQUIS of LOTHIAN.

EXTRAORDINARY DIRECTORS.
The Hon. Captain ANTHONY MAITLAND, R.N.
HENRY HOME DRUMMOND, Esq. of Blairdrummond.
SAMUEL LAING, Esq. of Papdale.
GEORGE MERCER, Esq. of Gorthy.
ROBERT JAMESON, Esq. Advocate.
ALEXANDER CONNEL, Esq. of Conheath.
JAMES WYLD, Esq. of Gilston.
ALEXANDER CLAPPERTON, Esq. of Spylaw.
STEWART SOUTER, Esq. of Melrose.
ADAM ROLLAND, Esq. younger of Gask.

ORDINARY DIRECTORS.
JAMES INGLIS, Esq. Banker.
EDWARD SANDEMAN, Esq. Merchant, Leith.
GEORGE PATTON, Esq. Advocate.
WILLIAM WALLACE, Esq. Professor of Mathematics.
ROBERT RENTON, Esq. M.D.
WILLIAM HENDERSON Esq. Merchant.
DAVID SMITH, Esq. W.S.[1]
WILLIAM WYLD, Esq. Merchant, Leith.
ANDREW CLASON, Esq. W.S.
GEORGE RITCHIE, Esq. W.S.
LINDSAY MACKERSY, Esq. Accountant.
WILLIAM BLACKWOOD, Esq. Bookseller.

ROBERT HAIG, Esq. Lochrin.
JAMES HAY, Esq. Merchant, Leith.
ALEXANDER KINNEAR, Esq. Banker.

Auditors.
WILLIAM WALLACE,[2] Esq. Professor of Mathematics, *Auditor of Rates.*
LINDSAY MACKERSY, Esq. Accountant, *Auditor of Accounts.*
JAMES A. CHEYNE,[3] *Manager.*
ARCHIBALD BORTHWICK,[4] *Secretary.*

LOCAL BOARDS OF MANAGEMENT.
Aberdeen.
LORD JAMES HAY of Seaton.
JOHN THORBURN, Esq. of Murtle.
The Rev. Dr. PATRICK FORBES of King's College.
Professor CRUICKSHANK of Marischal College.
GEORGE WATT, Esq. Surgeon.
Agents.
ADAM & ANDERSON, Advocates.
Perth.
PATRICK G. STEWART, Esq. Banker.
JAMES MURRAY PATTON, Esq. of Glenalmond.
JAMES CONDIE, Esq. Writer.
ARCHIBALD TURNBULL, Esq. Bellwood.
WILLIAM PEDDIE, Esq. Writer.
Agent.
GEORGE GRAY, Writer. /

PROPOSALS AND RATES
OF THE
Standard Life Assurance Company.

THE system of life assurance, though, like most of those discoveries which have proved to be of permanent and extensive utility to mankind, it was at first received with prejudice and opposition, is now, after a century's experience of its operation, justly regarded as one of the most beneficent and effectual means for increasing and securing the comforts of society, and mitigating the calamities arising from the uncertainty of life. An institution, indeed, which places it within the power of every man of ordinary prudence to decide whether he shall leave to his family the legacy of penury or independence, – which secures a provision for the future, without the sensible abridgment of present comforts, – which affords an advantageous investment to the capitalist, security to the money lender, accommodation to the borrower, and indulgence to the debtor, – and which, in short, adapts itself with such singular pliancy to all the wants and wishes of a highly cultivated state of society, – cannot fail, as soon as its principles are understood, to receive an ample share of encouragement and support.

These advantages life assurance is enabled to confer by means of co-operation. A single individual assuring a single life can do so only at a rate of profit proportioned to the greatness of his risk. His profit in the event of a long life would be great, but his loss in the event of a short one might be ruinous. The premium therefore must be high, from the absolute uncertainty of the contingency; and the transaction more resembles a wager than a mutually beneficial contract.

But the uncertainty which attends human life in an individual case, disappears in the case of large numbers of men. The number of deaths out of a thousand individuals within a given period now admits of being / reduced almost to certainty; and hence the assurer of a thousand lives knows before, with sufficient precision, the amount of his risk, and is enabled to assure at such a premium as will be sufficient to cover that risk, and leave merely a remunerating profit. This is effected by the formation of companies on such a scale as at once to embrace a great number of lives, and to afford a sufficient guarantee to the assured for the fulfilment of the company's obligations.

Perhaps the best and most familiar illustration of the beneficial effects of this system is afforded by assurances against fire. Every one perceives and admits the advantage of being able absolutely to secure himself against the consequences of a calamity which might in a moment reduce him from affluence to beggary, in return for a consideration so trifling as to be almost unfelt; and which, but for the burden of government duty,[5] would be diminished one half. But although, from the subject being a little more complex, the working of the same principle be less obvious in the case of life assurance, it is in fact not less striking; the rates in the latter case being truly, in proportion to the nature of the risk, as remarkable for their moderation as those for which assurance against fire may be obtained.

The number of those to whom assurances on lives hold out recommendations, is hardly less than those who are interested in assurances against fire. While the latter is a contingency which may or may not happen, and which every one flatters himself he will escape, death is a casualty which *must* happen; and the number of those who, without the security for the future which life assurance affords, can rely on their families being left in a state of independence at their death, can never, in a commercial country, and in the present condition and habits of society, be very great.

There are in truth but few persons who do not stand in one or other of two situations; either that *others* are dependent on *their* life for their subsistence or comfort; or that their own subsistence and comfort, with that of their families, depend to some extent on the lives of others.

In the first of these classes must be reckoned every married man, and every man who has connections or relations dependent upon him for support, and who derives his income from any profession or trade; – the barrister or man of business, the physician, the clergyman, the merchant, the soldier, the sailor, the annuitant, the man of literature, / the tradesman, the farmer, – all, in short, who have to trust to the annual return which their ability or exertions enable them to realize. That income, while life and health continue, may be sufficient to maintain themselves and their families in comfort and affluence; but their position in society generally renders any extensive saving impossible, even if length of days were allowed them; while a sudden visitation of disease may at once stop the source of income, or a premature death arrest their exertions before any provision has been made for the future. The conviction, too, that the amount of their annual savings, even if accumulated for many years, would not, at the present rate of interest, be likely to amount to any thing considerable, indisposes many even to save at all, who might act differently if they were aware of the strikingly favorable results of life assurance, and the extent to which a provision for the future might thus be acquired by a trifling present payment. To this most extensive class, who must always contemplate with anxiety the precarious tenure by which they hold the gifts of fortune, and the misery in which their families would be involved by their death, no greater boon can be imagined than an institution, which enables them, from their surplus income, without present inconvenience, to secure the possession of a competence for those they leave behind.

There are others in this class to whom life assurance has its advantages. Even as a mode of amassing wealth by compound interest, life assurance, in the present state of the money market, holds out no inconsiderable inducements to the capitalist; while, as such policies always have a marketable value, they are capable of being again turned into money should circumstances render it necessary.

Gentlemen of landed property whose estates are entailed, can thus, from their annual savings, secure comfortable provisions to their younger children, or ampler jointures to their wives.[6]

Persons who have right to succeed to an estate or to a legacy on their attaining majority or any other age, and whose chance of providing for their families or relations, or perhaps their own establishment by marriage, depends on their doing so, may, by assuring their lives for the intervening period, which may be done at a very small rate, give to this contingent interest all the security and nearly the same value with an absolute property. /

Scarcely less numerous is the other class who are interested in life assurance, namely, those whose income or whose chance of receiving payment of debts or funds depends on the life of others.

The lender, for instance, who advances money to a borrower, and whose chance of repayment depends on the borrower's continuing to live and labour, can thus secure indemnity in the event of death before repayment; while the borrower, again, by undertaking the payment of the premium of assurance, as well as the interest of the loan, will generally find it easy to raise money in circumstances where, but for the security afforded by assurance, it would have been impossible. And this may in both cases be done, either by an assurance of the life for a limited period, or by an absolute assurance of a sum payable on death.

The tenant of lands under an heir of entail or liferenter,[7] where the possession must depend on the lessor's life, may, by assuring the life of the granter of the lease, obtain compensation for its sudden termination, perhaps at the very time when he was beginning to reap the fruits of the labour and expense he had laid out upon the faith of it. Such leases are entered into, in consequence of their precarious duration, generally at a reduced rent, which enables the tenant to appropriate a small annual surplus for assuring, and thus to obtain substantially all the advantages of a lease for a time certain.

The person whose right of succession to an estate, a legacy, or property of any kind, depends upon his surviving another individual in possession, may secure an equivalent to his family, by effecting an assurance on the life of that individual; the sum to be payable only if the person effecting the assurance predeceases the person in possession; and as this is generally the assurance of a young life against an old one, a large sum may in this way be secured for a small premium.

Life assurance farther affords facilities for the perfecting of marriage contracts, and other family settlements, and security for the performance of their conditions. It affords the means of securing doubtful debts; of reimbursing parents or guardians for advances made by them for their children or wards, in the event of their premature death; of repaying to the purchaser of any office or annuity the sum paid for such office or annuity on the death of the person on whose life it depends; and, generally, it offers the means of indemnity / against any pecuniary loss or inconvenience to which one individual may become subject through the death of another.

Such are the more common and prominent cases, in which the benefits to be derived from life assurance are obvious; but there are few situations in life in which it may not be made the means of increasing comfort or averting distress. It is not therefore matter of wonder that institutions which tend so materially to the welfare of society should, in every case where they have been conducted on right principles, have been attended with complete success.

The Institutions for life assurance established in this country are comprised under one or other of three classes.

1. Societies for mutual assurance; which hold out to the assured the chance of profit beyond the fixed sum assured, but subject them also to the risk of loss to an indefinite extent.

2. Companies where the whole profits of the business are appropriated to the proprietors of the capital stock; the assured receiving exactly the sum assured without addition from profits. These afford perfect security, but exclude every chance of profit.

3. Companies formed by a combination of the principles of the other two. By means of a capital subscribed by the partners, of sufficient amount to cover any possible demand against the company, the security of the assured is guaranteed, while by participating in the profits, they derive the advantages possessed by societies constructed on the principle of mutual assurance.

Upon this last plan, which both theory and experience have stamped with popularity, the Standard Life Assurance Company has been established. The principle of its constitution is sanctioned by the highest authorities on the subject of life assurance, and is confirmed by the great success which has followed its adoption.

CAPITAL.

The Capital of the Company is Five Hundred Thousand Pounds Sterling;[8] besides which, the premiums and accumulating interest from an increasing fund, wholly applicable to the purposes of the institution under the Act of Parliament by which the Company is constituted.

While persons making assurances are thus provided with an undoubted / guarantee for the fulfilment of the Company's engagements, they will also have it in their power, without incurring responsibility, to participate largely in the profits of the business.

DIVISION OF PROFITS.

In the year 1835, being the termination of ten years from the establishment of the Company, the first periodical investigation of its affairs will be instituted; and from the surplus premiums, as then ascertained, additions will be made to the policies held by parties who may have assured under the condition of participating in the profits, in terms of the Company's Regulations; or, in their option, their future annual premiums will be diminished. At the end of each successive period of seven years thereafter a similar investigation will be instituted, and the profits apportioned in the like manner.

By this provision the assured have it in their power to secure the advantages which are held out by mutual assurance societies, without being subjected to the risk and responsibility which must necessarily attach to a connection with such institutions.

From the marked success with which the business of the Company has been carried on, there can be no doubt that large additions will be made to policies of this class.

REDUCED RATES OF PREMIUM.

In order to accommodate parties who may desire to secure only a certain fixed sum, payable on their own decease, or upon the death of any other person in whose life they may have an interest, without having any view to periodical additions to their Policies from the profits of the business, the Directors have caused a Table of Reduced Rates of Premiums to be constructed, applicable to this species of business; and parties have accordingly an opportunity of transacting on this basis with the Company on very favourable terms.

GENERAL REGULATIONS.

Being desirous to afford every safe encouragement to the extension of the system of Life Assurance, the Directors make it their study to conduct the business of the Company on the most liberal principles.

No charge is made on parties assuring, under the head of entry-money, admission fee, or otherwise. /

Military men are not charged with extra premiums, unless called into actual service.

Onerous Assignees to Policies opened by persons on their own lives, when duly admitted by the Company as the holders, will be held to stand in an equally favourable situation as if they had been the original assurers.

If any party desires to surrender an assurance entered into for the whole term of life, after three annual premiums have been paid, the Policy will be purchased by the Company at an equitable rate.

In cases where money is advanced by the Company by way of Redeemable Annuity, or in any similar manner, parties will be entitled, on redemption, to a Policy of Assurance to the extent of the whole sum advanced, upon the same beneficial footing as to the rate of Premium as if the Policy had been issued at the date when the transaction was originally entered into.

In order to avoid the possibility of defeating, or even protracting, the settlement of just claims upon the Company, by the delay and expense of legal proceedings, it is imperative on the Directors, in all cases, when required, to submit the matter of dispute to arbitration. /

The following Tables of the Company's Premiums will be found annexed:

Table I. – Rates either by a single payment, or annual payments during life, for an Assurance of L.100 to be paid on the death of the party, with periodical additions from profits.

Table II. – Rates either by a single payment, or annual payments during life, for an Assurance of L.100 to be paid on the death of the party, without additions from profits.

Table III. – Rates for single lives Assured for a term of years specified.

Table IV. – Annual premiums during the joint lives of two persons for the Assurance of L.100, payable on the death of either party.

Table V. – Annual premiums for an Assurance of L.100 to be paid on the death of one person, A, in the event of another, B, being then alive.

Table VI. – Premiums by a single payment, or annual payments to cease one year before the sum becomes payable, for L.100, to be paid when the party attains the respective ages mentioned in the Table. /

TABLE I.
SINGLE LIVES.

RATES by a Single Payment, or Annual Payments during Life, for an Assurance of £100, to be paid on the Death of the Party, with periodical additions from Profits.

AGE.	Annual Premiums.			Single Payment.		
	£	s.	d.	£	s.	d.
8 to 14	1	15	0	31	8	6
15	1	16	0	32	0	11
16	1	17	1	32	13	11
17	1	18	2	33	6	8
18	1	19	2	33	18	7
19	2	0	2	34	9	8
20	2	1	1	35	0	2
21	2	1	11	35	9	6
22	2	2	9	35	18	6
23	2	3	7	36	7	8
24	2	4	6	36	17	1
*25	2	5	4	37	6	7
26	2	6	5	37	16	5
27	2	7	4	38	6	5
28	2	8	5	38	16	8
29	2	9	5	39	7	2
30	2	10	7	39	17	10
31	2	11	9	40	8	11
32	2	12	11	41	0	2
33	2	14	2	41	11	9
34	2	15	6	42	3	8
35	2	16	11	42	15	10

36	2 18 4	43 8 3
37	2 19 10	44 1 0
38	3 1 6	44 14 2
39	3 3 2	45 7 8
40	3 4 11	46 1 7
41	3 6 9	46 15 6
42	3 8 7	47 9 7
43	3 10 7	48 3 8
44	3 12 7	48 18 1
45	3 14 9	49 12 11
46	3 17 1	50 9 1
47	3 19 7	51 5 7
48	4 2 2	52 1 8
49	4 4 11	52 19 2
50	4 7 10	53 16 8
51	4 10 8	54 12 11
52	4 13 9	55 10 4
53	4 16 11	56 8 1
54	5 0 3	57 5 0
55	5 3 10	58 3 5
56	5 7 9	59 2 2
57	5 11 8	60 0 1
58	5 16 0	60 19 8
59	6 0 7	61 19 5
60	6 5 4	62 18 6
61	6 10 7	63 19 0
62	6 16 2	64 19 10
63	7 2 3	66 1 4
64	7 8 9	67 3 3
65	7 15 11	68 5 10
66	8 3 8	69 8 10
67	8 12 0	70 12 2

* *Example.* – A person whose age does not exceed 25, may secure £100, payable upon his death to his heirs or assignees, increased by a proportional share of the profits, by annual payments of £2. 5s. 4d, or a single payment of £37, 6s. 7d, and so in proportion to a greater or lesser sum. /

TABLE II.
SINGLE LIVES.

RATES by a Single Payment, or Annual Payments during Life, for an Assurance of £100, to be paid on the Death of the Party, without addition from Profits.

AGE.	Annual Premiums.	Single Payment.
	£ s. d.	£ s. d.
8 to 14	1 11 11	28 12 10
15	1 12 10	29 4 1

AGE.	Annual Premiums.	Single Payment.
	£ s. d.	£ s. d.
16	1 13 10	29 15 11
17	1 14 10	30 7 6
18	1 15 9	30 18 5
19	1 16 8	31 8 6
20	1 17 6	31 18 1
21	1 18 3	32 6 8
22	1 19 0	32 14 10
23	1 19 9	33 3 2
24	2 0 7	33 11 8
*25	2 1 5	34 0 4
26	2 2 4	34 10 10
27	2 3 4	35 1 6
28	2 4 4	35 11 7
29	2 5 4	36 2 10
30	2 6 6	36 14 2
31	2 7 8	37 5 2
32	2 8 10	37 17 2
33	2 10 2	38 9 6
34	2 11 5	39 1 3
35	2 12 10	39 14 3
36	2 14 3	40 7 6
37	2 15 9	41 0 3
38	2 17 4	41 14 3
39	2 19 1	42 8 8
40	3 0 9	43 2 6
41	3 2 7	43 17 5
42	3 4 6	44 12 6
43	3 6 6	45 7 8
44	3 8 6	46 3 2
45	3 10 9	46 19 1
46	3 13 0	47 15 5
47	3 15 4	48 12 2
48	3 18 0	49 9 5
49	4 0 9	50 7 1
50	4 3 7	51 4 11
51	4 6 5	52 2 6
52	4 9 6	53 0 3
53	4 12 8	53 18 4
54	4 16 0	54 16 10
55	4 19 7	55 15 8
56	5 3 4	56 14 10
57	5 7 3	57 14 4
58	5 11 8	58 14 5
59	5 16 3	59 14 9
60	6 1 1	60 15 6

AGE.	Annual Premiums.	Single Payment.
	£ s. d.	£ s. d.
61	6 6 4	61 16 7
62	6 11 9	62 18 0
63	6 17 10	64 0 2
64	7 4 5	65 4 0
65	7 11 1	66 6 1
66	7 18 9	67 7 1
67	8 6 8	68 8 5

*   *Example.* – A person whose age does not exceed 25, may secure £100, payable upon his death to his heirs or assignees, by annual payments of £2. 1s. 5d., or a single payment of £34. 0s. 4d., and so on in proportion for a greater or lesser sum. /

TABLE III.
SINGLE LIVES ASSURED FOR A TERM OF YEARS SPECIFIED.

Premium for One and Seven Years.

AGE.	One Year.	Seven Years.
	£ s. d.	£ s. d.
8 to 14	0 15 3	0 16 9
15	0 15 6	0 17 4
16	0 15 11	0 18 3
17	0 16 9	0 19 2
18	0 17 7	1 0 2
19	0 18 4	1 1 0
20	0 19 4	1 1 9
21	1 0 9	1 2 6
22	1 2 0	1 3 4
23	1 2 10	1 4 2
24	1 3 6	1 4 11
*25	1 4 3	1 5 8
26	1 4 11	1 6 3
27	1 5 5	1 6 10
28	1 6 1	1 7 5
29	1 6 10	1 8 0
30	1 7 10	1 8 7
31	1 8 2	1 8 11
32	1 8 6	1 9 3
33	1 8 11	1 9 10
34	1 9 6	1 10 6
35	1 9 11	1 11 2
36	1 10 3	1 12 6
37	1 10 10	1 13 10
38	1 11 3	1 15 3

AGE.	One Year.	Seven Years.
	£ s. d.	£ s. d.
39	1 12 2	1 16 11
40	1 13 7	1 18 8
41	1 15 7	1 19 11
42	1 17 8	2 1 5
43	1 18 9	2 2 10
44	2 0 2	2 4 5
45	2 2 0	2 6 2
46	2 3 5	2 7 11
47	2 4 4	2 9 10
48	2 5 7	2 11 11
49	2 7 6	2 14 2
50	2 10 1	2 16 7
51	2 13 0	2 19 0
52	2 15 0	3 1 4
53	2 17 1	3 3 11
54	2 19 0	3 7 0
55	3 1 5	3 10 10
56	3 4 6	3 14 6
57	3 7 0	3 17 1
58	3 9 11	3 19 11
59	3 13 1	4 3 1
60	3 17 10	4 6 6

*   *Example.* – By a simple payment of £1. 4s. 3d. a person aged 25 may secure £100 to his representatives in case of his death within one year, – or a like sum by paying an yearly Premium of £1. 5s. 8d. in case of his death within seven years. /

TABLE IV.
JOINT LIVES.

Annual Premiums during the Joint Lives of two Persons, for an Assurance of £100, payable on the Death of either Party.

Ages of A.	B.	Premium.
		£ s. d.
10	10	2 17 1
	15	3 1 1
	20	3 5 7
	25	3 9 3
	30	3 13 9
	35	3 19 6
	40	4 6 10
	45	4 15 11
	50	5 7 10
	55	6 2 8

Ages of A.	B.	Premium.
		£ s. d.
	60	7 2 9
	67	9 6 3
15	15	3 5 0
	20	3 9 6
	25	3 13 1
	30	3 17 6
	35	4 3 1
	40	4 10 4
	45	4 19 5
	50	5 11 3
	55	6 6 1
	60	7 6 0
	67	9 9 5
20	20	3 13 11
	25	3 17 5
	30	4 1 9
	35	4 7 3
	40	4 14 6
	45	5 3 6
	50	5 15 4
	55	6 10 2
	60	7 10 2
	67	9 13 9
25	25	4 0 10
	30	4 5 0
	35	4 10 3
	40	4 17 4
	45	5 6 2
	50	5 17 10
	55	6 12 6
	60	7 12 5
	67	9 15 9
30	30	4 8 11
	35	4 14 1
	40	5 0 11
	45	5 9 6
	50	6 1 0
	55	6 15 5
	60	7 15 0
	67	9 18 1
35	35	4 19 1
	40	5 5 6
	45	5 13 10
	50	6 5 0

Ages of A.	B.	Premium.
		£ s. d.
	55	6 19 2
	60	7 18 6
	67	10 1 2
40	40	5 11 9
	45	5 19 9
	50	6 10 8
	55	7 4 5
	60	8 3 4
	67	10 5 6
45	45	6 7 4
	50	6 17 9
	55	7 11 0
	60	8 9 6
	67	10 11 1
50	50	7 7 8
	55	8 0 3
	60	8 18 2
	67	10 18 10
55	55	8 12 10
	60	9 9 0
	67	11 8 5
60	60	10 4 9
	67	12 2 1
67	67	13 15 8 /

TABLE V.
SURVIVORSHIPS.

Annual Premiums for an Assurance of £100, to be paid on the Death of one Person, A, in the event of another, B, being then alive.

Age of A.	B.	Premium.
		£ s. d.
10	10	1 8 7
	15	1 8 0
	20	1 7 5
	25	1 6 9
	30	1 6 2
	35	1 5 6
	40	1 4 10
	45	1 4 1
	50	1 3 4
	55	1 2 5

Age of A.	Age of B.	Premium.
		£ s. d.
	60	1 1 6
	65	1 0 5
15	10	1 13 1
	15	1 12 6
	20	1 11 11
	25	1 11 3
	30	1 10 7
	35	1 9 11
	40	1 9 1
	45	1 8 5
	50	1 7 7
	55	1 6 9
	60	1 5 10
	65	1 4 10
20	10	1 18 2
	15	1 17 7
	20	1 16 11
	25	1 16 4
	30	1 15 7
	35	1 14 9
	40	1 14 1
	45	1 13 3
	50	1 12 8
	55	1 11 7
	60	1 10 9
	65	1 9 11
25	10	2 2 6
	15	2 1 10
	20	2 1 1
	25	2 0 5
	30	1 19 7
	35	1 18 9
	40	1 17 9
	45	1 16 9
	50	1 15 10
	55	1 14 9
	60	1 13 9
	65	1 12 0
30	10	2 7 7
	15	2 6 11
	20	2 6 2
	25	2 5 4
	30	2 4 6
	35	2 3 5

Age of A.	B.	Premium. £ s. d.
	40	2 2 4
	45	2 1 1
	50	2 0 0
	55	1 18 9
	60	1 17 5
	65	1 16 2
35	10	2 13 11
	15	2 13 2
	20	2 12 6
	25	2 11 7
	30	2 10 8
	35	2 9 9
	40	2 8 2
	45	2 6 9
	50	2 5 3
	55	2 3 9
	60	2 2 3
	65	2 0 7
40	10	3 2 0
	15	3 1 3
	20	3 0 5
	25	2 19 7
	30	2 18 7
	35	2 17 4
	40	2 15 10
	45	2 14 3
	50	2 12 5
	55	2 10 7
	60	2 8 9
	65	2 6 8
45	10	3 11 10
	15	3 11 0
	20	3 10 3
	25	3 9 5
	30	3 8 5
	35	3 7 1
	40	3 5 6
	45	3 3 8
	50	3 1 7
	55	2 19 4
	60	2 16 11
	65	2 14 5
50	10	4 4 6
	15	4 3 8
	20	4 2 8
	25	4 2 1
	30	4 1 0

Age of		Premium.
A.	B.	
		£ s. d.
	35	3 19 10
	40	3 18 2
	45	3 16 2
	50	3 13 10
	55	3 11 1
	60	3 8 2
	65	3 5 1
55	10	5 0 3
	15	4 19 4
	20	4 18 6
	25	4 17 9
	30	4 16 8
	35	4 15 5
	40	4 13 9
	45	4 11 6
	50	4 9 2
	55	4 6 1
	60	4 2 5
	65	3 18 5
60	10	6 1 3
	15	6 0 3
	20	5 19 5
	25	5 18 8
	30	5 17 7
	35	5 16 3
	40	5 14 7
	45	5 12 7
	50	5 10 0
	55	5 6 7
	60	5 2 4
	65	4 17 2
65	10	7 10 9
	15	7 9 7
	20	7 8 8
	25	7 7 11
	30	7 7 0
	35	7 5 9
	40	7 4 2
	45	7 2 1
	50	6 19 5
	55	6 16 0
	60	6 11 6
	65	6 5 5 /

TABLE VI.
ENDOWMENTS.

Premiums, by a Single Payment or Annual Payments, to cease one year before the Sum becomes payable, for £100, to be paid when the Child attains the respective Ages mentioned in the Tables.

To be paid at Sixteen.

AGE.	Single Payment.	Annual.
	£ s. d.	£ s. d.
1	35 7 1	4 4 4
2	43 13 4	4 15 8
3	48 15 7	5 7 6
4	53 7 4	6 0 9
5	57 4 11	6 16 3
6	61 6 10	7 14 7
7	65 6 2	8 17 0
8	69 4 0	10 4 8
9	72 19 7	12 0 2
10	76 13 11	14 7 6

To be paid at Eighteen.

AGE.	Single Payment.	Annual.
	£ s. d.	£ s. d.
1	32 0 2	3 10 8
2	39 10 10	3 19 5
3	44 3 4	4 8 3
4	48 6 5	4 18 1
5	51 16 9	5 9 2
6	55 10 11	6 2 0
7	59 2 7	6 17 1
8	62 13 2	7 15 0
9	66 1 7	8 17 0
10	69 8 11	10 4 4
11	72 17 10	11 19 7
12	76 9 9	14 6 9
13	80 5 4	17 13 0

To be paid at Twenty-one.

AGE.	Single Payment.	Annual.
	£ s. d.	£ s. d.
1	27 7 3	2 15 0
2	33 16 0	3 1 2
3	37 15 1	3 7 3
4	41 6 1	3 13 10
5	44 6 4	4 1 0
6	47 9 8	4 9 2
7	50 11 0	4 18 5

To be paid at Twenty-one.

AGE.	Single Payment.			Annual.		
	£	s.	d.	£	s.	d.
8	53	11	4	5	9	0
9	56	9	9	6	1	5
10	59	7	3	6	16	1
11	62	6	3	7	13	7
12	65	7	9	8	15	3
13	68	12	3	10	2	4
14	72	0	3	11	17	4
15	75	11	8	14	4	1

NEW AMERICAN PROSPECTUSES

William Bard, *A Letter to David E. Evans, Esquire, of Batavia,*[1] *on Life Insurance* (New York: William Van Norden, 1832).

Life Insurance: Its Principles, Operations and Benefits, as Presented by the North Carolina Mutual Life Insurance Company (Raleigh, NC: Seaton Gales, 1849).

In contrast to Standard Life, which occupied a crowded market of dozens of British life insurers when it formed in 1825, the New York Life Insurance and Trust Company (NYL&T) was only the third major life insurance company to form in the United States when it opened its doors in 1830 (it was joined by Baltimore Life that same year). Its prospectus consequently performed many of the same basic educational functions as in the earlier Pennsylvania Company prospectus – with the twist, in the case of NYL&T, of making a special appeal to middle-class breadwinners. It also reflected the strong personality of William Bard (1778–1853), who served as the company's president from its formation until 1843, and as actuary until just before his death in the early 1850s.[2] From its inception, NYL&T made a point to challenge the older thinking of its competitors at every turn – starting with the appointment of a sizeable and aggressive sales force, most of whom received copies of this mass-published *Letter*.[3] Another example of Bard's forward thinking (though not on display in this letter, which did not include a premium table) was his unilateral move, in 1832, to switch from the Northampton to the cheaper Carlisle rates in order to attract more customers into his fold. His tactics were enormously successful over the succeeding decade: by 1840 NYL&T accounted for more than half of all life insurance sold in the United States.[4]

One innovation the NYL&T did not adopt was that of dividing part of its surplus income with policyholders. Among American insurers, only the Girard Life of Pennsylvania (1836) operated as a mixed company before the 1840s, when several mutual life offices burst onto the scene. These mutual firms supplemented Bard's focus on securing family fortunes against premature death with a new, more optimistic invitation for policyholders to participate in the rising tide of American investment.[5] Following in the successful wake of such offices as the Mutual of

New York (1842), New England Mutual (1835; no policies issued until 1844) and Mutual Benefit Life of New Jersey (1845), the North Carolina Mutual opened its doors in 1849 as the first life insurer in its state. Besides drawing attention to the long pedigree of mutual insurance in Britain, this prospectus also alluded to a unique feature of insurance offices in the southern United States: the coverage of slaves, which is discussed in more detail later in this volume.

Notes

1. David E. Evans (1788–1850) acted as agent between 1828 and 1837 for the Holland Land Company, which owned vast tracts in Genesee County, New York.
2. Bard traded the comfortable life of a Hyde Park gentleman for the more active profession of a New York City company promoter in 1830, after a lengthy lawsuit had eaten up much of his wife's inheritance.
3. Murphy, *Investing in Life*, pp. 13, 131. Bard originally wrote the letter as a response to Evans's pessimism regarding the sales potential for life insurance in the state of New York; with Evans's permission, he reprinted 10,000 copies of the letter for circulation by his agents, and he also reprinted it in several New York newspapers.
4. Ibid., pp. 14, 20, 47–50.
5. Ibid., pp. 6–7.

William Bard, *A Letter to David E. Evans, Esquire, of Batavia, on Life Insurance* (1832)

A LETTER.

December 1st, 1832.

TO DAVID E. EVANS, ESQ., BATAVIA,

Dear Sir,

I was lately shown a letter from you to a mutual friend in Albany, in which an opinion is expressed, that the business of Life Insurance will not meet much encouragement in your part of the country. I have often heard a similar one expressed in regard to other portions of the state. The growing business of this office, shows that such an opinion is not well founded, when applied to the city of New York. In June, last, the office had sixty-five running policies, and on the first of December, one hundred and fifty. It was natural its extension should commence where the office was situated, and where explanation and informa-tion could be more readily communicated, to those interested in securing their families against the vicissitudes to which all, and particularly men of business, are liable; but, I have no doubt, when the various means of security and conveni-ence an insurance affords in the business of life, are well understood, and this knowledge is widely spread, that the practice will extend through / the country and become equally, if not more generally, in use, than insurance against fire, or against risks at sea. Such has been the progress of Life Insurance in Great Britain, where the first office established, began with four insured on their books, and at the end of eight years counted only four hundred and ninety. There are now in England, over forty offices, and more than two hundred thousand lives insured. Life Insurance must have something in it peculiarly fitted to the circumstances of mankind, to have led to so great an increase. Will you permit me to occupy your attention for a short time, while I explain some of its operations; and then to ask whether it is not worthy the attention of our fellow citizens, and not likely to command it when use has made it familiar.

The nature of a Life Insurance is not always understood. It is a contract between a company and an individual, that in consideration of a sum paid down, or of a less sum paid annually by the individual to the company; his heirs or assigns shall receive from the company, a larger sum when he dies. An insurance against fire is a contract, that the individual whose house is insured shall receive payment for it, if it is destroyed by fire. A marine insurance is a contract that the individual whose vessel is insured shall receive a certain sum if his vessel is lost at sea. In neither case is there, as there has been supposed by some to be in Life Insurance, an impious attempt to prevent the will of Providence, but a wise and prudent endeavor to render such events as are beyond our control, less / calamitous than without such caution they would be. The amount to be paid by the company, and the amount to be received by the heirs or assigns, is settled by calculation, and is determined by observations made on the duration of life at different ages, and the interest allowed for money.

An insurance may be made for one year, for several years, or for the whole life. In the former cases, the money is paid by the company, if the individual insured, die within the period for which he is insured. In the latter case the money is to be paid whenever the insured dies. It may be made on one life, on two, or on more lives; to commence immediately or at a future day.

It would require much time to state all the cases in which Life Insurance may be employed for the benefit of families and individuals, and to facilitate and make secure operations otherwise hazardous. The most general use made of a Life Insurance, is, by persons living on income; to secure a family, by its means, a comfortable support after the death of its head or parent. This is accomplished by the payment annually to an insurance office, of such portion of the individual's income as can be spared, and for which payment the office contracts to pay, after the death of the insured, to his heirs or assigns, a fixed sum, the amount depending on the annual premium paid by the insured. We will suppose a married man, thirty years of age, clearing by his occupation one thousand dollars a year; that the support of his family costs him eight hundred / and eighty-two dollars, and that he has one hundred and eighteen dollars a year, to spare. It would take an individual a long time, by laying up this sum, to accumulate a moderate support for his family after his death, and should he die early, he must leave them in want; if he pays one hundred and eighteen dollars a year to the office for an insurance, he secures five thousand dollars for them when he dies, should his death happen the next day. A small sum, a few hundred dollars, to be received immediately on the death of a parent, would frequently be a great assistance to a family. The smallest sum may be secured by an insurance, and at a trifling outlay. If the parent is thirty years of age, four dollars and seventy-two cents a year will secure two hundred dollars, and eleven dollars and eighty cents will secure five hundred dollars.

To secure a family against want, on the death of the parent is the most general use made of a Life Insurance; but the cases in which it may be advantageously employed, are as numerous as the circumstances in the lives of individuals, are various.

If an individual has a debt hanging over him, and fears, should he die, his family may be injured by the forced payment of it, he can provide against such a calamity by insuring his life for an equal amount. Suppose the debt two thousand dollars, and the party forty years of age, sixty-four dollars per annum, provides for the debt when he dies.

A young merchant commencing business, may, by an insurance, add to his credit among those with whom / he deals, and would add to it, were it understood, that in case of his death, there were means provided for quickly settling his debts. Suppose an upright and industrious young man, twenty five years old, commencing business and obtaining a credit of five thousand dollars; one hundred and two dollars per annum will insure this, payable on his death, and thus secure a sum sufficient to satisfy all his creditors.

In our enterprising country where capital is wanting, and where credit and bank accommodations are among the means made use of to supply the want; where purchases of land, as well as of merchandise, are frequently founded on bank assistance, how anxious must those feel, who, dependant on endorsers, see their estates and the independence of their families, and the safety of their friends, all at hazard, should death suddenly overtake them; and should their involved affairs be left to the management of executors. Under such circumstances, a Life Insurance to the amount of their discounted paper, relieves them from uncertainty; and affords the means of immediately relieving endorsers from loss, their estates from the danger of being sacrificed, and their families from ruin.

A creditor, anxious about the safety of his debt, in case his debtor should die, may relieve himself from anxiety by insuring his debtor's life, by which means he will receive from the office, in case the event happen, the amount of his debt. Suppose A. is indebted to B. five thousand dollars, payable in seven years, and that A. is thirty-four years old, seventy-five dollars a / year will secure the debt, should A. die within that period.

An individual wishes to go into business. He has friends, who, having confidence in his skill, industry, and integrity, are willing to advance him money, but knowing the uncertainty of life, fear, if he should die, they would lose their money; if they insure his life to the amount advanced, this risk vanishes; if he die before they are repaid, the office insuring, pays the amount.

An individual is desirous of entering upon a hazardous enterprise, he sees in it a fair prospect of improving his circumstances, but it requires his personal skill and attention, he fears, should he die, his family will not be able, successfully, to conclude it. By a Life Insurance he puts himself at ease; a small part of his annual gains enables him to pay a Life Insurance – which secures his family a support should he die, and his enterprise fail in consequence of his death.

A farmer has a farm on life lease, depending on his own life, or on the lives of other persons; should he or they die, the support of his family will be gone. A small part of his gains applied to insuring his own life, or the lives on which the estate depends, will secure the means of buying another farm, or paying for another lease. A. purchases a farm for fifteen hundred dollars, depending on the life of B., aged fifty, sixty-nine dollars a year will secure to the purchaser fifteen hundred dollars, on the death of B., whenever it may happen.

A farmer possessed of a life lease farm, depending on / his own life, or on the lives of others, wishes to borrow money on the farm. By insuring at the office the party, on whose life the lease depends, for the amount he wishes to borrow, the office will lend him the money.

An individual has a wife, an aged parent, an infant child, an infirm friend, an old domestic, depending on him for support, a trifling sum paid annually for the insurance of his own life, will secure such parent, wife, child, friend, or domestic, from want, after the death of the insured.

A public spirited, or a charitable individual wishes to aid, by a legacy, a school, a college, a literary society, a church, or a charitable institution, his present means do not enable him to do so, to the extent of his wishes; they may be accomplished by an annual sum, paid for an insurance to the amount he wishes to leave to the favored object. Suppose such a person is sixty years of age, and wishes to leave, at his death, five hundred dollars to a church, a charity, or a mission; by insuring his life and paying thirty-five dollars a year, he can do so. How many worthy, pious, but poor clergymen, might be relieved from anxious care, relative to their families, would their congregations unite and raise a small sum for the insurance of their lives. Suppose the clergyman fifty years old, ninety-two dollars a year would secure to his widow two thousand dollars whenever he died.

A party expects to receive a property, provided he arrives at a certain age; it is lost to his family if he die before he arrives at that age; an insurance for the term / secures them against the consequences of his early death. A., aged nineteen, expects to receive a property valued at five thousand dollars, if he arrive at the age of twenty-one; his mother or sister will be without support, should he die before the end of the period; forty-five dollars a year will make them secure of receiving it.

These, sir, are a few of the innumerable instances in which Life Insurance may be made useful. It enables gentlemen in the army, the navy, the church, the law, or in office, medical, and other professional men, annuitants, tenants for life, tradesmen, and all other persons, whose income depends upon their lives, to make provision for a wife, children, or relations. It enables persons to raise money on loan, where real security cannot be offered; to provide for the renewal of leases held upon lives; to secure the eventual payment of doubtful debts due to individuals, or bodies of creditors. It enables proprietors of landed estates, and other persons whose property is charged with mortgages, or with portions for children, or other incumbrances, payable on events connected with the termination of their own, or of other lives, to answer the charges when they fall due. Parents may by this means, secure the return of money paid for education, apprenticeship, capital embarked in business, or other advances made for children, in the event of their premature death. It provides means to reimburse the sum expended in the purchase of any life estate, on the death of the person, during whose life it is held; to render contingent property / nearly equal, in point of security, with absolute property; and generally, it affords a certain indemnity against any pecuniary loss, claim, or inconvenience whatsoever, to which one individual may become subject, by reason of the death of another – Enough has been said to show the purposes to which Life Insurance may be applied, and enough, I think, to show, that there are in this country, as there are in every civilized country, materials sufficient to found a business as extensive as Fire or Marine Insurance; I should say, more extensive: for a Life Insurance may be made for one hundred dollars or for many thousands; it concerns the poor as well as the rich, the mechanic, the farmer, the man living on income, or the land-holder, the professional man, or the merchant – in short, all classes of men whatever.

An insurance for one or more years terminates with the period for which the insurance is made, but an insurance for the whole life is of a different character, and to one so insured, an insurance office becomes a savings bank with a peculiar advantage, in which the smallest annual savings may safely be deposited for the benefit of a family. An individual looking forward to accumulate something from his earnings for the support of his family after his death, feels discouraged when he thinks how many years he must live before a small sum, put out annually at interest, will amount to a moderate support for his family. Where could forty-seven dollars and eighty cents be put out, with security and with punctuality, annually, at compound interest / during a long life; and if it could be put out, what security is there, that early death may not frustrate the object intended; no where, except in a Life Insurance, where, supposing the party thirty years of age, the small sum of two dollars and thirty-six cents, paid annually, will secure to the individual's family one hundred dollars, on his death; or twenty-three dollars and sixty-six cents will secure them one thousand dollars; or forty-seven dollars twenty cents, will secure them two thousand dollars. In such cases, therefore, the office becomes a savings bank. The peculiar advantage alluded to, is, that in a common savings bank, the party depositing his money must live many years, supposing the interest of money five per cent., which is a very great interest to give for a long period, he must live nearly twenty four years, before two dollars and thirty-six cents per annum will amount to one hundred dollars, or twenty-three dollars and sixty cents to one thousand dollars, or forty-seven dollars and twenty cents to two thousand dollars, but by applying the same sums to an insurance he is secure, that die when he may, even the day after the insurance is made, his object is attained, his family receive immediately the money his prudence intended for them; he lives secure, that while his industry is providing for the support of those he loves, his small surplus gains are effectually guarding them against poverty, in the hour of distress.

There is one most valuable and important class of our fellow citizens, with whom my situation brings me in daily contact, and with whom you have been all / your life intimately acquainted, to whom Life Insurance appears to me so peculiarly applicable and advantageous, that I must beg leave, notwithstanding I have already occupied too much of your time, to notice them. It is the practice of our countrymen, arising from our prosperity and the facility with which a family is supported, to marry early. The children of our farmers, when married, pass a few years in accumulating, by their daily labour, a few hundred dollars, and then leave their homes, buy and settle on a farm. Let us suppose a young man and his wife, with two or three children, looking out for a farm. At twenty dollars an acre, he soon buys a good one. He pays down one thousand or twelve hundred dollars, and knows that to this office he can always apply for, and with certainty obtain the balance, on terms the most easy and convenient; if he is industrious, and lives, ten or fifteen years sees him out of debt and his farm clear, but if he die early, and who is secure against such an event? he leaves a young and rising family, the farm wants its owner, the interest never sleeps, and the property may be sacrificed. An insurance, costing, if the insured is thirty years of age, and the debt one thousand dollars, twenty-three dollars and sixty cents a year, guards against these fatal consequences; if the young farmer die, the office pays his debt, or rather, it is paid; his farm is free and descends unincumbered to his family; affording them a home and a comfortable support. Surely such an institution deserves the countenance, the support, and the consideration of all prudent and reflecting men, and is doubly / recommended, when it is considered how very small a sacrifice of some personal comfort or gratification, will secure, by its means, the independence and happiness of a poor man's family. In this view of the subject, an unnecessary journey, an idle amusement, a few wasted days in each year, is a sacrifice of the education and clothing, and food, of objects the nearest and dearest to us all, should it please our Maker to take us from them. The tobacco chewer will readily consume his two cents a day, which will secure to his family, in case of his death, and if he is twenty-five, three hundred and fifty-eight dollars. What shall we say to the tippler of twenty-five, who, if he drinks one shilling a day, sacrifices two thousand two hundred and forty dollars; a sum sufficient to make a poor family rich, at a moment when independence at least, is so important to them.

Nor should I forget to mention, if an individual insures for life, and after a lapse of years finds an insurance no longer necessary, or the payment of the premium convenient, that he does not lose the whole of what he has paid. The office fairly calculates what is the value of the risk it has run, and pays back to the insured all he has paid over this sum, and which went to make up the consideration for the risk to be run in future. After a number of years, the policy becomes of value to the insured; it is a part of his property; if he thinks proper to use it during his life, he receives back from the office no inconsiderable part of what has been paid, for the comfort of feeling secure and at ease during the previous years. /

Besides insuring lives, this office grants annuities. Excepting for some purpose of family convenience, few persons in early life will be inclined to purchase an annuity; the annuity before forty or fifty years of age not exceeding the legal interest of the money paid for it. This surprises many, as the capital invested is lost to the annuitant, but arises from this; that a reasonable compensation to the office, and the security of all parties, require that the annuity should be calculated at a much lower rate than legal interest. At sixty years of age, money applied to the purchase of an annuity at this office, will produce 9 35/100 per cent. At seventy years of age, 12 66/100 per cent. At seventy-four years of age, 13 33/100 per cent.

By purchasing an annuity, a person advanced in life may augment his annual income, or increase the income of some relative at a future period, or secure an allowance made to some dependant, or exonerate his estate from dower, or the incumbrance of a life charge.

The following modes occur for effecting these purposes:

1. The grant of an annuity on the life of one person, to commence immediately.
2. On the lives of two persons, to commence immediately, and to continue either wholly or in part, during the life of the survivor, or to cease on the death of either.
3. On the lives of infants, to commence at any period, either at the time of agreeing for the annuity, or at any future period; to continue for the remainder of life, or for any certain number of years, in case the life shall so long exist. /
4. On the lives of other persons, at any future periods.

And they may be obtained by the payment of a principal sum at the time the purchase is made, for such as are immediate, and for such as are prospective, either by that means, or the payment of a sum annually.

This office also affords an easy mode to parents or friends, of providing for children by endowment.

A parent wishing to provide for a son a sum of money to commence business with, when he arrives at twenty-one, or to provide a marriage portion for a daughter; for every hundred dollars he deposits with the company, the child being at the time of deposit, one year old, will receive, if he or she arrives at the age of twenty-one, three hundred and six dollars and fifty-eight cents.

If a parent, having a daughter one year old, should wish to provide for her an annuity at that period of life, should she arrive at it, when age will probably require indulgence and when an increasing family may make it doubly accept-able, say, when she arrives at forty years of age; he can do so, and place it beyond the control of a husband, by a deposit with the company. Let the annuity required, be three hundred dollars a year, a deposit of five hundred and eighty-seven dollars and fifty five cents will secure the payment of that annuity, from the company during her life, after she arrives at forty years of age.

I have troubled you, Dear Sir, with a long letter, but the remark mentioned in the beginning, induced me to / think you had not reflected on the importance and advantages of Life Insurance; and that you are among the thousand intelli-gent men, who, from other occupations, and from the novelty of the practice in this state, have not given it the attention it deserves.

Persuaded that the general habit of Life Insurance would contribute to the economy, virtue, and happiness of our citizens, and anxious that this institution affording to the Court of Chancery, and to the widow, and orphan, and to the wealthy, a place of safe and convenient deposit for their funds; and its assistance liberally in promoting the agriculture, the improvement, and the best interests of the state; should also supply the means of rendering the enterprise of its citi-zens secure, and free from hazard; I am glad to take every opportunity to extend the knowledge of the benefits to be derived form Life Insurance, and shall be pleased, if what I have said should lead you to a farther consideration of the subject, and to promoting the practice by your influence.

With sentiments of the highest respect and esteem,

I remain, sir,

Your ob'd't. serv't.

WM. BARD.

Life Insurance: Its Principles, Operations and Benefits, as Presented by the North Carolina Mutual Life Insurance Company (1849)

LIFE INSURANCE:
Its Principles, Operations and Benefits.

The Board of Directors of the North Carolina Mutual Life Insurance Company, owing to the increasing demand for information on the subject of Life Insurance, which has already exhausted an issue of 1000 Pamphlets, have deemed it necessary to make a new issue; and in doing so, have thought proper to revise the original, so as to embrace such alterations and additions to the rules and regulations, as have been found to be necessary.

It is gratifying to the Board to be able to state to the Members of the Company, that the business has been unexpectedly large, with a gradual and healthy increase. This success is not the result of any variation in practice from the mode of operations pursued by other well-regulated Companies, nor because the Directors have introduced any new or deceptive feature in the legitimate transactions of Life Insurance; but is plainly attributable to the fact, that the Company is organized on *purely mutual principles* – that its Charter is a *wise* and *liberal* one in its provisions, and that it is in truth, emphatically a HOME INSTITUTION. – Since the Company went into operation, in April last, it has, up to September, issued more than *two hundred and forty Policies!* nor has it yet sustained a single loss. This fact speaks for itself; and is most gratifying evidence, that the people of North Carolina and our neighbor States of the South, are satisfied of the necessity and policy of such an Institution; and furthermore, are both disposed and determined to give it a liberal patronage. – We do not mistake the public feeling in this regard. Many persons who, since they have become acquainted with the principles of our Institution and its plan of operations, and who for years past have been insured in "Foreign Companies,"[1] have transferred their Policies to this Company; and many others will doubtless / do likewise, as their annual premiums fall due. And why not? Why should the citizens of the Southern States leave *home* to seek insurance elsewhere? Our rates are as liberal as others: The privileges conferred by our Charter are as ample and acceptable, as others: The Institution is located in our own midst, and is subject to the immediate supervision and control of its members: And enjoying the advantages of the experience of others that have preceded it, similarly established on the principle of Mutual benefits and Mutual liabilities, it may reasonably hope, like every other well regulated Company in this Country and in Europe, that its purposes will be fully accomplished, and its efforts crowned with entire success. Indeed it cannot be denied that this Company has even thus early taken its stand among the oldest and best Institutions of the kind in this Country: and before the first annual meeting of its members, it is confidently expected to out-strip many companies that have been in operation for years; then why, we repeat, should our citizens annually send away thousands of dollars, which might be advantageously retained in our midst? It is estimated that more than $100,000 are annually sent from this State to be invested in life Policies; and the same amount, or more perhaps, from South Carolina, Georgia, Tennessee and Virginia. Surely these investments have not been made abroad from preference. On the contrary, they have rather been from the fact that there has been heretofore no Institution of the kind, near home, organized as this is, to claim the public confidence and support.

The Board have a high satisfaction in congratulating the Members of the North Carolina Mutual Life Insurance Company on the unexampled success which has thus far attended our efforts, and the cheering prospects of its continued growth, prosperity and usefulness.

Until within a very few years past, Life Insurance in this country was not known, except through the agencies of a few European companies in our more populous cities; and the first attempt to establish such companies in this country was regarded as an infringement upon the decrees of that Superintending Providence which hath "appointed unto all men once to die." Many supposed, that, being unwilling to confide our destinies to the Supreme / Ruler of the Universe we were about to transfer the safety of human life to the keeping of our fellow men.

In 1790, there were some six offices in Europe, and they were only doing a limited amount of business: now, since the Mutual feature has been generally introduced, there are 85 offices in operation, doing an incredibly large amount of business annually. One of these companies, viz. the Equitable, has accumulated a Capital of $50,000,000! This company was established in 1762, without Capital, and commenced operations with 15 policies of small amounts, and was wholly dependant upon incoming applications for a fund sufficient to enable them to meet any loss occurring by the death of a member. They struggled on slowly, but surely, and at the end of 12 years, they had 734 running policies; during the next ten years, this number was increased to 1608, and in 1792, just 30 years from its commencement, it had 4640 policies.

Many suppose that nothing like an accurate calculation of the mean duration of human life, can be made; and that any attempt to base the chances of success upon the average bills of mortality, would be exceedingly unsafe. In this opinion, however candidly entertained, there is a decided error. The experience of an accurate observation of nearly two hundred years, has proved that it is possible to make a calculation of human life, which will not in that time vary 6 per cent.

The first table made in England, showing the expectation of life at various ages, was by Dr. Price, from observations of the Bills of Mortality in Northampton: and fifty years subsequent to this time, the Carlisle table was made by Joshua Milne, from observations of Dr. Heysham of Carlisle, – this was from 1779 to 1787.

The decrements of life in these tables, differ very materially; the Northampton is much greater than the Carlisle: This discrepancy can readily be reconciled by taking into account the difference in the location of the places. The Northampton District is decidedly unhealthy; while the Carlisle has always been regarded as one of the most healthy Districts in England.

The Northampton table makes the whole number of persons embraced in their calculations, become extinct at the age of 96, / and the Carlisle at 104. Various other tabular views of the bills of mortality have been compiled in various districts of England, and on the European Continent, by men of deep research; and an immense amount of facts have thus been given to the world, which have formed the basis of the law of average of human Life, and the value of Annuities, and a corrent Scale, or Tariff, of Premiums, on Life Insurance.

Life insurance only guarantees the laws of average; it is not founded on the calculations whether death will, or will not happen. Death is inevitably the fate of all men. Every person born must die: but most live through a series of years; and the law of average, and duration of human life, is reduced almost to an exact science, and furnishes a data upon which to base the operations of a *Life Insurance Company*, without subjecting it to any contingency which can impair its ability to meet its losses. In this respect it is very different from all other species of insurance. The Insurer of a number of houses does not know whether a fire shall occur among his risks or not: the Underwriter for the vessel which leaves on a distant voyage, does not know whether the elements shall be prosperous for the safety of the noble bark or otherwise: the Health Insurer does not know whether his subject shall continue well, or be taken sick. There is no positive data upon which to base the calculations of success, in companies of this kind; but, in life insurance, death is regarded as a fixed fact – "dust thou art, and unto dust thou shalt return;"[2] and all the calculations are made in view of the final drama of human life.

Among the different tables in use with Insurance Companies, the "Carlisle" seems to be the favorite. Its calculations are found to apply with exceeding minuteness to the present experience of Insurance Companies in the middle States of our Union, and all that have adopted it, seem to be doing a safe and profitable business.

Life Insurance Companies are divided into three classes, viz. Joint Stock, Mixed, and Mutual. The Joint Stock Company has a Capital furnished by Subscription as a means of investing surplus funds; and whatever accumulation of profits occur, they are placed to the credit of each Stockholder as a speculation on his part. In a Mixed Company, there is a partial division of profits, / according to the mode fixed for a division of profits among themselves.

With the Mutual Company, all life insurers are equally entitled to the profits of the Company, in proportion to the amount of premiums by them respectively paid; and all members are entitled to a voice in the deliberations of the Company. The Mutual plan presents strong inducements to the insurer, whether in reference to early death or long protracted life. According to the Stock System, a person being 25 years of age and insuring $5,000, would have to pay $120, allowing this policy to fall due at 59 years of age, viz. 34 years after insuring. This annual amount is compounded according to standard tables at 4 per cent per annum. The value therefore, of these 34 annual payments, will amount to $8,382, and, at his death, his heirs will receive only the $5,000 originally insured, showing a loss to the insurer of $3,382, being the amount of premium and interest paid by him during the 34 years.

Let us now take an insurance of the same amount and same age, and trace its operations under the mutual system. At 25 years of age, his premium would be $120, the duration 34 years, the value of the 34 annual payments, compounded at 4 per cent. per annum, will be $8,382, the accumulated profits of this 34 years, by the data we have taken, viz. (the "Equitable" of London,) gives to this insurance $11,250, which, added to the sum insured, viz. $5,000, produce the amount of $16,350, payable at the death of the insured, being an excess over the cost of insurance of $7,868, and a nett gain in favor of the mutual system of $11,250. The rates of premium would of course very, according as a company charged more or less premiums; and the result would be varied by the difference of interest charged in the State where the office was located.

A peculiar case is mentioned in the Equitable Society of London, which we think further illustrates the signal benefits of insurance on the Mutual plan. An insurance of $5,000 in this company, effected in 1780, produced the following results: in 1793, the value was $7,600: in 1802, $10,050: and in 1834, a period of 50 years, the insurance originally of $5,000, was increased to the immense amount of $20,800, nearly six times that / of the insurance. These are results in a country where investments upon an average do not produce over 4 per cent. per annum, and, moreover, are not incidental to a few years of unusually prosperous business; but are the gradual growth, and continual experience, of three quarters of a century.

These enormous profits were, of course, not restricted solely to the regular interest of the funds of the company, but were increased by the following circumstances, to which Mr. Morgan,[3] the Actuary of this society, alludes, in an annual address, viz: The expired insurances and cancelled policies form a very material part of these profits; another which he considers a perpetual source of profit, is the probabilities of life among the members being much higher than those given by the table. It was found that where the table gave 4, the experience of the company gave only 3. This disparity arose principally from admitting none but good lives. To illustrate this matter still further – since the year 1800, this society has had an average of 8,000 members, the estimated annual number of deaths by the table is 247; whereas, the actual number was but 194, or 53 less than those in the table, which is made the foundation of its whole practice. The average amount of insurance on these individual lives, is $6,818; this sum, multiplied by 53, gives $361,354.

Their funds were further increased by large investments being made in stocks during the war[4] at greatly depressed prices, and after the restoration of peace, in 1815, these stocks were considerably advanced. But aside from these incidental causes of exorbitant profits to a mutual company, its principles, carefully carried out, will, in every case, produce eventually large dividends.

Circumstances occurring of such a nature as to render the continuance of a member impracticable, he may, after a few years, surrender his policy, and receive a certain valuation for it. The principle ordinarily used for determining the value of a policy is: take the premium at the age of surrender, and deduct from it the premium the party has been paying, multiply the difference by the value of an annuity at the age of surrender, and this will give the value; but, inasmuch as none but good lives ordinarily surrender, one third is deducted from this calculation. Take an example – a man 45 years of age takes out a policy for $1,000, / and at the age of 55, ten years afterwards, he surrenders it; during this time he has paid to the company $373.

Annual premium at surrender,	$57,80
Annual premium when taken out,	37,30
Difference,	$20,50

Multiply this difference by the value of an annuity at the age of surrender, and deduct one third, and the nett amount coming to the policy will be $167,10: this amount would be increased by any extra investments of the funds of the company.

In a calculation made by the Mutual Insurance Company of New York, a person at the age of 30 taking a policy of $1,000, and allowing that he lives through the expectation of life, i.e. 34 years and 4 months, by the Carlisle Table, at his death his family would receive $3,250. This insurance would of course yield a greater or less amount, as his life might fall short, or be prolonged beyond the expectation table.

We have thus presented to the public a brief and condensed account of the rise and progress of the Life Insurance principle; and the general reader will, no doubt, be forcibly reminded of the onward march of that elevated order of intellect, which has been able, with so much precision, to ascertain the average termination of human life.

It now remains for us to direct more especial attention to the precise principles upon which the North Carolina Mutual Life Insurance Company proposes to conduct its operations.

This company proposes to effect insurance on the lives of all sound and healthy individuals, during the whole period of life, or as much less as persons may desire; and in order to offer as strong inducements as may be consistent with the safety of the Mutual System to all insurers, they propose, that on all life policies, the premiums on which amount to $30 and upwards, that they will require only half to be paid in cash, and the balance in a note at 12 months with lawful interest.

The benefits of this regulation are very apparent, in view of the fact that many persons desirous of insuring their lives, have / limited means, and can only space a small amount at a time from their daily receipts. Another very important feature in this company is, that the charter gives the privilege to a Husband to insure his own life for the benefit of his Wife and Children, without any liability to have the amount diverted to the payment of any contracts, or debts of his own; and in like manner, the Wife may insure the life of her husband, subject to the same regulations; these are highly important features in our charter, which will no doubt readily commend themselves to the attention of the intelligent reader. This company also gives an annual division of profits to all life insurers, and proposes to charge no more for insurance than actual cost. The abundant success which has attended other companies, based upon similar principles, leaves no doubt as to the efficiency of the institution, and also its ability promptly to discharge all claims occurring against it.

The North Carolina Company will also insure the lives of all healthy slaves, for a period of from one to 5 years: but, in no case can their owners or insurers participate in the profits of the company.

All premiums for policies on slaves must be paid in cash. The insurance on slaves in this State opens a new field of thought to our Planters, and other slave owners, and proposes to secure them in the possession of that kind of property, which constitutes half of the actual wealth of the State.

This company will also grant policies on joint lives, to commence at any given time, the parties being in good health. An insurance may be effected on two joint lives, payable in the event of either of the lives failing, or payable upon the contingency of a life R surviving that of B, and it may, for a stipulated sum, be made payable at the death of R provided B should survive him; or it may be in the form of an annuity, payable to B, in the event of his surviving R, commencing at the death of R, and being continued during the life of B. This method is sometimes desirable. A man, for instance, might wish to make provision for his wife's benefit, in the event of her surviving him. This insurance would be made for a less premium than would be charged on condition of being payable at the death of R, without this contingency. /

We have abundantly shown in our previous remarks and examples, that the more desirable made of insurance is a life policy. This gives all the full benefits of the system, so far as profits are concerned, and also secures the party against the unpleasant contingency of being cut off from the benefits of the Company, at a time when his general health shall be so much impaired as to render it impracticable for the Company to renew his insurance. In this emergency, finding death staring him the face, the unhappy reflection is forced upon him, that he has to leave his wife and children to the charities of a selfish world.

The conditions of an Insurance for the whole continuance of life, are such as to admit of no contingency as to the final loss. The loss must come, and it cannot therefore be expected, that an Insurance for life will be taken at as low a rate, as for a term of years. Therefore, an adequate premium must be charged in view of a final loss; and in all such cases, our premium will be found to be at the maximum rates, varying of course, as the ages of the party may vary at the time of insuring.

Life Insurance is a subject every way worthy of your serious regard and most active labors. It is a noble and most beautiful science, and is destined, sooner or later, to work a mighty change in ameliorating the general state of society, and elevating its moral character; the gentle dawnings of the twilight which precede the coming day, are already sufficiently marked across the broad horizon of society, and soon, very soon, the pure effulgence of a meridian sun will disperse the last vestige of superstition and doubt, which has occupied the mind of the people, as to the propriety of this system; and its great benefits will stand boldly forth, challenging the admiration, and winning the approval, of all well regulated minds. /

BY-LAWS.

Sec. 1. The Officers of this Company shall consist of a President, Vice President, Secretary, Treasurer, Attorney, and a Medical Board of Consultation, consisting of three.

Sec. 2. There shall be an Executive Committee, consisting of three, appointed annually, from the Board of Directors.

Sec. 3. The Board of Directors shall have stated meetings, at the Office of the Company, on the first Saturdays in March, June, September and December.

Sec. 4. The President shall preside at all meetings of the Board of Directors, sign all Policies of Insurance, call special meetings of the Board of Directors, when he shall deem the same necessary, or when requested in writing, signed by three

Directors: and exercise a general superintendance over the affairs of the Company; and in his absence, the Vice President shall discharge the same duties.

Sec. 5. The Secretary shall keep a record of the proceedings of the Board of Directors, Ex. Committee, and of the Company; preserve the premium notes and applications; shall keep a General and Termination Register; a Journal and Ledger; a Book of Alienations and Surrenders; he shall collect all assessments that may be made, and once in thirty days pay over to the Treasurer, all monies in his hands belonging to the Company, and take his receipt for the same. It shall be his duty to give notice of the election of Directors as provided in the Act of Incorporation. He shall give a bond, with such sureties as the Executive Committee shall approve, in the penal sum of Five Thousand Dollars, conditioned for the faithful performance of his duty as Secretary.

Sec. 6. The Treasurer shall have the care of all the money belonging to the Company, and shall keep a correct account of all receipts and disbursements: all payments by the Treasurer shall be made upon warrant from the President, attested by the Secretary: and such payment, so attested, shall be a good and sufficient voucher for the Tresurer in the settlement of his account. / He shall give a bond to the Company, to be approved by the Ex. Committee, in the penal sum of Ten Thousand Dollars, conditioned for the faithful discharge of his duty as Treasurer. He shall render account of his trust, when requested by the Board or Executive Committee.

Sec. 7. The Executive Committee shall audit all accounts presented for payment, and possess the power to transact the business of the Company, in the absence of the Board of Directors, agreeably to such rules and regulations as may, from time to time, be adopted by the Board: may in their discretion give consent of the Company to any member who may wish to exceed the limits of travel, prescribed in the Policy, and such consent shall be signed by the President, attested by the Secretary: shall examine all applications for insurance, and if approved, the Secretary shall issue a Policy thereon.

Sec. 8. Persons proposing for Insurance, shall fill the application blanks furnished by the Company: the party to be Insured must be examined by the Family Physician of the party, and a Medical examiner of the Company, and previous to being insured, deposit his application and premium Note, if any, with the Secretary of said Company, and, if approved by the Executive Committee, the Policy shall bear date with such approval, and take effect at noon of that day.

Sec. 9. Premium on Policies for *Life,* for thirty dollars or *over.* per annum, may be paid as follows – viz: one half in cash, and one half in a Note, at twelve months, bearing interest at six per cent. per annum.

Premium on all Policies for a less period than the duration of life, shall be paid in cash. The applicant will in all cases pay one dollar for Policy, and one dollar for Application.

Sec. 10. Parties Insured at the table rates of premium, are not allowed to pass South of the Southern line of South Carolina and Tennessee, nor west of the Mississippi River, between the 15th of June and the 15th of October, without the written consent of the Company, but may reside or travel North of the lines named above, on any of the regular mail routes by Steam Boat or other conveyance.

Sec. 11. A party neglecting to settle his annual premium, to / pay the per centage when called for by the Directors, within forty days after it is due; or to pay assessments, when called for, within forty days, shall forfeit all the interest he has in the Policy; also, in case the party shall exceed the limits prescribed in Policy for residence, or travel upon the seas, without the written consent of the Company, and shall die in consequence thereof or shall die by the hands of justice, or in an attempt to violate any law of the land where he may happen to be, or in a duel, or by his own hand (except in case of insanity, whereof written notice has been previously given to the Company, or where it is clearly proven to have existed,) or if the party enters into any military or naval service, (the militia, not in actual service excepted,) he shall forfeit his Policy, all monies paid, and all profits due thereon.

Sec. 12. Within forty days from the first Monday in July, in each year, a statement, or annual report, of the affairs of the Company, shall be made out by the Secretary, and an annual dividend of the profits shall be made, when all Policies for Life, which have been renewed prior to said dividend, and then in force, shall have their per centage of profits carried to their credit, and all parties insured, whose Policies have been renewed as aforesaid, shall receive a notice from the Secretary of such profits, which shall be deducted from the amount of their premium at the next annual renewal. In case of the death of any Member, the amount then standing to his or her credit shall be paid over to the representative of said Party, after deducting all indebtedness to the Company.

Sec. 13. All claims for Insurance against the Company, shall be paid within ninety days after due notice, and proof of the death of the party – all indebtedness to the Company, upon said Policy, to be deducted.

Sec. 14. The funds of this Company shall, with the exception of what may, in the judgment of the President, Treasurer and Secretary, be reserved for contingencies, be invested, from time to time, by said Officers, in behalf of the Company, in Stock in any of the Banks of this State, in United States' Government Stock, or in State Bonds of North Carolina.

Sec. 15. It shall be the duty of the Board of Directors, at each annual meeting, to set apart such amount for a contingent, or / reserved fund, as shall in their judgment be deemed best for the interest and welfare of the Company.

Sec. 16. The Board of Directors, or Executive Committee, may appoint so many Agents as they may deem necessary, for the better management of the affairs of this Company; and such Agents shall give bonds to the Company, with such sureties as the Executive Committee shall approve, in the penal sum of $1000, conditioned for the faithful discharge of the duties of their Office.

Sec. 17. Slaves may be insured by their owners, or others interested, for two thirds of their value only, for a term not exceeding five years; and the Insurance on slaves shall be governed by the above rules and conditions, adopted for the regulation of this Company. But slaves are not allowed to travel beyond the limits of the State in which they are insured.

Sec. 18. Should the party insured, during the continuance of the Policy, die from drunkenness, he shall forfeit the Policy, and all claims upon the Company.

Sec. 19. If a Policy is assigned, notice is to be given the Company; and the party to whom the Policy is transferred, must sign all premium notes with the Insured.

Sec. 20. The members of this Company shall hold a meeting annually, for the purpose of electing a Board of Directors, on the first Monday in July in each year, at the Office of the Company.

Sec. 21. The Company will decline all applications for insurance, on persons whose pulse is uniformly over ninety.

EXTRA RATES OF INSURANCE ON SLAVES.

Slaves in Coal Pits,	1 ½ per cent. extra.
" Mining,	1 ½ " " "
" on Rail Roads,	½ " " "
" Steam Boat,	" " "
" Canal Boat,	1 " " "
" Fishing Boat,	1 " " "
" in Coasting,	1 " " "
" Hauling Seines,	1 " " "
" Getting Oysters,	½ " " "
" Rice fields,	1 " " "
" Rafting,	½ " " "/

PROOFS OF LOSS REQUIRED.

A certificate of the Physician who attended the Party in his last illness, stating particularly the nature of the disease, its duration, and the time he died.

A certificate of a friend or intimate acquaintance, stating how long he was sick, and that he was present during his illness, or at his death, and that he is knowing to his death.

A certificate of the undertaker, or sexton, who attended the funeral of the party, and saw his remains interred.

These several certificates must be sworn or affirmed to, before a Magistrate, or some one empowered to administer an oath or affirmation.

NECESSARY RECEIPT.

When it is a wife's Policy on the life of her husband, or of a Party Insuring the life of another, or in case of an assigned Policy, a receipt on the Policy is sufficient, from the parties holding such Policies. But when a party insures his own life, in case of loss, the Insurance must be collected by an Executor or Administrator legally authorized to settle the estate, and the Policy must be surrendered, receipted by the Executor or Administrator. /

CHARTER.

AN ACT to Incorporate a Mutual Life Insurance Company in the State of North Carolina.

1. *Be it enacted by the General Assembly of the State of North Carolina, and it is hereby enacted by the authority of the same,* That JOHN H. MANLY, HENRY W. MILLER, PERRIN BUSBEE, H. W. HUSTED, WM. H. MCKEE, WM. W. HOLDEN, WM. D. COOKE, WM. H. JONES, JAMES F. JORDAN, CHARLES B. ROOT, CHARLES E. JOHNSON, WILLIAM D. HAYWOOD, WILLIAM R. SCOTT, and others, their associates, successors and assigns, shall be and are hereby constituted and declared to be a body politic and corporate, in fact and in name, by the name of the North Carolina Mutual Life Insurance Company, to be located at such place in the City of Raleigh, as shall be designated by a majority of the Company present at any regular meeting; and by that name, they and their successors shall and may have succession during the continuance of this Act, and shall be capable of suing and being sued, pleading and being impleaded, answering and being answered unto, defending and being defended, in all manner of actions, suits, complaints, matters and causes whatsoever; and that they and their successors may have a common seal, and may alter and change the same at pleasure: And also, that they and their successors, by the name of "THE NORTH CAROLINA MUTUAL LIFE INSURANCE COMPANY" shall be in law capable of purchasing, holding and conveying any estate, real or personal, for the use of said corporation.

2. *Be it further enacted,* That all persons who shall at any time hereafter insure in or with the corporation, shall, while they continue so insured, be deemed and

taken as Members of the said corporation, and that the property and concerns of the said corporation shall be managed by thirteen Directors, all of whom shall be citizens of this State, to be chosen annually, by and from / among the members, and shall hold their office for one year, and until others are chosen: and that a meeting of the members of the corporation shall be held annually, for the purpose of electing a Board of Directors, at such time and place in the City of Raleigh, as the corporation in its by-laws shall appoint: of which election public notice shall be given in at least one of the Public Newspapers printed in said City, at least thirty days preceding such election; and such election shall be made by ballot and a plurality of the votes of the members present, allowing to each member one vote for every one hundred dollars insured in said company: and if any of the said Directors shall die, refuse to serve, or neglect to act in their said office, for the space of two months, then, and in every such case, the remaining Directors shall have power to fill such vacancies, until the next annual meeting.

3. *Be it further enacted,* That it shall and may be lawful for the said Corporation to insure their respective lives, and to make all and every insurance appertaining to or connected with Life risks of whatsoever kind or nature, as well of the sound in health as the infirm or invalid.

4. *Be it further enacted,* That it shall be lawful for any married woman, by herself and in her own name, or in the name of any third person, with his assent, as her trustee, to cause to be insured, for her sole use, the life of her husband, for any definite period, or for the time of his natural life; and in case of her surviving her husband, the same or nett amount of the insurance becoming payable to her, to and for her own use, free from the claims of the representatives of her husband or any of his creditors.[5]

5. *Be it further enacted,* That the husband may insure his own life, for the sole use and benefit of his wife or children, and in case of the death of the husband, the amount thus insured shall be paid over to the wife or children, or their guardian, if under age, for her or their own use, free from all the claims of the representatives of the husband or any of his creditors.

6. *Be it further enacted,* That the Directors for the time being, or a majority of them, shall have power to make and prescribe such by-laws, rules and regulations, as to them shall appear needful and proper for the management and disposition of the stock, / property, estate and effects of the said corporation, and for all such matters as appertain to the business thereof, and shall have power to appont such officers, clerk and agents for carrying on the business of the Corporation as they may select, with such allowances as to them shall appear just and satisfactory: Provided that such By-laws, rules and regulations, shall not be repugnant to the constitution or laws of the United States, or of this State.

7. *Be it further enacted,* That no policy shall be issued by this Corporation, until application shall be made for insurance for fifty thousand dollars at least.

8. *Be it further enacted,* That this Act shall continue in force for fifty years.

9. *Be it further enacted,* That this Act shall take effect immediately after its ratification. /

CASES ILLUSTRATING THE BENEFITS OF LIFE INSURANCE.

The following cases are selected from among hundreds of a similar character, as illustrating the advantages of Life Insurance, and the danger of delay in effecting it.

A highly respectable and wealthy Merchant, of New York, took out a Life Policy for the benefit of his wife, in the sum of 5,000, at the annual premium of 152,50; a few months thereafter, adverse fortune swept off his fortune, and a lingering disease terminated his life in less than eighteen months; two annual payments had been made to the Company, and his widow received from it, $5,000.

A Lawyer, residing in one of the Southern States, took out a policy on his life, in the sum of $5,000, at the annual premium of $150, for the benefit of his wife; his death occurred in fifteen months thereafter; two annual payments had been made to the Company, and his widow received from it, $5,000.

A Gentleman, residing in the State of Indiana, on the 19th of August, took out a policy on his life for $3,000; but one payment was made, of $102. He died on the 19th of September, and his widow received the sum insured, $3,000.

A Book-Keeper, in a highly respectable mercantile house in New York, through the persuasion of his employers, was induced to take out a policy on his life, for the benefit of his wife and children, in the sum of $1,000, at the annual premium of $25,70; a sudden illness from scarlet fever carried him off in ten days; two annual payments had been made, and his widow, in a few days after his death, received from the Company, 1,000 dollars; had it not been for this provision, she would have been left in destitute circumstances.

A Merchant, in one of the Southern States had a debt due him of 5,000 dollars; knowing that its ultimate payment depended on the continuance of the life of his debtor, he took out a policy on it in an office, for that sum \; one year's premium had been / paid, of $161,84. Soon after he was attacked with a severe illness, which terminated his life. The Company, on presentation of the requisite proofs of his death, paid the sum insured, and by this precautionary measure, be unexpectedly, and suddenly, realized a doubtful claim.

A young Lady effected an insurance on her own life for $2,000, for the benefit of her parents, who were aged, and entirely dependent upon the earnings of their daughter. She died during the year, and her parents were secured from want.

A Young Mechanic, in Boston, took out a joint insurance on his own life and that of his wife, so that whenever either should die, the other would receive the sum insured. Two years afterwards, the wife was attacked with Typhoid Fever, in the depth of a severe winter: at the time one of the children fell sick with Scarlet Fever. He was obliged to neglect his business, and watch day and night beside his afflicted family. His small stock of savings was soon exhausted, for he lived upon his daily labor. After several weeks his child recovered; but, worn out with watching and anxiety, he was seized with a fever which settled upon his lungs, although he had never been sick before in his life. He had now no money – and no prospect of receiving any. He sent for a friend, told him his circumstances, and requested him to loan him some money; at the same time assigning the policy to him and appointing him his Executor. His friend advanced the money, and, in two weeks more, the wife died, and the amount of their policy was paid to his friend, who immediately invested it for his benefit after deducting the amount advanced. After three months more, he died, and left $750 for his two children, who were adopted by relatives, and the money is now accumulating for them when they shall arrive at maturity.

A Clergyman, aged 30, possessed of an income of $2,500 per annum, desirous of securing his wife a sum sufficient for her support in the event of his death, insured his life for $10,000; the annual premium was $225, not a tenth of his income, and he having unexpectedly died after two payments had been made his widow received $10,000: which enabled her to maintain a state of comfortable independence during life. /

A Merchant, of Philadelphia made application for a policy upon his life; all the necessary papers were made out upon which to issue a policy, which was made by the company; but the premium was not settled previous to his departue for New York, where he was suddenly called upon business. Upon his return home, in crossing the Delaware, he was thrown into the river and drowned. Thus, by neglecting to settle the premium his family lost the benefit they would otherwise have derived from the insurance.

A Legal Gentleman took out a policy of $7,500, and having taken a severe cold, ruptured a blood vessel during a paroxysm of coughing, which caused his death; this occurred after only two annual payments had been made, and the wife received $7,500.

A Medical Gentleman whose practice gave $1,500 per annum, reflecting upon the precarious tenure of his health in the sphere of his duties, which necessarily exposed him to the constant vicissitudes of the weather, besides bringing him frequently in contact with persons having infections discuses, took out a policy for $5,000, and, after being insured 4 years; he died of a malignant fever, caught on a professional visit, and his widow thus obtained 5,000.

A young married man opened a drug store, and was induced, by his wife's friends, to insure his life for $5,000; shortly after this, the cholera made its appearance, and the party fell a victim. The assets of the deceased were little more than sufficient to pay his creditors, and had it not been for the insurance on his life, his family would have been left destitute; as it was, they received the $5,000 of Insurance.

A young man in a public office, with a salary of 1,000 dollars, having married at the age of twenty-five, very prudently insured his life for 6,000 dollars. At the age of twenty nine, he was unfortunately drowned in the endeavor to save his brother from the same fate; in this case four annual payments had been made which amounted to $416, and his widow received $6,000.

A farmer insured his life for $2000; during the next fall, at harvest time, he was thrown from his wagon and killed instantly. His widow received $2,500, which enabled her to carry on the farm.

JOHN FREESTONE, *WHERE TO INSURE: AN IMPARTIAL AND INDEPENDENT GUIDE* (1890), EXCERPT

John Freestone,[1] *Where to Insure: An Impartial and Independent Guide with Comparative Tables, Shewing the Security, Bonuses, and Expenses of the British Life Assurance Offices* (London: Simpkin, Marshall, Hamilton, Kent and Co., 1890), pp. 5–17.

Although life insurance offices continued to issue prospectuses into the twentieth century, prospective customers after 1870 increasingly turned to comparative guides such as Freestone's *Where to Insure* to help them make sense of the dizzying array of options that were available to them. If the increased competition of the late nineteenth century broadened the range of choices facing policyholders, the Life Assurance Companies Act of 1870 dramatically increased the amount of available information concerning the hundred or so insurance offices in existence.[2] Rendering that information even remotely intelligible to customers was the self-appointed task of writers such as Freestone, who, more often than not, stood to profit from offering such advice in their capacity as independent insurance brokers. The format of these guides varied, but most were produced in such a way as to channel prospective customers through the 'expert' who wrote them: Freestone did this by identifying offices by numbers instead of names. To bolster their expertise, many brokers added the academic credential of 'F.R.S.S.', or Fellow of the Royal Statistical Society, although none of them ever read scholarly papers there.[3]

In the United States, independent insurance brokers were rare by the late nineteenth century, since most firms required potential policyholders to apply through their exclusive company agents. Yet a similar impetus for publications like *Where to Insure* still existed, produced instead by the various state insurance commissions and focused mainly on the safety of the institutions. For example, beginning in the late 1850s, all companies operating in the state of Massachusetts were required to make a full report of their condition to the Massachusetts Board of Insurance Commissioners, which would then be published for the benefit of the public. Of course, the publication of raw balance sheets would be relatively useless to the average policyholder, so the Board processed this information in order to answer one basic question for policyholders: if the company were to go out of business today, do they have adequate reserves to purchase new policies for each of their current policyholders (at their current ages) in another company? This provided a succinct yet accurate picture of basic fiscal soundness for every company in operation, and it would enable potential applicants to compare the safety of insurers with widely varying premium rates.[4]

Notes

1. John Freestone was an insurance broker living in West Bridgford, which is a suburb south of Nottingham, separated from the city by the river Trent. He was elected Fellow of the Royal Statistical Society in February 1890 and was still a fellow in 1908, at which time he lived in Leicester.
2. See Volume 2 in this collection for more information on the Life Assurance Companies Act.
3. For more on British insurance guides, see Moss, *Standard Life 1825–2000*, pp. 125, 140.
4. Stalson, *Marketing Life Insurance*, pp. 385–97; and Murphy, *Investing in Life*, pp. 255–9.

John Freestone, *Where to Insure: An Impartial and Independent Guide* (1890), excerpt

WHERE TO INSURE.

No man wishing to make an intelligent selection of a Life Assurance Office can fail to have remarked the great number of difficulties that present themselves at the outset.

Before the investigation has proceeded far, finding himself bewildered by technicalities and the conflicting statements of the different agents canvassing him, the inquirer generally abandons the quest in despair, and insures with the agent whom he knows best, and in whose integrity he has most confidence.

How valuable at such a time would be impartial and independent advice from a competent and trustworthy source to the intending insurer!

THE FOLLOWING PAGES CLAIM TO SUPPLY EXACTLY THAT CLASS OF ADVICE.

The two main points to keep in view in comparing Life Assurance Offices, are,
FIRST: SECURITY.
SECOND: PROFIT. /

SECURITY.

Do not be misled by figures showing large funds. Large funds have large liabilities.

THE MAGNITUDE of an Office's operations, its premium income, or funds, is NO GUARANTEE for the security of the policy holder.

THEN WHAT ARE THE CRUCIAL TESTS OF SECURITY?

THE PRINCIPAL TEST is to be found in one of the schedules[1] which every Office is bound by Act of Parliament, to lodge with the Board of Trade, at intervals of 10 years, or less.

The Schedule in question shows, (a) The total Life Assurance and Annuity Funds (apart from Shareholder's capital).

(*b*) The present liability of the Office under its Life Assurance policies and annuity contracts.

Then, deducting (*b*) liabilities from (*a*) funds, shows,

(*c*) The amount of funds in hand OVER AND ABOVE present liabilities, and called SURPLUS.

It will be seen on reference to Table I (page 17) that the surplus in SOME of the Offices is MERELY NOMINAL, and WOULD DISAPPEAR, if the Offices in question failed to obtain the rate of interest that they have assumed in their calculations. /

REGARD MUST ALWAYS be had to the rate of interest assumed in making the valuations, as an Office assuming that it will make £4 per cent per annum interest of its funds, will be able to show a much better surplus than if it assumed £3 only.

The rate assumed by different Offices varies from £3 to £4.*

Those Offices valuing at £3 and showing good surpluses would be able to show LARGELY INCREASED SURPLUSES if they valued at £4.

ANOTHER IMPORTANT FACTOR in this computation of liabilities is the "Table of Mortality" used by each office.

There are about 8 different Tables used by the Offices, some adopting one, some another, in addition to Special Tables framed by Offices for their own use, and others for Annuities.

SOME OF THESE TABLES BEING MUCH MORE STRINGENT THAN OTHERS, RENDER IT OF THE GREATEST IMPORTANCE TO ASCERTAIN IF THE LIABILITY IS CALCULATED BY A STRINGENT TABLE OF MORTALITY, OR BY ONE OF A LAXER CHARACTER. /

An Office using one of the laxer "Tables of Mortality" and coming out with the same percentage of surplus as an Office using the most stringent Table is really NOT IN ANYTHING LIKE AS GOOD A POSITION as regards security.

For these reasons, the comparison in Table I. (page 17) must not be considered conclusive.

The Tables used by the respective Offices are not inserted in that schedule as they are known by names that convey no idea of the degree of stringency, and experience goes to show that even the more intelligent insurer invariably passes over the "Tables of Mortality" as hopelessly technical.

One would expect that the Offices having the largest surpluses would naturally attract the largest amount of business.

---

* Since the above was set up in type, one Office has adopted a valuation at the unprecedented rate of £2 10s.[2]

But either from the public not using the available means of information, or from the indefatigability of the Offices having smaller surpluses, THE REVERSE APPEARS TO BE THE CASE.

FOR INFORMATION Respecting Tables of Mortality used by any Office, enclose stamped envelope to J. FREESTONE, West Bridgford, Nottingham. /

Taking 10 of the Offices with the more slender surpluses, we find they not only obtain their share, but "the lion's share," of business. Their total amount of new policies for 1887 was £6,570,407, whereas the total for the same year in 10 OFFICES WITH THE LARGEST PERCENTAGES OF SURPLUS WAS ONLY £2,820,039, MERELY 42.92 PER CENT OF THAT OBTAINED BY THE 10 OFFICES HAVING VERY SLENDER SURPLUSES.

Truly it is the credit of the agent, and not the strength and merits of the Office, that secures the average insurer.

PROFIT.

It is frequently said, in reference to profit, or bonus, "You will do as well in one good, well-established Office as in another."

THAT NOTHING COULD BE FURTHER FROM THE FACTS OF THE CASE will be found as we proceed in our investigation.

YOU CAN Save Pounds by comparing prospectuses, etc. of assurance companies, before filling up proposal form. For assistance (gratis) write J. FREE-STONE, West Bridgford, Nottingham./

The profits in Life Assurance arise mainly from:–

(a) Light expenditure in obtaining and preserving business.

(b) Good selection of lives.

(c) Higher rate of interest obtained than that assumed in the valuation.

IN OTHER WORDS IT MAY BE SAID THAT THE PROFITS, OR BONUS, REPRESENT THE HANDING BACK TO THE INSURER OF SUCH PART OF HIS PREMIUM AS WAS NOT REQUIRED on account of the Office's experience having proved more favourable in respect of expenses, mortality, and interest, than was estimated when fixing the rate of premium.

Amongst other particulars, the Insurance Companies operating in Great Britain and Ireland, are required to render to the Board of Trade, particulars of bonus additions to policies at the latest valuation, or distribution of Profits.

Those bonus additions are in respect of the term of years covered by the valuation retrospectively, and as the term of years varies with the Offices, some being 3, others 5, 7, and 10 years, it is difficult even for an expert to discriminate, so that it is NOT SURPRISING THAT OUTSIDERS / SHOULD BE BEWIL-DERED IN ATTEMPTING A COMPARATIVE REVIEW.

TABLE II (page 20) HAS COMPLETELY REMOVED THIS DIFFI-
CULTY, as all the bonuses are there reduced to per annum, per £100, all the
companies being placed on the same basis where possible, so that COMPARI-
SONS MAY NOW BE FREELY INSTITUTED.

BONUS ADDITIONS ARE MADE ON 3 SCALES.

Division A. The increasing scale.

Offices allotting bonuses on this scale give a man a LARGER BONUS when
he has been insured 20 years, than when he had held his policy 10 years, and will
give a still LARGER BONUS at the next division of profits, provided the profits
have been equally good.

Division B. The uniform scale.

Offices adopting this plan give the same amount of bonus per £100 to all
policy holders, (generally omitting new entrants), irrespective of age, or premium paid. /

Division C. The decreasing scale.

This is the reverse of Division A. (increasing scale).[3] Here a policy holder is
credited with his largest bonus at the first division, and SMALLER BONUSES
at successive divisions of profits.

To one about to insure, the offices giving the largest bonuses are generally
attractive, but IT IS IMPORTANT TO ASCERTAIN WHETHER THE
OFFICES IN QUESTION CHARGE APPRECIABLY HIGHER RATES
OF PREMIUM THAN OTHERS.

If an office charges considerably more than others, it has less difficulty in
giving large bonuses.

TABLE IV. (page 35) showing the expenses of the various companies, HAS
AN IMPORTANT BEARING ON BONUSES, as if expenses are light, that
is, are well below 15 per cent of the premium income, BONUSES ARE USU-
ALLY HEAVY, and vice versâ.

Assuming 15 per cent of the premium income to be legitimately available
for expenses, an Office whose expenses are only 11 per cent. has 4 *per cent of that
income in hand as bonus* / where an office spending the full 15 per cent would
have nothing left from that source of bonuses.

YOU CAN Obtain the rates of any Office for all classes of Life Insurance
from JOHN FREESTONE, West Bridgport, Nottm.

TABLE III. (page 22) will be found a useful adjunct to Table II. as it will
show, by comparing the latest division of profits with the preceding divisions,

whether the bonuses in Table II. are larger or smaller than preceding bonuses in the same office.

In this table, no mention is made of age at entry or years in force, for the simple reason that the object of the Table is to show the total amount of profit or bonus divided amongst *all* participating policy holders, and gives AN AVERAGE of so much to each £100 insured.

This table also shows the progress of each company as regards the participating branch.

ENDOWMENT ASSURANCE.

Policies payable DURING LIFETIME at a given age, or at death, should that happen first, are technically called Endowment Assurance Policies.

I AM WILLING to answer any *bona fide* insurer's enquiries, state age and class of Policy contemplated. Enclose stamped envelope. J. FREESTONE, West Bridgport, Nottingham. /

AS THESE COMBINE THE ADVANTAGES OF AN INVESTMENT FOR OLD AGE, WITH PROVISION FOR PREMATURE DEATH, THEY ARE YEARLY GAINING IN FAVOR, AND DESERVEDLY SO.

They possess a further advantage which has only to be stated to be appreciated, viz.: that it sometimes happens that an insurer survives those for whose protection he insured in early manhood, and has to continue payment of premium when the reason for his insuring no longer exists, whereas AN ENDOWMENT ASSURANCE POLICY IS NOT DEPRECIATED IN SUCH A CONTINGENCY, being no less valuable to a single than to a married man.

THE SELECTION OF AN OFFICE FOR THIS CLASS OF POLICY REQUIRES EVEN MORE PAINS AND DISCRIMINATION THAN FOR A POLICY FOR THE WHOLE TERM OF LIFE.

THE REASON IS THIS,–

The premium charged for Endowment Assurance Policies is, as might be expected, much higher than for whole term policies. /

Supposing two men A.B. and C.D. when approaching their 30th birthday decided to insure their lives for £100, A.B. taking a policy payable at death with a yearly premium of 50/-, whilst C.D. takes a policy payable at 55 or death if earlier, paying 80/- annually until his 55th birthday.

Now if C.D. spent his 80/- yearly on a whole term policy (like A.B.'s), he would be insured for £160, instead of £100.

HOW WOULD THESE TWO MEN BE TREATED
AT THE DIVISION OF PROFITS?

C.D. paying (on Endowment Assurance Policy), so much more than A.B. might, not unreasonably, look for a larger bonus.

There has always been considerable divergence of opinion and practice amongst the Insurance Managers on the allotting of bonuses to Endowment Assurance Policies, some maintaining that those bonuses should be smaller than those on Whole Term Policies, others that they should be larger, whilst the greater number grant the same bonus, per £100, to Endowment Assurance and Whole Term Policies alike.

It is no business of the intending insurer to attempt a settlement of this disputed point. / If he is wanting to insure a sum payable at a specified age, or prior death, let him judge for himself from Table V. whether any of the offices which come out well under Tables I., II., III., and IV., will answer his purpose in respect of manner of giving endowment bonuses.

To show the importance of exercising the utmost care and caution in selecting an Office for Endowment Assurances, a letter appeared in an Insurance weekly paper last July, wherein a correspondent stated that after carefully selecting 12 of the best Life Assurance Offices, he wrote to each of the 12 asking them to state the total amount to which the £500 policy and accumulated bonuses might be expected to reach on maturity, 21 years hence.

The amounts named by the officials of the respective Companies were £600, £605, £619, £635, £647, £660, £677, £690, £700, £705, £710, £811.

NO WISE MAN Insures without carefully seeing where he can do best. If in doubt, enclose stamped envelope to J. FREESTONE, West Bridgport, Nottingham. /

TABLE I.

Shewing Percentage of Surplus over Liability. (Prepared from the Parliamentary Blue Books).

Office.	Date of Valuations.	Rate of Interest assumed in calculations.	Life Assurance and Annuity Funds.	Liability under Policies and Annuity Contracts.	Surplus.	Percentage of Surplus over Liability.
			£	£	£	
36	1879	£3	4,360,661	2,466,956	1,893,704	76.76
75	1885	£4	1,139,601	695,659	443,941	63.81
78	1884	£3, £3/15 & £2/10	836,415	522,934	313,481	59.94
66	1882	£3 & £4	2,106,115	1,495,587	610,528	40.82
47	1884	£3	338,670	243,360	95,309	39.16
25	1885	£3	3,817,338	2,762,246	1,055,092	38.19
72	1884	£3/10, £3	1,275	942	333	35.35
69	1883	£3/10	207,346	157,441	49,905	31.69
26	1887	£3	1011,722	776,692	235,030	30.26
50	1884	£3	21,103	16,325	4,778	29.26
37	1884	£3	2,002,652	1,573,503	429,148	27.27
27	1885	£3	974,387	772,525	201,862	26.13
86	1887	£3/10	2,365,270	1,914,146	451,123	23.56
12	1884	£3	1,494,726	1,211,948	282,778	23.33
60	1885	£3/10, £3	1,870,559	1,518,070	352,489	23.21
85	1886	£4, £3	324,240	267,572	57,428	21.46
63	1886	£3	1,765,193	1,458,466	306,727	21.03
45	1887	£4	6,109,541	5,058,505	1,051,035	20.77
64	1883	£3/10	490,286	406,752	83,534	20.53
18	1886	£3	3,372,940	2,799,520	573,420	20.48
22	1887	£3	1,825,032	1,518,942	306,090	20.15
79	1887	£3/10, £3	4,323,070	3,598,635	724,435	20.13
7	1887	£4	25,501	21,265	4,235	19.91
38	1887	£3	1,870,676	1,560,184	310,491	19.90
48	1887	£3/10	9,656,930	8,068,525	1,588,405	19.60
71	1884	£3	440,238	368,062	72,176	19.60
19	1886	£3	2,715,759	2,232,586	433,173	19.40
34	1885	£3/10	1,962,130	1,646,633	315,497	19.16
5	1885	£4	33,424	28,104	5,319	18.92
33	1883	£3/10	3,619,661	3,050,831	568,830	18.84

INSURERS can obtain further information (free) respecting the above Offices from J. Freestone, West Bridgford, Nottm.

RELIGION AND LIFE INSURANCE IN AMERICA

Charter of the Corporation for the Relief of the Widows and Children of Clergymen (1769; Philadelphia, 1814), pp. 3–4.

'Life Insurance', *Religious Intelligencer*, 18 July 1835, p. 103.

'Life Insurance – Ministers', *Christian Secretary*, 26 February 1847, p. 2.

'Life Insurance – A Scruple', *Christian Secretary*, 12 March 1847, p. 2.

'Life Insurance of Ministers', *Christian Secretary*, 23 April 1847, p. 2.

The first American life insurance firms were formed in the mid-eighteenth century to provide support for the widows and orphans of ministers. The Presbyterian synods in Philadelphia and New York set up the Corporation for Relief of Poor and Distressed Widows and Children of Presbyterian Ministers in 1759. Similar funds were organized by the colonial branch of the Anglican (later Episcopal) Church in 1769 (reproduced here in the first document) and by the Congregational churches of Massachusetts in 1786. The hierarchy of these organizations was concerned that the limited salaries paid to ministers left their families particularly vulnerable in the case of their untimely death. Rather than abandoning these widows and orphans to the mercy of charity, the various church leaders believed it was preferable to create insurance plans for this purpose. Although these policies were never particularly popular with the ministers they were intended to help, they established the precedent for clergy insuring their lives – and in turn drew on even longer-standing precedents established in Britain, by Anglicans in 1678 and by Scottish Presbyterians in 1743.[1]

For-profit companies likewise recognized that ministers formed an ideal market for their product. In editorials like the second document published in the *Religious Intelligencer* (a publication of various Bible and missionary societies) or the third document from the *Christian Secretary* (a Baptist periodical), insurance promoters highlighted the benefits of policies for the families of clergy. Although a few minority voices (as seen in the last two documents) expressed some concerns about the morality of life insurance, clergy across all

Protestant denominations constituted a significant clientele of the early American for-profit companies during the 1830s and 1840s.[2]

Notes

1. See A. Mackie, *Facile Princeps: The Story of the Beginning of Life Insurance in America* (Lancaster, PA: Lancaster Press, Inc., 1956). On the Corporation of the Sons of the Clergy, established by the Church of England to care for clergymen's widows, see M. R. Hunt, *The Middling Sort: Commerce, Gender and the Family in England, 1680–1780* (Berkeley, CA: University of California Press, 1996), pp. 165–6. On Scottish Presbyterians, see A. I. Dunlop, *The Scottish Ministers' Widows' Fund, 1743–1993* (Edinburgh: Saint Andrew Press, 1992).
2. Murphy, *Investing in Life*, pp. 211–14.

Charter of the Corporation for the Relief of the Widows and Children of Clergymen (1769), excerpt

CHARTER
OF THE CORPORATION FOR THE RELIEF OF WIDOWS
AND CHILDREN OF CLERGYMEN IN THE COMMUNION
OF THE CHURCH OF ENGLAND IN AMERICA

THOMAS AND RICHARD PENN, Esqrs. true and absolute Proprietaries and Governours in chief of the Province of Pennsylvania, and counties of New Castle, Kent and Sussex upon Delaware; TO all to whom these presents shall come, GREETING. Whereas, it hath been represented unto us, that the Clergy of the Church of England in our American Colonies, and especially the Missionaries in the service of the Society for the Propagation of the Gospel in foreign parts, have in general but a small support, and have always found it difficult to make any tolerable provision for their families, so that their widows and children are often left in great distress; and whereas, in order to provide a remedy for these growing difficulties, humble application hath been made to us, that we would erect and constitute a Corporation in our said Provinces and Counties, for receiving, managing and disposing such sums of money as may be subscribed and paid in from time to time by the Clergy and Missionaries themselves, and such benefactions as may be given by charitable / and well disposed persons, as a fund towards the support and relief of the widows and children of the Ministers of the Church of England in our said American colonies.

[...]

'Life Insurance', *Religious Intelligencer* (1835)

LIFE INSURANCE.

This means that the Life Insurance Company, in consideration of an annual premium, will pay to the heirs of any man a certain sum of money. For instance, a minister 40 years old having a family and no property but his salary, desires to provide for his family in case he should die. To such a man the Insurance Company says, "pay us $1,69 on a hundred dollars, and we will pay your family as many hundreds as you will insure, provided you die within the year. Or pay us $1,83 on the hundred annually, and we will do the same provided you die in seven years from this time. Or pay us annually $3,20 on the hundred, and we will do the same whensover you may die – the obligation continuing during your life." The premium varies with the age of the person – the older he is, the higher the premium. By this means the minister of 40 years old will secure to his family, in case of his death the current year, the payment of $1000 by paying in advance the premium of $16,90. Or the obligation may be prolonged for seven years by the annual payment of $18,30. Or it may be made permanent by the annual payment of $32.

The proposal seems to meet the exigency which poor ministers in our country have been trying to provide for. In Massachusetts, a fund is raised by the pastoral association from contributions after the annual sermon. The interest of this is paid to the widows of ministers in such proportion as the urgency of cases demands. In Connecticut we believe a sort of savings bank is instituted, by which the principal and interest of the deposits of any minister may be paid to his widow at his death. The same object may be accomplished through the Life Insurance Company with more certainty and ease. There are few ministers who cannot, by extra effort or extra economy, lay aside the annual premium which would secure to their families, in case of death, the payment of a thousand dollars. This, if it would not furnish them a support, would at least be a relief for the time most seasonable, and might by the means of helping them to situations of comfort and competency.

The Life Insurance Office affords advantages to another class of persons. A young man wishes to get an education, but he has neither money nor credit at all equal to the necessity. But he can raise the annual premium of a thousand dollars, which would be at 16 years old $8,40 for one year, or $9,00 annually for seven years. With this security he could borrow money equal to his necessities for getting through College. His life insurance adds so much to his credit.

This business is very various and extensive, affording facilities to persons of almost every condition. It is unquestionably a useful institution; and though many are shocked at the first annunciation of "life insurance," as if it were impious to get one's life insured for money it will be seen that such feelings are groundless. The company do not propose to prolong life, in any case, but to benefit survivors. – *Vt. Chron.*[1]

'Life Insurance – Ministers', *Christian Secretary* (1847)

LIFE INSURANCE – MINISTERS

We well remember that in our boyhood, we saw for the first time, "Life Insurance," on the door of an office in this city, and were startled by the presumption which those words seemed to imply. We could not see what insurance could have to do with human life, without attempting an interference with the prerogatives of the Almighty. And these feelings, we presume, have been experienced by others, and even after suitable explanations, have still occasioned an undefined repugnance to the scheme. We confess that the feelings of our childhood were not, in our case, easily overcome.

But what is this system of life insurance? Nothing is more certain than that each individual must die, but at what period he cannot know. He sees persons of every age falling around him, and feels that fatal arrow may strike him next. He has a wife, perhaps feeble and infirm, and perhaps children in the early years of life; and these are all so utterly dependent upon him, that if he were to die, they would at once be cast upon the charities of the world. He beholds around him widows and children thus bereft and destitute, and sighs deeply at the possibility that such an affliction may befall his own family. In this feeling stirs the life insurance system. A. B. C. and D. feel thus, and associate themselves to provide a remedy. A company is forged which becomes the repository of a common fund. Each member pays annually, according to his age and prospect of life, a certain sum into this fund; and in consideration of such payments, whether he dies in one year or in twenty, his wife and children are entitled to draw a specific amount from the company. He is, for example, 30 years old when he effects his insurance. In such case he pays into the company an annual premium of $2, and at his death his family receive $100. If he pays $20, his family receive $1000; if he pays $40, his family receive $2000; if he pays $100, his family receive $5000.

Now in order that this scheme may fulfill its purpose, it is necessary that the company should always be solvent – that is, able to pay its losses when the deaths of its members shall from time to time occur; and in order to maintain its solvency, it must graduate its premiums according to accurate calculations of the probability of human life. These calculations are made without difficulty, and insurance on lives becomes, therefore, as safe a business as any other. It is now considerably more than a hundred years since the establishment of the first life insurance company in England, and calculations of life and graduations of premiums have attained almost the certainty of mathematical demonstrations. A respectable life insurance company may therefore be trusted with as much confidence as any other moneyed corporation. Indeed, we regard it as the safest among such corporations.

Here then is a safe method by which a person may make greater or less provision for his family, according to the annual premium which he may be able to pay. How well adapted is such a scheme to meet the wishes of a husband and father, who feels that his wife's and children's daily bread is, to all human speaking, dependent on his life. How well adapted to the circumstances of all persons who are dependent on salaries – particularly to the circumstances of ministers of the gospel. Ministers, by the law of Christ, and by the acquiescence of their own feelings to that law, are prohibited from making the accumulation of wealth the end of their profession. As a matter of fact, their salaries rarely exceed their expenses; and though it is their duty to lay up a little something, if possible, every year, it will not be in their power to lay up much. What minister, as he looks on the destitute widow and children of some deceased ministering brother, is not rendered sick at heart by the thought that such may be the lot of his own wife and little ones that prattle on his knee. True, God gives to the widow and fatherless special promises, but he requires providence also; and he has so ordained events, that institutions have sprung up for the relief of such necessities, and it seems to us a plain duty of ministers to avail themselves of their aid. We have reflected much on this subject, and have felt deeply, and if our influence could move them, not one, who can command the means to pay a premium, would remain a month without an insurance on his life. If we could whisper a word to their wives, we would say to them, do not give your husbands peace until this thing is done.

Thus far from the New York Recorder. The importance of Life Insurance to ministers and others whose conditions require an expenditure of their ordinary means, without the ability of accumulating adequate provision for the support of their families in the event of their decease, would seem to be obvious. In the case of ministers especially, whose profession should engross their whole time and thoughts, if they would be *eminently* useful, we think as a matter of common prudence, some provision should be made for the support of their families, and how can this be done, more readily and securely than by an insurance upon life. What could be more satisfactory to a laborious and faithful minister than to know, that while all his energies are devoted to the good of his people, provision is made, in the event of his death, for the support of those dependent upon him, and perhaps *entirely* unable to provide for themselves. What better calculated to evince the respect of a people for their pastor, whose entire energies are devoted to their good, than provision like that referred to? and what is more likely to quicken, sustain and command the undivided consecration of those energies to the purpose of *doing good*? Formerly it was the usage at the ordination of a minister, to provide for his and his families necessities, by what was called a settlement. This was commendable. But now the same end would be more easily and perhaps advantageously obtained by effecting an insurance upon his life. Indeed, every minister should receive such a salary as would enable him to pay the premium himself, or else his society should be required to do it for his benefit. In almost all occupations, those engaged in them on attaining middle age, or before, with ordinary prudence, are enabled to make such provision from their own resources. And should the efforts of the clerical profession, of all others be paralized by the reflection, that whatever of good they may have accomplished for others, they are neglecting the prominent duty of providing for their own household.

Our attention has been called to this subject more particularly by the report of policies issued by the Connecticut Mutual Life Insurance Company established in this city, in which we find those of almost all classes except ministers, an institution as we are induced to believe presenting peculiar inducements to the assured, under the control of our own citizens, and thus far attended with unusual success, partaking of the character of a Savings Bank to those whose earnings might otherwise be dissipated, and affording to all classes by the payment of small sums annually, adequate provision is the *only* reliance. The office of the company is at 47 State street, where necessary information will be furnished and all inquiries answered.

'Life Insurance – A Scruple', *Christian Secretary* (1847)

Life Insurance – A Scruple.

A lengthy article having appeared in the Secretary of late commendatory of Life Insurance, I feel it my duty to present *a scruple* concerning it. I now refer to the propriety of Ministers engaging in any such compact. I have no superstitious feelings about it; nor have I the least disposition to injure the Conn. Life Insurance Co., or any other Company of the like character. The question whether Jesus Christ's Ministers should resort to such a method to obtain property for their families after their decease, is a question of *conscience*.

The following considerations prevail upon me to conclude that it is not right.

1. It supposes a valuable consideration to be received, without rendering a just equivalent for the same. Now is this right? Ought we not in all our commercial transactions with our fellow-men, to study, and act upon, the stern principles of rigid justice? Can we violate such principles and be guiltless? This question needs but to be put, to be answered, – in the full negative. Now, if I understand the policy of the Life Insurance compact, it is, that, upon the payment of a small premium, a larger sum shall be realized at death, than is deposited in the premium. In other words, property is expected, far exceeding in value, the equivalent rendered.

2. For Ministers of God to resort to such a method, is acting in contravention of the divinely appointed arrangement concerning their support; or their families' support.

It is recommended as *"good policy"* for a poor Minister, to obtain Insurance on his life. Let us look into this matter. If Ministers are poor generally, is it not because of the common Providence of God? Is it not the ordinary arrangement of Heaven, that the Ambassadors of Christ should not roll in wealth? What are we to understand by the express directions of Christ to the Twelve, and the Seventy, if not this, that they are not to expect an overflowing abundance of this world's goods? If it were for the best that they should generally be able to leave an abunance for their families, may we not suppose that the all-wise Provider would have so arranged the matter? Let ministers be contented with their general lot. If Divine Providence has so ordered it that they are to labor, not so much for the meat that perisheth, and *consequently*, live and die comparatively poor, why should they contend against their lot? Why abandon Heaven's policy, for the policy of earth? Why struggle, when they should remain quiet? As for the future, – and as for our families – we are forbidden to be over anxious. All we are responsible for, is, the discharge of present duty; and if the churches, through poverty, or through a covetous spirit, withhold the substance ministers need, with which to provide for themselves and their families, then should they submit, and *"go and tell Jesus,"* and He will take care of them and theirs. "There is no counsel or might against the Lord."[1] Bow to God's Eternal, All-Wise, Sovereign, and Far-Reaching Plan, – and all will be well. Die poor, as Lazarus, if the will of God be so, rather than become so dissatisfied, and so unreconciled to the poor lot of Jesus Christ's ambassadors. We should be willing to share the fate, even of our Lord him self if required, who had not where to lay his head! I know the bait held out by Life Insurance Companies, is tempting to our lower nature. But for one, I feel myself forbidden, – though I have been urged, and flattered by most encouraging prospects to engage in the compact, – forbidden by the conscientious scruple named above, by the general tenor of Scripture, and the superior though aresting arrangement of the Head of the Church, to resort to this policy of earth. All this, though perhaps, no one, and no one's family will need such help after death, more than your poor.

EUDOLPHUS.

We admire the conscientious scruples of "Eudolphus" for they indicate an honest and sincere heart; but after all, we do not discover the least occasion for such scruples in the matter under consideration. We have no disposition to encourage on the part of our ministers a desire for wealth; – on the contrary, we believe, as a general rule, that ministers who have property to any considerable amount are less valuable to the Church than those that are poor. But we cannot see the propriety of the conclusions to which our correspondent arrives. It is true that the Head of the Church was poor; – he had "not where to lay his head;"[2] and his disciples were also poor; but is this fact sufficient of itself to justify the conclusion that a minister of the gospel should wholly neglect the interests of his family and in case of his own sudden death, leave them to the world's cold charities? Paul was not unmindful of his own interests, and when arraigned before governors and kings, he defended them, to the extent of the law, using all the reason which God had given him for this purpose; nor can we conceive of any good reason why an ambassador of Jesus Christ should not at the present day, make use of his reason for the welfare of his family, provided he does it honestly and conscientiously.

But "Eudolphus" seems to think by getting his life insured he would be "abandoning Heaven's policy for the policy of earth," – that he would manifest "a dissatisfied and unreconciled spirit to the poor lot of Jesus Christ's ambassadors." If he himself was to reap the immediate benefits and thereby become rich by the operation, then his conclusions might be just and pertinent, but as the object of Life Insurance Companies is, not to benefit the insured, but his family *after* his own decease, the objection, to our mind, vanishes, provided the plan for accomplishing the object, is a fair and honest one. Our correspondent thinks it is not; for he supposes a valuable consideration to be received, without rendering a just equivalent for the same. We think he is mistaken in this. Suppose a man invests the sum of ten thousand dollars in some manufacturing establishment – a whale ship, or any other fair and honorable business and receives in return an annual dividend of twenty-five per cent; is he receiving a valuable consideration without rendering a just equivalent? Certainly not. Now suppose one thousand men of equal age, pay into a common fund, each one hundred dollars annually during their natural lives, and that others are allowed to unite with them upon equal terms from year to year. The money to be safely invested where it will pay the largest interest. It is also understood in the agreement, that at the death of each individual, his family is to receive the principal and interest on the whole amount of his investment. – This is in substance, a life insurance company, and we ask "Eudolphus," what there is about it, that looks like receiving a valuable consideration without rendering a just equivalent?

If the whole principle is wrong, and ministers of the gospel are forever cut off by their calling from making any provision for the wants of their families, why then we have nothing more to say; but we have yet to learn that this is so. Suppose our correspondent should be taken away in the meridian of life, and leave his wife and children without the means of support for a single month, when by getting an insurance on his life for the moderate sum of one thousand dollars he might have left them with a small pittance, enough to make them comfortable for a year or two; does he suppose his death would be more triumphant or happy by neglecting thus to provide for them, than if he had taken the precaution to make this provision? – We think not; on the contrary, it would be a consolation to him on a dying bed, to know that he was not about to leave them in destitute circumstances.

It may not be improper to add that we have no interest in insurance companies of any kind, nor do we desire to urge others to engage in them; – but when a plan is in operation, by which "valuable considerations" may be obtained at a fair price, we consider it but an act of duty to acquaint our readers of the fact.

'Life Insurance of Ministers', *Christian Secretary* (1847)

Life Insurance of Ministers.

Mr. EDITOR: – In a late number of the Secretary, I observed an article calling the attention of ministers to Life Insurance; and since that time the Prospectus of the 'Connecticut Mutual' has fallen into my hands. It appears to be an able and impartial document; and the perusal will enable one who takes out a policy, to do so understandingly. Whether a preacher should secure his family by Life Assurance seems to depend on the question, – Is it for his interest, under the restrictions, and on the terms proposed? There are obviously various considerations, a few of which opportunity is here taken to present. If mistaken in any point, the writer is ready to stand corrected.

1. A minister has had his life assured for $1000, and his death places that sum at the disposal of his widow. She may leave the $1000 with the Company, and for an equivalent, if her age be then fifty-one years, receive $80 a year during the remainder of her life. But should her health be infirm and feeble, prudence dictates that the assurance should be taken out, and placed where, in the event of a speedy demise, her children may have the principal. In this case she incurs, without a husband's assistance, the risk and trouble of a new investment.

2. A pastor, who has insured on the system of annual payments, is during his last years, superannuated. So far from continuing his yearly sums, he himself needs the benefit of his former deposits. But *failing to make payment at the time, the policy is forfeited,* and he loses the whole. To avoid this loss he may *seasonably* "surrender his policy and receive its equitable value in cash," to be invested elsewhere. Or in its stead, he may agree for an equivalent life annuity, or accept of a smaller joint annuity on his life and that of his consort, payable yearly as long as either shall survive. A European writer of celebrity lays down the general principle: – "That all savings from the earnings of labor ought to be made before the age of *fifty-five* years; that between the ages of 55 and 65, a man should expend

the labor barely sufficient for his maintenance; and that for the portion of life after the age of 65, he should subsist entirely on previous savings."[1]

3. The value of Life Insurance would be greater to ministers, were they as a class, short lived, or exposed like seamen, to fatal accidents, Statistics however, show, that of all professions, ministers have the longest lives. Prof. Caspar of Berlin made extensive researches,[2] and found, that of a hundred individuals in each calling, the numbers living at the age of seventy years, were –

Divines,	42
Agriculturalists,	40
Advocates,	29
Teachers and Professors,	27
Physicians,	24

The results indicate that divines have much the greatest probable duration of life. Dr. Nott of Franklin[3] is a well known example of this class. – But living beyond the average duration, so much the more costly becomes the normal Assurance.

4. Compare now deposits in a Saving's Bank. A pastor at the age of thirty years puts in $30 bearing interest at five per cent. He takes care to deposit the same amount every year, compounding the interest. The arithmetic of annuities will serve to determine the future amounts. Continuing the annual deposit regularly, as for Insurance, during thirty four years, (the expectation of life by Milne's Carlisle table,) he would then be the possessor of $2,550. The corresponding Assurance is but $1500; which however is increased by the variable dividends of the Company. "It is well known," Dr. Price strikingly remarks, "to what prodigious sums, money improved for some time at *compound interest* will increase. A penny so improved from our Saviour's birth at five per cent would in 1791 years amount to 144 millions of globes, each equal to the earth in magnitude, and all solid gold."[4] The illustration will not be without its use, to a systematic economist.

5. The current Assurances appear to be graduated on the principle of the English table, that the sums paid into the hands of the company avail them but three and a half per cent. This makes the premiums too high, or the final assurance in return, too small. The writer of the document before named, answers this objection (p. 11.) by saying, – "that the excess of premium is for the purpose of creating a fund to meet extraordinary losses. This excess of premium is not lost to the assured in this company, as they receive *all* the excess, after paying losses and expenses." But if all the assured are members of the company, and share in its gains and losses, higher rates than the equitable, appear much less necessary. There may be some reason not duly appreciated; but the explanation appears hardly sufficient. A long accumulation of capital in England has indeed reduced the rate of interest to three, or three and a half per cent: but the corresponding

rate with us, is not less than five per cent. Were our tables calculated with this rate, a smaller premium would secure $1000 assurance, and the company would still have a like security with the English: First there is advertised a present capital of $50,000, which like a balance-wheel serves to equalize the irregular failure of lives. And since the tables are graded for the mortality of the whole population indiscriminately, by insuring none but healthy lives, a constant gain will accrue from this source. Further, there is the income from expired insurances, cancelled policies, and the surplus interest on premium invested at a higher rate than that of the tables of assurance. It is therefore, believed that a set of new tables of assurance calculated at five per cent would be safe, enlarge the sphere of operations by reducing the cost, and prove *mutually advantageous*; – we are not prepared to call the present rates *disadvantageous*.

Should these considerations be found of service to any pastor, in deciding upon Life Insurance, the writer's design will not be unaccomplished.

March, 1847.   Vogel.

'PROSPECTUS OF THE DISSENTERS' AND GENERAL LIFE AND FIRE ASSURANCE COMPANY', *ECLECTIC REVIEW* (1839), EXCERPT

'Prospectus of the Dissenters' and General Life and Fire Assurance Company', *Eclectic Review*, 5 (1839), pp. 520–41, on pp. 520–1, 531–41.[1]

Among the large number of 'class' offices in Britain that appealed to specific social or occupational groups, several targeted different religious denominations. In addition to the Dissenters' and General, which included all non-Anglican Protestants in its target audience, other insurers appealed to Anglicans, Baptists, Catholics, Methodists and Quakers. The Friends' Provident was the first such office to form, in 1832, reaching out to Quakers from its head office in Bradford. By 1850 it had been joined by the Dissenters' and General (est. 1837), the Church of England (1840), the Star (founded by Methodists in 1843) and the Catholic Law and General (1850). Another firm, the Clergy Mutual, specifically targeted Anglican ministers, and most other religious offices included special features that were intended to benefit clergymen of their respective faiths. All such firms took advantage of the sense of community that existed within religious denominations, juxtaposing this with the communal side of life insurance. Many of them, for instance, promised to divert part of their income to Christian charities or proselytizing efforts, such as church-building. Several, including the Friends' Provident and the Clergy Mutual, offered lower premiums based on the allegedly superior vitality of their respective populations.[2]

Although there was an ample supply of insuring church-goers to keep most of these firms afloat through the nineteenth century (with the addition of a second Methodist office, the Sceptre, in 1864), the formula had built-in limitations to growth. One by one, denominational insurance offices either sold their business to more secular firms or broadened their own marketing efforts. For instance, the Dissenters' and General changed its name to General Fire and Life in 1847; the Star and Sceptre migrated from their Methodist roots before both became part of Eagle Star in 1917; and the Friends' Provident started admitting non-Quakers in 1914, shortly before absorbing the secular Century office in 1917.[3]

Notes

1. Author unknown, but most likely Thomas Price, who edited the *Eclectic Review* between 1837 and 1855, and was a founder and the first secretary of the Dissenters' and General. Founded by Dissenters, the *Eclectic Review* adhered to a non-denominational editorial policy, but did occasionally run articles (like this one) that appealed specifically to non-Anglican readers.

2. Alborn, *Regulated Lives*, p. 37.

3. Ibid.

'Prospectus of the Dissenters' and General Life and Fire Assurance Company', *Eclectic Review* (1839), excerpt

OUR readers have probably expected from us, before this, some account of the Institution, the Prospectus of which stands at the head of the present article. Devoted especially to the interests of the Protestant Dissenters of Great Britain, it pertains appropriately to the Eclectic to take cognizance of every use which is made of their name, and to subject to a severe though friendly scrutiny, whatever solicits their support, or proposes their advantage. To this duty we now address ourselves with a more ready mind and with fuller and more satisfactory information than if the attempt had been made at an earlier period. Time has been allowed for the Institution to settle down, and take its rank among kindred societies; while the measure of support it has obtained may be considered as a fair index of the degree in which it is likely to secure the confidence of the dissenting body, and thus become instrumental in effecting the benevolent object for which it was formed. The excellency of that object admits of no question, – the only doubt that has ever been raised respects the probability of its attainment by the means proposed. How far there was ground for this doubt was at first matter of uncertainty. Some were confident of success, and others predicted failure. The former pointed to the number, wealth, and intelligence of the great body of British Dissenters, and were certain of their rallying round a society which proposed so simple, feasible, and delicate a mode of providing for the comfort of the families of our ministers; – the latter insisted on the number of Insurance Companies already existing, and impugned the constitution of the projected association, as an approach to the reprehensible and most vicious practice of exclusive dealing. Before / closing our remarks we shall notice these objections: our present object is simply to remark, that the experiment has now been tried for upwards of twelve months, and that the evidence of fact has been supplied during that period, to determine the question thus raised. The progress made during this period demonstrates beyond doubt the feasibleness of the plan, and the certainty of its accomplishment, even beyond the early expectations of its supporters. This is a great step gained, and places us, as public journalists, in a position to speak freely of the well balanced constitution and admirable design of the Society. The certainty of its securing such a measure of support as will enable it materially to contribute to the mental repose and domestic happiness of a class of men whose claims are unrivalled, as their labors are most abundant; relieves us from the only ground of hesitation we have ever felt in proceeding to canvass its merits. Before entering on our more specific design, however, we shall avail ourselves of the opportunity offered, to furnish our readers with some little information on the subject of life assurance in general; – a subject, than which, none more important occurs in the whole economy of domestic life. We are the more disposed to this from the ignorance which prevails even among well informed men, respecting the data on which assurance transactions are based. We have found on some occasions, with no little surprise, that these transactions have been regarded as kindred, if not identical, with those of the gambler; a notion which could never have been entertained if the first rudiments of the science on which they proceed had been understood. As in numerous other cases, so in this, ignorance has confounded the dictates of wisdom, the arrangements of an honourable prudence, with the recklessness of an unprincipled speculation. Let the matter be placed in the clear light of day, and its integrity will be visible. A few remarks will suffice to put our readers in possession of sufficient information to decide the matter for themselves.

[...]

[T]he *Protestant Dissenters' and General Life and Fire Assurance Company* [...] was formed in the close 1837, and we shall occupy a brief space in explanation of its design and progress. It originated in a feeling of deep concern for the welfare of the Dissenting body, and of the Dissenting ministry especially. This is explicitly stated in the Prospectus before us, and we cannot do better than quote it.

'The Protestant Dissenters' and General Life and Fire Assurance Company, has been established with the view of calling the attention of a numerous and influential section of the community to the importance of providing, by means of Life Assurances, for the future interests of their families. Though the aggregate amount of Life Assurance has enormously increased, experience proves that this increase has principally taken place among professional men in good practice, persons enjoying comfortable incomes, and those who are engaged in the higher departments of trade and commerce; while individuals of limited means, and those occupied in the more ordinary pursuits of agriculture, manufactures, and trade, very generally neglect to assure their lives, seeking to provide for their dependent families by employing their surplus income in the slow process of gradual accumulation. Daily experience unfortunately furnishes too many instances where early death prevents the attainment of this object, and the members of a bereaved family are then left to deplore the consequences of rashly speculating upon the lengthened duration of life; when, by the employment of the same sum in an Assurance, they would have been entitled to its protection the moment after the Policy was effected.

The circumstances of the Protestant Dissenters of this country, are exactly such as render this mode of investment most advisable; while there is reason to conclude, that as yet they have availed themselves of it to a very limited extent. It was thought by the projectors of the present Company, that an Institution bearing their name, and conducted principally by members of their own body, would be more likely to awaken the attention and command the confidence of Dissenters, than the several Offices previously existing. Under this impression the Company has been formed, and it will be the peculiar care of the Directors to avail themselves of the extensive means of influence, and channels of communication, which they possess, to convey a knowledge of the advantages of Assurance to every town and village in the United Empire; and, in order that they may extend, as far as possible, the benefits now enjoyed by the more opulent, to classes which have as yet been scarcely reached – facilities will be given for effecting small policies – an object favoured by the legislature, which has recently *reduced the stamp duty* payable in respect to Policies of that description. /

It had long been felt, that the claims of the Ministry were very partially met. The fact was in every person's lips; it was obtruded on public attention in a thousand forms, some of which were exceedingly painful to every honourable and delicately minded member of the profession; and various expedients had been suggested in order to remedy the evil. Under the impression of this fact, several meetings were held, some three or four years since at the Congregational Library,[1] with the view of forming a Ministerial Assurance Society, in more immediate connexion, we believe, with the Congregational body. The design, however, fell through, – a circumstance which we do not now regret, as it left the ground open for an Institution of a more general nature, and of far wider scope. Several minor associations exist throughout the country, having for their object the comfort of the families of our deceased ministers, but their resources are exceedingly limited, and the eleemosynary principle on which, to a greater or less extent, they are based, induces evils of serious magnitude. Excellent in themselves, and worthy of all commendation, they minister partial relief in their several localities, to the widows and the orphans of our ministers, but are utterly incapable of meeting a twentieth part of the demand made upon them. Let us not be supposed – in making the reference we now do – to be disparaging the ministry, or lowering one tittle the public standing of its members. We know full well how sensitive some men are on this point, and to a great extent we sympathize with them. The feeling is an honourable and lofty one, and if it occasionally puts on a somewhat questionable garb, and looks more like pride than self-respect, we are only reminded of the tendency of human virtues to run into extremes. We know much of the great body of Dissenting ministers; we have seen them in their undress, have traced them in their families, have sat by their firesides, and after all our observations, extended through many years and diversified by an endless variety of circumstances, we say unhesitatingly, that they are not surpassed – nay, that they have never, as a body, been surpassed, since the age of inspiration closed. Endowed, in many instances, with rare abilities, and enriched with the fruits of assiduous study, they turn from the associations in which wealth and distinction are earned, and devote themselves, body, soul, and strength, to the unobstrusive engagements of their spiritual calling. It would be easy for many of them to obtain in other and more ambitious pursuits, such a share of the good things of this life, as would place their families beyond the reach of want, but necessity is laid upon them to preach the gospel, and they cheerfully obey the heavenly summons. Casting themselves and their families on the good providence of God, they find an ample solace in the spiritual benefits which they administer to others. This self-devotion is / entitled to a grateful recompense, hitherto but very partially rendered, and we rejoice in the formation of the present society as furnishing another, and as we anticipate, no trifling contribution to the comfort of this estimable class of men. Their own delicacy, joined with a noble-hearted devotion to their calling, prevents their doing justice to their own claims, and it is time, therefore, that their friends did it for them. Such is the design of the Dissenters' and General Assurance Company. The names of the Directors are for the most part well known, and will carry confidence with them into every part of the country. 'Most of them,' as is remarked in one of their publications, 'would instantly have declined to take part in a merely commercial undertaking, but the prospect of benefiting a body to which they are warmly attached, has overcome their reluctance, and induced them to incur the heavy responsibilities of their station.'[2] It is not too much to say, that it would be difficult, if not impossible, to combine together an equal number of gentlemen similarly distinguished by their wealth and position in the Dissenting body. By awakening an increased attention to the subject of life assurance among Dissenters generally, the directors hope to confer an immense benefit on the body at large, while by concentrating this business in one institution, they design the formation of a fund, from which a simple, delicate, and most honorable provision may be made for the comfort of the families of the Ministry. It is, therefore, made an integral part of the constitution of the company, and as such is inserted in their Deed of Settlement, that a tenth part of the profits of the business shall be set apart from year to year, to form what is called 'The Ministers' Fund.' Half of this fund is to be applied 'in the reduction of the premiums of assurances on the lives of Protestant Dissenting and Methodist

Ministers,' and the other half may be employed in the same way, or in such other modes as in the judgment of the Board shall be for the benefit of the families in question. By this arrangement it will be seen, that a moiety of the sum annually accruing to the 'Ministers' Fund' from the general profits of the business, must be applied to the benefit of the ministers actually assured, – or, in other words, to the reduction of the premiums payable on their policies. The other moiety of this fund is not so restricted, but may be used in granting annuities to widows, making provision for the settlement of ministers' orphans, or in other analogous modes, of beneficent operation. By this division of the fund two objects are gained, and each is admirable. The directors are enabled to hold out an inducement to congregations or individuals, to assure the lives of their ministers, by proffering such a yearly decrease of the sum to be paid, as shall gradually lighten the burden, thus rendering that facile which would otherwise be onerous and exhausting. We have known cases where / congregations have been deterred from assuring the lives of their minister from an apprehension of the extreme difficulty of maintaining the subscription list formed for that purpose. 'We could easily,' it has been remarked, 'obtain the requisite sum now, and for two, three, five, or it may be for seven years; but several of the original subscribers would be dropping off by death or removal, and it would be difficult to supply their place, until at length the matter would press heavily upon a few, and would give occasion, it may be, to the occurrence of serious evils.' This anticipation of a future burden has operated in a vast number of cases against an effort which might easily have been made, and which was called for by the claims both of justice and of kindness. To such a state of things the Dissenters' Assurance Company addresses itself. It obviates the very evil complained of, by applying a portion of its profits to a gradual liquidation of the burden; and thus brings within the reach of all what might otherwise be unattainable. The other object secured by the division of the 'Ministers' Fund' is the power granted to the Directors of meeting those cases of distress – unhappily not infrequent among us – which arise from the precariousness of human life. It sometimes happens, that a minister is cut down in the midst of his career, without having been able to make any provision, even the smallest, for the support of his family. His sorrowing household – the wife of his bosom, whose comfort was his daily study, and the children that enlivened his hearth and spread joyousness through his soul, are thus suddenly plunged into circumstances of extreme distress. Such cases would have been excluded from the benevolent operation of the fund in question but for the division adverted to, and the efficiency of the society, the comprehensiveness of its range, and the adaptation of its provisions to the actual exigencies of the Dissenting body would thus have been greatly impaired. It may possibly occur to some, that the proportion of a tenth is but a small contribution, whereby a very inconsiderable benefit will accrue to the parties whose advantage is designed. We have heard this objection mooted, while on the other hand it has been urged by some parties, that the subtraction of such a proportion of the profits must militate so seriously against the interests of the proprietors as to operate against the shares, into which the capital of the company is divided, being taken up. Both objections are unsound, as a few words will serve to evince. Respecting the latter, it is sufficient to remark, that without recurring to any of the ordinary means of pushing shares into the market; without a single advertisement, or the allotment of an individual share – save in the case of the broker of the Company – to a member of the Stock Exchange, the 10,000 shares have been actually issued to well-known and influential Dissenters throughout the country. Thousands more might have been disposed / of in the same way, and to similar parties – so general was the interest felt in the undertaking – and it will be for the proprietors on some future occasion to determine whether it will not be for the interests of the Institution to meet the demand still made for shares by the creation of an increased number. The Deed of Settlement gives the power to do this, – it will be for their wisdom to determine whether they shall avail themselves of it.

Respecting the other objection we remark, that the appropriation of a larger portion of the profits to the 'Ministers' Fund,' would probably have operated against the investment of such a capital as was requisite to insure the commercial integrity of the company, and thus have ruined the whole design. The proportion, therefore, was fixed at a tenth, provision being made by the thirtieth clause of the Deed, empowering the proprietors – while expressly prohibited from diminishing the proportion – to increase it to any extent they may see fit. Less than a tenth can never be so set apart, but more than this may, and we trust will be assigned to the object for which the Institution is formed. It is clearly as yet impossible to predict what will be the *measure* of the company's success. Sanguine anticipations are warranted, but it would be idle to attempt a specification of results. It is obvious, however, to remark, that the peculiar mode in which a large portion of the annual produce of the 'Ministers' Fund' is to be applied, increases vastly the pecuniary benefit conferred on the ministry. Suppose this produce be £500 or £1000. He will fall into a serious error, and will do great injustice to the society, who supposes that this sum represents the amount of the boon conferred. It would undoubtedly do so if the £500 or £1000 in question, were to be distributed in exhibitions of ten, twenty, or of any other given amount. A specific pecuniary contribution would in this case be made, the measure of which could easily be ascertained. But this is not the mode in which the fund in question is to be administered. Half of it, at the least, is to be employed as an inducement – and several cases already prove its efficiency – to churches or individuals to assure their ministers' lives. It thus operates as a motive to an outlay much larger than itself, *and the amount of the benefit conferred must therefore, in all fairness, be taken to be the sum total of all the ministerial policies which it has caused to be taken out.* Five hundred a year thus employed, may easily be made to produce many thousands for the service of the families of our ministers. And it should be remarked, in further elucidation of this plan, that it is the design of the Directors – a design already partially executed – to bring this subject fairly before that section of the religious world, whose welfare they specially seek. While desirous of giving every facility to ministers assuring their own lives, it is their special / aim, to urge upon the elders, deacons, and other leading members of our churches, the obligation under which they are placed to make provision for the comfort of those, who in seeking their spiritual benefit, are neglecting the secular interests of their children. They do not ask our ministers to deny themselves in order to protect their offspring from future want; but they say to the people among whom they labor, the people who share the benefits of their onerous and sanctified labors, 'Show your sense of your pastor's worth; your due appreciation of his services, your attachment to his person, by making some provision, according to the measure of your capability, for the maintenance and comfort of those whom he leaves unfriended and pennyless, in order to serve your good. Relieve his heart from the most painful and distracting of all earthly anticipations, that there may be no conflict in his breast between the feelings of the pastor and those of the parent, – no compunctious visitations lest in seeking your good he may be neglecting the claims of those beloved ones whom providence has made dependent on his care.' Such is the *animus* of the society's operations, and we cannot do better than illustrate it by an extract from a circular, bearing the names of four Directors, Thomas Challis, Joseph Fletcher, Thomas Piper, and Thomas Wilson, Esqs., and addressed extensively to the officers and members of our churches.

'In conformity with the general design of the Company,' say the Directors, 'it has been determined to appropriate a portion of its profits to the special benefit of the families of Dissenting Ministers. This is made an integral part of the Constitution of the Company, by being inserted in the Deed of Settlement, and can never, therefore, be departed from by the future Managers of its affairs. Among other ways of appropriating such profits, it is designed to apply them to the reduction of the premiums payable on the policies of Ministers. By this feature of their plan, the annual payment will be gradually diminished, and the sum ultimately required will in consequence, it is hoped, be so small as to bring the advantages of the Institution within the reach of a greatly extended class. It is the hope of the Directors that many Congregations and Churches will thus be induced to assure the lives of their Ministers. Hitherto little attention has been paid to this subject, and the evils which have followed are familiar to all who are acquainted with the Dissenting Body. It is well known that the incomes of Dissenting Ministers are, with few exceptions, barely adequate to the maintenance of their families. The wants of the passing moment may be met, but it is utterly out of their power to make provision for their families, when the Divine Disposer of events shall have summoned them to their reward. Cases of extreme distress are in consequence frequently occurring. The last hours of many Ministers who have laboured diligently, and with success, in their high vocation, are embittered / by a foresight of the privations and penury to which their dearest relatives will be subjected, and from which they see no earthly escape. Men of whom the world was not worthy, have sighed in deep bitterness of heart at the utter destitution to which they were leaving their weeping widow and her helpless orphans. The continual occurrence of such cases has long been felt to be a serious evil. It has grown with the extension of the Dissenting Body, and is now universally admitted to call for some vigorous, comprehensive, and speedy remedy. Such a remedy, it is believed, the present Institution will in part supply; and the Directors therefore solicit your zealous co-operation. A few individuals attached to the ministry and person of their pastor may easily realize a sufficient sum to effect an Assurance on his Life. This sum will be reduced from time to time by an appropriation of a portion of the profits of the Company; and the effort which might otherwise in the course of years prove burdensome, will thus be gradually diminished. Little need be said to enforce such an appeal. The voluntary seclusion of many of our Ministers from those paths of honourable pursuit which their talents would enable them successfully to prosecute, gives them and their families a powerful claim on the sympathy and gratitude of their people. If they minister spiritual things, as in many cases they do, to the cost of their families, it surely becomes such as are benefited by their labors to do every thing in their power to free them from anxiety, and to protect their dying hours from the bitterest earthly anticipations which can distract a husband or a father's heart. Allow us then, dear Sirs, to commend this subject to your grave consideration. It would be indelicate in us to do more than lay the case before you. In doing so, we have discharged our duty, and shall be amply recompensed for whatever trouble we may incur, if the Deacons, and other leading members of our Churches, are induced to carry out our suggestions.'

Several other topics remain, on all of which we had intended to say something, but our remarks have extended so far beyond our purpose, that we must omit some of them altogether, and only hastily allude to others. The pecuniary integrity of the Company is guaranteed by a capital of one million, which is divided into 10,000 shares of one hundred pounds each. Five pounds per share have been paid up, and the remainder is subject to the call of the Directors in case of need. No person can hold more than a hundred shares, and the great majority of them are distributed in allotments of five, ten, and twenty. The qualification for the Direction is one hundred shares; and the constitution of the Company is thoroughly popular. After the first of January, 1840, a general meeting of the proprietors is to take place annually in the month of April or May, and special meetings are to be convened on the requisition of twenty proprietors, holding not less than ten shares each. The holder of ten shares is entitled to one vote, of thirty, to two; of fifty, to three; and of eighty, to four votes. Proxies may be granted by one proprietor / to another, but must be renewed every six months in order to continue in force. It is needless to add, that a certain number of the Directors are to go out annually, and that the election of Directors, and all other matters pertaining to the Company, are in the hands, and subject to the decision of the proprietors.

One word respecting the life rates adopted by the Company, and we will pass on to the only other topic to which we shall advert. 'In calculating the Tables for Life Assurance,' their prospectus states, 'the Directors have adopted the course recommended by Mr. Babbage, as being in their judgment more equitable and business-like than the plan generally adopted. Having ascertained by the calculation of eminent mathematicians the real value of the risk, and consequently the amount of premium just sufficient to meet it,' they have added to this 'such a per centage as will defray the expenses of management, and allow of a sufficient dividend to the proprietors, whose capital is a guarantee to the assured.' This is clearly the only proper course, and we rejoice that the Directors have had wisdom to adopt it. The per centage they have added is a graduated one, and the result of their calculations is a set of tables standing midway between those of the older offices and the premiums of some younger competitors for public favor. The position they have thus taken up is at once liberal and prudent, and will command the confidence of reflecting men. It has happened with Life Assurance, as with other branches of commerce. The multiplication of traders has awakened a spirit of competition which has led to an improvident and, as we fear, a ruinous reduction of premiums. Terms are offered to the public below what the extent of the risk justifies, and a future failure is thus hazarded, where security – absolute, unerring security, is especially sought. What may be the result, it would be vain to conjecture; but it surely becomes wise men to reflect on the cost at which they effect a small annual saving, by assuring their lives with those offices whose only claim on public support is the low rates at which they issue policies. That their experience may justify the experiment they are making we shall be glad to learn; but it can be regarded only as an experiment, and as such necessarily militates against the security which a Life Assurance gives, and in which its value mainly consists. Two rates of premiums are published by the Dissenters' Company, the one fixed and unvarying, the other susceptible of reduction from an appropriation of the profits of the Company. Persons assuring on the latter table divide equally with the proprietors, the profits of that department of the business; and have the option of receiving their bonus in ready money, or of having it applied to the reduction of their premium, or added, in its *reversionary value*, to their policies. By a recent advertisement, we perceive, that other tables have been prepared, two of which / are specially designed to meet the case of superannuated ministers, and of other professional men. The policies taken out on these tables are made payable on a person attaining the age of sixty, so that provision may thus be easily made for the partial or complete retirement of those who are disqualified by increasing infirmities for the efficient discharge of their duties. The following statement of the distinctive features of the Company which has recently been issued as an advertisement, may appropriately close this part of our paper.

1. One tenth of the entire profits is appropriated by the Deed of Settlement in reducing the premiums payable for insuring the lives of Dissenting and Methodist Ministers, or in other ways similarly beneficial to their families.
2. Certificates of age, and character, and of the amount of loss in case of fire, not required from clergymen or churchwardens.
3. A Table of premiums for policies payable at the age of sixty, or of annuities to commence at that period, suitable to the case of superannuated Ministers, or of other professional men.
4. The lowest rates of premiums consistent with security, and the payment of policies guaranteed by a capital of one million.
5. Two Tables of premiums, the one giving an interest in the profits of the Company, the other not.
6. Every facility given on moderate terms to persons going beyond the prescribed limits of their policy.
7. Premiums may be paid either annually, half yearly, or quarterly, in a limited number of payments, or in one sum.
8. Loans advanced on policies of the value of £50, or policies purchased on liberal terms.
9. All claims payable in three months after satisfactory proof of death, or earlier on deduction of discount.
10. No entrance fee required.

There is only one other point to which our space permits us to advert, and that very briefly. Our readers may be desirous of knowing how far the support of the Dissenting body has been obtained, and what prospects are afforded of that support being continued and increased. This point has been already adverted to in the commencement of the present article, but we recur to it again in order to furnish more definite and satisfactory information. Upwards of 250 life policies, averaging about £700 each, have been issued during the brief period of the Society's existence, of which more than forty are on the lives of Ministers. In the fire department, the number of policies exceeds 2500, covering nearly £2,000,000 of property. Two hundred and thirty agents have been appointed, and in Bristol and Edinburgh organizations of resident proprietors have been formed. These facts constitute an ample justification of the hopes which prompted the / founders of the Company, and opens up a prospect of successful exertion, which, under the sanction of a favoring providence, cannot fail to be productive of great and lasting benefits. The principles of the Society have been approved, and its objects commended to support, by the resolutions of several of our most influential bodies. To say nothing at present of provincial associations, we should fail in doing justice to our theme, did we not place on record the following votes of the Congregational and Baptist Unions, and of Lady Huntingdon's Connexion.[3]

Baptist Union, May 1st, 1838.

The constitution and claims of the Protestant Dissenters' and General Life and Fire Assurance Company having been explained, it was Resolved unanimously –

That the benevolent feature of the Company, which secures to the families of Dissenting Ministers a portion of its profits, entitles it to the support of the Dissenting Body.

Congregational Union, Friday, 11th May, 1838.

Unanimously resolved –

That the design of the Protestant Dissenters' and General Life and Fire Assurance Company, in extending a knowledge of the advantages of Life Assurance in general, and of the various forms in which provision may thereby be made, by endowments and otherwise, for the benefit of Dissenting Ministers, and their families, is worthy of the attentive consideration of the Churches connected with this Union, and that the benevolent feature of the Company, which secures the appropriation of a portion of its profits to the furtherance and encouragement of this object, in behalf of their Ministers, entitles it to the support of the Dissenting Body at large.

Conference of Lady Huntingdon's Connexion, July 6th, 1838.

The object of the Protestant Dissenters' and General Life and Fire Assurance Company having been introduced to the consideration of the Brethren, it was Resolved unanimously –

That as the constitution and design of the Company offer considerable advantages to the families of Dissenting Ministers, and to the Churches which may entertain the benevolent intention of providing for the widows and children of their several Pastors, this Conference recommend it to the support of the Connexion at large.

As analogous to these resolutions, we must be permitted to transcribe the following brief letter, which, with the subjoined signatures of the Edinburgh Ministers, has been published in several of the Scotch papers. /

To Charles Spence, Esq., Agent for Edinburgh.

DEAR SIR, – We have perused the papers you sent us, explaining the objects of the Protestant Dissenters' and General Life and Fire Assurance Company. The favourable aspect this Office wears towards Dissenters, – the high respectability of its Directors, – the numerous classes whose support it is calculated to secure, – the extent of business it is thus likely to transact, – as well as the selected lives which these classes furnish, – unite in recommending this Institution to the favour of Dissenters generally, whose interests, in various ways, it seems highly fitted to advance.

Rev. JOHN BROWN, D.D.	Rev. JAMES KIRKWOOD.
WILLIAM INNES.	GEORGE JOHNSTONE.
C. D. CULLEN.	J. J. BATES.
JAMES ROBERTSON.	JOHN M'GILCHRIST.
HENRY WIGHT.	W. L. ALEXANDER, A.M.

The same letter, addressed to Messrs. Durham and Rough, the Company's agents at Dundee, has been advertised in the papers of that town, with the following signatures of Presbyterian and Independent Ministers.

Rev. DAVID RUSSELL, D.D.	Rev. GEORGE GILFILLAN.
D. K. SHOEBOTHAM.	SAMUEL, SPENCE.
MATTHEW FRAZER.	JAMES R. M' GAVIN.
J. CROSS.	

The operations of the Society embrace Fire as well as Life assurances, but we have left ourselves no space to advert to this branch of its business. We, therefore, merely remark in closing, that it affords an opportunity to almost every Dissenter in the kingdom, of contributing something towards that fund from the judicious appropriation of which we anticipate such benefits. Our colleges, and chapels, and school-rooms should, especially, and without delay, be transferred to the Dissenters' Company. Perfectly free from sectarianism – in the reprehensible sense of that word – the Society yet makes its appeal to, and mainly relies for support on, the great, enlightened, and virtuous body of Protestant Dissenters. In the conduct of its business it knows nothing of ecclesiastical distinctions. It opens its doors alike to Churchmen and Dissenters – to Peers and Commoners, and some of both are already ranked among its policy holders; but in the appropriation of a portion of its profits to a specific Dissenting purpose it sustains a character which places it apart from all similar institutions, and gives it an undeniable title to zealous and permanent support.

LIFE INSURANCE AS A DOMESTIC DUTY

'Life Insurance', *Macon Weekly Telegraph*,[1] 8 January 1838, p. 3.

John Neal, 'Life Assurance', *Columbian Lady's and Gentleman's Magazine*[2] (January 1846), pp. 8–12.

Arthur Scratchley, *Observations on Life Assurance Societies, and Savings Banks, in Two Parts, with a Mathematical Appendix and Tables* (London: John W. Parker and Son, 1851), pp. 63–71.

Arthur Reade, 'Before the Wedding Ring', *Policy-holder: An Insurance Journal*,[3] 16 (September 1885), pp. 297–8.

In the mid-nineteenth century, the most common marketing tactic used by life insurance companies on both sides of the Atlantic was the appeal to domestic duty, often embellished by melodramatic warnings about the fate of widows and orphans in uninsured households. This sales pitch was a mainstay of mid-century prospectuses, and it also appeared in lectures, newspaper paragraphs and short fiction. The people who produced such copy were most often employed by insurance companies or by trade journals. Typical in this regard was Arthur Scratchley (1821–97), a barrister who consulted extensively for insurance offices and building societies in the 1850s, and who served as secretary for the Western Life Assurance Society from 1847 to its dissolution in 1865. The two other authors represented here, John Neal and Arthur Reade, were freelance writers whose interest in the topic reflects the increasing currency of life insurance in everyday middle-class life. Neal (1793–1876) was a prolific novelist and critic who lived in Portland, Maine, for most of his life; his better-known novels were two decades behind him when he wrote this short dialogue on life insurance. Reade was a Manchester-based writer whose major themes included English composition and the use of stimulants; in 1885 the *Glasgow Herald* called him 'a literary busybody, whose chief occupation seems to be making books out of other people's brains'.[4]

Narratives that connected life insurance with domesticity tapped into two dominant genres in mid-nineteenth-century middle-class culture: the sentimental novel and the evangelical sermon. Insurance stories mirrored novels by mining the melodramatic potential of untimely death, and by foregrounding married women as the key to reconciling tensions between individual desire and moral responsibility. They also tapped into the evangelical obsession with death as a time of reckoning, prior to which all souls stood in urgent need of salvation. Life insurance stories departed from each of these genres at crucial points, however. Marriage typically came at the beginning of a life insurance story (followed inevitably by the breadwinner's death), whereas sentimental novels more often concluded their plots with a marriage or two, and scattered deaths at random intervals up to that point. And instead of being the 'angel of the house', dedicated to preserving domesticity and saving souls while the husband was alive, the insured wife played the important role of taking over as head of the household (with the company's silent assistance) after her husband died.[5]

In the course of dramatizing the prospects of dependants in the event of the breadwinner's premature death, life insurance rhetoric both overstated the penury facing widows and children of the uninsured, and understated the difficulties that often remained for policyholders' dependants. Charity, whether through an employer or relatives, often prevented the worst consequences of poverty in the first case, and the proceeds from an insurance policy were often diverted to pay off outstanding debts in the second case. This latter gap between the insurance company's promise and reality was especially common in Britain, where legislation to protect dependants from creditors' claims appeared on the scene three decades later than was the case in the United States.[6]

Notes

1. The *Macon Weekly Telegraph* was published between 1826 and 1895 in Macon, Georgia.
2. The *Columbian Lady's and Gentleman's Magazine* was a New York monthly published from 1844 to 1849.
3. The *Policy-holder* was published in Manchester starting in 1883, originally under the editorship of W. G. Walton.
4. *Glasgow Herald*, 17 February 1885, p. 3. On Neal, see E. Watts and D. J. Carlson (eds), *John Neal and Nineteenth-Century American Literature and Culture* (Lewisburg, PA: Bucknell University Press, 2012).
5. Alborn, *Regulated Lives*, pp. 154–7; Murphy, *Investing in Life*, pp. 150–1.
6. Alborn, *Regulated Lives*, pp. 157–62; Murphy, *Investing in Life*, pp. 137–41. On widow protection laws, see 'The Widow and the Fatherless' and articles by Arnold Scratchley and Thomas Bond Sprague, in Volume 2 of this collection.

'Life Insurance', *Macon Weekly Telegraph* (1838)

Life Insurance. – We are reminded of the beneficial effects of life insurance, by a recent instance which has come to our knowledge. A respectable lawyer in Georgia, having effected insurance on his life at the old Pennsylvania Life Insurance and Annuity office in Third-street, recently died, and the sum insured, nearly $5000 was promptly paid.

Such a relief at the moment of bereavement, when the income of a family is suddenly stopped by the decease of its responsible head, must be peculiarly welcome. – Those who know their families to be entirely dependent on their personal exertions would do well to set apart a small portion of their annual income towards securing some relief for them in the bitter hour of affliction. – *Weekly Messenger.*[1]

John Neal, 'Life Assurance', *Columbian Lady's and Gentleman's Magazine* (1846)

LIFE ASSURANCE.

BY JOHN NEAL.

"Ah! is that you? – how do you feel? – how's the weather?"

"Ugh – ugh! a damp cold day my love – ugh!"

"A what!" stopping on her way toward him, with outstretched arms, and a look of sorrowful astonishment.

"Well – what's the matter now?"

"Oh, Charles!" laying her little, soft plump hand, upon his arm, with a sweet smile, and shaking her loose hair and prettily-turned head at him, *so* piteously – "you needn't laugh, you brute you; it would have brought the tears into your eyes – *Oh Charles*, what did you promise me?"

"Promise you! – When? – *Where?*"

"When we were married, Charles."

"Upon my word, I've forgotten – what was it?"

"*Oh Charles!*" and her large dreaming eyes filled with tears, and she turned away from the offered kiss.

"What was it, Jenny?" – kicking off his boots, and fumbling about for his slippers, and talking all the time as fast as he could – "The old gallows! – that's the way with every thing now; upside down, or wrong end first; never get a pair of slippers, but they're inside out, or belong to somebody else – there now! But you haven't answered me, love – what was it I promised you at the time of our marriage? Really now – what was it Jenny? – *to love, honor and obey?*"

This was too much – 'much too much' – and the young wife hid her face in her perfumed handkerchief and wept aloud.

Whereupon her dutiful and loving husband fetched a long breath, flung off his coat, slipped into a dressing gown, and went softly up to her, and sat down upon the sofa, and tried to pull her into his lap.

But she only wept the louder – turning away her sweet lips, and refusing to be comforted; and when he would have put his arm round her waist, or toyed with her little dainty hand, as of yore, instead of jumping up with a cry of transport, as in duty bound, or dropping a low courtesy, or whispering thank ye, sir, she only pouted, and flung away from him and went and buried herself in the farthest corner of the farthest couch in the room – pulling a shawl over her face and drawing herself up and turning her back to him, as much as to say – *now for it! – I'll see!*

Whereupon, poor Charles, who had been rather inclined to a fit of the sulks himself, when he first entered the room, began to think that – *perhaps* – and here one little foot, after struggling through the scanty drapery of shawl and flounce, began swinging to and fro, with such a tantalizing uncertainty of purpose, that the poor fellow couldn't sit still – *perhaps* something might have happened; and having been solemnly cautioned over and over again, by nobody knows how many well-wishers of the family, to say nothing of his mother-in-law, never to thwart his young wife, lest he might have cause to be sorry for it the longest day he had to live – no matter why – he determined to gulp down the rising bitterness of his heart, and have another pull at the soothing system. But no – the more he tried – the more she wouldn't be comforted. The dear child was in its bridal tantrums – and lying flat on her face, with her head buried in the pillows of a low deep couch, and a magnificent shawl wrapped round her – and growing worse and worse every moment.

Well! thought her husband – there must be something to pay; and I'd give a trifle to know what. "Jenny! – Jenny dear!"

At this moment, the bell rang, and before Jenny could right herself, or get up a decent excuse for flushed cheeks, red eyes, and a rumpled dress – the door opened slowly, and in walked very slowly no less a personage than uncle Joe – a bachelor uncle, stout and free spoken – stately and testy – upon whom all the hopes of all the family were fixed.

"Halloo! – hoity-toity – what's in the wind now?" sung out uncle Joe, as he saw the lady of the house hurrying off at one door, while he entered at the other. "Ain't ye ashamed o' yourselves! – here Charles, here! – you great lubber, you! Haven't ye been married long enough to behave like a man – hey? – tut, tut – tut. Come here Jenny! What are you afraid of? Oh – ho – I see – crying hey? Well, well that's some comfort. Had enough o' billing and cooing – hey?"

"Take a chair uncle."

"'Take a chair, uncle!' too be sure I will. Just thought of it – pretty time o' day. What the plague have you been quarreling about?"

"Quarreling, uncle?"

"*Quarreling*! – yes, to be sure – quarreling! pulling hair. Can't I see? Don't I know? Haven't you been married well on to a twelve month – / hey?" setting down his huge knotted cane, as if he meant to force it through the floor, and pulling out a large gold snuff-box from his broad-flapped waistcoat-pocket and scattering the rappee right and left over the rich carpet, as he continued – "Come, come, now – none o' that, if you please. Here you, Jenny – stand up there, and take your fingers out of your mouth – and you, you great booby! – what are you grinning at! Look me in the face now, both of you – what in the plague were you quarreling about?"

No answer.

Uncle Joe fetched a stamp that shook the whole house.

"What! – ashamed to tell, hey? Pretty fellow for a husband, aint you?"

Here Charles looked at Jenny.

"And you, you jade – pretty fellow for a wife, ain't you?"

Here Jenny looked at Charles.

"That such children should dare to get married! Upon my life I wouldn't trust either of you with a rag baby."

Here both looked at uncle Joe – and after two or three wry faces, all three burst out a laughing together.

And then the glorious old fellow, who was a bit of a humorist in his way, and very fond of mischief, giving Jenny a pinch, and Charles a wink, which brought the color into her cheeks, and made him look like a simpleton, flung himself back into an old fashioned arm-chair they had just been patching at considerable expense, out of the small saving of the husband as a writer in some office, and upsetting a fancy table with a lamp on it that was never lighted, and a quantity of old china of no earthly use, fell a laughing with all his might, and kept on – and on – as if he would never stop, till the chair creaked and trembled in every joint, and the poor wife looked at her husband in dismay, expecting every moment to see his dear old good-for-nothing uncle Joe, pitching head foremost among the glittering fragments of her china, or sprawling at his whole length upon the floor.

And then there was a lull – and then another boisterous outbreak; and then there was a little playful questioning, and then it turned out that the marriage promise referred to by the wife, was about swearing; and that when the husband came into the room and she asked him about the weather, and he answered, a little pettishly perhaps, that it was a *damp cold day*, she had mistaken what he had said for something very naughty – very naughty indeed: and when she reminded him of the promise made to her literally on her marriage day, and not before, in the season of courtship – and she found not only that he had forgotten that promise, but that he was inclined to jest with it, and turn the whole off with a laugh – no wonder she had a swelling of the heart and lost her patience and threw herself upon her face and wrapped herself up in whatever happened to be nearest – and forgot her feet, and her husband.

This affair settled, and another long and hearty laugh – another yet, and yet another being over – uncle Joe turned suddenly upon his nephew and asked him, with the look of a thoughtful man of business, if he had made up his mind to insure.

The nephew seemed puzzled for a moment – and then he answered – no. He liked the plan – but really – uncle Joe must excuse him.

"But uncle Joe wont excuse you. You have no right to run such risks. What is to become of your *wife and children* – if you should have any; and happen to die in a hurry, as young men always do?"

Here Jenny caught her husband's hands between her's, and sat gazing into his eyes, with a look of unutterable tenderness. "Don't uncle, don't! I can't bear it!" she whispered.

"Hold your tongue child – you're a goose. You don't know what you're talking about. I want Charles to insure his life – it's all the property he's got, or is likely to have."

"Life – property – I don't understand you, uncle Joe."

"I dare say not. Allow me to make myself clear. People insure their ships, and houses, and profits – and leave what is more valuable to themselves, to their families, and to their creditors, uninsured – that is their lives. Life is not only property, but always the best property a man has – will not a man give all that he has for his life."

"Yes, uncle – but to assure one's *life* seems to me to be wicked, uncle Joe, our life is in the hands of our Maker – and it is for him to assure it."

"Nonsense, are not our ships and houses in the hands of our Maker? our crops? our health? our happiness? why not leave him to take the whole care of these off our hands? why sow? why reap? why take medicine? why provide for the morrow? why for our families?"

"I see, uncle – you do not mean to prevent death, by insuring against death."

"Certainly not, when we insure a ship, we don't say that she cannot go to the bottom – we only say, that if she does, we'll pay for her, and the owner shall not go to the bottom with her, a ruined and discouraged man. So with fire, we don't say, that if you insure, houses wont burn – but simply, that if they do burn we will pay for them, and save the owners from ruin. So – by insuring life, we do not mean to say that men shall not die – but only that *when* they die, their families shall not die with them – be scattered to the four winds of heaven – or starve and rot in cellars and work-houses; that accomplished women shall / not be turned adrift upon the world; or helpless children be smitten at once with bereavement and poverty."

"Yes uncle Joe – but" –

"But what, sir!"

"I haven't had time to think of it."

"A fiddlestick's end – yes, you have – how much time do you want? Thinking is of no use, I tell you, unless you have somebody at your elbow to answer your questions. You cannot even hope to understand the whole system, as I do, unless you give a month at least to the subject. Of course, therefore, if you were to put it off for a twelve-month, you would be just where you are now. No, no, Charles – decide *as* you may, and *when* you may, still you must depend upon somebody you have confidence in – just as we do upon a doctor. You take his drugs, every day, without understanding why or wherefore. Now – in one word – I tell you to insure. I say it is your *duty*."

"But how am I to pay the premium?"

"Fudge. You are young and in good health! Let me see – twenty-five last October. For one hundred dollars a year, you can be *certain* of leaving behind you, to your wife and children, Charles – think of that, my boy – to your wife and children – *five thousand dollars*, cash, die when you will – to-morrow if you like: and the longer you live, the larger the sum will be, unless you withdraw the profits; so that if you live to the average length of life at your age, and allow these profits to accumulate, you will leave not five thousand, but fifteen or sixteen thousand dollars to your family."

"Bravo! – but how am I to pay the hundred dollars a year?"

"Nothing easier. Pay one quarter cash, and the other three quarters at the end of the year – giving a good note on interest."

"But if I should not be able to pay the note at the end of the year."

"Then pay what you can – the interest if nothing more, and renew for the balance."

"And if I die – what becomes of the note?"

"It is deducted from the sum total due you on the books – made up of premiums, earnings and profits divided yearly, and averaging about ten per cent a year."

"And if I pay up every year?"

"Then you receive certificates of stock, bearing six per cent interest; upon which certificates the company are bound to loan you 66 2-3 per cent, in cash, whenever you need it, whether to pay your premiums, if a change of circumstances should occur, to educate your children, to provide for your family, or *for yourself*."

"I'll do it, uncle!"

"Don't, Charles, don't!" whispered his young wife.

"And why not, pray? If Charles will take my advice, he would never consult you – what do women know about such things?"

"Much, dear uncle – much more than you, old bachelors, ever give them credit for."

"Hold your tongue Jenny. Do as I bid you. You must insure his life – and then happen what may, the money will belong to you, and *to your children* – there, there – don't make a fool o' yourself. You must be looking for children – it is your duty – else what do you marry for? And it is your duty to provide for them too."

"But uncle" – thoughtfully – "how can this belong to a wife and to her children, if the husband and father is in debt?"

"Well done, my girl! Now I've some hope of you. You are not the simpleton I took you for – not by any means, and therefore I must answer you. The law is beginning to look upon the wife as a partner in business with her husband. She stays at home and takes care of the household – the children – the servants, and saves all she can. She has her little earnings and savings, and the law allows her to put them by *in this way*, and in no other, to the amount of three hundred dollars a year."[1]

"Ah! I see – but" –

"But what?"

"But a wife may have so much to gain by the death of her husband" – smiling faintly, but with tears in her beautiful eyes – "that – perhaps – in some cases – she might not watch over him so faithfully, as she ought –"

"Poh!"

"And if she did," continued the niece – "and if she *did*, how many there are who might charge her with neglecting her husband upon a sick-bed – perhaps upon a death-bed" – and here she began to sob, as if her very heart would break.

"Really, you have done it, now! Why not be afraid of growing rich? or of being suspected in the same way with a rich husband? – No, no, Jenny! A woman has always more to lose than to gain by the death of a husband, however wealthy he may leave her. But – *pshaw!* – I have wasted time enough with you on this subject; and I say that you have no more right to risk your life a single day without insurance, my boy, than you would have to risk your houses and ships, or other property without insurance, if you were over head and ears in debt. Good night – God bless you! – Good bye."

And the next moment uncle Joe had vanished. For a full half hour, not a loud word was spoken. The young wife and young husband sat holding each other by the hands – thinking what might be hereafter – and breathing low and trembling with every change of color and every change of thought. /

At last, he husband spoke. "Well Jenny," said he, "what do you say now?"

"Just what I said before, Charles – I am not convinced. We cannot well spare the money now – we have hardly enough to get along with decently. A part of our house, you know, is unfurnished; and we ought to have something put by – *dear* Charles, don't you think so?" and a large tear fell upon the hand she was holding to her lips – and her husband drew her up to his heart, and kissed her with more than the warmth of a bridegroom.

"True, dearest – very true. For whatever happens, we must be prepared and provided."

"And then too, dear Charles," continued the wife, sobbing, "what is the need of anybody insuring with your expectations?"

"We cannot hope to die together, my love."

"No, Charles – but happen what may, we shall be provided for, and so – and so," faltering, and hiding her face in her husband's bosom, and whispering just above her breath "and so will our dear children, if it should please our Heavenly Father to grant us children."

"Perhaps –"

"*Perhaps*, Charles. Your uncle is rich, and so is my father."

"True. But both are in business, and businessmen, you know, are always in the way of terrible vicissitudes."

"But you are young and healthy – and oh, I cannot but believe, with a long life before you."

"Tears! Nay, my dear girl – think no more of this matter. Let us talk no more of it – be cheerful and trusting, and, whether I live or die, it shall not be my fault if to the bitterness of death and the bereavements of widowhood there should be added the trials and temptations, the sorrow and abasement of poverty."

"What do you mean, Charles? – you'll break my heart, if you keep talking so. A plague on this life insurance, I say – I shall never hear the last of it, I am sure, now that Uncle Joe has taken it up."

"Assurance, my love – not insurance."

"Assurance! Well – It never entered my head before, that you wanted *assurance*."

"Not so bad! Kiss me – and then, if you have no other engagement and nothing better to do – and will promise to behave well, you may go to bed with me."

"Impertinence!"

Five years after this, Charles Hardy went into business with his father-in-law, and within eight years both failed. Uncle Joe married the mistress of a boarding-house, with a large family, and died, leaving his whole property to her; and not enough to his nephew to pay for the china he broke on the evening he spent there, laboring with him to get his life insured.

Soon after the failure, and while poor Hardy was trying to compound with his creditors, most of whom were disposed, not only to forgive him his debts, but even to help him forward again, for the sake of his dear little family, while others were unrelenting and merciless, not only withholding their sympathy but charging him with rashness and folly, and even his blessed wife with extravagance – the hardest thing poor Charles had to bear throughout all his trials; and just when he began to hold up his head and look about him, and feel encouraged – often lamenting that he had not followed the advice of uncle Joe, and put something by for a rainy day, which no mortal could touch, but his wife and her children, and as often declaring that, if his mind were relieved from that anxiety he should be happy – and then the eyes of his wife would glisten, and she would bid him be of good cheer, since he had health and character and experience and a family left, the best of capitals for beginning the world with. Just at this time, he was brought home speechless, over anxiety of mind had been too much for him – he could neither eat nor sleep; and after a long patient uncomplaining struggle with the cares and miseries that beset him – a struggle of which his poor wife knew nothing till long afterwards – his constitution gave way all at once, and he fell from his chair at the desk of a wealthy merchant, who, knowing his worth and deceived by the resignation and cheerfulness of the poor fellow, believed he was preparing him with certainty for a sphere of great usefulness – while he was dying by inches in his very presence.

The poor wife met the bearers of her husband at the door, without a cry or a tear. The children gathered about him – but even their wailings did not disturb him, and for many a long and weary day there was no hope – none whatever; but one evening, late in the summer, as he lay there with his lighted eyes fixed upon the open window – gasping for breath and evidently struggling with some great change at work within him – he turned suddenly toward his wife, and knew her, and pressed her hand between both of his, and then – while her heart was brimming with terror and joy, fearing that every breath would be his last, and full of thankfulness that reason had been vouchsafed to him to know his dear children and their mother once more – he lifted his thin hand towards the Western sky, and whispered "oh, that we might all go together!"

And there was nothing to be heard in reply, but the humble breathings of a broken-hearted wife, repeating the same prayer; and the sobbings of little children waiting to take leave of their dying father.

"If I could only be certain, my dear wife," he added after a short pause, "could I only be satisfied / that you and the children were provided for – that you were beyond the reach of want, I should die happy; but there! – it's no use talking; I might have forseen all this; I might have provided for it; and if I had done so, not only would it have made you and the dear children happy – but I do in my heart believe –"

"Happy! – oh Charles!"

"As happy, I mean as you could be, after we had been separated by death – at any rate your loss would not have been trebled to you as it must be now – but – I declare I don't know what I was going to say – ah – it was this – Had I done my duty, love, when it was very easy to do it – I should not only die happy now, but as I am a living man, I do believe it would have lengthened my own life – restored me to health perhaps. Ah! – why do you withdraw your hand? – why leave me at a moment like this! Merciful Heaven what's the matter with her! Run, children, run!"

The poor wife, who had been sitting by the side of her dying husband, with his head gathered to her bosom, smoothing his damp hair, and sobbing over his thin transparent hands, started up and sprang through the half open door; and after a few moments, they heard a drawer open and shut violently in the next room –

the sharp rustling of paper – hurried footsteps and cries – and before they knew which way to turn, she came back trembling and weeping to the bedside of the poor sufferer, and pressing her damp lips to his forehead she whispered to him to be of good cheer – to be comforted – and when he started up and gazed into her eyes with speechless terror, she told him that God had heard his prayer, and that his little ones and their mother were all provided for.

"Provided for! – how! – when! – where! – what has happened!" cried the husband, trying to lift himself up, and gazing at her with a bewildered look, and gasping for breath. "Oh speak to me! – let me be sure that I have understood you, and though I am ready and willing to die, still, as God is my judge, I believe it would bring me back to life again."

The poor wife answered not a word, but she fell upon her knees with a cry of joy and thankfulness, and her three children knelt with her, while from her uplifted hand fluttered a paper which her dying husband was just able to make out the meaning of. It was a life policy for five thousand dollars, taken out twelve years before in the name of the wife, and was now worth, after deducting the sums lent to her by the office to pay the yearly premiums with, and keep her sick husband after his failure, over *eight thousand dollars.* These were the savings of a prudent and thrifty housekeeper in the season of prosperity, when two dollars a week put aside for the purpose became the seed of a richer harvest than her husband had ever hoped for in the days of commercial change and overthrow. For a while she had forgotten the policy, believing it could be of no use to her or to the children till after the death of her husband; but when she discovered that, owing to a beneficial provision of the charter which entitled her to borrow back *two-thirds* of the whole amount she had paid in, together with *two-thirds* of all the profits she was entitled to, she bestirred herself and – prevented the forfeiture, and *now*, when there was no other help – no other hope under heaven – and the partner of her youth was dying of anxiety about his wife and his little ones, lo! they were provided for – and the husband's life saved – the broken heart healed – and the active man of business restored to usefulness; and all by the forecast of a young and fashionable, and up to a certain time, a frivolous and thoughtless woman.

P. S. Go thou and do likewise.

Arthur Scratchley, *Observations on Life Assurance Societies, and Savings Banks* (1851), excerpt

The Moral Urgency of Life Assurance.

[...] we would fain hope, that our readers are made sensible of the benefits to be derived, even as a mere matter of investment, from the application of the life assurance principle; and a few words may be suffered on its moral urgency, which alone affords earnest reasons why the system should be more extensively adopted.

It is needless to insist on that most necessary duty, which bids every man, both as a father and a husband, to promote the well-doing of his family, whilst he is alive to watch over them. With the exception of a solitary few, all men are conscious of its vital importance. It is a natural instinct or affection, intimately bound up with our existence, and often a source of intense pleasure. What we have rather to complain of, as deficient not in degree merely, but most often altogether, is, that, perhaps, even more binding duty, of providing for the *future* welfare of families. On the uncertainty of life we need not say anything; for, notwithstanding the incredulity of some men in respect to themselves, the *Bills of mortality* bear at once a startling testimony on the possible destruction of their hopes. And how many families are dependent entirely upon the income of a parent. How many have been thrown into irretrievable confusion by his sudden indisposition; – Or, still / oftener, how frequently has his sudden death reduced them to the most abject misery, so that their bread has been "dipped into tears," and they themselves brought "to sit on the margin of the grave."[1]

52. – It is true, many plans have been adopted by the more conscientious and thoughtful for the provision of their families. Perhaps they endeavoured to accumulate their savings by depositing them at interest in a bank, or they were laid aside for the purpose of being invested in stock. But nothing could be more precarious than either of these methods. There was the apprehension of sudden sickness, or sudden death; or the payment might be interrupted by circumstances, sometimes purely accidental, sometimes lying wholly in the conduct of the parties themselves. It was not unseasonably, therefore, that the first *life assurance office* was established in England; for the advantages offered were

immediate, evident, and most important. The great acquisition was this, that, instantly on effecting his assurance, or completing his first payment, however small, the individual secured the full object of his wishes; should he die at any moment after, his family were entitled to the *whole amount assured.*

53. – But it is remarkable, that, notwithstanding the manifest increase of late years in the numbers of life assurance societies, few individuals have, as yet, embraced the great advantage to be derived from them. It has been ascertained that, out of the very many families who are dependent entirely upon the mere *life* income of a parent or a husband, – that, in fact, out of upwards of thirty millions of people in the united kingdom, not more than two hundred and fifty thousand persons are assured, (excepting of course those who are members of mere benefit clubs, which mainly provide against sickness); and a large number of the policies effected in assurance companies are taken out as security in matters of business, not as provisions for families. Many reasons may be, however, assigned for this startling / fact. There appears to be a very great ignorance not only of the advantages which are afforded by the assurance system, but even of the very existence itself of such institutions. Even where there appears to be some knowledge, there yet exists an amount of prejudice, which, under the, now considered, too strict regulations of the more ancient companies might have been conceived, but certainly is not justified in the present day, and is altogether unworthy of these enlightened times. There are even a small party of silly *Illuminati* who view the system as irreligious, and consider it wrong to attempt to provide against the dispensations of Providence; but the feeling, which must be most taken into account, is that highly dangerous one of self-security,* which is so common – 'all men think all men mortal but themselves';[2] and that equally prevalent antipathy among older people to such subjects as are connected with death. Doubtless this last-mentioned feeling, more than would be imagined, deters men from the assurance of their lives; they will not engage in any duty which reminds them of their end; and, ashamed of a way of thinking, at once mean and contemptible, they invent, to satisfy their consciences, all sorts of petty excuses for the evasion of it.

54. – We remember a case, which has always appeared to us a melancholy instance of the evil that may arise from the omission of the important duty which we are advocating. It is that of a young man, a clergyman; – though married, and having a family, he had still the resources of a good living, amply sufficient for the most varied requirements. To profound scholarship, and the inexhaustible riches of a fine intellect, he added all those kindlier qualities of the heart, which would make a man estimable. But his character had its dark side too; his 'dazzling virtues' were not more numerous than his weaknesses. With thoughtlessness and

---

* See art. 36, page 39, for remarks on the experience of assurance societies in respect to premature deaths among sound lives.

irresolution he / lacked sound judgment; and it is not surprising, therefore, that he often took that course which was positively hurtful. Among other things, he had deferred, from day to day, the carrying into effect of a long contemplated intention to assure his life. Being in strong health, he was not sufficiently sensible of the precarious tenure of his existence, or of the common prudence of not leaving one day between the cognizance of a duty and the fulfillment thereof. This was the more unfortunate, as he was destined to leave this world at a period when it is most precious; when, for his children, all was laughter, buoyancy, and happiness. Of the solemn death-bed scene we will say nothing; yet, perhaps, he had quitted life with more peace, had he provided for his family.

Need we wonder that, when, in after years, 'the proud man's contumely'[3] had more than embittered the cold draught of poverty; – that, when, with the thousand natural ills which flesh is heir to, came the uncertainty of a precarious and toilsome existence, hard thoughts of that man fell even from the lips of his devoted wife? Need we wonder that, although gentle as any woman, yet she knew not how to repress at all times the murmurs of her children? Need we add, in fine, an account of her anxious watchings, of her endless toilings, her wasting melancholy; how she wept and struggled, struggled and wept, and, at last, was laid by the side of him, whose thoughtlessness had been the cause of all her sufferings.

The picture, we have here given, is not a mere outline, distinct perhaps, yet incapable of being filled up, – a sheer coinage of the brain; it is but a solitary example of a system which is loaded with evils the most palpable and pernicious:– so pernicious, that thousands upon thousands, we might say, of men's children are daily bearing testimony to its unfortunate consequences; but the most saddening point of reflection is, that, too frequently, the increase of their misery is in exact ratio with the extent of their merits. As they are the most virtuous and the most amiable, so does the blow of sudden change / from comparative affluence to penury fall the harder; and the more delicate the nurture of the children during the life-time of their thoughtless parent, the more painful do they feel the pressure of their altered circumstances. Oh, if every man, as a father and as a husband, were not only *conscious* of the duty which he owes to his family, but determined also to put into *practice* every expedient that might promote the exercise of it, how much harrowing misery would be spared to the unfortunate; what a large mass of moral and physical suffering could be obviated.

55. – But it will be objected by some that the "times are bad;" and that they are ill-able to afford so considerable a sum as would be necessary for the assurance of their lives. We would reply, that, even supposing they are unable to assure for the sum of £1000, or £700, or £500, – cannot they therefore secure £100, when this last can be obtained by the payment of little more than eighteenpence weekly? Of a truth, a life assurance society is adapted no less for the rich nobleman, than for

the tradesman; while the former may make use of its full benefits for the provision of the younger members of his family, it need not be said how much both of benefit and of happiness may accrue to the latter by the payment of the small sum above-mentioned. Wives and mothers should see to it; – should reflect that no delicacy of sentiment should stand in the way of that duty by which the future welfare of their children can be so greatly affected. If unwilling to add to their expenses, or to urge the husband and father to greater efforts, let them economise from their weekly expenditure; let them lay by sums, however small, which may be appropriated to the completion of the desired object. Let those, who have but recently entered the married state, bear this in mind equally with others, who may be surrounded with a family. Let them remember, that the payments of an assurance are so equitably graduated according to age on entry, that the earlier a man begins the discharge of this excellent duty, the less will / be his future payments, and the easier the continuance of the self-imposed economy. The old man at sixty would have to pay £6. 15s. 3d. a year for the same sum which would cost £4.3s.3d. a year to the man at fifty, or £2. 4s. 8d. a year to that of thirty (see Table 1, page 51[4]); and, where a participation in the profits of the society is purchased, instances are frequent where the allotment of Bonus, applied to the reduction of future payments, has, in policies begun when young, almost reduced to nothing the subsequent annual cost to the assurer.

56. – All, therefore, whose incomes are wholly dependent on their personal exertions, or upon their continuing in existence, should neglect no longer to lay aside a sufficient portion, by means of which some provision may be created for the maintenance of those they would leave behind them. The wretchedness of a family, reduced from easy circumstances to a painfully necessitous condition, which even though not equivalent to starvation, may deprive the widow of the means of educating her sons and daughters; of fitting them to earn their livelihood, and to contend with the competition of numerous others in similar positions, – that wretchedness, we repeat, can be prevented by comparatively so small an outlay, that the abstaining from a few indulgencies would give the head of the family the means of meeting it. To our mind, nothing can be more selfish than the manner in which thousands in good employment neglect altogether the facilities, which the life assurance system would afford to them. There might be some excuse for the deficiency of a provident spirit, if the only accumulation, which could be secured to a man's family, in the case of premature decease, were simply the amount of the actual savings themselves which he had put by; but, by the system of co-operation in question, he can secure not merely those savings, but the larger amount to which they would have accumulated in a long term of years. – Take the case of a man aged thirty, who lays aside £50 a-year from his / income. Suppose him to die unexpectedly, say in three years. If his savings had

been merely invested at interest, his family would receive little more than £150; but, if he had subscribed to an assurance company (the charge for which at age thirty is £2. 4s. 8d. per cent.) they would receive £2238, nearly. This example must speak for itself, but in the words of an able periodical devoted to the life assurance cause, we would add, that, 'although in the great number of instances in which men fail to insure their lives as a provision for their wives and children, the neglect arises from the difficulty of withdrawing from a limited income even the small sum requisite for the annual payment of premium, yet it cannot fail, to occur to every person anxious for the welfare of his family, that this very difficulty is the strongest argument that can be advanced in support of life insurance. If a man whose income arises solely from his exertions, or from any other source terminating with his existence, finds the whole of that income absorbed in sustaining his position in society, let him contemplate the dreadful situation of those who are dependent upon his labours, when cut off, by his decease, from their sole means of support. Who is there who would not abstract something from his present enjoyments in order to protect a beloved wife, and the affectionate offspring around him, from so frightful a state of dependence upon the cold charity of the world! When it is considered, indeed, by what* small increments of saving the means of insurance may be obtained, it / is surprising that any instance should exist in which it is not effected – a few tavern visits less, an occasional mislaying of the key of the wine cellar, a tight stopper in the spirit bottle, a water side visit put off till next year, a party omitted to be given, a slight forgetfulness of the length of time a coat or a silk gown has been in wear, and a score other things of the kind, present an ample variety of sources for furnishing the small annual sum requisite to place a family in security. Many men who have a strong perception of the importance of insuring their lives, unfortunately neglect to do so from the belief that in a little time they will be in a better position to do so – next year, trade may be more brisk, or an official salary may be

---

* For example:– The weekly payment for a £25 policy at age 36, would be only 3 1/4*d.*

One pint of ale per day costs about 1s. 6d. per week, or 3l. 18s. per annum, which would assure to a man, aged twenty-five, the sum of £200, whenever his death might occur. By a similar payment, a person aged forty-nine could secure to his widow or children the sum of £100, in like manner. By a resolution to forego an useless luxury, a lad might secure to himself, not long after attaining his majority, one hundred pounds! By a like saving, a person aged thirty-three could in fifteen years become possessed of £100.

A married couple, about middle age, by denying themselves the pint of beer which they usually take at dinner or supper, could secure to the survivor of the two, upon the death of the first, upwards of £100; or they might secure to a child of two years of age, a like sum when it came of age.

An ordinary smoker consumes fully one pennyworth of tobacco per day; but the sum thus spent in an useless and dirty habit, if applied in a proper manner by a person at the age of twenty-five, would secure to him £100 on his attaining the age of sixty years.

increased, or an old aunt may die – but next year brings with it its own necessities; and even if it did not, what peril is encountered in the delay? It should be borne in mind that people can only insure when they are in the most perfect state of health – a whitened tongue, or a quickened pulse, find no passport of admission to a life office; and who shall say he is secure, for a single hour, from some derangement of system, that may bring these symptoms upon him. What anxiety must he who is waiting for the proper moment to insure, sustain at every incipient approach of illness? The spasm he feels may be the herald of cholera – the sudden ache in the temple may be the courier of death.'[5]

57. – The insurance of life in all cases is wise – in many, absolutely necessary – in some, an imperative duty. How many of our readers, who at this moment possess a comfortable competency, would, in the event of death, leave their families in a state of destitution. How many family circles, the heads of which are in the receipt of a liberal salary, living in handsomely / furnished houses, and keeping excellent tables, would by a single death, be suddenly deprived of all, and doomed to penury and wretchedness. How many wives and children have exchanged their happy homes to become the inmates of union workhouses, from the neglecting of life assurance by that person through whose means they were enabled to live in comparative affluence.

58. – One word to the Insurance companies themselves, – the majority of their publications in support of life assurance have addressed themselves mainly to making an impression upon the minds of the middle and higher classes, and even there they only partially succeed in their object. The humble operatives, whose circumstances are more precarious, have not been addressed with the same anxiety to produce conviction. To the managers we would say that, if their object be truly to make life assurance universal, they must first remove, as far as the principle of the system will allow, many imperfections in the practice upon which they apply it. They must cease to consider that the industrial portion of the community are for ever to be exposed to leave their successors no better off than they themselves have been. They must induce the industrious mechanic, the small tradesman, and others in a similar position, to give the subject more careful consideration, as a matter coming home to themselves, and within the reach of their narrow resources; and we doubt not, that when they see existing obstacles removed, they will turn to the system with anxious desire.

Arthur Reade, 'Before the Wedding Ring', *Policy-holder: An Insurance Journal* (1885)

"AND so, Wedgewood has gone at last," I said to my friend Fairfield.

"Yes! poor fellow," be replied, "Southport did him a deal of good, but when he left Manchester for the South we all feared that he would never return. He had the best medical advice; but his was a hopeless case from the first."

"What family has he left?"

"A wife and four children."

"Are they provided for?"

"Alas! No! He was a very careful man and didn't trouble the tailors once in five years, and nobody ever saw him with a new hat; but all his savings went during his six months' illness."

"Was his life insured?"

"No! for the very simple reason that nobody would accept him when he wanted to insure. The fact is, when he was well his wife objected."

"His wife objected!" I said. "Do you mean to say that any woman in her senses would stop her husband from insuring his life?"

"Yes!" he replied, "it seems queer but it's true. Some women rush to the conclusion that their husbands are going to die; others think there is no necessity for *their* husbands to insure, because they have always had a good situation and are likely to have; to others, the money to be paid when the policy becomes a claim seems like the price of blood, and they could never, never touch it. I know a lady who opposed the insurance of her husband's life, and would not listen to such a thing. One day her husband's life was instantly dashed out. What is the sequel? The widow is dragging out a miserable existence, and her children have been taken away from her to be clothed, fed, and educated for cold charity's sake."

"She was a foolish woman," I remarked.

"Yes," said Fairfield, "but she is a type of thousands. Mrs. Wedgewood, for instance, was a woman of this character. Her husband was healthy when they were married; why, then, should *he* insure? She never dreamed of the possibility of *his* falling ill. When he recovered from a very serious illness she wanted him to insure; he did his best, poor fellow, to insure his life, but was rejected as a bad life."

"Well, then, if the man did all he could to insure his life, we must do something for his family. He did a great deal of work for the public good, although his zeal often outran his discretion in the extent of the labours which he undertook."

"Let us appeal to the public, by all means," said Mr. Fairfield.

"All right, we will begin with yourself. How much will you give?"

"I'll give £10, and here's my cheque."

"Thank you, and now we'll draw up an appeal to the public."

"And tell them," chimed in Fairfield, "that he took the most obvious means of providing for his family, but no insurance company would accept him. Don't tell them that if he had proposed before his illness he would doubtless have been accepted as a first-class life. With the record of his illness against him, it was impossible for any office to accept him."

The appeal, signed by a number of well-known men, went forth to the philanthropic public. All Wedgewood's friends were privately written to, and about £100 collected.

"A very small sum," he remarked.

"Yes," I replied. "The fact is, the public are being appealed to sadly too often on behalf of some minister or some public man who has lived up to his income, and left his family penniless at his death. Now, I do not know what you think of men who thus ignore their duties to their families."

"Well," he replied, "I think with St. Paul, 'He that provideth not for his own, and especially those of his own household, has denied the faith, and is worse than an infidel.'"[1]

"Precisely so. And what do you consider the best way of providing for a household?"

"The easiest, as well as the only way," replied Fairfield, "is by means of life insurance; for the moment a man has paid his premium his family becomes entitled to the amount for which he has insured, whenever death may occur."

"When is the best time to insure?"

"Why, certainly, when young. Life assurance is not always possible; therefore it should be secured when it is. The earlier a policy is taken out the better. *It should always come before the wedding ring.* I once heard the late George Dawson say, that if he had the power he would not suffer a young man to marry unless his life was insured; and I know many fathers who have refused to sanction the marriage of their daughters until the young men had given a proof of their love in the shape of an insurance policy.[2] Nay, more, a life insurance policy is a certificate of character and of health. It is a proof of forethought."

"Yes, it is," I admitted, "and if all fathers insisted upon the production of such a certificate before giving their consent to the marriage of their daughters, there would be fewer unhappy marriages and fewer destitute families. Death is a terrible thing under any circumstances; but its terrors are increased when a young man leaves a wife and children to the tender mercies of the world."

"Just so," said Mr. Fairfield, "and as charity begins at home, – may I ask whether you are insured?"

"What do you take me for?" I asked. "Why I insured when I got married, when I was barely twenty-one, and earning only a guinea a week; but an agent bothered me so much that I was obliged to insure, and I now feel thankful to him for bothering me."

"Then you insured to oblige the agent?"

"Not exactly; but you know I thought it would do some other day equally well, and when I could better afford."

"You were not alone," he said, "the tendency to put off insuring to a more 'convenient season' prevails to a very large extent among all classes. Some men plead that they cannot afford to insure when they spend more than the premium required in beer and tobacco; others say, 'wait till next birthday!' The thought that when that arrives, health, and even life itself, may be parted with, does not occur to their mind. As a matter of fact, all men think all men mortal but themselves; and those who seem the likeliest to live to a green old age are frequently cut off earlier than those who do not look so promising. The reason is, that the strong and healthy do not take enough care of themselves; whereas, the men who know their weak points husband their strength and respect the laws of health. I have mentioned that the best time to insure is in youth. As the late Dr. Norman Macleod put it, it is not a wise thing to defer assurance till a man's hair is becoming grey, for in an assurance office a man has to pay for his grey hairs."

"What office do you recommend a young man to insure in?"

"Well, I am not an assurance agent, but I can safely recommend my own office."

"Why did you insure in that office?"

"Because I believe it is conducted on a sound basis."

"What do you mean by a 'sound basis?'"

"I mean that its funds exceed its liabilities; that its expenses of management are moderate; and that the conditions attached to its policies are liberal. In joining an office it is important to remember that you may at some future time feel a difficulty in meeting your premiums, or even find it necessary to surrender / your policy, and you should, therefore, take care to select an office which would treat you liberally in such a case."

"Do you think life insurance a good investment?"

"Certainly. In a well managed office it may safely be said that no one under fifty, taking out a policy entitled to profits, contributes as much as he receives. As a matter of fact, it is only in exceptional cases of very old people that the premiums have been known to exceed the sum assured, including bonus additions."

"How can an office afford to pay more than it receives?"

"Because it invests the premiums, and owing to the interest which it makes upon its investments is thereby enabled to meet all claims."

"But I don't want to propose. Didn't I tell you that I am already assured?"

"But are you insured for a sufficient amount? You told me that you insured when you were twenty-one. Since then your responsibilities have increased. Have you thought how far the present assurance will serve as a provision in the event of your death"?

"Yes, I know I am not sufficiently covered, and I will at once take out an additional policy, because I am more than ever convinced of its value; and I will urge others to insure their lives, as during the last ten years, I have seen many of my friends cut off in the prime of life, and their families have had to face a cruel world almost penniless and friendless."

BENEFIT SOCIETIES VERSUS SAVING BANKS AND INSURANCE COMPANIES: AN ADDRESS TO THE MEMBERS OF BENEFIT SOCIETIES AND THE PUBLIC IN GENERAL (1822)

Benefit Societies versus Saving Banks and Insurance Companies: An Address to the Members of Benefit Societies and the Public in General, Showing the Utility that Benefit Societies are to the Community at Large – the Assistance They Are to the Already Overburdened Poor's Rates – the Contrast between a Benefit Society and an Insurance Company – also, the Deception, Pains, and Penalties of the Latter, and the Necessity of All Classes Encouraging Benefit Societies in Preference to Saving Banks or Insurance Companies. By the Founder of the St. Ann's Union, True Sons of Equity, Oxford Good Intent, Provident Fund, &c. 2nd ed. To be had of J. Beswick, 2, Brown's Buildings, Stanhope Street (London, 1822).

John James Beswick, the likely author of this pamphlet, was typical of an early nineteenth-century British 'clubman' or friendly society member: he was the secretary of the St Ann's Union, which held its meetings in the Crown and Barley Mow, a pub in Gray's Inn Lane, and he helped found three other self-help societies[1] catering to working men, none of which had more than a few dozen members. Small, congenial and informal, friendly societies offered a version of self-help that was markedly distinct from savings banks and life insurance offices, both in the nature of the provision against contingencies and the manner in which they delivered that service. Formed largely among specific occupational groups, their main focus was to provide for members when illness or injury prevented them from earning a wage; many also saved up dues to pay pensions to members when they grew too old to work. With a few exceptions, they were self-governing bodies, proudly proclaiming their independence in rituals and parades.[2]

Upper-class response to benefit clubs was ambivalent at best. Ratepayers saw the virtue in clubs that might reduce dependence on poor relief, but they also tended to identify clubs with political radicalism, intemperance and a dangerous ignorance of actuarial principles. As a result, early friendly society legislation in Britain combined mild encouragement (in particular, tax-exempt status and the power to lodge their funds with the National Debt Office) with mild surveillance (e.g. requiring clubs to report their rules, which needed to include an approved actuarial plan).[3]

In contrast to friendly societies, savings banks in Britain mainly grew out of charitable efforts by upper-class reformers, most notably the Tory MP George Rose. By making it easier for workers to gain access to their money, they presented saving and spending as complementary virtues, which in tandem would reinforce the development of a thriving consumer culture and a loyal populace. Although a series of supportive laws between 1817 and 1850 spurred rapid growth of this sector, a wave of embezzlement scandals led to the establishment in 1861 of a competing state savings bank run by the Post Office, which primarily preached thrift to working-class children. The surviving charitable banks, which were especially successful in Scotland and Yorkshire, supplemented this new appeal by encouraging the establishment of 'penny banks'. The Post Office attracted £135 million in deposits by 1900, at which point their voluntary counterparts held £51 million in working-class savings.[4]

Prior to 1850, working-class life insurance in Britain occupied a space somewhere between friendly societies and savings banks. Commercial insurers that targeted working families initially assumed that workers needed to be persuaded to insure for their own good, lest they be tempted to squander their savings prematurely and thereby leave their relatives penniless. This was the message of companies like the General Benefit Insurance Company (est. 1820), the National Provident (1835) and the Provident Clerks (1840), all of which took advantage of special privileges by registering as friendly societies, but which otherwise operated much like other offices that appealed to higher-class customers. Most of these firms were successful enough to prosper through the end of the century, but further waves of start-ups in the 1840s and 1850s failed to make any additional dents into their chosen market.[5] The real explosion in British working-class life insurance, as will be discussed later in this volume, came after the 1860s with the rise of 'industrial' companies like the Prudential, Pearl and Refuge.

Notes

1. The four benefit clubs mentioned as being founded by the author were all based in London; the True Sons of Equity lasted from 1814 to 1878 and had between 100 and 200 members in the 1860s (this is probably the club referred to in the pamphlet that formed in 1814). The other three clubs still existed in 1837 but did not survive into the 1860s.
2. S. Cordery, *British Friendly Societies, 1750–1914* (New York: Palgrave Macmillan, 2003), pp. 12–64.
3. Ibid., pp. 85–96.
4. Gosden, *Self-Help*, pp. 209–25, 256–7; P. L. Payne, 'The Savings Bank of Glasgow, 1836–1914', in P. L. Payne (ed.), *Studies in Scottish Business History* (New York: Kelley, 1967), pp. 152–86, on pp. 175–80.
5. Alborn, *Regulated Lives*, pp. 203–5.

Benefit Societies versus Saving Banks and Insurance Companies: An Address to the Members of Benefit Societies and the Public in General (1822)

MAN by nature being subject to various diseases, cannot supply his own wants without the assistance of his fellow-creatures. A conviction of this well known axiom first united men together in bonds of friendship. But as affliction often prevents man from following his daily labour (without which few men can support themselves or families), it became necessary to seek some resource, that would preserve that sort of independent spirit, which every human being should endeavour to promote, and prevent the degradation and humiliation of applying to a parish for relief.

A consideration of these circumstances, caused *Friendly*, or *Benefit Societies*, to be instituted; the nature and beneficial advantages of which, being so generally known, the Legislature gave them all the encouragement possible. In 1793 an Act was passed for their protection; and many, in various parts of the kingdom, were commenced, varying their payments and benefits, as suited the pecuniary circumstances of their members.

The good effect of Benefit Societies, in relieving parishes, may be seen by the returns made to Parliament in 1803, in which it appears, that the number of persons belonging to Benefit Societies was 704,350, and the number of persons permanently and occasionally relieved in England and Wales was 725,566, including children; if the children were deducted from this number, without doubt the number in Societies would exceed those relieved. The expence / of the above to the parishes (independent of their earnings, and the charitable donations left to each parish for their relief) was £4,033,444 14s 2d. The poor's rates to pay this sum were excessive; but let it be remembered what they would have been, had not Benefit Societies been in existence!

A better proof cannot be given than a statement of the following fact. A Society, averaging 460 members, in the course of seven years, paid annually on an average £1150, being at the rate of £2 10s per member; therefore, allowing for the variation in the benefits of different Societies, – say two-thirds of the above as the average, – and taking only the number in Benefit Societies in 1803, there would be annually paid by Societies the sum of £1,173,916 13s 4d. This seasonable relief, in aid of the poor's rates, we should conceive, would be a grand object with all classes to encourage.

These laudable institutions, for a series of years, were supported; and might have gone on with every advantage, had they been left, uninterruptedly, to proceed with those benevolent views for which they were originally intended; but in 1816, the idea of a number of men congregating together, was not deemed proper, there being a possibility of their conversing on other topics than those immediately connected with the Society's concerns; a remedy was therefore sought for, and some of *those*, who were particularly *strenuous* in procuring the passing of the various Acts *in favour of Benefit Societies*, now deserted their offspring, and *adopted* the novel scheme of *Saving Banks*.[1] This, for a time, was a serious check to Benefit Societies, as many healthy members left them, and placed the amount of their contributions into those Banks; considering / that, as they had not been, probably they never might be, afflicted: therefore they could save *all* the money they paid to a society, and use it for some other purpose. The consequent result of this, was soon experienced – Societies being left with the heavily afflicted members, the stock was shortly expended, and the Societies were dissolved. In such cases, what became of the members? – Many were compelled, if affliction continued, to apply to the parish for relief. A part of those who had left Societies, and placed their money in these Banks, now, in turn, met with affliction; they then had recourse to their own fund. But alas! in a few weeks, they drew the contributions of a year or two, or the whole of their savings: their illness continuing, they, as well as others, were compelled to seek relief from their parish. When recovered, many saw their fatal error, and again cheerfully joined a Benefit Society.

The Saving Bank system therefore not being complete, other measures were speedily adopted; for in July, 1819, a further Act was made[2] (to which all future Societies must conform) – the restrictions in which are such, that very few Benefit Societies are likely to be thereafter established. Suffice it to say, that before a Society can be established, *a memorial must be presented* to the Justices *at the Quarter Sessions for leave* so to do; the memorial must also have *the signature of at least three persons to be Trustees* of the Society, the majority of whom must be *substantial householders assessed to the relief of the poor upon a sum of not less than £50. Householders of this description are not likely to join a* BENEFIT SOCIETY, therefore the Trustees very probably will be strangers. But mark – when these Trustees are once elected, *they cannot / be removed from their office*, though disapproved of by the whole Society, *without their own, (the Trustees) consent*, unless application is made to the Sessions, and the *Justices approve of the removal.*

Soon after this Act had passed, the town was covered with bills, and lottery-like puffs, stating that an Institution was about to be formed[3] far preferable to Benefit Societies. Prospectuses soon followed, which were sent forth in great quantities; couched in language which, no doubt, was intended to crush Benefit Societies (since which others have commenced), and by such means prevent (if possible) hard-working men from enjoying a pint of porter with each other, once in a month, or a quarter of a year. But these, as well as Saving Banks, will probably not have the desired effect. These Insurance Companies boast of their immense capitals, and their patronage; but were the patrons of one of them applied to generally, from the gentlemen named, it might be questioned if they knew much of the concern; as, from their public characters, oil and water might as soon unite, as such persons be expected to associate together. But neither this, nor any other Hydra* need be feared, if members of Benefit Societies are but firm and united; for when their system is exposed, their career will, most probably, be of short duration.

It will now be necessary to explain some of their views, in order that members of Benefit Societies may not be drawn into their snares; it therefore requires to be shown what these Insurance Companies are, and the urgent necessity of all classes supporting Benefit Societies in preference to them, it appearing to be their object to deprive / the tradesman, mechanic, labourer, and others, from having any immediate controul over their own property. But it may not be long before they find that they have made false calculations; their payments and restrictions being so enormous and arbitrary, compared with those of Benefit Societies, that, in all probability, many will forego the blessings, or comforts, of the Hydra, and return to their old Society, or some other.

In the introduction to the Companies' rules it is said, that *they expect* part of their *plan* will, in all probability, be *pirated* by some of the crafty managers of *Enrolled Benefit Societies*. But let it be asked, if this *monster* has not *notoriously pirated* from *the general rules of Societies, with the exception of the heavy contributions, that the Hydra requires to satisfy its voracious appetite?* It is also said, that the fines and extra contributions are great, and are a long complained-of grievance, and only profitable to secretaries, and other officers, who are a great expence to Benefit Societies.

As the *Hydra has examined Benefit Societies*, it may, of course, *be examined in its turn*, to see if it has not *extravagant expences*, and such as a Benefit Society would never expect to provide for. There is a large office, fitted up with a counter and desks, for a MR. SECRETARY, and it may not be wrong to say, house rent, coals and candles, with a gentleman's salary besides. There is also a number of clerks, whether wanted or not. But the *Hydra* conceives *these trifles* will be overlooked, when speaking of other Secretaries. There are also *Doctors to pay*, and these gentlemen seldom go far or near without being well paid. They have their regular *Solitors* [sic], from which it may be inferred, that they do not expect / their concern to be con-

---

* As the Insurance Companies boast of many heads, it may not be inapplicable to call them by this name,

ducted without *law suits;* but whether the Solicitors' services will be required or not, they are in readiness, and, it may be presumed, will *be paid,* as lawyers seldom work for nothing. But these expences, it is supposed, must not be noticed. Then there is the Patron, President, Vice-Presidents, Treasurer, Trustees, and Directors; (mighty great sounds to be sure!) but what controul has any of the members over them? When you pay your money, you must withdraw, and may, if you can, believe that it is carried on at a small expence; but if endowed with rationality, you will very probably consider that the *expence* must be *very great.* The printing alone, in announcing where this Hydra is to be seen, must be enormous.

It also attempts to persuade you, there is *no entrance money.* It is true it does not call it entrance money. But ask common sense, if any one engages for benefits in this Insurance, for which, by the tables, they are to pay 5s 5d per month, – and upon being admitted, they have to pay a month's money, – *what can this* 5s 5d *be called but entrance money?* A member *when free,* has to take out *a policy* for himself and his wife, for which he has to pay a *stamp duty.*[4] Does not this again add to the entrance money? The Company also wishes to make it appear, that the *payments* to it are *less* than to *Benefit Societies.* This is *not the case;* the *tables* for payment *prove it;* it is there stated, that a person 33 years of age, to receive the following benefits,

In Sickness, per week	£1 0 0
Superannuated, ditto	0 5 0
At a Member's Death	20 0 0
At a Member's Wife's ditto	10 0 0 /

must pay 5s 5d per month, which is 16s 3d per quarter. – *O how wonderfully low, for the above benefits!!!*

Again, referring to the boasted *Capital,* may not this be *a shadow?* for, if *real,* surely the subscribers to it must expect an *interest* for their *money,* – not one word of which is mentioned; and if the Company is established (as the Hydra states) to prevent artful and designing men forming Societies to suit their own purposes, *why do they wish for more contributions than are likely to meet the claims?* which experience proves to be the case by the following Societies. One was commenced in 1812, to which members were to pay 2s 6d per month, and contributions to births, deaths, &c., and to allow as follows:–

In Sickness, per week	£1 0 0
Superannuated, ditto	0 5 0
In a Workhouse, ditto	0 3 6
In Prison for Debt, ditto	0 5 0
Member's Death	20 0 0
Member's Wife's ditto	15 0 0
Member's Wife's Lying-in	3 0 0
Child's Death	3 0 0
At a Loss by Fire	15 0 0

The contributions, and fines of every description, paid to this Society by one of the members (who entered on the first night) to December 1821, being nine years and a half, were £25 9s 9d, which averages 13s 5d *per quarter* for all the above benefits. Is this not *less than the Insurance Company?*

Another Society was commenced in 1814, to which members were to pay 2s 6d per month, and contributions to births, deaths, &c., and to allow the following benefits:–

In Sickness, /

In Sickness, per week	£0 18 0
Superannuated, ditto	0 5 0
In a Workhouse, ditto	0 3 6
In Prison for Debt, ditto	0 4 0
If drawn for the Militia	2 10 0
At a Member's Death	18 0 0
At a Member's Wife's ditto	9 0 0
At a Member's Wife's Lying-in	2 2 0
At a Child's Death	2 2 0
At a Loss by Fire	15 0 0

The above benefits are less than the before-mentioned Society, and so are the members' contributions. One of its members has paid, for contributions and fines of every description, from the first night to Jan. 1822, being seven years and three quarters, £15 2s 4d, which averages 9s 9d per quarter. Is this not *less, and more Benefits allowed, than in the Insurance Company?* These two Societies have paid in the above time £3664 16s 11d for various claims, and still have a surplus in hand of £932 14s sterling money.

If this is not sufficient proof, the following will leave no doubt upon any one's mind. A Society was commenced in 1815, to which members were to pay *no extra contributions* whatever (and from which the Hydra probably has taken his plan), the monthly payments were fixed at 3s 4d, and the following benefits were to be allowed:–

In Sickness, per week	£1 1 0
Superannuated, ditto	0 7 0
At a Member's Death	20 0 0
At a Member's Wife's ditto	10 0 0

One of the members, who entered on the first night, has never served any office, but paid for his omissions, which to Feb. 1822, (being six years and a half,) has amounted / to £1 6s, – this is 4d per month, making his total payment 3s 8d *per month*. After paying all claims, this Society has *a surplus of £445*, and only 85 members. *This* having been *gained by so few members at 3s 8d, what is likely to be the gain of the Insurance Company,* who require you, *for less Benefits,* to pay 5s 5d *per month!*

As a further proof of the enormous sum which is required by the Insurance Company, to insure for funeral money, a plan was submitted, a few years ago, to a Benefit Society of about 400 members, to allow an extra benefit at the funeral of a member, in addition to their regular allowance, by the members paying 1s per lunar month for the same (taking all ages). The additional benefit was to be £24. To show what was likely to be the result, the exact number of members, in each quarter, from 1809 to 1813, was taken, being five years previous, when the amount from them as above (at 1s per lunar month, for all ages) would have been £1158 1s. The number of deaths in the same time was 16. This, allowing £24 for each, would have been £384, which, deducted from the £1158 1s collected, would have left in hand £774 1s, by this simple collection! With the Hydra, or puffing and boasting Institution, for an equal number of all ages, and to allow £25 at a death, (which would have been £16 more to pay,) they require 2s 0 1/2d per month! If the like had occurred with them in the above five years, their gain, (deducting the extra £16,) would have been £1964 7s 1/2d.

The foregoing facts, the correctness of which is incontrovertible, it is trusted will be sufficient to show the public at large that Benefit Societies are far preferable to Insurance Companies. But if enough has not been already said on the subject, let their *pains and penalties* be *described* / and *explained*. In the first place, you cannot insure for more than *three-fourths* of your average *earnings*, a *certificate* of which is to be *produced*. On admission, you must *sign* a *déclaration* of your *trade or calling*; and should you, at any time after, *help a friend*; or, by chance, for want of employ in your regular business, work at *any thing else*, till your work comes in; and during that time meet with an accident, or become ill, *no benefit whatever* will be allowed you. If you are taken ill while at your regular employ, and your shopmates are willing to give you a sixpence, or make a *collection* to assist you, it must *not be received*, nor any *relief from your trade club*, or *any other fund whatever*, without deducting the amount from the sum allowed by the Company. Should you not conform to this, and it be afterwards known, *exclusion* from the Company will be the result. Should any person be permanently *disabled*, by loss of sight or limb, or through apoplexy, paralysis, or otherwise, they are *immediately* placed on the *superannuated* list, by which they are deprived of three-fourths of the allowance (at least for some time). *If*, while receiving their benefit, you wish to *go out*, you cannot do it without a *certificate* from your overseer, the *doctor*, in which is to be stated where you are going to, and the time you will return; and *should you, while out, go a greater distance than, or in a contrary direction to, the place named*, or shall *not return at the time specified therein*, or *drink in a public-house, or any part of the premises, for either offence you will be excluded*. When *afflicted* there is *no one* to *bring* you your *money*; so that, far or near, you must fetch it, or be *at the expence of sending for it*. If you omit to pay within fourteen days after your *quarter* becomes *due* – of which you have *no notice* to inform you of your danger – *all benefits / are immediately withheld.* In short, the plans of this Monster are so surrounded with snares, that few, when claiming benefit, can escape them; and there is but little or no chance of members saving themselves from being *excluded,* there being *no arbitration or appeal*; nor can any one be re-entered, without the consent of the Board of Directors.

Having thus described the deception, pains, and penalties, of one Institution, little need be said upon the others. The restrictions and payments to them are a shade lighter: the contributions for funeral money being one halfpenny per month less for each sum.

From this plain statement of facts, it is hoped that the *preference* will hereafter be given to well regulated *Benefit Societies:* and those who are now members of Benefit Societies will keep so, and endeavour to recommend as many as they can to join them. Those who have hitherto neglected to make a provision for the day of affliction, would do well to examine the various articles of Benefit Societies, and join one where they can take upon themselves any office they please, and where they can see how their money is expended.

It is stated by these Institutions, that Benefit Societies frequently dissolve, leaving the members destitute, after having paid in their contributions for a series of years. It is true, many have so done: but what was the cause of all this? It is well known, that formerly Societies consisted of only 50 or 60 members, and no more were admitted, although many young and healthy men offered. In a few years, affliction and death overtook several, consequently they wanted members; but then no one would join them, their numbers continuing to decrease, and their funds lessening in proportion. A few deaths swept away the remainder / of the funds, and the Society was necessitated to dissolve. This, in all probability, would not have been the case, had there been a continual supply of a few members, as their contributions, until free, would have been a support to the outgoings.

Another cause which often reduces Societies is, that from want of employ, many are, though reluctantly, compelled to leave, not being able to clear the books; to remedy this evil, it would be a praise-worthy act, for the members of each Society, to form a fund, to assist those who may be so situated. This is done in several, and generally approved of.

Having thus endeavoured to explain and show, that *Benefit Societies* are *less expence,* and ought to be *encouraged in preference to Saving Banks or Insurance Companies,* it is hoped that it will, when read, have the desired effect. Parish Officers, and others, would do well, were they to offer premiums for a certain number of members; in which case it would assist the poor-rates, and thereby in time reduce them. These rates, in England and Wales, in 1820, amounted to £7,322,591. 7s.

LIFE INSURANCE AND SAVINGS BANKS
IN AMERICA

A. B. Johnson,[1] 'The Relative Merits of Life Insurance and Savings Banks', *Hunt's Merchants' Magazine and Commercial Review* (January 1851), pp. 670–7.

Joseph B. Collins,[2] 'Life Insurance', *Hunt's Merchants' Magazine and Commercial Review* (February 1852), pp. 196–8.

Savings banks emerged in the United States somewhat later than in Britain, but with similarly philanthropic trappings: the Philadelphia Saving Fund Society (est. 1816) and New York's Bank for Savings (1819) both targeted the growing class of low-income workers as their primary clientele. As in Britain, the emphasis among philanthropists broadened over the course of the century to inculcate the saving habit in children as well as adults: the Penny Provident Fund in New York attracted over 100,000 depositors by 1900 by selling stamps to the city's children.[3] Most state legislatures followed British precedent by capping the level of deposits, in an effort to limit savings bank customers to the working classes. In contrast to Britain, where these laws were generally effective at shunting middle-class deposits to commercial banks, many American savings banks continued to attract deposits from wealthier customers.[4] This was the case for A. B. Johnson's Ontario Bank in upstate New York, and it was also the case for Boston's first savings bank, the Provident Institution for Savings, which quickly became a major player in the city's financial dealings.[5]

In contrast to Britain, where debates between savings banks and life insurance companies subsided after the 1840s, American advocates of these two forms of thrift continued to wage fierce battle throughout the nineteenth century. One reason for this was that savings banks in the United States continued to target the same middle-class and lower-middle-class breadwinners who were being courted by life insurance companies, whereas the largest customer base for the Post Office Savings Bank and its voluntarist competitors in Britain after 1850 was women and children. Another reason related to the much later appearance in the United States of mutual life insurance, which only took hold in the 1840s, after savings banks were firmly established. In Britain, in contrast, the Equitable had entrenched the idea of mutual life insurance by 1800, and even most joint-stock companies were sharing part of their surplus with policyholders by 1840. As a result British life insurers did not feel a need to protest as loudly as their American counterparts regarding their advantages relative to savings banks.

Notes

1. Alexander Bryan Johnson (1786–1867) emigrated from England to Utica, New York, in 1801 and founded the Utica Insurance Company in 1815. After the state revoked his charter for that firm in 1818 on the grounds that it unlawfully combined banking and insurance, he became president of the Utica branch of the Ontario Bank (the head office of which was based in Canandaigua, NY, 100 miles west of Utica), a position he held until 1857. Besides writing several books and articles on banking, he also published widely on the philosophy of language. On his life, see C. L. Todd and R. Sonkin, *Alexander Bryan Johnson, Philosophical Banker* (Syracuse, NY: Syracuse University Press, 1977). Johnson reprinted this essay in *A Guide to the Right Understanding of our American Union; or, Political, Economical and Literary Miscellanies* (New York: Derby and Jackson, 1857), pp. 263–76.
2. Joseph Budd Collins (1794–1867) was a founding trustee of the Mutual of New York from 1845 and its president between 1850 and 1853, before taking over as president of the United States Life Insurance Company of New York until his death.
3. J. Schwartz, *Fighting Poverty with Virtue: Moral Reform and America's Urban Poor, 1825–2000* (Bloomington, IN: Indiana University Press, 2000), pp. 46–9.
4. Murphy, *Investing in Life*, p. 166; T. Alborn, *Conceiving Companies: Joint-Stock Politics in Victorian England* (London: Routledge, 1998), pp. 137–40.
5. B. Farrell, *Elite Families: Class and Power in Nineteenth-Century Boston* (Albany, NY: State University of New York Press, 1993), pp. 49–52. For more detail on American savings banks, see R. D. Wadhwani, 'Citizen Savers: The Family Economy, Financial Institutions, and Social Policy in the Northeastern US from the Market Revolution to the Great Depression' (PhD dissertation, University of Pennsylvania, 2002).

A. B. Johnson, 'The Relative Merits of Life Insurance and Savings Banks', *Hunt's Merchants' Magazine and Commercial Review* (1851)

FREEMAN HUNT, ESQ., *Editor of the Merchants' Magazine, etc.*

DEAR SIR:– A clergyman, possessed of only a small annual salary, inquired recently of me, the comparative merits of Life Insurance and deposits in Savings Banks, as a provision for his wife and children against his death, superannuation, or loss of health. The following thoughts are the result, and you may insert them in your valuable Magazine, if they will interest any of your numerous readers. Life is so short, and man's actions so diversified, that every man founds many of his practices on precepts he has never investigated, and on examples he has never tested; hence, disquisitions on conduct are like ready-made clothes, they may not fit a wearer as well as garments made to his measure, but they are better than nudity. Nor need we be over-scrupulous in publishing our disquisitions, from any fear that we may unconsciously promulgate error. Providence has provided for such infirmity of our judgment, by so organizing us, intellectually, that speculative error can never be engrafted ineradicably on our thoughts, any more than the Siamese twins can propagate their physical deformity on human bodies. Very respectfully, your obedient servant,
  A. B. JOHNSON.

LIFE INSURANCE POSSESSES MANY OF THE ELEMENTS OF GAMBLING – MEN NEED THE COERCION OF NECESSITY, NOT THE ANODYNE OF SECURITY – WHATEVER SUPPLIES THE OFFICE OF THRIFT SUPERCEDES THRIFT – A MAN'S PERFORMANCES ARE GRADUATED BY HIS EFFORTS – EVERY MAN'S EFFORTS ARE GRADUATED BY HIS NECESSITIES – LIFE INSURANCE SUBSTITUTES A REMOTE GOOD IN PLACE OF A PRESENT EXIGENCY – LIFE INSURANCE IS UNFAVORABLE TO DOMESTIC PURITY – SAVINGS BANKS ARE AS CONDUCIVE TO THRIFT AS LIFE INSURANCE IS TO UNTHRIFT – ACCUMULATION IS A MORE SALUTARY RELIANCE AGAINST WANT THAN LIFE INSURANCE – TO TEACH THE POOR SELF-DEPENDENCE IS A BETTER CHARITY THAN ALMS –

THE EXPENDITURE OF MONEY IS THE MOST TO NOBLE OF ITS USES – THE
SLOW ACCUMULATION OF PROPERTY PRODUCES BETTER MORAL EFFECTS
THAN THE SUDDEN ACQUISITION OF PROPERTY – SAVINGS BANKS SHOULD
PAY DEPOSITORS AS MUCH INTEREST AS PRACTICABLE, ETC.

LIFE INSURANCE POSSESSES MANY OF THE ELEMENTS OF GAMBLING.

The characteristic of gambling consists in the absence of mutual benefit to the players. So in life insurance, no party thereto will usually gain, except at the loss of the correlative party. The chance of gain is also adverse to the insured, as is demonstrated by the large surplus profits which life insurance companies announce the possession of; and which profits, like the foot-prints around a slaughter-house, may admonish those who are entering that the current inwards exceeds greatly the current outwards. Life insurance is promoted by the same artifice as lotteries, – the publication of every case where an adventurer dies soon after the commencement of his insurance: while nothing is said where the insured abandons his policy in disgust, or from sickness, poverty, or inadvertence, after having distressed himself for years, by annual premiums; – nor where a person pays much more than his heirs are to receive back on his death. A gentleman of this city, who became married at the age of twenty-five years, and whose support consisted of a small annuity, insured five thousand dollars on his life, at an annual premium of eighty dollars, which he could badly spare.

As the premium is paid in advance, it at the end of the year, amounted, with legal interest, to	$85 60
He then paid another	80 00
The interest on which, with the interest on the former $85 60, was	11 59
Making, at the end of two years	$177 19 /

Should he continue the process twenty-four years, he will have paid, in principal and interest, $5,038 86, being $38 86 more than his widow is to receive at his death; but he is young and robust, and should he live till he shall become seventy-five years old, his payments, and compound interest thereon, will amount to more than $37,000; – consequently, after his widow shall receive the stipulated $5,000, his loss on the transaction will be $32,000.

MEN NEED THE COERCION OF NECESSITY, NOT THE ANODYNE OF SECURITY.

But gambling lures men from industry, frugality, and accumulation, by hopes of gain, through processes less slow than these, and less self-denying; and in this result, also, life insurance assimilates with gambling. "Eat, drink, and be merry, for to-morrow we die," and a life insurance will provide for our family, is the tendency of life insurance, whether conducted by corporations which catch large adventurers, or by clubs that catch humble people, or by health societies, that wring from manual laborers their pettiest surplus earnings. To paralyze a man's efforts, no surer means can be devised, than companies and clubs which shall care for him in sickness, bury him when dead, and provide for his widow and orphans. By like influences, the heirs of rich men rarely exhibit self-denial in expenditures, or energy in business, and become drones in society. Necessity is nature's expedient to vanquish man's love of ease. Providence intends that we shall take care of the future by taking care of the present, and take care of our descendants by taking care of ourselves; just as a horse takes care of his hind steps, by taking heed where he places his fore feet.

WHATEVER SUPPLIES THE OFFICE OF THRIFT SUPERCEDES THRIFT.

Ignorant of human nature is he who believes punishment can be wholesomely disconnected from crime, evil from vice, or poverty from anything but self-denial. If, like our Indians, we possessed no artificial melioration of pauperism, we, like them, should possess no voluntary paupers. The Bavarian government punishes, not only beggars, but persons who give alms, either in money or victuals.[1] No man is so reckless as to remain in bed, when the house in which he is lying is on fire; but he may reside in a dilapidated house till it fall and crush him, if the catastrophe is not imminent. So, if no life insurance would provide for our families, after our decease, no health insurance or club would provide for ourselves during disease, and bury us decently when dead, we should provide for these purposes by self-denying accumulations.

A MAN'S PERFORMANCES ARE GRADUATED BY HIS EFFORTS.

A civilized man's wants are numerous, an Indian's, comparatively few; hence, the civilized man labors more than the savage, and thence proceeds the difference in their performances. Every man's productions will, ordinarily, be thus proportioned to his efforts, therefore, some governments stimulate late efforts by protective duties and honorary distinctions; but where a man aspires to only present necessaries, and to a club for assistance in sickness, and a life insurance for his widow and orphans, he will accomplish only what he aspires to. A man's efforts dilate, like the atmosphere, in proportion to the vacuum which the efforts are required to fill; hence, the man who strives for present affluence, as his only provision against sickness and death, will find his efforts expand with his aspirations, and his accomplishments will increase / with his efforts. These principles are true of states and nations. The federal government refused to construct the Erie Canal, and, thereby, induced the State of New York to invoke its own energies, from whence soon proceeded the Erie Canal. A long train of kindred public works immediately followed, by reason, that when men discover their own efficiency, they continue the exercise of it after the occasion by which it was originally induced. The conflagrations of San Francisco[2] have been severally succeeded by a new city of increased solidity; and the mechanics of that region, acting under the excitement of great demand for labor, and high remunerative wages, seem to e a race of giants; though, when driven, by lack of encouragement, from our Atlantic cities, they went out a race of pigmies. Men are, however, slow to learn, and our States are continually importuning Congress for improvements of rivers and harbors, and, thereby, tranquilizing State aspirations, that would otherwise soon accomplish the desired improvements.

EVERY MAN'S EFFORTS ARE GRADUATED BY HIS NECESSITIES.

What the poor expend in tobacco we lament, forgetting that men labor by only the coercion of wants, and that Diogenes, who disciplined himself to live without wants, lived without labor also. Tobacco, and other coarse superfluities, perform for the poor what equipages and gorgeous furniture perform for the rich. Our organization is so admirably adapted to keep us active, by the coercion of wants, that new wants arise in every man spontaneously, as fast as he can satisfy old ones. Napoleon, in the zenith of his prosperity, craved more dominion, with an intensity augmented by his present possessions, instead of being thereby mitigated. The design of Providence, to thus keep men active, by the pressure of wants, life insurance and assistance clubs counteract. All sumptuary laws contain the same error, and all Malthusian restraints on marriage. Railroads would never have been invented, had we coercively limited the operations of every man to his local neighborhood, as a means of obviating the disadvantages of distance. To evolve good out of apparent evil, is one of the most striking characteristics of Providence; and one which man's short sightedness is continually endeavoring to counteract, by diminishing his wants instead of gratifying them by increasing efforts.

LIFE INSURANCE SUBSTITUTES A REMOTE GOOD IN PLACE OF A PRESENT EXIGENCY.

A man who labors to purchase an insurance on his life for the future benefit of his widow and orphans, cannot command the energy which he would feel were he laboring for his own present affluence:– distance of time operating on man's energies like distance of space operates on the attraction of a magnet. This effect of distance every man feels when, in the midst of health, he indites his last will and testament. Aware of this natural difficulty, when a celebrated English judge wrote his own will, he took ten guineas from his purse and laid them on a table, that he might stimulate his intellect by the semblance of a present interest. And let no man suppose that life insurance is not obstructive of present affluence. A man's early annual savings are ordinarily small, and whether he is to grow affluent or remain poor, depends, usually, on whether he employs his small savings in processes of increase, or extinguishes them in annual premiums of life insurance, or some other way; just as whether a man shall make money in the purchase of wheat, wool, or cotton, depends, usually, on petty savings of expense in the management of his purchases, rather than on any great increase of / marketable price, between the time of his purchase and sales. Imagine, now, a father who shall keep himself poor, by an annual drain of his savings to some life insurance, for the remote benefit of his wife. He dies, and she commences a like process for the benefit of her children. She dies, and the children severally begin the same process for the benefit of their descendants; and thus, like a cat in chase of its tail, the world is made to revolve round a life insurance in pursuit of an always future competency, instead of a present affluence; whereby a less motive is continually substituted for a greater.

LIFE INSURANCE IS UNFAVORABLE TO DOMESTIC PURITY.

In England, mothers have been convicted of murdering their infants to obtain some petty sum which certain clubs bestow for funeral expenses on members whose children die.

Not long since, a man in London killed with strychnia his wife's sister, after having induced her to insure her life largely for the benefit of his wife.[3] The motive to such murders is so operative, that English companies reject all insurances when the applicant cannot show that the beneficiary possesses as much interest in the life of the insured as he is to gain by his death. If our insurance companies are not equally cautious, every life policy which contravenes the precaution, is the tender of a bounty for the commission of murder, and the tender may be fearfully effectual when pestilence makes sudden deaths escape scrutiny:– to say nothing of ordinary diseases, in which, whether the issue shall be life or death, often depends on ministrations whose precise quality cannot be apparent to observers; and much of the attendance on the sick is secluded from all observation. A man, well known in New York, was prostrate with disease, when his life insurance became renewable. His wife knew the contingency, but she possessed no means of paying the required premium. The policy would expire on the morrow, and, though his recovery was possible, the support of his family depended, probably, on his speedy death. Conjugal duty and pecuniary interest were in demoralizing conflict. Was the wife to attempt a prolongation of his life under the hazard of a widowhood of penury; or was she to intermit ministrations on which alone a prolongation was possible? He died before the hour at which his policy was to expire, and though charity may hope the result was produced by Providence, against the best efforts of the widow, the less human nature is thus tempted, the purer will be our domestic relations.

SAVINGS BANKS ARE AS CONDUCIVE TO THRIFT AS LIFE INSURANCE IS TO UNTHRIFT.

The disadvantages of life insurance and clubs proceed from our organization, and, therefore, are inevitable. The advantages of savings banks are equally organic. A boy who makes snow-balls will throw them away as fast as he makes them, but should he chance to roll up one of more than ordinary size, it will excite in him an ambition to enlarge it, instead of throwing it away; and the bigger it becomes under his efforts, the stronger will become his desire for its further increase. The principle applies to money. The day's earnings of a poor man are cast away as soon as earned; a man's recklessness being as great as his poverty; but should he deposit any of his earnings in a saving bank, an appetite for accumulation is immediately produced by the unusual possession of a surplus: and the appetite, growing by what it feeds on, will add an impulse to the industry and frugality of the depositor. "Eat, drink, and be merry, for to-morrow we die," is no longer / the maxim of such a man; but rather, "refrain from *expenditure* to day, that we may add to our deposites to-morrow."

ACCUMULATION IS A MORE SALUTARY RELIANCE AGAINST WANT THAN LIFE INSURANCE.

To become fonder of accumulation than of expenditure, is the first step towards wealth. An agriculturist will receive a few grains of an improved species of corn, which he will not eat, but will plant them, and replant the product from year to year, till his few grains will become hundreds of bushels. Money is increasable by analogous processes, and success is within the power of every man who shall attain to ordinary longevity. If a man at the age of twenty years can save from his earnings twenty-six cents every working day, and annually invest the aggregate at compound legal 7 per cent interest, he will, at the age of seventy, possess $32,000. Many men who resort to life insurance, can save several times twenty-six cents daily, and thus accumulate several times the above sum, long before the age of seventy. Nearly all large fortunes are the result of such accumulations; hence the men who amass great fortunes are usually those only who live long. The last few years of Girard's and Astor's lives[4] increased their wealth more than scores of early years. To be in haste to become rich by a few great operations, is a direct road to eventual poverty. We cannot, however, command long life, but we can approximate thereto by commencing early the process of accumulation – an elongation by extending backward being as efficacious as an elongation forward. Every hundred dollars expended by a man of the age of twenty years, is an expenditure of what, at our legal rate of interest, would, by compounding it annually, become $3,000, should he live to the age of seventy. This lesson is taught practically by savings banks, and well counteracts the fatal notion of the young, that old age is the period for accumulation, and youth the period for expenditure. By like principles, a young man who pays annually a premium for life insurance, loses not the premiums only, but the immense increase which the money would produce, should he invest it at compound interest, and live to the ordinary limit of man's life. Extremely old men, who have no length of life in prospect, are the only persons, if any, who should insure their lives, for the expense of their insurance would be but little more than the annual premiums.

TO TEACH THE POOR SELF-DEPENDENCE, IS A BETTER CHARITY THAN ALMS.

"The poverty of the poor is their destruction,"[5] says the Bible; but savings banks correct this evil, by enabling them to accumulate their savings, and become rich by the means which, ordinarily, alone make the rich richer. That no class of persons may be excluded from the vivifying process of accumulation, savings banks for the reception of penny deposits have recently been instituted in London, and numerous are the reported instances of the salutary change they have produced in the habits and pecuniary condition of the depositors. Nature kindly aids the improvement by the organic mode in which every man estimates his possessions – not by comparing himself with other people, but by comparing his present possessions with his former; so that a man who possesses a surplus of two pence will feel rich, (as we experience in children,) if he never before possessed a greater surplus than a penny. We have long sought to benefit the poor by administering free soup to the destitute, penitentiaries to the wayward, clubs and life insurance to the thriftless; but if we induce the poor man to accumulate his occasional surplus earnings, we shall enable him to cook his own soup, support / his family better by his life than by his death, and diminish the inmates of penitentiaries.

THE EXPENDITURE OF MONEY IS
THE MOST IGNOBLE OF ITS USES.

The highest value of affluence is the social influence which it confers, whereby the possessor may become useful to society by his example and precept. Many persons keep themselves poor by lavish expenditures, in the hope of being deemed rich, and enjoying the superiority which riches confer. The deception is necessarily of short duration; but had the party carefully saved and accumulated, he might soon have become permanently rich. The mental anguish which a man feels when he loses part of a large fortune, proceeds from an imagined diminution of his influence and power, not from any physical privations that the lost wealth will create. Nor is such a notion fanciful: men who have been esteemed wise counsellors while rich, lose commonly their reputed wisdom, if they lose their property. This phenomenon was observed by Shakespeare, who accounts for it by saying –

> "Men's judgments are
> A parcel of their fortunes; and things outward
> Do draw the inward quality after them,
> To suffer all alike."[6]

That money is useless except for the physical enjoyments which its expenditure will produce, is the error of the poor; while persons who have experienced the intellectual gratifications which result from the retention of money, gain a better estimate of its value. The respect that attends wealth is as old as the Bible, which says – "If a man come unto your assembly with a gold ring and goodly apparel; and there come in also a poor man in vile appeared, and ye have respect to him that weareth the gay clothing, and say unto him, Sit thou here in a good place; and say to the poor, Stand thou there, are ye not partial?"[7] If two men arrive at the Astor House,[8] where the charge for board and lodging is the same for both, yet the man who is known to possess the most property will be lodged in a better room than the other, and receive, in every way, a preference. If the two take passage in a steamboat, the like preference will be accorded to the man of superior wealth; and these instances are but exemplifications of a general custom.

THE SLOW ACCUMULATION OF PROPERTY PRODUCES
BETTER MORAL EFFECTS THAN THE SUDDEN
ACQUISITION OF PROPERTY.

A man's self-respect, and the respect of his wife and children for him and themselves, will increase continually as his savings augment. The gradual increase of wealth which attends the accumulation of a man's savings, is also more favorable to its preservation and to the possessor's equanimity than any sudden accumulation of prosperity. The upstart is a well-known genus of repulsive and pernicious peculiarities. A family who succeeds to the slowly accumulated savings of a deceased father, know his modes of investment, (a knowledge almost as valuable as the property he may leave them,) and the family will be more likely to retain the property permanently, than a widow or orphans suddenly enriched by a life insurance, which will be paid them in money, of whose proper uses and safe investment they will be ignorant. Besides, the parent whose savings are safely accumulated in a savings bank feels not the anxiety which sometimes attends life insurance, lest / he may be incapacitated by sickness, inadvertence or disappointment, from paying his burdensome and insidious renewal premium. He is, on the contrary, master at all times of his deposits, and can recall them all or a part, as his necessities may require, or as more lucrative investments may become known to him – savings banks being a school to teach the art of accumulation to the poor, rather than a resort for experienced capitalists. Nor is a savings bank depositor a sort of prisoner under bonds not to travel into foreign countries without the consent of some life insurance company; his freedom nor his money is lost to him; nor, in case of his death, are his deposits liable to be wrested from his family by any quibble such as life insurance companies occasionally will and always can interpose, where the company happens to believe that the insured person was not so robust as he or some physician represented at the commencement of his insurance.

SAVINGS BANKS SHOULD PAY DEPOSITORS AS MUCH INTEREST AS PRACTICABLE.

As savings banks are the laboring man's only mode of accumulation, they should pay depositors as high a rate of interest as practicable; for the more productive a poor man's mite can be made, the stronger will be his motive for frugality and industry. Some savings banks in Connecticut pay depositors 5 1/2 per cent interest, while our banks pay only 5 per cent, though our legal interest is 1 per cent more than in Connecticut; consequently, our long-established city savings banks have accumulated enormously large surplus profits which exist without a legal owner or a legitimate object. These banks are required by their charters[9] "to regulate the rate of interest so that depositors shall receive a *ratable* proportion of all the profits, after deducting necessary expenses;" but the provision fails to effect its object, (as is manifested by the accrued surplus profits,) though portions thereof have in some cases been invested in the erection of expensive banking-houses, and the purchase of valuable city grounds. The depositors from whose hard earnings these costly investments were abstracted, have received their stipulated 5 per cent interest, drawn out their deposits, and are heard of no more forever. Like other property for whom no owner exists, erections of the above character belong to the State, and are subject to legislative disposals, together with all other surplus profits possessed by these institutions. Why, then, should not all savings banks be compelled to honestly divide annually (as a bonus) among its depositors the total amount of its net earnings, beyond the stipulated 5 per cent? The surplus which any bank may own at the time of the enactment of the law, can be reserved from distribution, except the income which may thereafter be annually earned therefrom. Every savings bank possessing a surplus, will thus present to new depositors an inducement which will be salutary to the thrifty poor who may avail themselves of the common benefit; and as the existing large surpluses are owned mostly in cities, the inducement will be presented to the class of poor persons who are locally (by reason of surrounding temptations) most in need of inducements to self-denying accumulations. The law will be beneficial to depositors also, who reside where new savings banks are located, by reason that the depositors will receive more than 5 per cent interest, as soon as the bank shall possess deposits enough to neutralize the contingent expenses; and thus every depositor will become a quasi bank stockholder to the amount of his deposits, and feel a common interest in increasing the number of depositors so as to diminish ratably the per centage of contingent expenses. /

CONCLUSION.

Finally, in our legislation towards savings banks, we must remember that the conception of them originated in abstract benevolence, but they achieve good only as an incident of machinery which is instituted for the personal gain of salaried officers, or for some kindred private benefit. To the Legislature we must look for laws that shall coercively carry into practice the public benevolence which the institutions are capable of effecting, or they will continue to accomplish only as much public benefit as shall be necessary to secure private gains.

Joseph B. Collins, 'Life Insurance', *Hunt's Merchants' Magazine and Commercial Review* (1852)

Art. VII. – Life Insurance.*

To Freeman Hunt, Esq., *Editor of the Merchants' Magazine, etc.*:–

Sir:– The reputation which Mr. Johnson has long enjoyed as an experienced and successful banker, and as an essayist in matters pertaining to his profession, would seem to entitle his opinion in the premises to consideration and weight. But the numerous and gross errors he has committed in the article alluded to, have destroyed wholly our confidence in his views regarding the one, and gone far to weaken it in reference to the other.

His first position is thus stated:–

"Life Insurance possesses many of the elements of gambling." "The characteristic of gambling consists in the absence of mutual benefit to the players. So in life insurance, no party thereto, will usually gain, except at the loss of the correlative party. The chance of gain is also adverse to the insured, as is demonstrated by the large surplus profits which life insurance companies announce the possession of; and which profits, like the foot-prints around a slaughter-house, may admonish those who are entering that the current inward exceeds greatly the current outward. Life insurance is promoted by the same artifice as lotteries, the publication of every case where an adventurer dies soon after the commencement of his insurance; while nothing is said where the insured abandons his policy in disgust, or from sickness, poverty, or inadvertance, after having distressed himself for years, by annual premiums; nor where a person pays much more than his heirs are to receive back on his death." To this we reply:–

---

* We published in the *Merchants' Magazine* for December, 1851, an article on *"The Relative Merits of Life Insurance and Savings Banks,"* from the pen of a highly esteemed contributor, A B. Johnson, Esq., President of the Ontario Branch Bank at Utica, and we now chearfully give place to a reply by Joseph B. Collins, Esq., the President of the Mutual Life Insurance Company of New York. This correspondence opens a field of discussion that can scarcely fail of eliciting truth, or at least of becoming a source of many valuable suggestions touching the ethics and economy of Life Insurance, and other corporations connected with the commercial enterprises and spirit of the times. – *Ed. Mer. Mag.*

It is not true that in life insurance no party thereto can gain but at the expense of another party; for the large amounts paid upon policies as they mature result from the premiums improved as interest, which have been paid upon them. The premium exacted upon every policy is the sum which, invested annually during the life-time of the assured, will produce, at an assumed rate of interest, the amount insured for and payable at his death. Life insurance is simply a system of deposits for accumulation, over which the principle of average is extended for the protection of those who would otherwise suffer from the premature death of the insured. The application of the law of average, so far from giving it the character of a gambling transaction, in reality goes far to equalize among all connected with it, a participation in all the chances of life, whether fortunate or adverse, and while his argument might in a degree apply to fire and marine insurance companies, of whose aid and benefits he is doubtless glad to avail himself, it is almost wholly inapplicable to life companies. For in the former the mass of their contributions save the few from ruin. The former must lose, that the latter may gain.

A man may, and often does, insure his house, or store and merchandise, for a long series of years, pay out premiums of insurance, and never meeting / with an accident, may, in a sense, throw away large sums of money, and get no return. And so, only on a much larger scale, in marine insurance. But in life insurance, if the policy be kept up, the assured survivor will inevitably draw the sum insured, with, in many cases, handsome advances in the way of dividends. And here we may insert, as a proof of Mr. Johnson's great ignorance of existing facts, or obliquity of view, that all or nearly all the leading life insurance companies being on the mutual principle, "the large surplus profits they announce" go to the policy-holders, and their *"foot-print"'* are seen in the policies. Was the omission of this cardinal feature casual or intentional? In England a life policy for £5,000, after a continuance of forty years or more, had more than £30,000 paid upon it at the death of the assured.

In gambling no man can win unless another loses. Just so in banking: a bank cannot make large gains by discounts unless taken from the pockets of those that pay. What the bank gains the individual loses. In life insurance all pay in, and all draw out. Those that die early are greatly benefited – those that live longer in a less ratio.

The insinuation that life insurance is promoted "by artifice," is unworthy of the writer. We might as fairly charge upon banks that the directors reject notes at their counter, when they can only take legal interest, that they may shave them at double the rate, in the street.[1]

But Mr. Johnson's main effort seems to be to degrade life insurance, and to elevate savings banks. He asserts that the one makes a man thriftless, and the other frugal; as if it did not require as much self-sacrifice to provide twenty-five dollars to pay the premium on a life policy, as to make a like deposit in a savings bank; and as if the stimulus in the one case were not much greater than the other, since the deposit in the one case may tomorrow be worth a thousand to the laborer's family, and in the other but twenty-five dollars. Moreover, a life policy has always a definite nominal value, just as much as a deposit in a savings bank, and in a case of need can be sold and made available for present purposes, or a loan can be had on it for a temporary period. Again, the depositor is more likely to be tempted to withdraw his money from a savings bank, and hazard it, perchance with fatal loss, than to sell, or drop his life policy.

Mr. Johnson, too, is singularly unfortunate in his illustration of a case arithmetically considered, as we proceed to show. He says:–

> A gentleman of this city, who became married at the age of twenty-five years, and whose support consisted of a small annuity, insured five thousand dollars on his life, at an annual premium of eighty dollars, which he could badly spare.
>
> As the premium is paid in advance, it at the end of the year,
> amounted, with legal interest, to $85 60
> He then paid another $80 00
> The interest on which, with the interest on the former $85 60, was   11 59
> Making, at the end of two years $177 10
> Should he continue the process twenty-four years, he will have paid, in principal and interest, $5,038 86, being $38 86 more than his widow is to receive at his death; but he is young and robust, and should he live till he shall become seventy-five years old, his payments, and compound interest thereon, will amount to more than $37,000; – consequently, after his widow shall receive the stipulated $5,000, his loss on the transaction will be $32,000.

A payment of $80 a year for 50 years, compounded at 7 per cent per annum, will produce not $37,000, but $34,800 15. The calculation, how / ever, is so much nearer right than the argument, that we dismiss the error with the remark, that, if Mr. Johnson uses in his banking operations the same interest tables from which these calculations are drawn, his house is in a prosperous way, and the "footprints should admonish those who are entering, that the current inwards exceeds greatly the current outwards."

Mr. Johnson tells us a doleful story of a woman hastening, by neglect, the death of her husband, in order to secure the avails of a life policy. Improbable as the story is, will he deny that the same woman would as readily have suffered *her* husband to die, could she thereby hasten the possession of a clever sum lying in a savings bank? Again, Mr. J. avers that life and health and other mutual benefit associations are immoral in their tendency, making the several parties careless of the future. It may be urged on the same principle that fire insurance is immoral, because the selfish unprincipled policy holder says, "Let the house or goods burn, I am insured." Why provide hospitals and other benevolent institutions, as a resource in case of inevitable sickness, or other misfortune, "Let each party look out for himself."

But no, Mr. Editor, Mr. Johnson has wholly mistaken his vocation in attempting to decry life insurance. So far from promoting thriftlessness, or immorality, it will be found on a scrutinizing inquiry, that life insurance, no less than deposits in savings banks, is sought by the reflecting, prudent husband and father, the affectionate care-taker of his dependent family. Life insurance is one of the happiest and most beneficent results of philosophical observation and mathematical deduction. Subject, as is our race, to a thousand contingencies, in this age of intense activity and energy, by which multitudes of families are exposed to sufferings resulting from death and poverty, with its attendant ills; but for the suggestions of this benevolent invention, these sufferings would in vain seek relief. And among those happy thoughts, none has accomplished so great good, at so little sacrifice, as life insurance. It was very emphatically declared, by a policy-holder, "But for a policy on my life I should have died long ago. When tossing on my uneasy pillow with severed pulse and throbbing temples, the consciousness that while yet in health I had secured my loved ones from penury, by procuring a policy on my life, diminished that fever, and calmed that pulse, and through the blessing of an over-ruling Providence I am restored to health, and am again able to exert myself for my endeared relatives."

We might here, perhaps, close our strictures upon Mr. Johnson's assault upon life insurance, but there is one more objection that may seem to call for reply. He most disingenuously insinuates that it is no uncommon occurrence for a life company to wrest from a surviving family its just due, by a "quibble." Let him point out the company or the case. We profess to know the operations of a number of life companies, and we have never known a just claim resisted, or a "quibble" resorted to as a defense.

We appeal to the grateful hearts of ten thousand widows, and their dependent children, to disprove this groundless imputing charge.

We should regret, exceedingly, to impute, or even suspect unworthy motives in any one, but we are wholly unable to account for so uncalled for, so unnecessary, so harsh a denunciation of life insurance companies, upon any general principles. We hope – shall be glad to believe that public good alone has been the prompter, but we do earnestly desire, that when he again wields the pen he will write on subjects that he understands, and is disposed to treat fairly.

J. B. C.

INSURANCE AND SELF-HELP IN BRITAIN

'Insurance amongst the Working Classes', *Economist*, 2 October 1858, pp. 1090–1.

Frank Ives Scudamore,[1] *Life Insurance by Small Payments: A Few Plain Words Concerning It* (London: Emily Faithfull and Co., 1861).

In 1858 friendly societies were in the middle of a transition from being important sites of working-class (usually, but not always, male) sociability at the start of the nineteenth century to being sprawling, fairly efficient providers of sick pay and pensions by the century's end. As they grew into prominence, insuring around half of all British working men as of 1900, they generated a variety of tensions: as members lived longer, they faced an uphill battle to remain solvent; as actuaries appeared on the scene to help solve this problem, members rebelled against this threat to their traditional informality; and paternalistic employers as well as government regulators recurrently threatened their commitment to autonomy. Abetting this process was a major amalgamation movement involving several of Britain's largest friendly societies, which adopted a federal model that enabled hundreds of local clubs to pool their resources; between 1845 and 1875 the Odd Fellows, Foresters and Shepherds increased their combined membership from 339,685 to more than a million by that means. The Office of the Registrar of Friendly Societies, created by Parliament in 1852, produced annual reports that enabled interested outsiders to watch this transition unfold. Middle-class advocates of self-help generally applauded the vibrant activity recorded in these reports, but they could not resist scolding friendly societies for failing to conform to their own preferred business practices and moral behaviours.[2]

Throughout this period most British friendly societies continued to focus exclusively on paying benefits to members who were prevented from working due to illness, injury or old age. Life insurance companies, for their part, studiously avoided diversifying into sick pay, and seldom sold pensions before 1900. Consequently, with the major exception of 'collecting societies' (which provided burial insurance to millions of Britons), friendly societies and commercial life insurance rarely crossed paths. The same could be said about savings banks – despite the best efforts of Frank Scudamore, who spent the 1860s trying to popularize working-class life insurance through the Post Office Savings Bank. His first such effort, documented in *Life Insurance by Small Payments*, offered the Post Office as a temporary repository for working-class savings, to be earmarked as annual premium payments to participating companies. Although many life offices cooperated with Scudamore, few employers heeded his call to set up group schemes for their workers. When employer-sponsored group life insurance did get off the ground after 1890, the employers in question (including the Association of Civil Servants, the National Union of Teachers, and several banks) preferred working directly with individual insurance companies.[3] Another brainchild of Scudamore's was to issue life insurance policies directly from the Post Office, but this was even less successful; the Government Insurances and Annuities Act of 1864, sponsored by William Gladstone, sold fewer than 500 policies a year into the 1890s, and has been described as 'an abysmal failure' by a recent historian of the Post Office.[4]

Notes
1. Frank Ives Scudamore (1823–84) joined the British Post Office in 1840 and was picked over Anthony Trollope to serve as Assistant Secretary from 1864; he was Receiver and Accountant-General from 1861. He was a leading architect of the Post Office Savings Bank network, which first took root in 1861 and generated 180,000 accounts in its first year.
2. Cordery, *British Friendly Societies, 1750–1914*, pp. 87–93, 104–5, 125–52.
3. Alborn, *Regulated Lives*, p. 42.
4. M. Daunton, *Royal Mail: The Post Office since 1840* (London: Athlone, 1985), pp. 106–9; C. R. Perry, *The Victorian Post Office: The Growth of a Bureaucracy* (Woodbridge: Boydell Press, 1992), p. 77.

'Insurance amongst the Working Classes', *Economist* (1858)

FRIENDLY Societies are, as our readers are aware, the Insurance Companies of the poorer classes. The three Annual Reports[1] which have now been put forth by the Registrar of Friendly Societies in Great Britain are full of curious and interesting information, throwing as much light on the state of those great masses on which all English society rests, as any series of authentic political facts to which we have access. Few people probably are aware how deeply-rooted the principle of Insurance is amongst even the poorer classes of Great Britain. The Registrar states in one of his Reports,[2] and not without adducing adequate evidence of so striking a fact, that "there are more Friendly Societies for mutual relief in sickness, &c., in England and Wales, than in the whole of the rest of Europe or elsewhere." Between the years 1795 and 1857 no less than 26,000 Friendly Societies have been registered according to law in England and Wales, and no subsidy from the State has been granted to them as has generally been the case on the Continent; and, though so large a number have never existed at any one time in England and Wales, – many of them having been established on insecure principles, – there seems to be no reason to doubt that from 15,000 to 20,000 must be in active existence at the present time. There are certainly upwards of 9,000 such societies which invest a portion of their funds in English and Welsh Savings Banks alone; and recent inquiries show it to be highly probable that at least as many more have chosen other and some of them much less safe modes of investment. The Registrar estimates the whole funds of such societies at not less than 9,000,000*l*, the number of the members at 2,000,000, giving an average stock of 4*l* 10s per member, and he estimates the annual sum expended in relief for sickness alone at 1,000,000*l*. Nor is this in all probability anything but a minimum estimate. It [is] worth while to compare the result with the accounts received from continental countries.[3] In France, whose population is about double that of England and Wales, there were at the end of 1856, 426,453 members of Friendly Societies, with funds to the amount of 661,292*l*, or 1*l* 16s per member. In Belgium, with a population of about 4 1/2 millions, there are 211 Mutual Aid Societies, about as many as in Bedfordshire, – there are, however, some special Miners' and other Provident

Societies largely assisted by Government, as well. In Austria and in Bavaria, perhaps in Germany generally, the principle of union appears to be more grounded on common trades than common localities. In Bavaria, with a population nearly the same as that of Belgium, there are 119 of such societies, not apparently averaging more than 100 members each. In Spain they exist only in Catalonia. In Poland and Italy there seems to be no general institution of the kind.

It is clear, therefore, that the principle of mutual insurance amongst the lower classes has taken root among the English as it has taken root in no other nation.[4] In England there has been no temptation held out by the Government, and scarcely any by generous people in the richer classes to form such associations. Here, again, the difference is remarkable in France. In France the subscriptions of Government and of honorary members, who subscribe only to increase the profit for the poorer members, appear to be more than 20 per cent. of the whole contributions. Among the English Societies it seems there are about 1 1/2 per cent. honorary members. Thus the number of members of Friendly Societies in England is at least eight times as many in proportion to her population as in France, and this without any temptation beyond the natural advantages of mutual aid. It is not as yet possible to compare the English with the Welsh and Scotch Societies, as the Registrar has not yet been able to form any accurate estimate of the number of societies still in existence, but it is already evident that neither in Scotland nor Ireland has this institution taken a much deeper root than on the Continent, while in Wales, on the other hand, as far as we can yet form any judgment, it is quite as popular as in England. During the 63 years from 1793-1855 inclusive, during which 26,000 Friendly Societies were registered in England and Wales, only 700 had been registered in Scotland. Again, it is some slight test of their prevalence to know the number of these societies which deposit any portion of their funds in Savings Banks, because, though this is a very uncertain index to their actual / numbers, it is probably a fair criterion of their *relative* numbers in the different sections of the kingdom. It will be seen by the following return that the Welsh Societies have the largest credits of this kind in proportion to population, and the Irish the smallest: –

	England.	Wales.	Ireland.	Scotland.
Population in 1851	16,700,000	1,000,000	6,500,000	3,000,000
No. of Friendly Societies depositing with Savings Banks in 1856	8,241	488	220	97
The total deposits of these societies in Savings Banks	£1,287,324	£93,782	£11,006	£16,150
Average amount deposited by each society	£156	£192	£50	£166

This result may only indicate, however, that the Welsh Societies are more cautious *how* they invest their money than the English, and, consequently, invest a larger proportion of it in Savings Banks, the safest and best investments easily accessible for small sums. And this leads us to a branch of the subject of great practical importance.

It would seem from the Registrar's last Report that the small Friendly Societies are exceedingly incautious in the investment of their money, placing it at random in any local firm that seems to offer a good rate of interest with reasonable security. Thus, in the published accounts of a bankrupt estate which passed through the Bankruptcy Court in the present year, it was found that no less than 36 Friendly Societies were creditors of this firm, in which they had invested a total amount of 4,085*l*, at an average of about 144*l* for each society. Another large brewer's firm recently bankrupt had 44 such societies amongst their creditors, – and it is found that these unsafe investments of small sums are extremely common. Now the Acts of Parliament relating to Friendly Societies have given them many special privileges, especially the right to take precedence of any other creditor in case of the insolvency of any of their own officers having funds of the society in his hands, – but Parliament grants this special protection only on condition that the investments be limited to a certain small and safe class; and this is necessary, since the most terrible losses of the hard-earned savings of the poor have been incurred in this way. And it is necessary that it should be widely known that any losses incurred through unsafe investments, unauthorised by the recent Act, may be recovered from the trustees so investing them. The authorised investments are in Savings Banks, the Public Funds, with the Commissioners for the Reduction of the National Debt, and such other security specially authorised by the rules of the society, *not being* the purchase of house or land (except only of the building wherein the meetings of the society are held), nor shares in any joint stock or other company, nor personal security, except in the case of members of a full year's standing at least, and then only to an amount not exceeding one-half of that member's life assurance in the society. Unsafe investment has been one great cause of failure in these societies, – the funds being so small and the managers so often ignorant of their duties, that any considerable firm in the locality of the society offering an investment has been eagerly closed with.

The second risk, and one of far greater moment, because a danger of *principle* in the constitution of these societies, has been insufficient provision in the outset for the claims to which they become liable as years go on. The principle of insurance no doubt is, that by collecting men into large masses, the sudden pecuniary calamities and responsibilities which would overwhelm any single man may be subdivided till they weigh very lightly on the mass, so that all may be relieved from the *fear* of ruin, and the few who would actually incur it, may be saved from it. But, then, in proportion as these claims are to weigh *lightly* on the whole society, the society must be so formed as to accumulate in its youth a large reserve fund against the time when the full strain of its liabilities begins. If all who joined it were already middle-aged or old men, – already constantly liable to sickness, – the contribution from each would have to be very considerable indeed in order to cover all the responsibilities incurred, and so far the object of the society, – that of lightening the pressure of calamity, – would not be answered nearly as well as if men began to contribute at an earlier period of life.

The losses would be divided amongst many, and so *equalised*, indeed, but it is also needful for the money to be saved during the period of youth and health. This accordingly is the principle with most Friendly Societies. The age of entrance is usually limited to 35. But then the effect of this is that for some 20 or 30 years the annual strain on the society is constantly on the increase, until the *average* age of the members has reached the highest point to which, in a mixed society of new or younger members and members already grown old, it is likely to attain. It is generally found that this point is not reached for 30 years after the formation of the society. Accordingly, for the first 30 years the funds of the society ought to be regularly accumulating. There is, therefore, nothing more false in principle than the rule adopted by the class of Birmingham, Dividend, or Tontine Societies, to which attention is called by the Registrar in his last Report. These societies divide all the reserve fund every year, leaving a balance often not above 2s 6d per member to add to the annual subscriptions of the next year. The consequence is, that there is no provision for increasing liabilities, and of 50 of such societies established in London during the last 20 years, the Registrar found on inquiry only 12 surviving. The dividend principle, if it commences before the *maximum* liabilities of the society are reached and provided for, is essentially unsound.

On the whole, it is a matter for a really national pride to find the principle of insurance so firmly rooted amongst our lower classes. Societies are instituted all over the country, hundreds in almost every county some of them in a state of high prosperity, – having on an average reserve funds amounting to 4*l* 10s per member, and often reaching above 10*l* per member, by which members are secured against sickness, old age, loss by fire, the expense of militia substitutes, funerals, or like liabilities. It is not easy to overrate the importance of the advantages thus secured. To take a single instance. The following are the *monthly* payments by which a man of 30 years of age can secure provision against sickness up to the age of 65, 8s a week for life after that age, and the payment of 5*l* to his family on his death: –

	Monthly Payments for a Man aged 30.	
	s	d
For 10s a week in sickness until 65	1	2 ¼
For 8s a week for life after	2	10 ½
For 5*l* payable at death	0	2 ½
Total	4	3 ¼

But if it be difficult to overrate the physical advantages thus secured, it is impossible to overrate the importance of the principle of provident self-restraint thus cherished in the minds of the masses of the English people. When continental thinkers wonder at the peculiar prosperity of England, it is sufficient to point to such habits as these in the families of about 2,000,000 of her working men to explain the secret of that prosperity.

Frank Ives Scudamore, *Life Insurance by Small Payments: A Few Plain Words Concerning It* (1861)

I. *The Advantages of Life Insurance.* – These are so generally known and admitted that no lengthened description of them need be given. The man whose income will cease when he dies, may, by insuring his life for such a sum as his means will justify and permit, secure to his family the continued enjoyment after his death of a proportionate part of his income. He cannot leave to them his wages or his salary, but, by insuring his life, he may leave to them a sum of money, which will to a certain extent take the place of his wages or salary.

It is sometimes asserted that a prudent and frugal man may do as much for himself as an insurance company can do for him, if he will steadily lay by and put out to interest the sums which he would have to pay to the insurance company if he insured his life. But this assertion is untrue. Even if the prudent and frugal man could invest the amount of his small premium as profitably as the insurance company can invest the total amount of all the small sums which they receive from a large number of persons, and if he had leisure and skill to search for the means of employing his little savings profitably and securely, he might still be unable to do for himself what the insurance company can do for him. Before he can do as much for himself as they can do for him, he must be able to invest £2 or £3 as profitably as they can invest £20,000 or £30,000; he must have time to seek / the means of investing his money, and skill to know whether they are safe or unsafe when he has found them, and he must live for many years. If he lays by, and puts out to interest, those sums only which he would pay to an insurance company if he insured his life, and does not live to be an old man, he will not, at his death, have done for himself as much as an insurance company would have done for him. If he undertakes the investment of his little savings, the amount of provision for his family will depend upon the length of his life; but if he insures his life for the benefit of his family, the amount of his provision for them will not be reduced by his early or untimely death. Thus, Life Insurance not only enables the man whose salary or wages cease on his death to extend some of the benefits of his salary or wages to his family after his death, but also gives to the family of the man who dies early in life some of the advantages which are enjoyed by the families of those who live for many years.

II. *The Advantages of Life Insurance may be purchased cheaply.* – A man in his twentieth year may insure his life for £100 in any one of many highly respectable offices by an annual payment of from £1 16s. to £2. A man in his thirtieth year may insure his life for the same sum by an annual payment of from £2 5s. to £2 10s. These annual payments also purchase for those whose lives are insured a share in the profits of the insurance offices, and this share is sometimes a considerable addition to the amount of the policy.

III. *The Benefits of Life Insurance may be purchased most advantageously by the Young.* – The man who insures his life in his twentieth year pays about ten shillings less for every £100 insured than is paid by the man who commences Life Insurance in his thirtieth year. In the long course of years the man who begins to insure early in life may pay as / much as, or more than, he who postpones his insurance to a later period; but the advantages of an early commencement are very great.

First, because by spreading the payment over a greater number of years we have a smaller annual payment to make during that half of our lives which is charged with the cost and care of a family; and next, because every man should insure his life whilst his health is good, and before the unhealthiness of his occupation or any of the ills and accidents to which he is liable have had time to weaken his constitution and lessen his chances of acceptance by insurance companies. Many men who would have had no difficulty in insuring their lives at twenty years of age have failed to seize the opportunity, and have discovered at thirty that their opportunity was gone.

IV. *Circumstances have hitherto prevented the Working Classes and Persons of Small Income from purchasing the Advantages of Life Insurance.* – The premium on a policy of insurance is payable annually in one amount and in advance. A working man who is in receipt of weekly wages, and who wishes to insure his life, must either pay down the whole of his wages for one or two weeks or must save up the premium little by little from week to week. It is almost impossible for him to take the first of these two courses; and until lately the facilities afforded to the poor throughout the country for the investment of small savings were so slight and so few in number as to make the second course one of considerable difficulty. To lay by week after week the one or two shillings which will make up the annual premium, to have the little fund always in the house and yet to resist the many and strong temptations to spend it, demands a steadfastness of purpose which very few men possess. Yet, unless working men had possessed this steadfastness of purpose, they could not until / very recently have purchased the advantages of Life Insurance. Obstacles, alike in kind, but somewhat less in degree, have prevented a vast number of persons who receive their small incomes by monthly instalments from insuring their lives.

V. *By the Establishment of Post Office Savings' Banks, the advantages of Life Insurance have been placed within reach of the Working Classes, and of all those Persons whose small Incomes are paid to them by small but frequent Instalments.* Thus: –

1. The Post Office Savings' Banks, which are already established at 1,700 Money Order Offices in England and Wales, and will eventually be established at every Money Order Office in the United Kingdom, are open for the receipt of deposits during from seven to eight hours of every working day, and consequently give very great facilities for the investment of small savings.

2. In these banks, deposits of one shilling or of any number of shillings will be received.

3. The security of these deposits is guaranteed by Act of Parliament.

4. Any man whose age does not exceed thirty years, may, by depositing one shilling per week in a Post Office Savings' Bank, accumulate by the end of a year as much as will enable him to insure his life in a respectable office for £100. For the price of six pints of beer per week he may insure his life for £100. A larger weekly saving will, of course, enable him to effect an Insurance for a larger amount, or at a later period of life.

5. At the end of the year, when his premium becomes due to the insurance office, he can draw the required amount out of the Post Office Savings' Bank, and, as that bank is also a Money Order Office, he can at once remit the premium by means of a Money Order to the proper person. The interest which he will receive for his deposits from the Post Office / Savings' Bank will be nearly sufficient to pay for the charge on the Money Order.

6. The mode of depositing money in and withdrawing it from Post Office Savings' Banks is fully explained in a little tract entitled "Post Office Savings' Banks: a Few Plain Words concerning them,"[1] to which is added a complete list of all the Post Office Savings' Banks in England and Wales.

It is probable that as the advantages of the Post Office Savings' Banks, and the facilities which they afford for the easy and gradual accumulation of premiums on policies of insurance, become more generally known, a very large number of persons will hasten to obtain through the instrumentality of the banks the benefits of Life Insurance. It is probable that parents will encourage their children to insure their lives at a much earlier age than is customary now that the obstacles to the collection of the premium are so great. A lad of sixteen, by a deposit of one shilling per week in a Post Office Savings' Bank, may accumulate in a year the premium on a policy of £150; and when a policy of that amount has been acquired and maintained for several years it becomes a marketable security, and may either be retained to serve its original purpose, or used, legitimately, to further the advancement in life of the person on whose life it is effected, or deposited as a guarantee for his fidelity. If any support be required for the statement that many persons would readily purchase the benefits of Life Insurance if they could purchase them by small payments, that support may be found in the marked success of the arrangements which are now to be described.

VI. *The Plan adopted in the Post Office, with a view to promote Life Insurance amongst the Officers of that Department.* – With a view to facilitate the payment of premiums of insurance by officers of the Post Office, and to encourage those officers to insure their lives, the Postmaster-General, in September, 1859, / proposed, and certain Insurance Offices, about twenty-nine in all, have agreed: –

1. That the insurance offices should advance policies of insurance to the officers of the Post Office without requiring them to make any preliminary payment whatever.

2. That the Postmaster-General should collect the premiums by weekly or monthly deductions from the wages or salaries of the persons concerned, and pay the collections over quarterly to the insurance offices.

The arrangement includes some other provisions for the advantage of the officers of the Post Office, and others for the protection of the insurance offices; but the noticeable features of the scheme are, that under it officers of the Post Office may obtain a policy of insurance without incurring one farthing of preliminary expense, and may keep it up by permitting small and convenient deductions from their wages or salary. That the advantages of the scheme have been appreciated[2] will be evident when it is stated that under it upwards of 1,200 policies have been effected in the course of two years.

VII. *Difference between the Plan adopted in the Post Office and that recommended in Section V. of this Tract.* – Under the plan adopted in the Post Office, the person who is desirous of insuring his life obtains his policy without preliminary payment, and is not called upon to exercise any prudence or economy until after the reward for that prudence and economy has been placed in his hands. Under the plan recommended in Section V. of this Tract, the person who desires to insure his life must save one premium before he can effect his purpose, and must exercise prudence and economy for a considerable period before he can obtain his reward. The Post Office plan, therefore, is the more attractive of the two; indeed, it would be difficult to hold out greater inducements to Life Insurance than are held out under / this plan. And large employers of labour who have many men under their control would do well to consider whether they might not introduce the Post Office plan into their factories, mills, workshops, or counting houses. In such an undertaking the insurance offices would of course gladly co-operate whenever there was reasonable prospect that a fair amount of business would be done, and that the premiums would be collected with befitting regularity.

Still, let the employers of labour do what they will, there will always be a vast number of persons to whom the advantages of a plan such as that which is in operation in the Post Office cannot be extended, but who will be anxious to participate in the advantages of Life Insurance. To these persons the plan described in Section V. of this Tract is strongly recommended, since, though not so favourable to them as that which is in operation in the Post Office, it will enable them to enjoy "Life Insurance by Small Payments."

INSURANCE AND SELF-HELP IN AMERICA

George D. Eldridge,[1] 'Assessment Life Insurance', *North American Review* (October 1890), pp. 507–10.

B. H. Meyer,[2] 'Fraternal Beneficiary Societies in the United States', *American Journal of Sociology*, 6 (1901), pp. 646–61.

In the aftermath of the Civil War, the surging popularity of life insurance in the United States led to the chartering of numerous new companies. Yet the resulting market saturation, combined with the general economic downturn of the 1870s, created problems for the entire industry. While the more well-established companies were strong enough to weather the depression with few problems, ninety-eight firms – most of which had been chartered in the 1860s – went out of business between 1868 and 1877. Taking advantage of these problems within the ordinary life insurance industry, numerous fraternal societies and assessment companies emerged as major competitors to the American companies.

Assessment or cooperative companies, as they were sometimes called, were associations in which each member was assessed a flat fee to provide the death benefit when another member died, rather than paying an annual level premium based on age. Promoters of these plans, like the author of the first document, argued that the level-premium system adopted by the ordinary industry was too expensive, necessitating the overpayment of premiums and tempting managers to misuse these funds. The two main problems with assessment organizations were the uncertain number of assessments which would be required each year and the difficulty of maintaining membership levels. As members aged and death rates rose, the assessment societies found it difficult to recruit younger members willing to take on the increasing risk of assessments. By the turn of the century, most assessment companies had collapsed or reorganized as mutual companies.[3] If their popularity in the United States was short-lived, it was practically non-existent in Britain, where the only office selling that variety of insurance with any success was Eldridge's Mutual Reserve Fund, which opened a branch in Liverpool in 1886 and closed in 1905.[4] The market vacuum that led to the assessment companies' rise in the United States was largely absent in Britain, where surviving insurance offices outnumbered failed ones and were effective both at absorbing dislocated customers and shooting down the alleged merits of 'assessmentism'.

Fraternal organizations, described in the second document, were voluntary associations of people affiliated through ethnicity, religion, profession or some other tie. Although fraternal societies had existed throughout the history of the United States, it was only in the late nineteenth century that they mushroomed in number and emerged as a major provider of life insurance, mainly for working-class Americans. While many fraternal societies initially issued insurance on an assessment basis, most soon switched to mutual insurance. By the turn of the century, the approximately 600 fraternal societies in existence provided over $5 billion in life insurance to their members, making them direct competitors of the major stock and mutual companies. Just five years later, membership was over 6 million with $8 billion of insurance in force – a development that stood in stark contrast with Britain, where friendly societies never actively engaged in life insurance despite boasting millions of loyal members.[5] Along with British industrial companies, these fraternal societies would serve as a model for the emerging American industrial insurance companies beginning in the mid-1870s (discussed later in this volume).

Notes

1. George Dyre Eldridge was vice president and actuary of the Mutual Reserve Life Insurance Company; he also published the *Guardian*, a monthly journal devoted to promoting assessment life insurance.

2. Balthasar Henry Meyer (1866–1954) was a professor first of sociology and then of political economy at the University of Wisconsin from 1897 to 1910, where he specialized in the study of railroad legislation. He would later serve on the Wisconsin Railroad Commission (1905–11), the US Railroad Securities Commission (1910–11) and the Interstate Commerce Commission (1911–39).

3. Murphy, 'Life Insurance in the United States before World War I'.

4. *Policy-holder*, 4 (1886), p. 304; *Report from the Select Committee of the House of Lords on Life Assurance Companies* (London: HMSO, 1906), question 228.

5. D. T. Beito, '"This Enormous Army": The Mutual-Aid Tradition of American Fraternal Societies before the Twentieth Century', in D. T. Beito, P. Gordon and A. Tabarrok (eds), *The Voluntary City: Choice, Community, and Civil Society* (Ann Arbor, MI: University of Michigan Press, 2002), pp. 182–203.

George D. Eldridge, 'Assessment Life Insurance', *North American Review* (1890)

IV.
ASSESSMENT LIFE INSURANCE.

A POLICY of life insurance is a contract agreeing to pay a certain sum upon the death of a specified person, provided death occur within a specified period. In practice the business is carried on by aggregations of policy-holders called "companies," and the guarantee of the sum assured rests upon the obligation of the mass of policy-holders to contribute for death-claims the equivalent of the aggregate amounts which the company is obligated to pay to the individual policy-holders. In addition to this the policy-holders must pay the cost of transacting the business.

These propositions are true of life insurance regardless of method, and unless there is equivalence between the risk assumed by the company and the liability assumed by the policy-holder, there can be no such thing as security.

When one has to deal with the liquidation of the obligation of the individual to the company and the security for deferred payments from the former to the latter, difference of method is developed, and this, in common parlance, is dignified into difference in system, whereas in reality there is but one system, and that the system of life insurance.

There have thus come to be recognized two "systems" – the "level-premium" and the "assessment." The first essential difference is that, while the "level-premium" company limits the liability of the policy-holder to a predetermined sum, the "assessment" company limits it only by his *pro rata* of the actual claims. Each recognizes the standard mortality tables, but one uses them to determine in advance a maximum rate of premium for each age, while the other uses them as a standard for adjusting losses incurred among the policy-holders of different attained ages. The equation of liability in the case of the level-premium company is, therefore, between the present value of the amount of the insurance and the present value of the premiums which the policy-holder is obligated to pay, it being assumed, for the purpose of calculating these present values, that the deaths will occur in accordance with a certain table of mortality and that invested funds will earn a certain rate of interest. As the payment of the sums insured depends wholly upon the realization of enough from the policy-holders to meet them as they fall due, and as the payments by the policy-holders are limited by contract, safety is possible only on a basis of assumption, as to mortality and interest, less favorable than the future will show; and as many of these contracts extend over a long term of years, allowance must be made for contingencies. Therefore one of two things is inevitable: either the liability of the policy-holder to the company must be excessive, or the security less than absolute. /

The equation of liability in the case of the assessment company is between the cost which the risk will actually entail and the payment which the policy-holder must make, and is determinable as events develop and the payments are needed. This, however, does not imply that payments can be made by the policy-holder only as the money is needed for the liquidation of actual claims. On the contrary, there may be many variations in the method of making payments, provided the following essentials be kept in view:

(*a*) That funds contributed for the payment of death-claims be held inviolate for that purpose.

(*b*) That each policy-holder's contribution to the current claims of a given period be determined by the actual amount of such claims and his attained age, whether that contribution be made by him by direct payment or partly by direct payment and partly by diminution of his interest in any reserved fund that the company may hold.

(*c*) That each policy-holder receive the benefit of the payments actually made by him and the accretions thereon, and pay the cost of the entire benefits which he receives.

Since the limit of each policy-holder's liability in a given period is not a predetermined sum, the assessment company may take cognizance of the fact that all men who insure do not die insured – a fact that the level-premium company cannot take into account. In practice many assessment companies determine a payment which each policy-holder is to make at stated dates by discounting the sum assured by an assumed rate of interest and a table of the number that, from an initial number insured, will be living and insured at each succeeding age of life. This table is computed from the standard mortality tables, and from a table of discontinuances from other causes than death, made up from the tabulated experience of other insurance companies. This last element has a material effect in reducing the amount of the payment.

A payment thus determined is not to be confounded with the level premium of the other plan. It is not a limit of liability and, consequently, of security, but a deposit with the company of a sum on account of future death-cost, which is always available for and sacred to the payment of claims. The different aspect which it must hold in the eyes of the law from that of the "reserve" accumulation of the level-premium company is an additional distinction between the two methods. As the liability of the policy-holder in the level-premium company is absolutely limited by contract, any payment that he may make over and above the current death-cost is a diminution of the present value of the future contributions which he can be called upon to make. The present value of these contributions is, at the outset, the equivalent of the present value of the insurance granted, and if only the amount of current death-claims was paid by the policy-holder as time went on, these two present values would advance by equal steps. Therefore when anything more than this current cost is paid, the result is that the present value of the policy-holder's liability to the company is reduced below that of the company's obligation to the policy-holder, and unless the company holds the difference in hand in invested assets, it is and must be insolvent. The amount of these overpayments, together with the accretions thereon, is, therefore, available only for the payment of the claim under the individual policy to which it belongs, and if the company uses it for other purposes, even though it be the payment of other death-claims, it is insolvent and its insurance-granting power is destroyed; a receivership being the only alternative. It is because of this fact that failures have occurred in such numbers among companies operating on this plan.

In the case of overpayments to the assessment company no such liability exists. The money is received as a trust deposit made for a specific purpose – the payment of death-claims – and for that it is available. Its misuse renders the trustees criminally liable, but does not involve the destruction of the company's insurance-granting power. Thus in the level-premium company the impairment of the reserve fund means the loss to the policy-holder of the future insurance for which he has contracted, and this without returning to him the money that has been lost; in the assessment company, his future insurance is still secure, on the payment by him of its / cost, so that the loss of the money is not supplemented by the loss of what may be worth to him many times more.

Two corollaries follow from the distinction noted between the two plans:

(*a*) The cost of doing the business in an assessment company must be fixed by contract. This is the requirement of the law in all States that have legislated on the subject. Moneys that are collected for the purpose of paying death-claims must be held inviolate for that purpose, and though the policy that contributed them lapses and they are forfeited as a penalty, they are still available only for the purpose for which they were paid, and the persistent policy-holders must have the benefit of them in that direction.

(*b*) Savings in death-losses, surrender-charges on lapsed policies, gain in interest, and other profits in a level-premium company may be used for expenses or as the management determine. By the assumption on which the level premium is made up there is an excess over the requirements. The excess can be used for expenses. When the policy lapses, the liability under it is cancelled and the funds that were held to offset that liability are released, to be used as the management see fit. They are in no sense inviolate to the payment of claims or the benefit of the persistent policy-holders.

A large portion of the resources of every active life-insurance company must consist of the obligations of the policy-holders for payments on account of future death-claims, and this must especially be the case with an assessment company, which proscutes its business without the accumulation of large sums of money. Upon the security of these resources rests the integrity of the contracts entered into. That security, under all plans, is the same – namely, such provision that the policy-holder who refuses to pay shall forfeit to the company more than the loss that he inflicts upon it. Theoretically, the lapse of a policy cancels an obligation to the company no greater than the obligation of the company to the policy-holder which is cancelled at the same time; but practically the matter of lapse is wholly in the hands of the policy-holder, who has it in his power to say whether the company shall be required to continue the contract that it has entered into with him, while the company has no election in the matter. Common-sense points to what experience attests – that lapse will occur when it is to the advantage of the member that it should, and that when a lapse would be to the advantage of the company, the policy will be kept in force. The company must, therefore, as an offset to the privilege granted the policy-holder, exact of him, in event of his lapse, a penalty sufficient to protect the persistent policy-holders against any loss that his act may cause. If it has always in hand the means of imposing this penalty, the security of that portion of the resources represented by the future payments of policy-holders is as secure under the one plan as under the other.

This statement of the principles underlying assessment life insurance is confined to the merest outlines. The plan is one that deals with pure life insurance – the protection of the family or the dependent against the loss that would be caused by the death of the father, the husband, or the provider. It shapes itself to many modifications; such, for instance, as creditor and partnership insurance. It furnishes, distinctively, insurance for the productive period of life, the period of the dependent family, the education of children, and the hazards of active business. It leaves the combination of insurance and investment, the seductive "tontine" and endowment, to the other plan. That its chosen and appropriate field is broad beyond even the need of a great business, the record that it has made proves.

Starting twenty years ago under the form of fraternal insurance, it has developed into a great business, recognized by the laws of almost every State as of equal legitimacy with its level-premium rival. It has formulated its methods, corrected its crudities, and to-day enrols in its list of policy-holders more than two and a half million citizens. During 1889 it paid over $42,000,000 in death-claims, swelling the total paid since organization, by the companies in active existence, to $300,000,000. That it has become the recognized plan of life, as distinct from investment, insurance, is attested by the fact that it paid more in death-claims in each of the last two years than did the level-premium companies. Thirteen millions of people in this country are interested directly in its present and future, while the whole people / have a common interest in the lessons of thrift which it teaches. It is far from necessarily antagonistic to the level-premium plan. Its true rivalry is to accomplish better than that plan can the work of life insurance. There is abundant room for both. As compared with the level-premium method, the assessment plan bases its claims upon the following propositions:

(*a*) Equal or greater security, without resort to excessive charges.

(*b*) Pure life insurance without the concomitant of vast accumulation, with the resultant dangers of poor investments and misuse of funds.

(*c*) A limited, as against an unlimited, expense charge.

(*d*) Funds paid for death-claim purposes held inviolate therefor.

(*e*) Equal security for that portion of the resources of the company which consists in the obligations of policy-holders to pay on account of future death-claims.

(*f*) Reserve funds available at all times as a conservator of the insurance-granting power of the company, rather than as a menace to that function.

(*g*) Equal accountability to the State for the proper conduct of affairs, and equal recognition under the law as life insurance.

GEORGE D. ELDRIDGE.

B. H. Meyer, 'Fraternal Beneficiary Societies in the United States', *American Journal of Sociology* (1901)

FRATERNAL BENEFICIARY SOCIETIES
IN THE UNITED STATES.*

WE are fond of saying that there is nothing new under the sun. Men less wise than Solomon, if they will but look and see, may discover that the world itself is new. The elements which compose land and water have remained unchanged, and the natural laws which they obey are eternal. But the relations which mankind bears to the animate and inanimate world surrounding it are continually changing. It is in these changed relations that one may discover the newness of the present world, and it is also in these changed relations that every significant political and social question of the present has taken its rise. Most of the earlier economic, political, and religious systems were based upon the principles of authority and dependence. The banner of independence was carried high by the leaders of the revolutions which one by one broke up the old systems. The eras of revolutions – religious, political, and industrial – were transitional in their nature, and paved the way for a system of society having for its watchword neither dependence nor independence, but interdependence. Present society had its beginnings in dependence; its intermediary was independence; and the keynote of the future will probably always remain interdependence. Interdependence is the prime characteristic of the new world of which we are a part. Old institutions have been modified, the "cake of custom" has been broken, and new institutions have been created to bring about a proper readjustment among men in these changed relations. Among the institutions which have performed and are performing services in this respect, the network of fraternal beneficiary societies in the United States deserves full recognition. The social history of the United States cannot be written without taking notice of a / system which includes one out of every fifteen of our population, and which involves the expenditure of

---

* The investigation of which this paper is a by-product was conducted under the auspices of the Ethical Subcommittee of the Committee of Fifty.[1] This publication is by permission of that body.

millions of dollars annually. These societies constitute a complex of organizations which embraces in its scope the most diverse elements with respect to race affinity, material possessions, religious beliefs, political affiliations, intellectual attainment, and social position. The thread of fraternity joins them all in one great round table of equality and democracy.

Fraternal beneficiary societies, as the name suggests, are dual in their nature. Because they are both fraternal and beneficiary, these societies are really composed of two organizations each: a fraternity and an insurance company. The National Fraternal Congress[2] declares the following to be the distinctive features of a fraternal beneficiary society: (1) the lodge system; (2) representative government; (3) ritualistic work; (4) fraternal assistance to living members in sickness and destitution; (5) the payment of benefits to living members for total physical disability; (6) the payment of benefits at the death of members to the families, heirs, blood-relatives, or dependents of such deceased members. In other words, a typical fraternal society rests upon three things: *first*, voluntary organization on a basis of equality; *second*, some ritualistic system; and *third*, a system of benefits. These three are united in different proportions in different societies, and in not a few of them a struggle for predominance is taking place between the first and third. This is the battle between "fraternalism and commercialism." No such antagonism should exist, for some system of relief is a natural out-growth of the idea of fraternity. As a matter of fact, it does not exist except where the benefit features are made so prominent that the fraternal element is lost from sight, and the fraternal society becomes an insurance company, perhaps wrapping the fraternal mantle about the decrepit body of a tottering insurance scheme.

The lodge system characteristic of fraternal societies goes hand in hand with the representative form of government. The term "lodge" may be used to designate the lowest unit of organization; in it direct representation is the rule, while indirect / representation prevails in the higher lodges, usually termed grand (state) and supreme (national) lodges. Elementary lodges, or lodges of the first degree, have various names in different fraternal societies. There are camps, castles, chapters, clans, colonies, conclaves, divisions, rulings, hives, and tents. Lodges of the higher order generally have the same name, modified by some syllable, word, or phrase; such as high, superior, supreme, grand. Other societies have adopted special terms for their compound lodges. The higher bodies customarily exercise some supervision over the lower, and are legally responsible as principals of the latter.

The highest lodges usually meet biennially, the intermediate ones annually, and the local lodges weekly, biweekly, or monthly. Numerically the biweekly meetings appear to prevail. At the local meetings routine business is transacted in a manner similar to that in which any other society would do its business. Initiations and the granting of degrees are accompanied by ritualistic exercises.

The rituals of fraternal societies are based upon sacred as well as secular themes, the latter being rather the exception. Among the former may be mentioned: the story of the cross, the building of the temple, David and Jonathan, Joseph, Maccabaeus, Ben Hur. Facts of United States history, the life of the nomad, the friendship between Damon and Pythias, are employed by other societies for their rituals. It has been said that most rituals are the very quintessence of dryness. In reply it may be urged that rituals are not to be read in one's study, but that they must be seen and heard in order to be appreciated. The ritual aims to reach the human soul through both the avenues of sight and hearing. By appealing to two senses at the same time the impression is likely to be much more abiding. Ritualism cultivates certain attitudes of mind and leads the participant mentally through scenes and experiences associated with lofty themes. It arouses the imagination and teaches objectively what many a learner through ritual could scarcely acquire through private reading, even if he possessed both ability and time, neither of which is probable. The value of ritualistic exercises can be properly estimated only / when we take into consideration the multitudes to whom such ceremonies appeal with all the force of reality. Other features of the programs of fraternal societies are essentially similar to those of literary clubs – readings, essays, debates, musical selections, etc. In addition, fraternal solicitude and the work which grows out of it find a permanent place in these meetings. It is customary in several great orders for the presiding officer to open the meeting with the question, "Does any brother know of a brother or a brother's family in need?" or words to that effect. Other societies adopt analogous forms. This is a truly beautiful custom, which can hardly fail to teach that in modern society vital relations exist among men, and that, in a sense at least, every man is every other man's keeper. The unobtrusive manner in which relief is given affords practical illustrations of true charity, in which every piece of silver is accompanied by golden, loving words and more loving deeds.

The relief work of some of the orders is magnificent, as the following statistics, recording the activity of a single society for the last year, will testify: brothers relieved, 87,546; weeks' benefits paid, 568,094; widowed families relieved, 5,685; brothers buried, 8,997; paid for the relief of brothers, $2,111,646.26; paid for the relief of widowed families, $124,836.81; paid for the relief of orphans, $33,130.46; paid for the education of orphans, $6,823.33; paid for burying the dead, $583,556.96; special relief, $259,131.65; total relief, $3,119,125.47. While this order pays small death benefits, it by no means belongs to the insurance type of fraternal societies; yet it is expending nearly $8,500 per day, over $350 per hour, and approximately $6 per minute. Surely this kind of charity is more than "sounding brass or a tinkling cymbal."

Relief work of this kind is not to be confused with the systems of "benefits" adopted by the great majority of the newer societies, and which differ in name only, but not in substance, from mutual insurance. There exists much opposition among some fraternal societies to the use of such "old-line" terms as "premium," "policy," "reserve," etc. They prefer the terms /"contribution," "certificate," "emergency fund," etc. Nevertheless, whenever a definite sum of money is promised at the end of a fixed period of time in return for specified contributions, an insurance contract is entered into, and the transaction is insurance. No amount of sophistry can cover an escape from this conclusion, and such a contract must ultimately rest upon the same fundamental principles upon which all other insurance contracts rest. There are fraternal societies whose beneficiary system stands as firm as the pyramids of Egypt, and the fraternal spirit of which has not been dwarfed in consequence. There is no fundamental antagonism between the noblest aspirations of fraternity and the demands for absolute safety and permanency on part of benefit features of fraternal societies; indeed, without the latter the former may become an illusion capable of drawing multitudes into bitter disappointments, if not worse.

There are in the neighborhood of six hundred fraternal beneficiary societies in the United States, with an aggregate membership of five and a half millions, two and a quarter of which are included in the three greatest and oldest and most purely fraternal orders – the Independent Order of Odd Fellows, the Freemasons, and the Knights of Pythias – two and a half millions in the forty-seven which together form the National Fraternal Congress, and the remaining membership is distributed among the five hundred or more smaller societies. Collectively these societies have an annual income of sixty millions and carry certificates – insurance policies – aggregating nearly five thousand millions of dollars. About 5 per cent. of their income is derived from admission fees and other dues, and the remainder is raised by assessments and annual dues. Fees for admission vary from $1 to $50 in different societies, $5 being most common; and annual dues usually range between $2 and $10 and over, depending upon the amount of benefit carried. Only "benefit" members pay all the dues. "Social" members, constituting about 14 per cent. of the aggregate membership of the societies in which such a class is maintained, generally pay the regular admission fees, dues, etc., but do not contribute / for benefits, except, perhaps, to relief, widows' and orphans', and similar charity funds. "Honorary" and "invited" members are commonly exempt from financial obligations to the society.

The weakest spot of the fraternal beneficiary system is found in its protective features. Not that there are no fraternal societies whose systems of benefits are not thoroughly reliable, for there are such; but rather that there are so many of them that persistently and consciously ignore those fundamental and elementary principles without which anything in the nature of insurance can never endure. So often has this been done that the whole fraternal system of benefits has fallen into disrepute among many thinking people, and will require radical reforms and heroic work on the part of its friends to dispel the cloud which has been hanging over it. A brilliant Frenchman has said that people will not learn from experience unless this experience is repeated *on a large scale* through successive generations. The history of benefit systems of fraternal societies lends support to the generalization of the Frenchman. It would be neither agreeable nor very profitable to rehearse the many tales of disaster connected with the history of fraternal societies. However, it is worth our while to take a brief survey of the plans which are at present pursued by many of them in operating their benefit departments.

A speaker before the National Fraternal Congress, in 1899, presented the following statistics, illustrating the many different rates charged by different societies for the same amount of protection at the same age:

At age 30: $0.25, .35, .37 1/2, .44, .45, .46, .50, .55, .56, .60, .62, .64, .65, .69, .70, .80, .82, .84, .85, .90, .92, 1.00, 1.04, 1.10, 1.11, 1.14, 1.16, 1.19, 1.21, 1.22, 1.40.

At age 50: $0.65, .75, .80, .85, .90, 1.00, 1.10, 1.16, 1.20, 1.25, 1.33, 1.38, 1.40, 1.42, 1.45, 1.50, 1.53, 1.55, 1.58, 1.60, 1.65, 1.72, 1.78, 1.80, 1.85, 1.86, 1.90, 1.96, 2.00, 2.07, 2.08, 2.15, 2.35, 2.45, 2.52, 2.56, 2.86, 2.90, 3.00, 3.30, 3.80.

These figures tell their own story. The speaker also found that there were twenty-one orders charging less at age fifty than another order charges for age thirty. When large numbers of men are considered, health experiences are as certain, although not as definite, as the laws of natural science, and any system of / benefits which ignores this fact cannot be sound. It seems almost incredible that in this late day men should be found who deny the certainty of mortality experience, yet in fraternal literature one may find proof thereof. In justice to those who, it is hoped, constitute a majority among fraternalists, it should be said that notes of warning from within the ranks have not been wanting. They have been sounded loud and clear in unmistakable tones. The National Fraternal Congress has taken the bull by the horns by repudiating the hand-to-mouth "levy" schemes and elaborating a table of level rates, step-rates, and of two modified step-rate plans. These tables have been recommended to members by successive congresses. The table of level rates is approximately one-sixth lower than the net premiums (*i.e.*, premiums including only the mortuary and reserve elements, but not the "loading" or expense) based on the American Experience Table at 4 per cent. interest, for corresponding ages up to thirty-five; and nearly 10 per cent. below the same above age thirty-five. Whatever may be said with respect to the adequacy or inadequacy of the rates recommended by the Fraternal Congress, it must at least be admitted that it shows a conscious attempt on part of influential fraternal societies to base rates of contributions on actual experiences in health and expense items. One fraternal society has adopted for its basis of rates the combined experience tables of four great orders, and intends to continue on this basis until it has accumulated experience of its own adequate for the formulation of reliable tables. This is a rational method of procedure. If fraternal societies can furnish protection at lower rates than those which have hitherto seemed possible, they should have an opportunity to do so, provided that the experiment does not involve inevitable ruin. Experimentation is justifiable, both ethically and socially considered, only within certain limits. We may encourage a man to become an expert marksman, but we have no right to condemn his fellow-beings to serve as targets, nor should our statutes permit him to go unpunished in case he persists in continuing such target practice. Some societies are doing business today at rates less than one-half and one-third of those recommended by the congress. This / is nothing short of criminal. There is something radically wrong somewhere when a small organization can slide along in a happy-go-lucky fashion with its liabilities half a million in excess of its assets; yet such is the case today. To wipe out so large an unfavorable balance requires special assessments. These are unpopular and threaten to reduce membership. The infusion-of-new-blood hobby is held up as an encouragement to the faithful members, until the inevitable must be faced. Relatively few fraternalists seem to realize that the only safe way is to charge whatever is necessary to cover the risk at whichever age a person may enter; in other words, that the only way to do an insurance business is to conduct the same in accordance with well-established principles and business methods. If the standard mortality tables used by old-line companies are too high for the experience of fraternal societies, let their own experience serve as a guide; but until experience tables of individual societies have been actually established the use of some other reliable tables should be made compulsory. If fraternal societies can bring about a more favorable health experience, they should have an opportunity to do so. If they can reduce the cost of insurance, they will benefit society by extending the blessings of protection to ever-widening circles. If the expense element is at present too high, let them have free rein, consistent with safety, to demonstrate that it can be reduced. Their present weaknesses should not lead us into intolerance.

These remarks in regard to the safety of benefit systems apply only to those societies which promise a fixed sum to beneficiaries in certain contingencies. Although the exact number could not be ascertained, a careful estimate places the number of societies which will be excluded by this last limitation at from one-third to one-half of the whole number, so that approximately only 50 per cent. of the fraternal societies will be directly affected by radical changes in protective features. The original fraternal idea was to have members contribute equal sums in specified contingencies, and the proceeds of such contributions, not exceeding a certain maximum nor the amount of a single assessment, to be paid to the beneficiary. This is not insurance, / but relief work, to which the principles of insurance do not apply. If "fraternal insurance" had never been made to stand for anything else, it is probable that much of the confusion and many of the erroneous notions which prevail today could never have arisen. Many people seem to believe that there is one thing called "insurance" and another and a different thing known as "fraternal insurance." As a theory this is vicious; as practice it is criminal. Whatever the methods of organization employed, whether stock companies, mutuals or coöperative associations, assessment or stipulated-premium organizations, or any combination of these, ultimately all insurance, irrespective of external forms, must rest upon the same fundamental principles; if not, it is not insurance nor anything worthy of the prestige which this term has gained. "Insurance" which does not protect is no insurance at all. The old fraternal idea was chiefly remedial; insurance in the modern sense is primarily preventive.

While differences of opinion may exist with respect to the efficiency of legislation in bringing about reforms, there can be no question about the necessity of more adequate insurance legislation in general, and statutes relating to fraternal societies in particular. The inference should not be drawn that general insurance laws should not apply to fraternal societies. They should, in so far as these societies are insurance organizations; but because of their dual nature, uniform statutes relating to fraternal beneficiary societies exclusively should be enacted. Insurance legislation is in a chaotic state. The greatest diversities and antagonisms exist in law where conditions are essentially the same. The lack of uniformity is one of the greatest evils. The National Fraternal Congress has for a number of years recommended a uniform law, which has been enacted by the Congress of the United States for the District of Columbia, and which has also been adopted by the legislatures of several states. Only fifteen states have fairly complete legal provisions relating to fraternal societies, four of these having special laws governing the same. Six states are silent on the matter, and twenty others exempt fraternal societies from statutes regulating assessment societies, while four others require compliance / with either the assessment or the regular insurance laws. Considering the magnitude of the interests involved, the urgent necessity of uniform general laws must be apparent. Either the United States Congress should establish a federal bureau for the national supervision of all fraternal and insurance organizations, or the states should bring about essential uniformity by voluntary coöperation. There exists much apathy among politicians toward this subject, for very few of them, it seems, have the moral courage to advocate measures which can bring about those radical reforms which are necessary in order to place fraternal beneficiary societies on a permanent footing. There are those in public life who believe that, because of the large membership of fraternal societies and the influence which they are capable of exerting, a man who would venture upon such an undertaking would thereafter be politically "dead." Many things in this "new world" of ours have to be borne vicariously, and this may be one of them; yet there are reasons for believing that any man in public life who would show the courage necessary to do this in a rational and fair-minded way would ultimately be the gainer thereby. Once let the illusion be thoroughly exposed, and a grateful public will remember its benefactors.

An excuse for the legislative neglect of fraternal beneficiary orders is found in the relative newness of the entire system. To be sure, a few orders count the period of their existence by centuries, but, with the exception of the three greatest fraternal orders and several smaller ones, the fraternal system, as it exists today, is but a quarter-century old. The fanciful connection between modern fraternities and mediæval guilds has no significance from a social point of view, even if it could be established as a historic fact. The godfather of modern fraternal beneficiary societies is the Ancient Order of United Workmen, founded by "Father" Upchurch, a wage-earner at Meadville, Pa., in 1868. This society served as a model for the hundreds which have followed. Of 568 fraternal societies, the date of whose organization could be ascertained, 78 only were founded before 1880, 124 between 1880 and 1890, 136 between 1890 and 1895, and / 230 since 1895. In other words, 86 per cent. of the fraternal societies are only twenty years old, nearly one-fourth are between ages of five and ten, and over 40 per cent. are either infants or children below five. The aggregate membership has risen from 3,707,947 in 1893 to 5,339,075 in 1900. The increase during the last five years has been 25 per cent., and during the past ten years it has doubled. The membership in two orders approximates one million each, and in two others it is about half a million each. There are a dozen societies with a hundred thousand or more members, ten which average over fifty thousand, and a second dozen with an average of about twenty-five thousand.

This large membership raises the question of the effect of fraternal societies upon modern life.

The "jiner" is a familiar character. Like some of the "poor" who puzzle charity workers, they distribute their fraternal affiliations in such a way as to secure the largest revenue. "Fraternity for revenue only" is their motto. They join one society to gain a *clientèle*; a second to secure customers; a third to win influence. If they do not join more, it is "because there is nothing in it." We need scarcely spend time with this abnormal type. It does not represent the "brother."

It has been asserted, however, that membership in a lodge frequently involves expenditures which should have taken another direction. Regalia and the like cost money, and the husband may spend five or ten dollars for a uniform while his wife must be satisfied with a cheap calico dress. Picnics and excursions and celebrations under the auspices of the lodge cost money, and money which, it is asserted, should in many instances be paid for better food and clothing and higher types of amusement and recreation. Whatever may be the ultimate truth in the matter, fraternal societies have here a problem which is worthy of their serious consideration. When membership in the lodge brings sorrow and pain into the family circle, the spirit of fraternity is violated at the very outset.

This applies chiefly, if not exclusively, to men. But women have also founded fraternal beneficiary societies. There are less / than ten societies composed of women only, and about fifty admitting both men and women. Mixed societies may be passed over with the remark that their experience appears, on the whole, to be favorable. Women add an important social element, and seem to counteract that tendency toward "commercialism" which has made its way so far to the front in some of the newer societies. Fraternities composed entirely of women aim to accomplish pretty much the same thing which men's societies attempt. They operate systems of benefits and generally conduct their lodges in an analogous manner. The very rapid increase in the number of members of several women's societies is sufficient to show both some degree of success and of popular favor. In view of the fact that there are several millions of wage-earning women in the United States, the gradual extension of the fraternal system among women seems capable of accomplishing much good. Not only can these societies direct and cultivate the social habits of women, but they can maintain systems of benefits which will add security to woman's position in society. What has been said in an earlier paragraph in regard to protective features of fraternal societies applies also here. When multitudes of women are not only dependent upon themselves, but have also others dependent upon them, any system which adds certainty and stability to their status must be looked upon with favor. Even in far-off New Zealand, that experiment station of the world, women's fraternal societies, says the *Registrar of Friendly Societies*, "are growing in public favor." An important element in this problem is the matter of insurance risks. Extensive testimony brought before the National Fraternal Congress seems to indicate that on the whole women constitute as good insurance risks as men under the same climatic and industrial conditions, and that under certain circumstances the mortuary experience among women is even more favorable than among men. An extension of insurance among women is to be regarded as most desirable.

From a social point of view there are other important considerations which enter into the question of fraternal beneficiary societies. Whether meetings occur biweekly, as most of them / do, or more or less frequently, the atmosphere of the lodge-room leaves its mark upon the brother. It is impossible for a person to visit year after year the same precincts, see and hear the same ritual, participate in the same unpretentious charitable work, hear the same gentle counsel, and be exhorted by the same lofty injunction, without being affected in his inmost soul. The very fiber of his being must show all this in its structure. Within the lodge-room all men are equal in both theory and practice. Questions of religion, politics, nationality, etc., are scrupulously avoided. Every brother must, it is true, believe in a supreme being; but he may worship where and how he pleases. A candidate is not admitted if he is addicted to drink, or if he is engaged in the manufacture or sale of liquor. Some are prohibitionists, but as a class fraternal societies stand for moderation rather than absolute prohibition. If a brother takes to drink after he has joined an order, he is privately admonished by his fellows. This unobtrusive personal work of fraternal societies is one of their greatest elements of strength. A brother has a definite place in the world. No matter what may befall him, he finds sympathy and assistance in the lodge, provided he does nothing contrary to the law. And even if he has seriously erred, his brothers will try to help him on his feet again and support him in his attempt to live an upright manly life. Many beautiful concrete illustrations could be cited to show this.

An important element in the fraternal beneficiary system of the United States is the National Fraternal Congress, organized at Washington, D. C., November 16, 1896. The congress started out with seventeen orders, representing 535,000 members, and carrying $1,200,000 benefits or insurance. At the close of 1899 the congress represented forty-seven orders, an aggregate membership of 2,668,649, and insurance risks amounting to $4,021,869,290. Last year the societies represented in the congress paid over thirty-eight millions in benefits.

The idea of such a congress originated in New York, in which state the fraternal orders had united in a similar way and had won much praise from the friends of the system by the able manner in which they had antagonized hostile legislation. It is / a fact worthy of notice that the Ancient Order of United Workmen, which is the prototype of so many later societies, was also the promoter of the congress, for it was pursuant to a notice sent out by its supreme master-workman that the Washington meeting was held. In its organization the National Fraternal Congress presents no novel features. It has the usual set of officers and the customary methods of doing business. Its scope of work is indicated in the names of the standing committees on statutory legislation, medical examinations, statistics, and good of the order, and others. Along all of these lines it has done a large work. Much valuable statistical material has been gathered, which may ultimately serve as a basis for the insurance business of the orders. Reports have been made from year to year on legislation in the different states; and the discussions of the medical section have resulted in greater thoroughness and uniformity in examinations. Among the special committees which from time to time have been appointed, none has accomplished a better task than the committee on rates, to which reference was made in a preceding paragraph. The congress has done a great deal to clarify opinion among the orders in regard to their financial affairs. It has also brought together the fraternal press of some three hundred members and a total circulation of more than a million and a half. A similar body, the American Fraternal Congress, was organized at Omaha, in 1898, by the representatives of eighteen orders. The chief point of difference between the two congresses seems to be the reserve fund upon which the latter insists. This is significant as indicating a strong tendency toward the employment of well-established business methods. In one way or another a number of societies have established a reserve fund, although, because of their dislike for old-line terms, it is usually called an "emergency fund." The federation of fraternal societies has given a strong impetus to reform.

Opposition to fraternal societies is based upon a number of different things. The imperfections of their benefit systems have called forth bitter attacks, which have only too often been justifiable. Those fraternal societies which do an insurance / business on a sound basis do not seem to be able to control the system, and nothing but the most radical changes can prevent many others from moving steadily to certain destruction which has so often heretofore brought the whole system into disrepute. Secrecy is another source of opposition both on part of some churches and on part of private citizens. Attacks based upon this ground generally find much of their inspiration in the literature of the anti-masonic agitation following the abduction of Morgan,[3] as anyone who will take the trouble to compare magazine articles of the last ten years with the pamphlets and articles of that period may convince himself. Some critics seem to assume that everything secret is bad and of the evil one, and everything open is of the light and good. "Disloyal oaths" even are mentioned. There is absolutely no evidence available anywhere which would even arouse the suspicion that secrecy as now practiced by fraternal societies is anything more than a prudent method of self-protection against imposters and designers. It is the most convenient and efficient method by which a person may establish his identity with a certain order in an unmistakable way in every part of the world. The oath, too, comes in for its share of the condemnation. The form in which some oaths are expressed is said to be barbarous and revolting. The investigations of history easily dispel such notions, by showing that these forms are survivals, and that all the oaths aim to accomplish is to impel every member to do his very utmost in living up to his obligations. No covenant is to be left unfulfilled so long as there is a single thing untried in the attempt to redeem a pledge once given. Some of the orthodox denominations object to the threefold count of secrecy, ritualism, and insurance. Ritualism is "counterfeit religion;" hence the church cannot tolerate it. "Insurance is against the first commandment, because it takes a man's trust from God and places it on the insurance company; it is against the eighth commandment, because by it the beneficiary gets something not paid for by him, therefore it is stolen; and it is against the tenth commandment, because the person who invests in life insurance is taught to covet something not his own. . . . Money procured through life / insurance is obtained by good luck or a species of a game of chance." The church cannot be held responsible for the action of a particular synod; yet those high in the councils of the church can render a great service by disowning such arrant nonsense and enlightening their benighted brethren who are capable of passing such asinine resolutions.

The fraternal beneficiary system, then, like most institutions, embodies both elements of strengh and of weakness. Its weaknesses are found chiefly in unsound financiering, the inimical possibilities of conviviality, undue multiplication of orders and the competition among them, encroachment upon family life by calling for large sacrifices in time and money, and in the utter lack of uniformity and the incompleteness of the statutes governing the orders. It is strong in its great relief work, its fraternal solicitude for members, its rules of equality, its unselfish and self-sacrificing acts of personal devotion, and in its teaching of right ideals, habits of thought and action. The first part of the duality constituting the system – fraternity – deserves unstinted praise; the second part – benefit – must be subjected to a process of metamorphosis (excepting, of course, individual societies) before it can meet the unqualified approval of thoughtful men. The fraternal beneficiary system of the United States deserves, as a whole, to be well thought of.

B. H. MEYER.
UNIVERSITY OF WISCONSIN.

JOSIAH C. NOTT, 'STATISTICS OF SOUTHERN SLAVE POPULATION, WITH ESPECIAL REFERENCE TO LIFE INSURANCE', *DEBOW'S COMMERCIAL REVIEW* (1847)

Josiah Clark Nott,[1] 'Statistics of Southern Slave Population, with Especial Reference to Life Insurance', *DeBow's Commercial Review*, 4:3 (November 1847), pp. 275–89.

Just as life insurance was spreading throughout the north-eastern United States during the first half of the nineteenth century, southern slaveholders began seeking policies to underwrite their human chattel, particularly their skilled artisans, those hired out to work in industry, or those engaged in especially hazardous occupations such as mining, railroad construction or steamboat employment. Reflecting the dual status of slaves as persons and property, owners sought and received policies from both life and fire insurance companies. While it is impossible to determine the full extent of this line of business, there is substantial evidence that slave policies were firmly established among the urban slave owners of the Upper South by the eve of the Civil War, and that the major southern companies, including Baltimore Life (1830–67), North Carolina Mutual Life (1849–65), Mutual Benefit Life and Fire of Louisiana (1849–53), Greensboro Mutual Life (1853–65) and Virginia Life of Richmond (1860–3), all underwrote a substantial number of slaves. By the late 1850s two-thirds to three-quarters of all policies for both North Carolina Mutual and Baltimore Life were on slaves. While several northern companies refused to engage at all in this line of insurance, numerous other northern companies did agree to underwrite slaves, although these policies only formed a fraction of their overall business.

In the document reproduced here, Dr Josiah Nott (1804–73) – a prominent Alabama physician and medical examiner for several southern insurers – expressed his concern about the financial safety of underwriting slaves, given the sparse knowledge of slave mortality and the potential for moral hazard. Most companies heeded his warnings, setting premium levels much higher than those on white lives, and putting in place stricter policy conditions with regard to slaves. Most insurers granted slave policies for no more than seven years and for no higher than two-thirds to three-quarters the market value of the slave in question; additional policies on the same life in different firms were strictly forbidden. Beyond the usual underwriting restrictions, policies were also void if the slave died due to the mistreatment of the master, during an insurrection, or while attempting to escape.[2]

Notes
1. Dr Josiah Clark Nott (1804–73) was a well-known racial theorist and a medical examiner for several insurance companies in Mobile, Alabama.
2. Murphy, 'Securing Human Property'.

Josiah C. Nott, 'Statistics of Southern Slave Population, with Especial Reference to Life Insurance', *DeBow's Commercial Review* (1847)

Art. I. – STATISTICS OF SOUTHERN SLAVE POPULATION.

WITH ESPECIAL REFERENCE TO LIFE INSURANCE.

My communication in the May Number of your Review on "LIFE INSURANCE AT THE SOUTH," had reference only to the white population.* I now, in compliance with your request, give you a few remarks on the value of life among the colored population, which is becoming a very important subject for consideration. My time is much occupied with yellow fever, and I might very fairly claim indulgence for the hasty and imperfect manner in which I am performing my task; but I may, with still more propriety, offer as an excuse a deficiency of material, from the universal neglect of VITAL STATISTICS in the United States. We have already seen that there is by no means a redundancy of information as regards the whites; but the neglect, North and South, of statistics of blacks, is positively disreputable in this enlightened epoch.

Though there is a want of data, by which we can fix with accuracy the value of life among the colored population, there are still sufficient to show that insurance companies are going into this branch of their business pell-mell, without knowing anything of the probabilities. If I can bring them to a halt, and give a better direction to this part of the investigation, it is all I can now hope.

No one can be more fully alive than myself to the vast importance of insurance on negroes, to the South; yet, though I may be severely censured by some,

* The article to which our friend Dr. Nott adverts, was a very valuable and interesting communication which should be read and studied by every insurance company and agency in the Union. It occupies a large space in the volume, and abounds with the most valuable statistics of life and mortality to be had in the Southern States. Dr. Nott will continue these valuable papers; and it is our purpose to aid him by the collection of material at the North wherever it can be had. These subjects are entirely new among us, and their full and elaborate discussion is very much a question of American interest. – EDITOR.

I shall express myself freely without regard to the opinions of others, as I believe the truth alone can be beneficial on the whole. If risks on this class were taken alone by joint stock companies, formed of heavy capitalists who were disposed to gamble on the chances, I should have no objection to see a course of experiments which might lead to a discovery of the true value of life among the colored population; but it should not be forgotten that the life insurance companies now preferred are the *Mutual*, and that unless all the risks work well, the interest of every individual must be jeoparded, / as *all* are stockholders under this system. Suppose, for example, 1,000 lives are insured in a mutual company, one-half whites, the other colored. If the risks upon the latter are badly selected, upon whom would fall the losses? Not upon the owners of the slaves alone, or rich members of the company, but upon the poor, honest, industrious, and I may add unsuspicious man, who at the end of the year scrapes together a few of his hard-earned dollars to invest in an insurance company, with the hope of saving his wife and children from beggary when he is no longer able to toil for them.

The data given in my former paper go strongly to prove that the acclimated population of our southern sea-ports *are taxed too high* for life insurance, and I hope I shall at least gain credit for honesty of intention if I now express my doubts whether we are taxed enough on the colored population.

The general fact that there is less mortality South than North among the colored class is sufficiently established; but there are no statistics by which the chances of life can be calculated with sufficient accuracy to form the basis of insurance operations in any city in the Union. At the South, vital statistics have been so neglected by local authorities, that, with the exception of Charleston, South Carolina, we are left wholly in the dark, and even here there has been a great deficiency of details. Within the last year or two, however, important improvements have been made in the manner of keeping tables of mortality in Charleston and Mobile, and we may in a few years expect important results.

Though the white and black races stand diametrically opposed to each other as to the influence of climate on health and longevity, and the necessity for so doing is manifest, yet in most cities no attention has been paid to separating the two classes in their bills of mortality. Even in the large cities of the North the bills of mortality are so badly kept, or so concealed from the public, that nothing can be ascertained on this point. I have made repeated but fruitless efforts to procure bills of mortality of the colored population from Baltimore, New York, and Boston. I have, however, been fortunate enough, through the kindness of Dr. G. Emerson[1] (who has taken the trouble to ransack the records for me), to procure the bills of Philadelphia for 20 years.

I am really at a loss how to account for the silence of Boston on this subject. The statistics of that city, embracing everything which the statesman, physician, or philanthropist could ask, as births, marriages, deaths, sexes, occupations, ages, diseases, manufactures, etc., etc., are all given with admirable system and detail annually, and yet no allusion whatever is made to the mortality of the colored. I have before me the census for each year since 1840, and the last of them, viz., for 1845, is accompanied by a long and able report by Dr. Shattuck[2] on vital statistics, making altogether an octavo volume of 300 pages, and yet not a fact can be found bearing on our subject. Can it be that the mortality of the colored population is concealed on account of its connection with the question of abolition? When I see the intelligence with which these statistics have been conceived and executed – when I see that these details were once carefully kept, and then of late years abandoned – and when I reflect on the improbability / of the importance of such facts being overlooked in a city like Boston, I cannot help indulging such a suspicion.*

I have on a former occasion, in the Southern Quarterly Review,[3] discussed at some length the question of the unity of the races, and shall not here open that question again; but no one at all familiar with the past history of the negro and his present peculiarities, can entertain a doubt that he is now very widely separated, both in *physique* and *morale*, from the white man, and that it would require a combination of circumstances not likely to occur, and a long series of years, to bring him up to the Caucasian standard.

The extreme antiquity of Egypt as a civilized nation, taught by Champollion, Young, Vyse, Birch,[4] and others, has not only been confirmed by the recent important discoveries of Baron Bunsen and Lepsius,[5] but these gentlemen have fixed beyond dispute the epoch of Menes, the first king of Egypt, at more than 3600 years before Christ. It is equally well settled by the monumental history of that country, that the negroes existed at that early day with all the physical characteristics they now possess, and that they were treated and spoken of as slaves and barbarians. No one familiar with this discussion, will question these statements, and I think we may conclude that if, the Negro has never, in the course of 5,000 years, been thrown into a position to develop his equality, we have no right to expect any great advance in the next few hundred years. The good old Bishop of Blois (H. Gregoire),[6] in his work on the "Literature of Negroes," after exhausting the history of the past, has only been able to collect a few examples who had attained a certain degree of proficiency in the literature of the whites; but not one of them can bear comparison with the better specimens of the Caucasian race; and all attempts made in the present century at bettering the condition of the slaves have but added to their ignorance and unhappiness.

But, passing by the physical history of the negro in the old world, I shall confine myself to the influence of climate as exhibited in this country over this race, so far as it is connected with the subject of life insurance.

---

* We should be greatly obliged to Dr. Shattuck for any information in these matters it may be in his power to give. This is a matter of universal interest. – ED.

All testimony combines to establish the fact, that cold climates are most unfavorable to the health and longevity of the blacks; and as some of our readers may not be familiar with vital statistics, I will precede those of the colored class by tables, showing the mortality among the whites in various parts of the world, which may serve for comparison. The deaths from recent and authentic tables, were as follows:

STATISTICS OF MORTALITY – AVERAGE FOR ONE YEAR.

Boston	1 in 47
Philadelphia	1 in 42
England	1 in 45
France	1 in 42
Austria	1 in 33
Prussia	1 in 38
Russia	1 in 38
London	1 in 37
Birmingham	1 in 36
Sheffield	1 in 32
Leeds	1 in 37
Bristol	1 in 32
Manchester	1 in 29
Liverpool	1 in 28

I have not been able to get any tables from the towns in Canada, / showing the mortality of the negroes. Rankin, in his "Visit to Sierra Leone,"[7] informs us, that the negroes who deserted their masters during the Revolutionary war, and joined the British army, were afterward colonized in Nova Scotia, but finding it impossible to stand the climate, they were removed to the colony in Africa by the British government. They there, in their state of liberty, showed their constitutional indolence and improvidence, and most of them have had the good fortune to be kidnapped and sold back to the United States. If I recollect correctly, Rankin states, that of 1,100 taken to Sierra Leone, but about 600 of them and their descendants remained at the end of thirty years.

As before stated, I have been unable to procure from Boston and New York tables exhibiting the mortality of the negroes for late years, but I have so often seen it stated at 1 in 15, and 1 in 18 respectively, that I presume, these figures may be assumed as substantially correct.*

Philadelphia may be placed intermediate in point of climate between the extremes of heat and cold in the United States, and we should accordingly expect to find here an intermediate mortality in this class. The tables below (furnished me by Dr. G. Emerson), when placed beside those of Charleston and Boston, will confirm such a result. As the climate on the gulf approaches still more

---

*   If there is any one who has information to the contrary, we would gladly welcome the
     facts. – ED.

closely that of the tropic, it is not improbable that the longevity of the blacks is still greater (as it certainly is of mulattoes) here, than in the city of Charleston. The tables of mortality for Charleston and Philadelphia are as follows:

MORTALITY OF CHARLESTON.

Years.	Whites.	Blacks.	Years.	Whites.	Blacks.
1830	1 in 39.4	40.0	1838	1 in 18.3	33.0 Y. Fever.
1831	1 in 46.6	37.9	1839	1 in 29.9	39.0 "
1832	1 in 51.9	55.3	1840	1 in 50.7	46.6
1833	1 in 55.0	55.7	1841	1 in 65.1	44.8
1834	1 in 42.1	44.1 Y. Fever.	1842	1 in 50.3	47.8
1835	1 in 43.1	46.4 "	1843	1 in 60.8	32.9
1836	1 in 40.6	19.6 Cholera.	1844	1 in 69.3	43.3
1837	1 in 47.3	46.7	1845	1 in 52.9	48.5

MORTALITY OF PHILADELPHIA.

Years.	Blacks.	Years.	Whites.	Blacks.
1821	1 in 16.9	1831	1 in 39.6	33.6
1822	1 in 21.5	1832	1 in 28.8	22.6
1823	1 in 17.5	1833	1 in 47.3	35.2
1824	1 in 17.5	1834	1 in 41.4	33.3
1825	1 in 27.0	1835	1 in 38.3	31.2
1826	1 in 26.1	1836	1 in 43.8	21.4
1827	1 in 18.9	1837	1 in 45.1	32.7
1828	1 in 20.8	1838	1 in 45.0	29.2
1829	1 in 23.7	1839	1 in 49.4	31.3
1830	1 in 27.2	1840	1 in 52.2	38.6

It appears from the above tables, that the average mortality in Philadelphia, among the colored population, was 1 in 26, and in Charleston, 1 in 44. Certainly a very marked contrast, and there can be no doubt, that, could the free colored be separated from the slaves, / the latter in Charleston would show a still more favorable result.* There is a considerable number of mulattoes, and free colored in Charleston. The mortality in Philadelphia has been decreasing among both whites and colored, no doubt from the improved condition of the city.

I have marked above the years in which Yellow Fever prevailed in Charleston, and it will be seen that the mortality in those years among the negroes was lower than among the whites, on account of their exemption from this disease. In my former article, I gave evidence of the fact, that the mortality from this disease falls on the *unacclimated whites*.

---

*   We have the authority of Dr. Niles,[8] then a citizen of New York (now of Paris), in a pamphlet published by him in 1827, for giving the mortality of Baltimore in 1823–24–25, as follows – Whites, 1 in 44; free blacks, 1 in 32; slaves 1 in 77–8. This result is probably attributable to two causes – 1st, there is a large proportion of mulattoes among the free colored; 2d, the physical wants of the slaves are better supplied, and they are infinitely more cheerful and happy than the free colored.

I have given in the above tables the mortality of whites and blacks together, in each city, in order to contrast the influence of climate on the races. The greatest mortality ever known in Charleston, in the colored class, was in 1836, when it was raised by the Cholera to 1 in 19 – more than double the average; but even Cholera and Slavery combined, here, are far less destructive to the negro, than liberty and climate in Boston, where the mortality is said to average 1 in 15.

To arrive at a fair estimate of the mortality of this class in northern and southern cities, we must take into consideration, not only the influence of climate, but social condition also. The negro, is by nature indolent and improvident, everywhere and under all climates; and has nowhere in a state of freedom shown a high degree of longevity, or prolificacy, though by nature the longest lived, I believe, of all the human family. These facts should not be overlooked in estimating their mortality at the North, where they are enjoying all the abstract delights of liberty. In the West Indies, we have a strong illustration of the effect of emancipation, and in their native state, in Africa, the average longevity of the blacks (as in all barbarous nations) will be less than among our slaves. In our northern States, where they, to a great extent, fail to provide against the severe winters, the diseases arising from cold and want must add much to their misery and mortality.

History cannot point to any epoch, or spot on the earth, where the condition of the negro race, either physical or moral, has been at all comparable with that of the slaves of the United States. Mr. Lyell,[9] who seems to have reflected much and honestly on the evils of slavery, during his last visit to this country, expressed to me decidedly his conviction, that the negroes could only be civilized through slavery. They are here brought into forced contact with a civilized race, from whom they imbibe new and more enlarged ideas – they are taught a rational religion – many learn to read and write – all are taught the agricultural, or mechanic arts, or some other useful employment – they not only become more intellectual, but improve in physical appearance; and if they are capable of civilization at all, they are thus admirably prepared for a farther advance. Their progress has certainly been infinitely more rapid than it could have been / under any missionary or colonial system. Mr. Lyell thinks, from all this, that they may be brought up to the Caucasian standard, but if he will live among them as I have, and study well their history, from the palmy days of Egypt down, he will find abundant reason to change this opinion. The races of men, like animals in a wild, uncultivated state, may, if docile, be tamed, educated and vastly improved, but there are limits set to each by nature, beyond which no advance can be made. Although there may be an occasional example where a negro will show a degree of intelligence and capacity for improvement beyond the mass, yet no negro has ever left behind him any intellectual effort worthy of being preserved. The negro is naturally mild and docile; the Indian, on the contrary, is an untamable, carnivorous animal, which is fading away before civilization, in spite of the efforts of missionaries. Can any man who knows anything about the present condition of the Indians and their past history, propose a scheme for their improvement, which would offer the least prospect of success – the race must soon be extinct – even the pure blood Mexicans, who I have no question are a different race from the aboriginal savage, are going down in darkness to their long home.[*]

The negro will reach, I may say *has* reached, his highest degree of civilization, and emancipation has so far only proved what I think is inevitable, that when removed from compulsion he relapses into barbarism. The Indian can be made to do nothing "on compulsion" – he would rather die than be a slave.

When a race (as the negroes) has had possession of a continent for at least 5,000 years, and no monument stands to designate a single civilized spot – when we see that it held constant intercourse with Egypt in her glory – when, too, we see the result of all recent experiments of abolitionists – I think we may safely conclude, that the negro attains his greatest perfection, physical and moral, and also his greatest longevity, in a state of slavery. The single fact of the longevity of the colored class in Charleston is a very significant one, and should be pondered on by the philanthropist. The colored population of this city show, not only a lower ratio of mortality than any laboring class of any country, but a lower mortality than the aggregate population (including nobility and all) of any country in Europe, except England, with which it is about on a par, and would surpass even England were the slaves taken separate from the free colored. The mortality of the aggregate colored population of Charleston now is less than that of the aggregate of any *town* in Europe.

That the negro, even when placed under the most favorable circumstances, as to physical wants, &c., is unfavorably affected by cold climates, is a fact which admits of no dispute. All the hospital practitioners of the Northern cities must acknowledge the fact. So sensitive are they to cold, and so little are they affected by that fell-destroyer of the white race, *malaria*, which kills more than war and famine, that they suffer in the Southern States more from diseases of winter than those of summer. They are, I am informed, exempt / from the violent congestive fevers of our interior districts, and other violent forms of marsh fever; and so exempt are they from yellow fever, that I am now attending my first case of this disease in a full-blooded negro. In fact, it would seem that the negro blood is an antidote against yellow fever, for the smallest admixture of it with the white will protect against this disease, even though the subject come from a healthy northern latitude, in the midst of an epidemic. There are some exceptions, but they are rare. I will not fatigue the reader by an elaborate comparison of the diseases of the two races, as influenced by climate, but will allude to a single one – consumption.

[*] The Peruvian and Mexican, the most civilized races found in America, had smaller heads than the savage tribes. How did their heads get smaller by cultivating their intellects, if they are the same race with the latter? This is a question I should like to see solved.

In Charleston they have but recently commenced separating the white and colored population in their bills of mortality, with full details, and I have the deaths from consumption in the latter class for but one year, viz.: 1846; but the ratio of deaths from this disease is so uniform, that it fluctuates but little when undisturbed by epidemic diseases. In Charleston the deaths from consumption in 1846 were 1 in 7 of all the deaths; and in Mobile the average for the three years 1844–'45–'46, the ratio was 1 in 8, in the colored population.

The following extract is from the "New York Medical and Surgical Reporter," February 27, 1847:

> "*Colored Home*.[10] – The report of the resident physician, James D. Fitch, M. D., for the year ending 1st January, 1847, is just published. By the tabular account of the inmates during that time, which specifies the sex, age, history and diseases of all who have come under the supervision of Dr. Fitch, we find that the total number in charge, during the year, was 464, and the number of deaths, 89. *** The disease most prominent is consumption, by which more than one-half of the deaths have been caused, the number being 47," &c.

Now, how near this astounding mortality from consumption may be to the general result of other years in New York and Boston, I have not the data to determine. I can only say, that I have no disposition to plead one side, but, on the contrary, would be very glad if some gentleman of the North would give me, or the public, all the information possible. Why do they not give us the facts fully?

The combined influence of climate and social condition is again illustrated by the comparative increase of the colored class North and South. It has been already stated, that the *whole* population of Philadelphia, including white and colored, in the decennial period from 1830 to 1840, increased 35 per cent., while the colored, taken alone, shows an increase of but 18 per cent. From the constant escape of negroes from the slave States, and the protection offered them in Philadelphia, we should have expected a different result. I will here introduce an extract, bearing on this point, from my article in the Southern Quarterly Review, January, 1846, on the Unity of the Human Race.

It occurred to me that one of the best methods of testing the influence of climate on the negro race, would be to ascertain the relative proportion of children, in different States, to the free colored women between 15 and 45 years (the fruitful age). I have accordingly constructed the following table from the census of 1840, in which is given all the free colored children under 10 years, and the colored females as near as possible. The census gives the free colored females between 10 and 24, between 24 and 36, and between / 36 and 55. I have, therefore, taken half of the aggregate of the first and last, and added this amount to the whole of those between 24 and 36, which must give a sufficiently near approximation to the truth.

I have, in the fourth column of the table, placed the per centage of excess or deficiency of children compared with the females; and the excess or deficiency in each State is expressed by placing the sign *plus* or *minus* before the number expressing the per centage.

I have confined these statistics to the *free* colored population, because they are the most stationary; and similarity of habits and other circumstances, render them the fairest test. There are some irregularities in these statistics which are difficult to explain, but if we take the aggregate of sections, or any rational view of the matter, I think they are not unsatisfactory. I give them for what they are worth, hoping they will at least lead the way to other observations.

	Number of free colored women between 15 and 45 years.	Free colored children under 10 years.	Percentage of excess or deficiency of children under 10 compared with the females.		Number of free colored women between 15 and 45 years.	Free colored children under 10 years.	Percentage of excess or deficiency of children under 10 compared with the females.
Maine	280	296	+5	Georgia	515	802	+55
New Hampshire	117	107	−9	Alabama	406	572	+40
Massachusetts	1,782	1,807	+1	Mississippi	269	409	+50
Rhode Island	850	673	−26	Louisiana	5,892	8,178	+38
Connecticut	1,836	1,902	+3	Tennessee	999	1,854	+95
Vermont	156	167	+7	Kentucky	1,276	1,984	+55
New York	12,511	12,040	−3	Ohio	3,558	5,190	+43
New Jersey	4,374	5,853	+33	Indiana	1,348	2,370	+75
Pennsylvania	11,687	12,509	+7	Illinois	696	1,084	+55
Delaware	3,207	5,358	+33	Missouri	298	345	+15
Maryland	13,727	18,548	+35	Florida	177	216	+23
Virginia	10,457	15,857	+53	Arkansas	81	144	+77
North Carolina	5,507	7,666	+39	Michigan	148	173	+17
South Carolina	1,776	2,795	+57	Dist. of Columbia	2,161	2,376	+9

The only line which can be drawn across the United States without intersecting States, is one about thirty-six and a half degrees of latitude, which very nearly bounds on the north, North Carolina. Tennessee, and Arkansas. The States of North Carolina, South Carolina, Tennessee, Arkansas, Georgia, Alabama, Mississippi, Louisiana, and Florida, are all south of this line, and the other States all north of it. From the abundance of provisions, the absence of malaria, the protection here given to the colored class, we might reasonably infer that they would be most prosperous and prolific in the northern division. The southern division comprises all the most sickly portions of our country, and the free negroes have less liberty and indulgence than at the North. A calculation made from the above table gives but about 25 per cent. more children than females in the northern division, while in the southern the excess is 44 per cent. The New England States alone show 3 *per cent. less children than females of the child-bearing age.* /

By the census of 1800 there were in the New England States, of all ages, 17,317 free colored, and in 1840 there were but 22,633, or an increase only of 5,316 in 40 years! If climate and social condition have nothing to do with this result, I must leave it to others to show what becomes of the natural increase, and of the colored immigrants constantly coming in.

But, had we all the data necessary for fixing the value of life in the pure whites and blacks, another question arises with regard to the longevity of the mixed bloods or *mulattoes.* This question presents many ramifications, which are not only curious, but deeply important to the philanthropist. It has been more fully treated in some of its bearings than I have room for here, in the article alluded to in the Southern Quarterly, and I now shall merely touch it so far as it is connected with the value of life. Whether it be primitive or not, the white and black races are to all intents and purposes *specifically different*, and it is our business now to treat them as we find them in reference to our subject.

A writer in the Boston Medical and Surgical Journal, Nov., 1842, under the signature of "Philanthropist," who seems to be an earnest seeker after truth, uses the following language:

"From authentic statistics and extensive corroborating information, obtained from sources to me of unquestionable authority, together with my own observations, I am led to believe that the following statements are substantially correct:

"1st. That the longevity of the Africans is greater than that of the inhabitants of any other part of the globe.

"2d. That mulattoes, *i.e.*, those born of parents one being African and the other white or Caucasian, are the shortest lived of any class of the human race.

"3d. That the mulattoes are not more liable to die under the age of 25 than the whites or blacks; but from 25 to 40 their deaths are as 10 to 1 of either the whites or blacks between those ages; from 40 to 55, the deaths are as 50 to 1: and from 55 to 70, 100 to 1.

"4th. That the mortality of the free people of color is more than 100 per cent. greater than that of slaves.

"5th. That those of unmixed extraction in the free States are not more liable to sickness or premature death than the whites of their rank and condition in society; but that the striking mortality so manifest among the free people of color, is in every community and section of the country invariably confined to the mulattoes.

"It was remarked by a gentleman from the South, eminent for his intellectual attainments, and distinguished for his correct observation, and who has lived many years in the Southern States, that he did not believe that he had ever seen a mulatto of 70 years of age.

"From a correspondence published in the Boston Spectator, in April last, are taken the following statistics:

"In a colored population of 2.634.348, including free blacks, there are 1,980 over 100 years of age; whereas there are but 647 whites over 100 in a population of 14,581,000.

"In Boston, the number of deaths annually among the colored population is about 1 in 15, and there are fewer pure blacks in this city than any other. The same comparative mortality between mulattoes and blacks exists in the West Indies and in Guiana, where unfavorable social causes do not operate against the mulattoes as in the United States."

Though they do substantially, my observations at the South will not fully corroborate all the above conclusions of "Philanthropist." My belief is that the mulattoes *do* die more than whites or blacks under 25, as they *certainly* do above this age, and that the pure / blacks are destroyed by cold climate as well as the mulattoes, though the latter may be most sensitive.

I will here give the results of my own professional observation during 20 years at the South, which I feel assured time and experience will substantially confirm. The facts were forced upon me during my intercourse with the colored class, and attracted my attention long before I had formed any theory on the subject, and at a time when my convictions were the opposite of what they now are.

1st. The mulattoes are intermediate in intelligence between the blacks and whites.

2d. They are less capable of enduring fatigue, exposure, and hardships of all kinds, than either blacks or whites.

3d. The mulatto women are peculiarly delicate, and more subject to a variety of chronic diseases peculiar to females.

4th. The women are bad breeders and bad nurses – many do not conceive, and most are subject to abortions, or premature births.

5th. The two sexes, when they marry, are less prolific than when crossed on one of the parent stocks.

6th. The specific difference of the races is strongly illustrated in the exemption of the negroes from yellow, and congestive fevers; not only the negro, but the quarteroon, though a native of a cold latitude, is to a great extent exempt; there are occasional exceptions, and it is well known that yellow fever, like cholera, has often been fatal to domestic animals.

The above facts, which I think will in the main hold good in all the Atlantic States, and are more marked the farther north we look, would seem to be contradicted to a considerable extent, if not wholly refuted by an opposite state of things on the Gulf. I hope the contradiction, however, will prove to be only apparent.

The mulattoes, by which I mean all grades of mixture, derived from the early population of Pensacola, Mobile, and New Orleans, and who are a mixture principally of French and Spanish blood with that of the negro, present very different physical characters from the mulattoes seen in the Atlantic States, who are derived mainly from the Anglo-Saxon race. The complexion on the Gulf of the colored creoles (as they are called) is a strong copper, or bronze of different shades, which is agreeable to the eye, and strikingly different from the chalky, sickly hue of the others; they excite at once in the mind the idea of a *new*, or *distinct race* – are well formed, more robust and hardy, and their features often regular and handsome, partaking little of the contour of the negro; they are also much more prolific and long-lived than the mulattoes of the colder States. A stranger coming to Mobile, or New Orleans, could not fail to be forcibly struck by the physical peculiarities of these colored creoles, many of whom resemble so closely certain Mongol tribes, as to give strong support to the suggestion of Dr. S. G. Morton,[11] that the latter *may* possibly be a mixed race of Caucasians and negroes; an idea which will be much strengthened by his remarks on the influence of climate on hybridity. Their hair is often as straight, black, and glossy as that of the Chinese or Indian – the high cheek bone, and obliquity of the eyes is not uncommon. In looking over the well-executed heads in Richards' physical history of man,[12] I can find no type of the colored races of / the *old world*, as the Mongol, Hindoo, Malay, &c., of which I have not seen a good imitation in real life, among the colored creoles of Mobile and New Orleans – but it is remarkable that they show *no resemblance to the aborigines of the new world* – these stand out from the rest of mankind, as Dr. Morton's Crania Americana will show, as boldly as a new and distinct creation.

It is perhaps a difficult task to account for the above differences between these creoles and the mulattoes of colder climates; it is possible that a reason may be found in certain affinities or repulsions of certain races, which fits or unfits them for perfect amalgamation. The population of Germany, France, Spain, Italy, England, Ireland, and Scotland, is such a heterogeneous compound at the present day of aborigines, Celts, Sclavonians, and Germans, that there are now endless disputes as to the original physical character of each of these latter races; and as to the blood which now predominates in each country. The modern Britons, and Germans, from whom they are principally descended, are usually much more fair in complexion than the French, Spaniards, Italians, Russians, Poles, &c., who, Lawrence[13] and others, maintain, are derived from the Celts, and Slavons, of dark skin, hair and eyes. Explain the fact as we may, it is to my mind evident that negroes amalgamate much better with the dark than the fair races.

When we reflect on the specific differences between the two races (Caucasian and Negro) and the many peculiarities which belong to the mulatto, I think we are justifiable in regarding the latter as a hybrid. I have shown on a former occasion that naturalists have been able to lay down no rule which could offer the slightest objection to this idea. We have shown also that different hybrids are subject to very different laws; some are prolific and others not, &c. Why may it not be a law of the human hybrid, that it is a more delicate, less hardy, and long-lived than the parent stocks? there are facts in natural history which lend support to this idea.

Dr. Morton, the distinguished author of the Crania Americana, and Egyptica, in a paper read last November before the Academy of Natural Sciences in Philadelphia, on "hybridity in animals and plants, considered in reference to the question of the unity of the human species," gives us some interesting facts, which may account more satisfactorily for the distinctive character of the mulattoes North and South. After showing that not only different *species*, but *genera* produce prolific hybrids, he gives facts to prove that climate has much to do with the fecundity of certain hybrids; they may not breed, for example, in a cold climate, but will in a warm one, which is more congenial to their nature. Such would seem to be the case with the mulatto or hybrid offspring of the Caucasian and Negro races; the facts can be clearly established that the mulattoes (the colored creoles at least) of Mobile and New Orleans, are more prolific, more hardy, longer lived, and in every respect a superior race to those of the North. My observations for some years were made on the mulattoes of South Carolina, and even as far South as this, their inferiority is manifest.

The facts and deductions thus far presented would lead very strongly to the conclusion that the black slaves of the South are very / safe risks for insurance; but though fully persuaded of the favorable position of this class, both as to climate and social condition in reference to health and longevity, and though deeply impressed with the importance of this branch of life insurance to the slave States, still I must say that I believe there are yet no data by which the value of these lives can be fixed with sufficient accuracy to justify the thoughtless procedure of some companies.

The mortality among the colored class in Charleston, including blacks, mulattoes, slaves, and free, is 1 in 44 annually; and though this is a more favorable table than can be found in any laboring class in the world, and though even this mortality might be greatly diminished could we separate the free and the hybrids from the black slaves; yet it must be remembered that among the whites it is only the better class that apply for policies; and that the negroes are the laboring class of the South. It is a well-known fact, that as you rise in the scale of society so does the longevity increase, simply because the upper classes are less exposed to the causes of diseases, and can command comforts and prompt medical advice in sickness. The experience too of insurance companies in Europe, shows that there is far less mortality in their selected lives, than in the aggregate population of a nation. It cannot be reasonably expected, then, that the slaves at the South can equal in longevity the better classes of Europe, or the selected lives of insurance companies.

The black slaves, though generally treated with kindness and indulgence, are the laboring class – are exposed much to the causes of disease, and are less protected in sickness than the higher classes; like the man-servant and maid-servant of the free States, they are less cared for in sickness and health than the master and mistress. The longest lived class in England are the nobility; and though poverty in itself may not be a sin, it is not only a disgrace, but tempts many a poor fellow to sell soul and body both.

"Lord lead us not into temptation," is the wisest prayer ever uttered – it contains a profound reflection on human nature. Men are prone to become very good and pious when they get too old to be tempted, and we should therefore pray daily not to be tempted. Life insurance on negroes offers strong temptations to be feared, many of which I have not time to enumerate.

When a company insures the life of a free man, it has the best of all guaranties against foul play, viz.: the innate love of life of the insured party. But on the other hand, we occasionally see at the South unfeeling masters, as we do unfeeling husbands, cruel fathers, and cruel masters to apprentices, in the free States; and such individuals will not show any increase of kindness during sickness, should their interest be opposed to humanity. As long as the negro is sound, and worth more than the amount insured, self-interest will prompt the owner to preserve the life of the slave; but, if the slave become unsound and there is little prospect of perfect recovery, the underwriters cannot expect fair play – the insurance money is worth more than the slave, and the latter is regarded rather in the light of a superannuated horse.

Human nature is the same everywhere, and at all times. See how the English manufacturer coins his guineas out of the exhausted / frames of his wretched operatives – after one set of victims is worked to death, another is at hand ready for the sacrifice. So with the Southern masters, though their slaves, as a general rule, meet with more kindness than any laboring class in the world; yet when it ceases to be the interest of the owner to preserve the life of the slave, he will in many instances cease to be careful of it. Any man who will drive a horse cruelly, will drive a negro or operative to death, if he can gain anything by so doing.

Suppose a thousand slaves to be insured for seven years, and at the end of one, two, three, four, or five years, a portion of them should become unsound, and it is no longer the interest of the owners that they should live out the seven years; would not many be like the Yankee Captain with the insured ship, "damn the old hulk, let her sink – I am safe." That "Almighty Dollar" would soon silence the soft, small voice of humanity.

We have every reason to believe that many unsound negroes would be insured fraudulently, which could be easily done – and it is a singular fact, that the negroes who will nurse the master with untiring devotion and kindness, night and day, are like dogs, utterly regardless of each other's wants in sickness – this is a characteristic in freedom or slavery.

It would be unsafe to insure negroes on plantations in the country, because it is impossible, I fear, to get competent and reliable medical examiners, and for other reasons. Most of the applications would probably be from the towns. It has not been, nor do I think it is likely to become, the custom of masters to insure slaves, except in those instances where they suppose some extraordinary risk to life is incurred, and if such risks alone be taken, the chances must be against the underwriters. I will mention for example the fact, that most of the negroes presented to me for insurance, have been deck-hands of steam-boats, who, besides the danger of being blown up, are exposed to other dangers much greater; at one moment they are employed as firemen, and at the next, they are rolling cotton bales down the river bank at midnight in a cold rain. Many are consequently attacked by pleurisy,[14] and other acute diseases – they are not unfrequently seriously injured by blows from the cotton bales while rolling down the high bluffs, and lastly, they often become intemperate, and contract other bad habits which lead to disturbance of health.

Since the above was printed we have received the following letter from Dr. Nott, which is worthy of attention:

THE SLAVE QUESTION.

Mobile, Sept. 20, 1847.

With what intense anxiety are the eyes of the whole country fixed upon the meeting of our next national assembly? Do we not all feel that we are on the verge of a struggle which must shake the Union to its very foundations? The social position of the negro race, and its influences on the various sections of the country, is to be discussed, and, in my opinion, most of the leaders of public opinion, North and South, are wholly unprepared to meet the great difficulties which complicate this subject; and the facts I have here and on former occasions alluded to, call loudly upon the attention of the statesman, the patriot, and philanthropist. All the reasoning and action of legislators heretofore have been deduced / too much from the history of the Caucasian race, as if the question were settled that the white man and negro are essentially the same, and demand the same course of policy. When we ask for *facts* – for some clear light of experience, drawn from the history of the past, to lead us out of the labyrinth in which fate has placed us – we are answered by the sentimental abstractions of the closet. But, Mr. Editor, these great difficulties cannot be met and overcome by abstractions. We must look to the natural history of the races for light; and I have no hesitation in asserting, that nothing wise – nothing productive of substantial good to the negro race – can be effected without a full knowledge of their physical and intellectual character.

Can humanity look without a shudder upon the reckless impetuosity with which demagogues and fanatics decide great questions like this, involving the lives, fortunes and happiness of millions of human beings, without the slightest knowledge of those facts which are indispensable to the formation of a rational opinion? The angry and senseless discussions on negro emancipation, which have agitated Christendom for the last half century, were commenced in ignorance, and the abolitionists have only become more angry and unreasonable, as facts have risen up against their theories.

It has become evident that this controversy, as now conducted, must lead to consequences fraught with evil both to the white and black races. Is it not time, then, that good and wise men should rise up, inform themselves thoroughly, and, looking the difficulties full in the face, adopt such a course as reason and humanity shall dictate?

The object of the honest abolitionist must certainly be, to better the condition either of the white or black races. How are the whites to be benefited? What the distant future may bring forth, human sagacity cannot foretell; but we know that all great and sudden changes in the policy of a country must be productive of distress; and no one can doubt that emancipation of the Southern slaves would, for a long series of years, be followed by utter destruction of the great staples of the South, and a corresponding destruction of the manufacturing and other interests of the North. It would not stop here; but the older nations who are fed by our commerce would suffer, even more perhaps than ourselves. Should such consequences be hazarded without good and sufficient reasons? But how are the blacks to be benefited by emancipation? This is the great point on which the controversy should turn. Where are we to look for light on this point, either in the history of the past or in the teachings of the present day? Will some abolitionist talk to us sober sense and reason, and demonstrate some plan by which the negro can be made free, prosperous and happy? I am a slave owner, and while on the one hand I shall, in common with the Southern people, resist all encroachments on our constitutional and natural rights, I am, on the other hand, free to say that I am ready to advocate any scheme of emancipation which will insure to the slaves of the South greater happiness than they now enjoy. Every candid and intelligent man, who has examined the facts, must acknowledge that the negroes of the Southern States are infinitely better off than those of Africa, all of whom are the slaves of barbarian chiefs; that they are in a far better condition, morally and physically, and more happy, than those of the free States; that they are in every respect in a better condition than the emancipated blacks of the West Indies; and that African colonization, and the long and painful labors of missionaries, have so far resulted in no good.

Whether the negro be of distinct origin – whether he be a descendant of Adam, changed by the long-continued action of physical causes, or whether the

Almighty has, by a direct curse, blackened his skin and clouded his intellect, it is not our intention here to inquire; but it cannot be denied that the negro *now* presents peculiar physical and intellectual characters. We must therefore, take him as we find him, and for all practical purposes it is immaterial which theory we adopt. The true questions to be decided are – To what position among mankind is he *now* best suited? and, to what position more exalted can time and experience elevate him?

Though many contend that mental cultivation, continued through several generations, may greatly improve a race, no one of our authoritative writers on the natural history of man, whether Christian or Infidel, whether advocating or opposing the unity of the human race, can be found to maintain the intellectual equality of the black and white races.

Experience teaches that none but an intelligent people are fit for any form of government short of an absolute despotism, and it is difficult to imagine how the negro is to be sufficiently enlightened to qualify him for self-government. He / cannot be educated to any extent while a slave, because he becomes unfit for slavery and dangerous to the master. He cannot be liberated and allowed to remain where he now is, because a large population, so indolent, improvident and vicious as free negroes everywhere are, could not be tolerated in any country. Could Alabama, for example, permit her 300,000 slaves to be freed and turned loose within her borders? And I would ask the States north of the Potomac, if they would vote for the emancipation of three millions of slaves, with the "*proviso*," that when liberated they should all settle at the North? I have no doubt that the abolitionists of the North would sooner vote that all the tribes of Africa should be turned over to the devil without benefit of clergy. Self-preservation equally forbids that such an idea should be entertained for the Southern States.

But one scheme, then, can be seriously entertained, viz.: that of colonization, and it is much to be desired that some one would give us a project by which these millions of ignorant, stupid negroes can be successfully colonized, and kept from relapsing (as they are rapidly doing in St. Domingo) into African barbarism. The experiments in colonization, and even the gigantic efforts to suppress the slave-trade, have so far been productive of nothing but evil; and we have every reason to believe, that if the negro *can be* so improved as to qualify him for self-government, a long series of years will be required to effect such a result. The monumental history of Egypt, according to recent researches of Bunsen, Lepsius and other learned hierologists, shows, beyond dispute, that the negro presented the same physical and intellectual characters 5,000 years ago that he does now; and how long, may it be asked, will it take to bring him up to the Caucasian standard? I deny, positively, that there is any evidence in the history of the past, or the experience of our own times, to prove that the brain of a race can be enlarged and the intellect expanded by cultivation through a series of generations. The skulls of the untutored Germans of antiquity – of the Greek peasants – of the ancient Britons, and of the wandering Circassians,[15] who are now bidding defiance to the Emperor of Russia, are as well formed as those of the nobility of England of the present day. Baron Larrey,[16] whose authority will not be questioned in this matter, tells us that the wandering Arabs have the finest formed brains he ever saw. The Caucasian head is always ready formed, and when the spark is applied the intellect blazes forth. Wherever this race is brought under a good government, great men spring up from the very forests. Can any one believe for a moment that the genius of Alexander, Cæsar, Napoleon, Hannibal, Newton, La Place, Cuvier, Shakespeare, &c., is attributable to cultivated ancestry? No – the same blood has been coursing through the veins of the race from Adam down to the present day.

But let us suppose, for a moment, that the negro really is susceptible of progressive improvement. Where is the nation willing to devote the time and money necessary for the perfection of three millions of negroes? Will Old England? No. Will New England? No. They may both be ready to sacrifice both the whites and blacks of the South on the altar of false humanity, but neither will stretch out his hand to offer substantial aid in the cause.

I must bring this hasty letter to a close, but hope I have said enough to make apparent the paramount importance of *negro statistics.* If the blacks are intellectually inferior to the whites – if the whites are deteriorated by amalgamation with the blacks – if the longevity and physical perfection of the mixed race is below that of either of the pure races, and if the negro is by nature unfit for self-government, these are grave matters for consideration. These conclusions I solemnly believe to be true, and that full investigation will only tend to confirm them; and I may add, that my conviction is the result of much personal observation and careful perusal of every work of note on the natural history of man in the French and English languages.

The negroes have attained a greater moral and intellectual elevation – greater physical development and longevity, and incomparably more happiness, in our slave States, than they have ever enjoyed under any other circumstances. Every feeling of humanity, then, and every motive of policy, should bid us handle gently a question of such extreme delicacy. We have yet no light to guide us safely in a change; and as we know that the Southern people are responsible to God alone for their sins, and that it is his hand at last that rules the destinies of nations, it would be better, far, to leave this question to the slow but certain work of time and experience.

Yours, &c.,

JOSIAH C. NOTT, M.D.

W. E. BURGHARDT DU BOIS (ED.), *SOME EFFORTS OF AMERICAN NEGROES FOR THEIR OWN SOCIAL BETTERMENT* (1898), EXCERPT

Du Bois, W. E. Burghardt (ed.), *Some Efforts of American Negroes for their Own Social Betterment* (Atlanta, GA: Atlanta University Press, 1898), pp. 18–21, 54–6.

William Edward Burghardt Du Bois (1868–1963), better known as W. E. B. Du Bois, was a leading civil rights activist and a prominent writer, historian, sociologist and journalist. He was a founder in 1909 of the National Association for the Advancement of Colored People, its director of research in the period 1910–34, and later chair of the department of sociology at Atlanta University (1934–44). His most famous works are *The Souls of Black Folk: Essays and Sketches* (1903) and *Black Reconstruction in America, 1860–1880* (1935). During his tenure as a professor of economics and history at Atlanta University from 1897 to 1910, he organized a long series of conferences called the Atlanta University Studies of the Negro Problem. The document excerpted here is from one of the sixteen publications produced as a result of this conference series.

In the aftermath of the Civil War, most life insurance companies treated black applicants as undesirable risks, choosing either to charge discriminatory rates based on their race or deny them coverage altogether. With the emergence of industrial companies during the 1870s and 1880s, blacks became a much larger proportion of potential policyholders. The two major industrial companies, Metropolitan Life and Prudential of America, both eventually adopted the rule of charging the same rates for all policyholders, but only paying claimants on black policies two-thirds of the stated death benefit. As had been the case during the antebellum period, companies justified all of these discriminatory measures by arguing that black mortality rates were substantially higher than white rates. However, several lawsuits during the 1880s and 1890s successfully challenged this rate discrimination as being in violation of the Fourteenth Amendment. Companies responded by either dropping blacks from their insurance roles or rating them as substandard risks (ostensibly based on non-racial factors, for which it was still legal to discriminate). By the end of the nineteenth century, blacks were finding it increasingly difficult to obtain life insurance at reasonable rates.[1]

Mirroring the explosive growth of fraternal societies offering small burial and life policies to whites in the postbellum period were black fraternal benefit societies. Like their white counterparts, these organizations emerged to provide social and economic support to their members. One of these societies, the True Reformers (founded in 1881 in Richmond, Virginia) attracted over 100,000 members in eighteen states; unlike many associations run on the assessment plan, the True Reformers set insurance rates based on the fragmentary mortality evidence available on blacks. Almost every other black insurance organization established over the ensuing decades had its roots in the True Reformers, with most organizers being former agents hoping to mimic the success of this initial society. Many of these societies suffered the same fate as white fraternal and assessment societies, collapsing under the weight of an inadequate fee structure and an ageing membership. Yet two of them, the North Carolina Mutual and Provident Association and the Atlanta Mutual Insurance Association, both made successful transitions to become legal reserve life insurance companies (North Carolina Mutual Life and Atlanta Life) catering to a black clientele by the early decades of the twentieth century.[2]

Notes
1. Bouk, 'The Science of Difference', pp. 169–80.
2. W. B. Weare, *Black Business in the New South: A Social History of the North Carolina Mutual Life Insurance Company* (Durham, NC: Duke University Press, 1993), pp. 12–16.

W. E. Burghardt Du Bois (ed.), *Some Efforts of American Negroes for their Own Social Betterment* (1898), excerpt

SOME
EFFORTS OF AMERICAN NEGROES FOR THEIR OWN
SOCIAL BETTERMENT.

Report of an investigation under the direction of Atlanta University; together with the proceedings of the Third Conference for the study of the Negro Problems, held at Atlanta University, May 25–26, 1898.

Edited by
W. E. BURGHARDT DU BOIS, Ph. D.,
Corresponding Secretary of the Conference.

ATLANTA, GA.
ATLANTA UNIVERSITY PRESS.
1898. /

[...]

5. *Beneficial and Insurance Societies.* – The beneficial society sprang directly from the church organizations and has developed in four characteristic directions. First, by taking on ritual, oaths and secrecy it became the secret society just mentioned. Secondly, by emphasizing and enlarging the beneficial and insurance feature and substituting a board of directors for general membership control, many of these societies coalesced into, or were replaced by, insurance societies. Thirdly, the training in business methods thus received is now, in an increasing number of cases leading to co-operative business enterprise. Fourthly, the distribution of aid and succor tended to pass beyond the immediately contributing members, and become pure charity in the shape of Homes, Asylums and Benevolent Societies of various sorts.

In number of organizations the secret societies outstripped the benevolent societies, while the others naturally are still but partially developed. Nevertheless the beneficial society antedates emancipation; some now in existence are fifty years old or more, and others now extinct can be traced back to the Eighteenth century.

These societies, of all kinds, sizes and states of efficiency, are still very numerous. Take, for instance, Petersburg, Va. There alone we have reports from twenty-two, as follows:

BENEFICIAL SOCIETIES OF PETERSBURG, VA.

	NAME.	When Organized.	No. Members.	Assessments per Year.	Total Annual Income.	Sick and Death Benefits.	Cash and Property.
1	Young Men's	1884	40	$7 00	$275 00	$150 00	$175 00
2	Sisters of Friendship, etc.	*	22	3 00	68 55	43 78	
3	Union Working Club	1893	15	3 00	45 00	23 00	
4	Sisters of Charity	1884	17	3 00	51 00	30 00	
5	Ladies' Union	1896	47	3 00	135 00		128 25
6	Beneficial Association	1893	163	†25c. 5 20	1,005 64	808 46	440 00
7	Daughters of Bethlehem		39	†12c. 3 00	129 48	110 04	
8	Loving Sisters	1884	16	†25c. 3 00	22 50	30 50	62 00
9	Ladies' Working Club	1888	37	†12c. 3 00	95 11	52 65	214 09
10	St. Mark	1874	28	†12c. 3 00	84 00	32 00	150 00
11	Consolation	1845	26	†12c. 3 00	68 00	27 00	100 00
12	Daughters of Zion	1867	22	†12c. 3 00	66 00	40 00	36 00
13	Young Sisters of Charity.	1869	30	†12c. 3 00	90 00	30 00	100 00
14	Humble Christian	1868	26	†12c. 3 00	68 00	35 50	75 00
15	Sisters of David	1885	30	3 00	90 00	60 00	130 00
16	Sisters of Rebeccah	1893	40	3 00	120 00	85 00	175 00
17	Petersburg	1872	29	†12 1/2c. 3 00	85 00	11 00	99 53
18	Petersburg Beneficial	1892	35	†50c. 5 20	182 00	158 00	118 00
19	1st Baptist Church Ass'n	1893	100	60	60 00	40 00	80 00
20	Young Men's	1894	44	†25c. 3 00	211 00	202 25	100 00
21	Oak St. Church Society	1894	38	1 20	42 60	112 63	50 00
22	Endeavor, etc.	1894	98	3 00	120 00	96 00	43 00
	Total		942		$3,113 88	$2,177 81	$2 275 87

*   Organized before the war.
†   Assessment upon each member in case any member dies. /

Returns from other places are not so full, not because of the lack of such societies, but because of the difficulty of getting exact reports from them. They are small, have no public office and must be searched for. Probably there are at least one hundred such societies in the nine cities. Some are small and weak, others flourishing. Of the latter class the condition of six typical ones is given in the next table.

SOME TYPICAL BENEFICIAL SOCIETIES.

PLACE.	NAME.	When Organized.	Number Members.	Assessments per Year.	Total Annual Income.	Sick and Death Benefits.	Cash and Property.
Galveston, Tex	Daughters of Rebecca	1866	53	$12 00	$900	$800	$3,000
Augusta, Ga.	Trinity Moral Reform	1850	240	1 00	960	500	100
" "	Union Relief	1894	100	1 20	800	300	1,000
" "	Young Mutual	1886	475		661	498	87
Atlanta, Ga.	Helping Hand	1879	50		140	100	1 lot.
" "	Coachman's Benefit	1896	40		240		
	Six Societies		958		$3,701	$2,198	$4.187

The business methods of beneficial societies are extremely simple. A group of mutually known persons, members of the same church or neighbors, unite in an organization and agree to pay weekly 25 cents or more into a common treasury; a portion of the fund thus secured is paid to any member who may be taken sick, and, too, the other members in such case give their services in caring for the sick one. In case a member dies each of the other members is assessed from 12 1/2 to 50 cents – usually 25 cents – in addition to their regular fee, to help defray funeral expenses. This simple and safe insurance business has everything to commend it as a method of self-help, and it has without doubt had much to do with the social education of the Negro, both before and since emancipation.

The indications are that ten or fifteen years ago the number of these societies was twice as great as at present. Over half of those reported in this inquiry were established before 1890, and are probably survivals of a very large number of enterprises. The insurance societies have come in to replace the activities of these societies, and the change, while indicating higher economic development, is at present having many disastrous results. The impulse towards insurance societies was given by the large number of white societies organized to defraud and exploit the Negroes. Everywhere the Freedman is noted for his effort to ward off accident and a pauper's grave by insurance against sickness and death. In New York city a canvass of one slum district showed that 15% of the Negro fathers and 52% of the mothers belonged to insurance societies.* In Philadelphia the situation is similar, although the disparity between the sexes is not so great.† So, too, throughout the South the operations of these societies has been wide-spread. Partly in self-defence therefore / and partly in obedience to a natural desire to unite small economic efforts into larger, the Negro insurance societies began to arise about 1890, and now have throughout the country a membership running into the hundred thousands. Some of the secret societies are in reality insurance

---

*   Laidlaw, 2nd Sociological Canvass, 1897.[1]

†   DuBois, The Philadelphia Negro.[2]

societies with a ritual to make membership more attractive. The True Reformers' order, for instance, was started in Richmond, Va., not over fifteen years ago; it now extends widely over the East and South, owns considerable real estate and conducts a banking and annual premium insurance business at Richmond.

Three typical Virginia insurance societies are the Workers' Mutual Aid Association, the Colored Mutual Aid Association and the United Aid and Insurance Company. The Workers' Mutual Aid Association was organized in 1894. It is conducted by twelve stockholders and has two salaried officers, besides the agents. It claims 10,053 members, an annual income of $3,600, and sick and death benefits paid during the year to the amount of $1,700. It owns property to the amount of $550. Its rates of insurance are as follows:

Weekly Premiums.	Weekly Sick Benefits.	Death Benefits.
$05	$1 25	$17 00
10	2 00	35 00
15	2 75	45 00
20	3 50	55 00
25	4 25	65 00
30	5 00	75 00
35	5 75	85 00
40	6 50	95 00
45	7 25	105 00
50	8 00	115 00

The agent reporting declares: "This class of enterprises do well, but the great drawback is they are too numerous, and it is hard to find young men who are willing to do the work necessary to make them a success; and then the class who are willing to take hold honestly, is at a *very grea* premium." The headquarters of this association is in Petersburg, Va.

The Colored Mutual Aid Association was organized in 1895; the number of stockholders is sixteen; the number of salaried officers, three; the number of members, 5,000; the total annual income, $1,172 82; the total expenditures for sick and death benefits, $800. The rates of insurance are:

Weekly premiums.	Weekly Sick Benefits.	Death Benefits.
$05	$1 50	$15 00
10	3 25	35 00
15	3 50	40 00
20	4 50	50 00
25	5 25	60 00
30	6 00	75 00
35	7 00	85 00
40	8 00	95 00
45	9 00	100 00
50	10 00	115 00 /

The United Aid and Insurance Company, according to its report, "was organized in Richmond, Va., four years ago; we have a total membership of 21,500 members. We are doing business in all the cities of this State and also in some other States. The financial condition of the company is good; it pays all claims promptly." The company occupies its own building in Richmond.

The membership of these societies is naturally much smaller than reported, but nevertheless it is large. The insurance charged is of course very high. A thousand dollar life policy costs about $250 a year premium, against $30 to $40 for a middle aged man in the regular life insurance companies.* This high rate is to cover the weekly benefits in case of sickness, and as there is no age classification and practically no medical examination, it represents the gambler's risk. Such business, of course, opens wide the door for cheating on both sides. The educational value of conducting these enterprises is, among the Negroes, very great, and considering their lack of business training, the experiment has been quite successful. On the part of the insured, the old beneficial society was a more wholesome method of saving. The insurance society savors too much of gambling and discourages the savings bank habit.

[...]

ORGANIZED EFFORTS OF NEGROES FOR THEIR OWN SOCIAL BETTERMENT IN PETERSBURG, VA.

Paper Submitted by James M. Colson,[3] Professor of Natural Science in the Virginia Normal and Collegiate Institute.

I. THE CHURCH.

The colored population of Petersburg is 13,000. There are 12 colored churches – 8 Baptist, 2 Methodist, 1 Presbyterian and 1 Episcopal. All the churches save one own their places of worship. The total enrollment is 7,768, and the active membership is 4,032; the church property is valued at $114,760; the indebtedness is $4,579; the income for the past year was $11,653.72; the annual expense was $11,045; the sum of $900.35 was expended for charity by nine churches, the other churches keeping no record of their charitable work; 81 persons and an orphan home are reported as having been helped.

The organization of church work is far from being complete. Christian Endeavor and young people's denominational societies are slowly growing in favor. Such relief work as is attempted is carried on by each congregation mainly for its own members. Benevolent societies exist in most of the churches for the

---

* Mutual Benefit Life Ins. Co.'s rate for a man of 45 is $37.42. /

purpose of helping the sick and burying the dead. Their members pay from 5 to 10 cents monthly; they receive $1.50, $1.00 and 50 cents per week, according to the number of weeks sick, and $15.00 and $20.00 death benefits. Only members of the church society get assistance. Nearly all the churches make some effort to care for the aged and poor sick. Outside of this there is little or no organized charitable work. Two churches have branch or mission Sunday-schools. In the true sense of the term there is no local missionary work supported by our churches – the missionary societies scheduled are adjuncts of the Home and Foreign Missionary Societies of their respective denominations.

In all the churches the constant struggle to obtain money to pay current expenses is so great that little energy is left to look after the spiritual development of the people.

The only recognition of the social needs of the young people is evidenced in the annual picnic and Christmas tree. Two good signs are to be noted; The growing sentiment against the use of the church edifice for anything else than religious exercises and the demand for an educated and clean ministry.

II. SECRET SOCIETIES.

Reports have been obtained from more than 40 secret societies. Their actual membership is 1,246; they own real estate to the value of $7,450; their income for last year amounted to $4,746.27; they paid out for sick benefits $770.25; for death benefits, $1,369.05; and aided 250 persons. These societies pay sick benefits of $1.00 or $2.00 weekly, and death benefits ranging from $20 to $125. The orders are establishing "endowment / funds," so that it is possible to give a much larger death benefit than could otherwise be given. For example, the local society pays $25 out of its treasury and the order $100 to the heirs of the beneficiary in the case of a $125 death claim. Two of the orders scheduled are attempting very praiseworthy organized charity work in the way of Old Folks' Homes.

Besides the care of the sick and the burial of the dead these societies are accomplishing much good in the development of our people. The keeping of records, the transaction of business in the local and general gatherings, the contact with one another, etc., are training us in a manner quite as important as that obtained in the school. It is worthy of note that our women share with our men the advantages of the organizations, for they are eligible to membership in all excepting the Masons and Odd Fellows. The place of these institutions in our social life is not fully appreciated.

III. BENEFICIAL SOCIETIES AND INSURANCE COMPANIES.

Beneficial or benevolent societies, as they are called, date back more than fifty years. There are still many, but the insurance companies, white and colored, are taking their places. Twenty-one beneficial societies, with a membership of 1,542, and three mutual aid associations, with a membership of 19,553, are reported. The twenty-one beneficial societies reported a total annual income of $3,076.49, total expenditure for sick and death benefits, $2,478.81; amount of real estate or other property, $1,735.87. Some of these societies have a large membership; with but few exceptions, the members pay 25 cents monthly, or 5 cents per week, with a small tax quarterly or semi-annually, and an assessment of 12 or 25 cents on the death of a member. These are local organizations and many of them under proper management could be easily transformed into strong cooperative business enterprises.

Petersburg has four Negro insurance companies; two have their home offices here and two are branch offices. Three of them report 19,553 members; if this membership is reduced by 50% the actual number will be more nearly represented; their income for last year was $8,869.82; they expended for sick and death benefits the sum of $3,500; they own no real estate; their other property is valued at $675. These companies pay sick and death benefits. The death benefit is small in proportion to the premiums; their drawing feature is the sick benefits, which the beneficiary can get without dying to win. Their rates are from 5 to 50 cents weekly for sick benefits ranging from $1.50 to $10.00 per week and death benefits from $15.00 to $110.00. They employ twenty-five or more agents or clerks, and are closely imitating the white industrial insurance companies, which are partly responsible for this new enterprise since they refused to employ colored agents. Here is a very promising field, both for business and the application of sound methods of insurance. The True Reformers, besides their work as an order, carry on an insurance business. They issue two policies of $200 and $500 respectively.

IV. COOPERATIVE BUSINESS.

Petersburg has no cooperative stores now, though such enterprises have been founded from time to time in the past. Ignorance of busines methods / and lack of moral basis rather than the failure of the people to patronize them, is responsible for their non-existence.

V. MISCELLANEOUS SOCIETIES AND INSTITUTIONS.

There are many children's societies, an increasing number of clubs, and other organizations in the city, which have not been reported for various reasons. Three children's societies are reported under this head; their membership is 59;

their income for the last twelve months was $114.61; and their expenditures for sick and death benefits amounted to $66.60.

Excepting a Baptist academy and an orphan home conducted under the same management, our educational institutions are supported by the city, State or white church societies.

CONCLUSION.

Leaving out the clubs, the tendencies of all these societies are good. They are unifying and educating our people, and, in a simple yet effective way, are rendering much needed help. No great effort has been organized in our midst, but there is abroad a spirit that something must be done. This feeling will crystalize into action. Under intelligent and honest leadership these organizations can be made the nucleus for grand business concerns which can give us assistance and opportunity for the use of energy for which, at present, no provision is made.

[...]

ARTHUR WYNDHAM TARN, 'SOME NOTES ON LIFE ASSURANCE IN GREATER BRITAIN', *JOURNAL OF THE INSTITUTE OF ACTUARIES* (1899), EXCERPT

Arthur Windham Tarn,[1] 'Some Notes on Life Assurance in Greater Britain, Particularly with Reference to the Work and Development of the Native Offices', *Journal of the Institute of Actuaries*, 34 (1899), pp. 517–61, on pp. 518–34.

The development of life insurance in the British colonies was most often a story of a handful of British firms entering a previously untapped market, followed by a flourishing set of home-grown competitors that increased their market share owing to protective legislation, advantages in underwriting and better access to profitable investments. The number of British insurers that sought business in the colonies was never large: of sixty firms with more than £50,000 in premium income in 1910, more than half operated exclusively in Britain, another sixteen did less than 5 per cent of their business abroad, and only six collected more than 30 per cent of their premiums outside Britain. Standard Life led the way among British offices that specialized in overseas business, with more than half its premium income coming from that source; other major players included the Commercial Union, Gresham and Norwich Union. Colonial business could carry higher risks, as when the Sepoy Rebellion in 1857 damaged the two leading insurers in India, the Family Endowment and the Medical Invalid, both of which transferred their ailing business to the soon-to-be insolvent Albert. Despite that setback, India remained an attractive market for several British offices, although few of them took the initiative to cater to the growing class of middle-class Indian natives. This failure, as well as rising Indian nationalism, led to the formation of several new home-grown offices there after 1900, a process that paralleled in many regards the emergence of African-American insurance offices in the United States.[2]

By that point British firms had largely ceded ground to indigenous life insurers in its other colonies as well – starting with the Barbados Mutual in the 1840s, and followed by offices in Canada, Australia and finally South Africa. Some of these offices' success was due to protective legislation, which arose alongside limited self-government in Canada (after 1841), Australia (starting in the 1850s) and the Cape Colony (in 1852). A more serious obstacle to success for British life insurance companies in the colonies was the higher costs associated with this form of business. Salesmen expected higher commissions, and mortality often exceeded British results – owing to unhealthier climates, gatekeeping problems or both.[3] Increasingly, British insurers also faced competition in their colonies and other foreign markets from American insurers, which greatly expanded their foreign presence after 1870. American offices focused much of their attention on the Latin American market, where the British presence was minimal, and on Canada, where their 30 per cent market share in 1890 compared to 13 per cent for British firms. New York Life additionally emphasized central Europe (where it vied with the Gresham for business), and the Mutual of New York had thriving agencies in Cape Town and Sydney.[4]

Notes

1. Arthur Wyndham Tarn worked for the London-based Westminster and General Life Assurance Association when he delivered this paper to the Institute of Actuaries in February 1899; he moved to the Guardian in 1906 following a merger, and remained there into the 1930s.
2. Alborn, *Regulated Lives*, pp. 27–33.
3. Ibid., pp. 31–3. Gatekeeping refers to efforts by firms to avoid subpar risks through careful selection methods. On colonial life insurance regulations, see H. R. Harding, 'British Life Assurance Companies and Colonial Legislation', in Volume 2 of this collection.
4. Keller, *The Life Insurance Enterprise*, p. 84; J. M. Hudnut, *Semi-Centennial History of the New-York Life Insurance Company 1845–1895* (New York: The Company, 1895), p. 356; S. B. Clough, *A Century of American Life Insurance: A History of the Mutual Life Insurance Company of New York 1843–1943* (New York: Columbia University Press, 1946), p. 162.

Arthur Wyndham Tarn, 'Some Notes on Life Assurance in Greater Britain', *Journal of the Institute of Actuaries* (1899), excerpt

[...]

The history of life assurance in the Colonies is necessarily of a modern character – at any rate as regards native offices, which for the most part have sprung into being within the last 30 years. The oldest existing Colonial life office is the Barbadoes Mutual Life Assurance Society, which was established in 1840, and has ever since enjoyed uninterrupted prosperity. The office next in seniority is the South African Mutual Life Assurance Society, instituted in 1845, and till 1888 known as the "Mutual Life Assurance Society of the Cape of Good Hope." In 1847 the Canada Life Assurance Company was established, and two years later saw the birth of the Australian Mutual Provident Life Assurance Society.[1] Each of these institutions, representing life assurance in four of the principal sections of the British Empire, has therefore been actively engaged in the promotion of thrift in the Colonies for 50 years and upwards; and each, it may be added, has done good service to actuarial science by publishing its mortality experience throughout the greater part of its existence. In other important possessions of / the Empire, such as India and New Zealand, life assurance has been conducted on lines entirely distinct from those prevailing either in this country or in the four groups of Colonies already referred to. In the former country native prejudices and other obstacles have had to be contended against, so that it is only within the last quarter of a century that societies of this nature have met with any appreciable favour. In the latter Colony native life assurance is entirely monopolized by the Government.

In connection with the establishment of native offices in the Colonies, it should be mentioned that a considerable impetus was given to life assurance in different parts of the Empire by an office founded at Edinburgh in 1846, and called the Colonial Life Assurance Company,[2] the main purpose of its promoters being that of extending to the Colonies of Great Britain and to India the full benefit of life assurance. Being conducted on sound business principles, this company proved eminently successful, and to its example may be traced the pop-

Earliest Colonial Life Offices.

ularity of life assurance in the Colonies. After an active existence of 20 years this company was transferred to the Standard Life Office.

Their Progress and Development.

Having shown the origin of native life offices in Greater Britain, I will now proceed to give a brief account of their progress and development. Commencing

In the West Indies.

with the group of Colonies where life assurance dates furthest back, namely, the West Indies, I may observe that here the Barbadoes Mutual, which confines its business to the assurance of lives resident in these islands, reigns supreme. To the members of this Institute the work of this society is not unfamiliar, since on two occasions within comparatively recent years its operations have been deemed of sufficient interest to form the subject of a paper read at our sessional meetings.*

In South Africa.

In South Africa, up to the year 1891, when the Southern Life Assurance Society was established, the South African Mutual was the sole native office. Of late years, however, branches have been formed in this rapidly-developing part of the world by offices from Great Britain, the United States, and Australia. In 1897 the numbers of such offices were 21 British, 2 American, and 2 Australian. The competition and enterprise thus engendered has had a beneficial effect upon the native / offices, which have extended their operations beyond the British Colonies into the Orange Free State and the Transvaal Republic. In the mortality experience published by the South African Mutual last year, the rapid extension of the business of that office is strikingly illustrated by the circumstance that during the last 16 years covered by the experience the number of lives under observation had increased to nearly four times that of the first 34 years. To reach the scattered outlying districts of these parts, a system of canvassing is employed which was imported from Australia, and of which a description will be given when speaking of that group of Colonies. In 1894, an Industrial Life Office was established, being worked on lines somewhat similar to those of institutions of the kind in this country. It may be mentioned that, at the last annual meeting of one of the native offices, the chairman stated that not more than three policies had been drawn from that part of South Africa known as Rhodesia, and that the policy of the office for the present was to restrict business to persons living in the principal towns and in settled occupations, and then only at a substantial extra premium. Hence miners, prospectors, police, transport riders, and such people who have no settled homes, have been excluded from the risks of this society. From the Annual Reports of the Government Actuary at the Cape, it would appear that new business, both as regards numbers of policies and sums assured, is about equally divided between the native and foreign companies.† The average sum assured per head in South Africa is over £25, and the average amount per policy is about £400.

---

*   *J.I.A.*, xxiv, 373,[3] and xxvii, 161.

†   The figures for 1895 were:
      Foreign Companies, £5,762,008 under 13,184 policies;
      Native Companies £5,044,026 under 14,637 policies

In the Dominion of Canada, from the year 1847 to 1866, life assurance business was of a very limited character, there being only two offices actively working in that Colony, namely, the Canada Life and the Colonial of Edinburgh. In the latter year, however, Canada was invaded by offices from the United States, which infused into the business an amount of enterprise never before experienced, and within a few years other native offices sprang into existence. In 1877 an Act of the Dominion Parliament was passed, containing provisions drawn with a view to protect native companies. As a result of this Act, many foreign companies either withdrew altogether from the Dominion / or ceased to transact new business, and the annual reports of the Insurance Superintendent show a steady increase in the numbers of Canadian companies, as well as in the amount of new business transacted, and the proportion which it bears to that of British and American offices. This increase is best illustrated by a comparison between the new business obtained by Canadian, British, and American companies during the years 1876, 1886, and 1896.

Year	Canadian Companies	British Companies	American Companies
	$	$	$
1876	5,465,966	1,683,357	6,740,804
1886	19,289,694	4,054,279	11,827,375
1896	26,171,830	2,869,971	13,582,769

As regards relative numbers of companies in active work in the Dominion, it may be stated that in 1876 there were 37 offices, of which 7 were Canadian, 17 British, and 13 American; while in 1896 there were 39 offices, of which 11 were Canadian, 8 British, and 10 American. Since then 4 more Canadian offices have been licensed to carry on business in the Dominion, thus bringing up the number to 15.* Of these 15 companies, 12 have their head office in the Province of Ontario, 2 in that of Quebec, and 1 in Manitoba. The reason of so large a number having been established in Ontario is that, not only does that Province consist almost entirely of a population of British origin, whereas the inhabitants of Quebec are mostly of French descent, and hence not so familiar with the principles of life assurance as their neighbours, but the great centres of trade, such as Toronto, Hamilton, and London, are situated in Ontario, and this circumstance greatly facilitates the transaction of life business. It may be added that all life assurance companies in Canada are under the supervision of the Superintendent of Insurance for the Dominion, who year by year issues an elaborate publication containing detailed statistics relating to the various companies, which, after being duly licensed, are required to make an annual return to the Government. The Insurance Department, on its part, institutes a most searching investigation into the accounts and securities / of each company, which, upon the officials

In Canada.

---

*   All these companies, with one exception, are proprietary.

being satisfied that everything connected with the company's business is as it should be, receives an annual license. Notwithstanding, however, the unquestionable security possessed by Canadian offices, life assurance appears to be less general in the Dominion than in other parts of the British Empire, the average amount per head being only about £12, or about half that of South Africa. This low average is, no doubt, due in great measure to the fact that nearly one-third of the population of Canada is of French extraction, while of the remainder a large proportion are of mixed nationality.

In the Australasian Colonies. In Australasia life assurance for 20 years was practically monopolized by the Australian Mutual Provident Society, the other native offices then in existence being purely local in character. In the year 1869, however, the marvellous success of this office appears to have induced three of these Colonies to establish other societies of a similar kind. Accordingly, in July of that year, a rival office to the Australian Mutual Provident in New South Wales, called the Mutual Life Association of Australasia, came into existence, and in a few years justified the comprehensiveness of its title by establishing branches in five of the other six Australasian Colonies. A month later, not to be outdone in this direction by the sister Colony, Victoria was able to boast of possessing a life office with an equally comprehensive title, namely, the National Mutual Life Association of Australasia, which has also branches throughout the Australasian Colonies, and which owed its foundation mainly to the efforts of its present Managing Director, Colonel Templeton, C.M.G.[4] The third Colony to establish a life office of this type was New Zealand. This democratic Colony, however, determined that, as security was the most important element in life assurance, the office should possess a Government guarantee. It was established at the end of 1869,* and commenced business in the following March. It would appear that up to that date there was no branch of any life office in the Colony, and hence the start was made under the most favourable conditions. An attempt was made to conduct the business by means of a Board partly elected by the policyholders, but, this experiment proving unsatisfactory, / the management became exclusively that of Government officials. The progress of the Department may be best judged from the fact that, at the end of 1897, it had on its books 36,174 policies, insuring, with bonus additions, close upon ten millions sterling. Its work, however, which is strictly confined to New Zealand, is so well known to members of this Institute, both from repeated references to it in the *Journal* and the insurance papers, and also from the very graphic account of the details of the management given at the Congress by its head, Mr. J. H. Richardson,[5] that it is unnecessary for me to dwell on it. While the Government has, by means of repeated legislation,

---

* This year witnessed the failure of the Albert Life Office in England, which caused such a sensation throughout the insurance world.

taken steps to make it impossible for any native office to be established in the Colony, the latest returns show that branches of six Australian, one British, and two American offices have been formed there. At the end of 1895 a comparison between the total business in force and the European population in this Colony brings out an average sum assured per policy of £267, and an average amount per head of £26.14s. 1d., this latter sum being the highest in any Colony.

On the Continent of Australia the progress of life assurance has been rapid, especially since the year 1869, when it received a fresh impetus by the formation of the two offices already referred to. During the last 30 years a number of societies have been established, and there are now 11 native offices actively at work,* besides branches of the three principal American Companies. Six of these offices have their headquarters in Victoria, four in New South Wales, and one in South Australia. Since the total population of Australia is only four millions, it may be imagined that competition in this part of the world is exceptionally severe. In spite of this, however, the native offices succeeded in 1896 in obtaining over seven millions in new business. In the course of an interview by a leading American insurance paper[6] a few years ago, Mr. Richard Teece, the well-known Australian Actuary, gave the following description of the method adopted in the interior of Australia by enterprising offices in search of new business. He says:– "When a trip of this nature is proposed, the agent secures his buggy and horses, which he pays for himself, and also a black boy to ride the spare horses, for, as he may / be going to drive for several days right across the Continent, he has to take along about thirty horses. He notifies the company of his intentions, and they send a doctor with him, whose expenses they pay, but the agent is not allowed a cent for expenses. The agent starts off, driving four horses in his buggy, and they go out into the country to get applications. A man is seen ploughing in the field; the agent goes to him, talks to him, and perhaps gets his application. The doctor is at hand, and makes an examination. The agent takes the premium, issues a binding receipt for it, and then they drive to the next person in sight; and so they keep on to the end of the trip, covering the country from station to station, and driving often over 100 miles a day."

The principal trouble, however, in Australia is not so much the obtaining of new business as the keeping it on the books when once it is secured. It is a constant source of complaint that some individuals make it a practice of becoming assured over and over again, taking out policies and dropping them after a year or two, since they find that they can be assured as often as they please with but little trouble. A serious obstacle in the way of maintaining a permanent business by offices is the facility with which loans are granted on policies, the tendency

Side note: Method of obtaining Business in Australia.

Side note: High Rate of Lapses.

---

* A summary of the revenue accounts and new business of these offices, for the year 1886, appears in *J.I.A.*, xxvi, 476. For their present position, see list in Appendix to this Paper.

of which is undoubtedly to encourage lapses. A striking illustration of the high rate of lapses in the Colonies during the early years of assurance is given in the recently-published Mortality Experience of the Canada Life Office. Here the percentage of discontinuances in each year of assurance is traced in various experiences, from which it appears that whereas during the years of assurance 0 and 1 the percentage to the total in the H^M experience is only 9.7, that in the Canada and A.M.P. Experiences is 17.8 and 25.9 respectively.

Crisis of 1893. The financial crisis which took place in Australia during the spring of 1893, when 14 banks in New South Wales, Victoria, and Queensland either failed or temporarily suspended payment, naturally gave a severe blow to life offices in those Colonies, from the effects of which they are only now recovering. For some length of time before this date all forms of life business had shown evidence of great expansion. During the two years succeeding the crisis, however, the offices had a severe struggle to maintain the position they had already acquired, the lapses and surrenders exceeding the new business. / It was, I believe, to some extent owing to the depression caused by this crisis, that towards the end of 1896* two of the Victorian life offices decided to join forces, and after a short delay the sanction of the Supreme Court was obtained for the amalgamation, which took place at the beginning of the following year, the business, assets, and liabilities of the smaller society being transferred to the larger, which in consequence was placed in a much stronger position than before.

Life assurance in Australia is more prevalent among the masses than is the case in most other countries. The average sum assured per policy is certainly less than in either Great Britain or Canada, being about £290. This average, it may be added, is highest in Western Australia and lowest in South Australia. The number of policies in proportion to the population, however, is much greater than elsewhere, the ratio being 66 per 1,000 of the population as against 32 in the United Kingdom and 38 in Canada, and the average sum assured per head being £21.†

Early Life Assurance in India. The last of our Possessions that calls for notice with regard to the progress of life assurance is the Empire of India. Here, owing to the entirely different conditions of life prevailing in that vast country, life assurance has been placed in a position totally distinct from that of the Colonies of which we have been speaking. It would appear, however, that so far back as 1833 the establishment of a life assurance office was contemplated by the Government of Bengal, which was to be of an official character, but on political grounds the scheme was successfully opposed by the East India Company.‡ During the last 60 years a few

---

*   Shortly before this date, another Victorian company took over the business of one of the two existing South Australian offices.

†   *Wealth and Progress of New South Wales,* 1896–7.

‡   Slater – *Rise and Progress of Native Life Assurance in India.* In his work on India in 1880, Sir Richard Temple observes: "It has sometimes been strongly recommended that the

native offices have been started in India, the oldest still in existence being the Madras Equitable, founded in 1842, which assures the lives of Europeans, East Indians, Eurasians, and Parsees. The business transacted by this Society, however, is of a very small / character, the average number of policies effected during the last three years being only 27. In the course of a report on this Society, made in 1881,* Mr. A. H. Bailey observes that the general rate of mortality experienced in the Society coincided almost exactly with that of the Uncovenanted Service Fund, published by Mr. A. J. Finlaison in 1874, which accordingly was adopted as the basis of the valuation. In an article which appeared in the *Calcutta Review*, in 1855, and which was reprinted in vol. vi of the *Journal*, the writer complains that the rates of premium for residents in India were too high, and suggests that an addition of three years to the age for the extra risk was quite sufficient. The following rates were at that time charged for an assurance of Rs. 1,000 for civil and military officials respectively by the native offices:†

Age	PREMIUM	
	Civil	Military
	Rs.	Rs.
20	28	31
25	30	34
30	33	38
35	37	42
40	41	47
45	45	53
50	50	58
55	59	68
60	72	84

On comparing the above rates with those contained in Mr. Bailey's report just referred to, I find that the latter, which are described as being a reduced scale, are considerably higher throughout the Table.

As an illustration of native ideas of life assurance in India, the following remarks are of interest: "It is certain that our remote ancestors had no idea of   Native Opinion. life assurance. Their joint family system afforded all the comforts, conveniences, and assurance they needed. English ideas have, however, of late undermined the system, and the necessity for a substitute in an artificial contrivance like

---

Government in India should undertake life insurance to a moderate and limited extent. The measure was designed for the benefit of the natives, as being calculated to teach them habits of thrifty forethought, and to form ties of the happiest kind between them and the State. Owing to various practical difficulties, and also to objections against interference with private enterprise in this respect, the Government has not yet seen its way to under-taking business of this nature, however desirable that may be on many grounds."

*   *J.I.A.*, xxiii, 52.

†   All these offices, it may be noted, have long since passed out of existence.

life assurance is being daily more and more felt. A quarter of a century ago an attempt was made by some Bengali gentlemen to establish a regular Indian Life Office, but it failed. The / late Albert Life Office next opened its doors for the admission of Indian lives, and several Bengali gentlemen eagerly subscribed, but the loss which its unfortunate – not to say disgraceful – failure brought on, cast a damper from which the Indian mind has not yet fully recovered."*

Establishment of the 'Oriental.' In their modern form the principles of life assurance may be said to have been first introduced into India 25 years ago, when Mr. D. M. Slater founded the Oriental Life Office at Bombay. The policy of this Company was then, as it still continues to be, that of assuring the lives of every race in India, whether European, Parsee, Hindoo, Mohammedan, Cingalese, Burmese, or Chinese, at precisely the same rates of premium, provided, of course, that they are able to pass a satisfactory medical examination. From various pamphlets and criticisms which have been published regarding this policy, it would appear that the management of a native life assurance company in India is not altogether a bed of roses. In a recent monograph which Mr. Slater has written upon his experiences upon the subject, however, he assures us that "no other single measure undertaken by private enterprise has conferred greater social blessings upon both the European and native populations."†

Evidence before the Opium Commission. Some interesting information with regard to the modern growth of life assurance in India may also be found in the evidence of Mr. Slater and of various medical men resident in that country, given before the Opium Commission in 1893. From this evidence we learn that the practice of life assurance among the natives is considerably increasing, and that assurance companies will accept a proposal from a man who takes opium as readily as if he did not, if in other respects his life is an eligible one. During the first decade of the history of the Oriental it was considered expedient to make a small extra for opium consumers in moderate quantities, more, however, as an extra precautionary measure than on account of any proved ill effects of the opium habit. At the end of this period an investigation was made into the matter, and it was then ascertained that out of 167 deaths not a single one was due either directly or indirectly / to opium. The ratio experienced for every 100 deaths computed by the H^M Table was – British 154, Eurasian 82, native 103. Hence, while British lives experienced 54 per-cent greater mortality than what was the case in this country, that of the aggregate Indian lives had been precisely the same as that shown by the H^M Table. The result of this investigation modified the practice of imposing extras, and it was

---

*   *Hindoo Patriot*, 14 June 1886.

†   *Rise and Progress of Native Life Assurance in India*. It may be here mentioned that, on last New Year's Day, the King of Portugal conferred on Mr. Slater the honour of a Knight of the Order of Christ, in consideration of his long and laborious services in the cause of life assurance in India.

stated that it sometimes happened that when a life proved exceptionally healthy no extra at all was made for opium smoking. A further investigation took place six years later, the number of deaths being 779, when it was found that the mortality of British lives in India was 52 per-cent greater than that of the H^M Table, while that of the aggregate native lives was only 16 per-cent greater. Here, again, it appeared that no death was due to opium, and in view of the additional light thrown upon the subject by this experience, the management decided in future to charge no extra whatever to opium eaters. It may be added that two years ago another native life office under British management was established in India with the object of conducting business on lines similar to those of the Oriental. While, however, the policy of accepting native lives on the same lines as those of Europeans has been a successful one in Mr. Slater's office, it by no means follows that it would be equally so when pursued by British offices, which, indeed, have been very chary as to accepting this class of risk, and have limited operations of this kind to men of prominent position, and hence easily traced. It has been stated that the natives of India are to a great extent devoid of the moral sense of truth, regarding the business of life assurance as a mere game of skill, and any fraud in connection with it as a meritorious act. Another difficulty, as regards the general population, is that of identifying a particular life on a claim arising, owing to the similarity in names borne by the natives.

The foregoing description of the origin, progress, and development of the native offices in Greater Britain, though necessarily of the briefest character, will, I think, be considered sufficient to illustrate the growth of life assurance amongst our kindred in different parts of the Empire. I will now proceed to examine in a general way the position of these offices as regards the nature of their assets, the decline that has taken place in the rate of interest yielded by their funds, the stringency observed in the calculation of their reserves, and the rate of expenditure with which their management is conducted. In doing so, it will, of / course, be necessary before making comparison with life offices in this country to take into consideration the very different circumstances surrounding societies in such comparatively newly-formed countries as our possessions in Canada, Australasia, and South Africa. These different circumstances are perhaps seen most clearly when we look at the first of the items I have mentioned, namely, the assets set down in the balance-sheet, and hence this subject seems not unnaturally to form the next most appropriate for our notice.

Assets of Life Offices.

In Canada, life offices claim to possess absolute Government security, since, as we have seen, every item in their accounts is carefully investigated by, and has to receive the approval of, the Insurance Department of the Dominion. From the summary of the assets of all the Canadian companies tabulated in the report of the Insurance Superintendent for the year 1896, I have calculated the percentages of the various classes of securities as follows:

In Canada.

Security	Percentage
Real Estate	9.5
Loans on Real Estate	37.3
Loans on Collaterals	7.1
Cash Loans and Premium Obligations on Policies	10.5
Stocks, Bonds, and Debentures	27
Cash in Hand and in Banks	2.5
Other Assets	6.1
	100

If we compare these percentages with those relating to securities of a corresponding nature in the assets of British companies, we find a very marked similarity, especially as regards the two principal items – "Loans on Real Estate", which is very little higher than our "Loans on Mortgage", and "Stocks, Bonds, and Debentures", which is rather lower than that in British companies.

On the Austral-
ian Continent.   When we turn to the balance-sheet of Australian offices, we find that a much greater contrast in the character of the assets prevails here than in the Canadian offices, when the percentages of those of British offices are placed alongside. This contrast will be readily seen in the following Table,* which is taken from a very interesting paper on / "Australian Investments", read three years ago by Mr. W. R. Day before the Insurance Institute of New South Wales.

Security	PERCENTAGES	
	British	Australasian
Mortgages	37.2	50.7*
Loans on Policies	4.7	20.7*
Government and Municipal Securities	21.6	7.6*
Property owned	6.8	10.9
Stocks, Shares, and Debentures	20.3	.6
Cash in Hand and at Bankers'	3.4	6.2
Other Items	6	3.3
	100	100

The most striking features in the percentages of the Australian companies' assets are the very large proportion borne by "Loans on Policies" and the very insignificant one represented by "Stocks, Shares, and Debentures." As regards the former item, the explanation is to be found in the operation of the non-forfeiture system. This system, which in its present form was founded some thirty years ago in the Colony of Victoria, has been universal throughout Australasia for many years, and, it has been estimated by Mr. W. R. Dovey, accounts for three-quarters of the total amount set down against this particular asset. The extremely small proportion borne by the latter item is due to the fact that this class of securities scarcely exists in Australasia – at least, in a form suitable for life office investments – on

---

*   The Assets marked thus (*) were, in 1897, 48.6, 20.4, and 10.3, respectively per-cent of the total.

account of Government control prevailing to so great an extent in commercial undertakings. In fact, the favourite securities of Australian life offices may be said to be mortgages of land and fixed deposits in banks. Such investments as life interests and reversions are naturally almost unknown in the Colonies.*

In the New Zealand Insurance Department the assets at the end of 1896 were invested as follows: /

Security	Percentage
Government Securities	32.9
Mortgage on Freehold Property	30.7
Loans on Policies	17.6
Local Bodies' Debentures	6.3
Landed and House Property	5.5
Cash on Current Account	4.1
Miscellaneous Assets	2.9
	100

As regards the second item in this table, it may be remarked that by the constitution of the Department the investment of all funds in securities of this nature is controlled by a Board consisting of leading Government officials, who are restricted to lending not more than three-fifths of the value of the property. The constitution also provides that one-quarter of the total funds must be invested in Government securities and loans to local authorities approved by the Governor in Council. It will be seen on reference to the Appendix to this Paper that the total assets of the Department amount to more than 2 1/2 millions sterling.

In New Zealand.

In South Africa the assets of the two native offices may be classified as follows:

Security	PERCENTAGES		
	In Cape Colony	Elsewhere than in Cape Colony	Total
Government and Municipal Securities	5.5	6	11.5
Mortgages	39	20.1	59.1
Loans on Policies	7.9	3.3	11.2
Transvaal Debentures		2.6	2.6
House Property	2.3	3.8	6.1
Cash in Hand and at Bankers'	3	2	5
Other Items	2.7	1.8	4.5
	60.4	39.6	100

Here we see that mortgages again bear a very high proportion to the total assets – higher, in fact, than in any other group of Colonies. The non-forfeiture system is also prevalent in the South African Colonies, and hence the same remarks which have been already made with regard to the item "Loans on Policies" also apply in this case.

In South Africa.

---

*   One office in New South Wales, and two in Victoria, appear to include among their assets securities of this nature, but the total amount at the end of 1897 was under £100,000.

Average Rates of
Interest yielded
by Funds.

From the consideration of the nature of the assets of Colonial life offices we naturally pass to a comparison of the rates of / interest yielded by them in the past and at the present time. It need hardly be said that throughout the Colonies, with the exception apparently of those in South Africa, this rate has declined rapidly within recent years. In Canada the funds of life offices, which in 1880 yielded an average of nearly 6 $^3/_4$ per-cent, produced in 1891 a mean rate of only 5 $^1/_2$ per-cent, and at the present time 4 $^1/_2$ per-cent may be taken as above rather than below the average yield, and this, too, in spite of the fact that not less than 6 per-cent is charged on loans on policies. In Australasia the rate of interest has been maintained better than in Canada, probably on account of the higher percentage which policy loans bear to the total assets, the rate charged in these Colonies for such loans being either 6 or 7 per-cent. The rapid nature of the decline in these Colonies may be judged of by the fact that in 1891 the funds of the combined Australian offices yielded an average of £5. 19s. 1d. per-cent, while in 1896 the average yield had fallen to £4. 18s. 10d. per-cent.* During the same period the New Zealand Government Department had experienced a fall from £5. 8s. 2d. per-cent to £4. 19s. per-cent. In the course of his Inaugural Address before the Insurance Institute of Victoria in 1897, the President (Mr. Gillison) gave some striking illustrations with regard to this rapid decline, and arrived at the conclusion that, after making an allowance of 1 per-cent per annum for the depreciation which has taken place in Australian securities, the average rate is very little above that of British offices.† As already remarked, these securities usually consist of landed property, whereas the assets of British offices include a large proportion of Stock Exchange securities, from which a profit may be realized from time to time sufficient to neutralize to a great extent the fall in the rate of interest. The South African offices have, on the other hand, been fortunate in not only maintaining the average rate of interest at a respectable figure, but have even increased it, since while 20 years ago this rate appears to have been 4 $^3/_4$ per-cent, it now stands at about 5 $^1/_4$ per-cent.

Standards of
Valuation.

In view of the general decline in the average rate of interest / yielded by the funds of Colonial life offices, it is satisfactory to observe that these offices are fully alive to the importance of meeting this decline by strengthening their reserves. In Canada, the standard rate of 4 $^1/_2$ per-cent, fixed by Statute for valuation purposes as long ago as 1877, is still in force. Most of the life offices in the Dominion have, however, wisely reduced their valuation rate to 4 per-cent; and it is to be hoped that the standard rate in Canada will before long be reduced to this lower rate, as

---

* A table in the *Australian Insurance and Banking Record* for January 1899, gives the following percentages relating to the average rate of interest:– 1889, 6.29 per-cent; 1894, 5.44 per-cent; 1898, 4.82 per-cent.

† In a Paper read before the same Institute in October last, Mr. Pullar discusses this subject at some length, though without expressing any definite opinion as to the future.

was done some years ago in the United States. In Australia, where no standard rate prevails, the offices value their liabilities at 4 or even $3\,^1/_2$ per-cent, while in the last valuation of the New Zealand Government Department the rate adopted was also 4 per-cent, special reserves being made in addition, which reduced the rate to $3\,^5/_8$ per-cent. Of the two native life offices in South Africa, the older, which has hitherto valued at 4 per-cent, has now lowered its rate to $3\,^3/_4$ per-cent with the object of making a further reduction of $^1/_4$ per-cent at its next valuation. The younger, however, on the advice of two well-known British actuaries who were consulted on the matter, has decided to continue for the present the rate adopted at its first valuation, namely, 4 per-cent, which is more than 1 per-cent below the mean rate yielded by its funds. It may be added that, with a few exceptions in Canada, where the Table of the American Offices is occasionally used, the Institute of Actuaries' Tables of Mortality are universal in the Colonial offices.*

The rate of expenditure in life offices throughout the Colonies is, it need hardly be stated, considerably greater in proportion to the premium income than in the old country. In Canada this rate is nearly 20 per-cent in the most economically-managed office, the average being a little over 25 per-cent. Here the keen competition with expensively-managed American companies, together with the fact that most of the offices are of recent growth, sufficiently accounts for the expenditure appearing abnormally high. In the Australasian Colonies the percentages / vary from 13 to 33, that of the New Zealand Government Department being 23. The average of all the Australasian office was, in 1897, a little under 20 per-cent. From a table published in the *Australasian Insurance and Banking Record* for January 1898, where an analysis of the various items of expenditure is given, it appears that the proportion of the expenditure for obtaining new business may be put down at about 76 per-cent of the new premium income.[1] In these Colonies the competition is also very severe, though it is principally among the native offices which absorb the bulk of the Australasian business.

In South Africa, where the same method of obtaining business is employed as in Australasia, the average rate of expenditure is somewhat less, being about 17 per-cent of the premium income.

Ratios of Expenditure to Premium Income.

[...]

---

*   At least three Australian offices now employ the $H^{M(5)}$ Table, either wholly or partially. One of these offices states:– "The H^M and $H^{M(5)}$ Tables have been specially blended for the use of this society. For the early years of the policy the H^M Table only is employed, and for its later years the $H^{M(5)}$ Table. Between these periods the values have been graduated, and lie between the H^M and $H^{M(5)}$ values. Such middle period embraces, for over three-fourths of the policies, all durations between three and ten years, while for less than one-fourth of the policies, being a portion of the endowment assurances only, it includes all durations between four and eight years. For assurances on joint lives and term assurances the H^M Table alone has been employed."

INDUSTRIAL INSURANCE IN BRITAIN

Joseph Burn,[1] 'Industrial Life Assurance', *Journal of Federated Insurance Institutes*, 5 (1902), pp. 345–66.

J. F. Williams,[2] *Life Insurance of the Poor: An Illustration of Economic Disadvantage* (London: P. S. King and Son, 1912).

Despite proclamations to the contrary by countless company promoters, it appeared in the 1850s that the market for British life insurance could not be extended very far into the working classes, who comprised the overwhelming majority of British consumers. A decade later, it was clear to most observers that such a market did exist, but that breaking into it required radically different products and marketing strategies. The first firm to figure this out was the London-based Prudential Life Assurance Company, which formed in 1848 and converted to an 'industrial' office in 1854, focusing almost exclusively on providing funeral benefits for the working poor. Prior to its entry into this field, burial insurance had been the province of a handful of small companies and self-help societies; the Prudential soon dominated, and greatly expanded, this market by creating an army of door-to-door canvassers who doubled as weekly collectors of customers' premiums. Another London firm, the Pearl, rose to prominence in the 1870s by closely modelling itself on the Prudential, and a third, the Refuge, pursued the same path after converting from a friendly society in 1881. All three of these firms were tightly held joint-stock companies, which generated large fortunes for their business partners;[3] but mutual offices also took up the new model of selling industrial life insurance, in the form of 'collecting societies' that formed under the Friendly Societies Act. The two largest of these, the Royal Liver and Liverpool Victoria Legal, had more than 1.5 million members each by the turn of the century.[4]

Although the insurance press and many members of the general public were full of praise for the success of the Prudential and other industrial firms, this sector of life insurance also invited its share of criticism. Child welfare advocates, led by the Bishop of Peterborough and Benjamin Waugh, painted them as promoting neglect by diverting parents' funds to pay for the anticipated burial of their children. A Parliamentary investigation in 1889 generated a good deal of publicity but no major legislation, and charges linking industrial life insurance with 'child murder' receded by 1900. After the turn of the century, critics turned to the allegedly exorbitant expenses that industrial firms passed along to their millions of customers. This was the focus of a major Parliamentary investigation in 1920 (known as the Parmoor Committee), which led to reforms in 1923.[5]

Industrial offices responded to such charges by claiming that the habit of saving that they instilled in their working-class customers persisted as those people and their children moved up the social scale. They could back this up with an impressive record of selling a growing volume of larger 'ordinary' policies, a branch of their business that started to take off after 1880. Industrial offices also pioneered the sale of endowment insurance, which combined term life insurance with annuities. In 1908, when Parliament introduced state-subsidized old age pensions for the first time, industrial insurance companies had more than a million of these policies in force, which had the likely effect of saving taxpayers millions of pounds.[6] With the establishment in 1901 of the Association of Industrial Assurance Companies and Collecting Friendly Societies, this sector developed a powerful lobbying group to defend their interests in Parliament and in the courts.[7]

Although friendly society advocates mainly stayed on the sidelines during these controversies, they persisted in celebrating their own definition of thrift and self-help as superior to that on offer by industrial life insurance. For most of the century, they could afford to look down on industrial insurance from a distance, since the two groups generally stayed out of each other's way: standard friendly societies hardly ever paid funeral benefits, and life insurers mostly avoided offering pensions or sick pay. When industrial firms aggressively added endowment insurance to their offerings in the 1880s, and signed up under the National Insurance Act of 1911 to administer state-subsidized sick pay, their substance as well as style came into direct conflict with friendly societies, ultimately spelling the demise of the latter form of thrift.[8]

Notes

1. Joseph Burn (1871–1950) joined the Prudential Life Assurance Company as a clerk in 1886. In 1901 he became head of the company's investment department, was joint assistant actuary from 1908, actuary from 1912, general manager from 1920 and president from 1941–50. He was instrumental in introducing the 'block system' of agency organization to the Prudential in 1913. President of the Institute of Actuaries from 1926 to 1928, Burn served on several important Parliamentary commissions during and after World War I, including the National War Savings Committee, for which he was knighted in 1918.

2. John Fischer Williams (1870–1947) graduated from New College, Oxford, in 1892 and became a barrister in 1894, practising at Chancery into the 1920s. His primary claims to fame came after the appearance of this pamphlet: first as the author of *Proportional Representation and British Politics* (1914), and then as legal adviser to the British team

that oversaw war reparation payments from Germany in the 1920s. After retiring from the bar in 1930, he continued to write and speak extensively on international law.

3. L. Dennett, *A Sense of Security: 150 Years of Prudential* (Cambridge: Granta Editions, 1998), pp. 13, 39–40, 121–31; *Pearl Assurance: An Illustrated History* (Peterborough: Pearl Assurance Plc, 1990), pp. 9–16; C. Clegg, *Friend in Deed: The History of ... the Refuge Assurance Company* (London: Stone and Cox, 1958), pp. 6–15.

4. *Reports of the Chief Registrar of Friendly Societies, Workmen's Compensation Schemes, Industrial and Provident Societies, and Trades Unions, for 1900* (London: HMSO, 1901), pp. 179–80.

5. G. K. Behlmer, *Child Abuse and Moral Reform in England, 1870–1908* (Stanford, CA: Stanford University Press, 1982), pp. 119–37; D. Morrah, *A History of Industrial Life Assurance* (London: George Allen and Unwin, 1955), pp. 87–121.

6. Alborn, *Regulated Lives*, pp. 40–1, 215.

7. B. Gilbert, *The Evolution of National Insurance in Great Britain: The Origins of the Welfare State* (London: Joseph, 1966), pp. 337–43.

8. Alborn, 'Senses of Belonging'.

Joseph Burn, 'Industrial Life Assurance', *Journal of Federated Insurance Institutes* (1902)

THE great love of independence and the dread of pauperism among the English working classes is manifested in no more striking manner than by their own persistent efforts to make provision for the extra expense occasioned by sickness and death. These early efforts to obtain some form of provident insurance were peculiar to the English-speaking people; it was their own invention, and arose from what they themselves felt to be an absolute necessity. Recognizing this truly fine national characteristic, it is pitiable to recall the many difficulties which were met with before the eventful evolution of a reliable and equitable form of Industrial Assurance.

In endeavouring to trace the history of Industrial Assurance we find that, although Burial Clubs and Friendly Societies in various forms have existed for many years, yet Industrial Insurance, as we now know it, is a matter of quite recent history, and its tremendously rapid growth would certainly seem to show that what was for so many years persistently sought after by the English people has at length been attained. We find, by reference to the Charters of the Guilds, which existed in the middle ages, that provision was made for the burial of the dead as one of the most important duties to be discharged by members of the association to one another. In the reign of Henry VIII, the property of these Guilds was confiscated, and their place was eventually taken by various Burial Clubs and Friendly Societies, in which little or no attempt was made to fix the amount of premium to be paid so that it should be an equivalent of the benefit to be received. Uniform premiums for all ages at entry were most usual, and consequently it generally happened that as members grew old younger men did not care to join, and bankruptcy often resulted. Of course there was no such thing as an actuarial valuation, for even if such had been thought necessary there was no actuarial knowledge available for the purpose, and if a Society *did* happen to accumulate what was considered a large fund, the benefits were generally increased and feasting of the members / was freely indulged in. Towards the end of the eighteenth century various attempts were made at Government supervision, and undoubtedly the several Acts passed during the nineteenth century have had a most salutary effect in exposing the unsound financial position of many Societies and inducing them to take the necessary steps to place their business on a safer basis, but even at the present time it is notorious that there are many of the smaller Friendly Societies whose financial position is anything but satisfactory.

The first Industrial Life Assurance Company was founded in 1849 under the title of the Industrial and General, and is thus referred to by the *Liverpool Chronicle* of that date:– "We have had our attention directed to a brochure bearing the title "What is Life Insurance?" written by the Rev. J. B. Beade. It is in the form of a dialogue between two labouring men, and is mainly calculated to show the illiterate and unthinking the great advantages offered by well regulated and stable assurance associations. The Industrial and General Life Insurance and Deposit Company has been instituted and arranged on a plan expressly to meet the requirements of persons of limited incomes accruing at short periods. With a view of adapting it to the wants and wishes of the industrial classes, the directors have arranged to grant assurances and annuities as low as £5, at premiums payable weekly, monthly, quarterly, or annually."[1] In 1852 an offshoot of the above Company – namely, The British Industry Life Assurance Company – was founded, and contained in its prospectus the following advertisement:– "Adapted to meet the requirements of the middle and industrial classes by granting policies as low as £5 or under that amount according to age; by accepting premiums in weekly, monthly, quarterly, half-yearly, and annual payments; by protecting the assurers when circumstances arise to interfere with their regular payments; and other decided advantages unattainable by the rules of general assurance offices. . . .

"Clothing life assurance in the humblest possible habiliments, disguising its virtues under the most retreating form that ingenuity could invent, it would be difficult to prevent the most unpracticed eye from discovering the presence of a true friend; indeed, a guardian angel whose ministering objects cannot but be considered little less than divine. . . .

"An inspection of the following table will show that the interests of all classes have been consulted in their formation, and / that the poor man may follow the dictates of affection and duty by using the road now thrown open to his use. It is to be hoped he will not neglect or delay embracing the means thus afforded him of showing to a discerning public, that the coarser cloth does not always cover the coarsest heart, and that the poor man's affection for his offspring issues from as pure a source, and flows as determinedly along, as may that of the generality of those who are termed the better classes."[2]

But notwithstanding this high-toned announcement we find that the "poor man's" premiums were mostly wasted in exorbitant salaries to incompetent officials. In 1853 there was a tea meeting at the Town Hall of Birmingham[3] at which some "nasty" things appear to have been said. Subsequently there was a change of management and the business was put upon a sound footing.

In 1854 the directors of an ordinary Assurance Company,[4] after having made many enquiries and careful investigations, decided to commence the transaction of Industrial business. They recognised from the first the great difficulty of deciding upon a scale of premiums which should be equitable from the assured's point of view as well as sufficient to ensure the security of the contract. The actuaries of the day had practically no experience of Industrial Assurance or data upon which to base reliable tables of premiums. Very little help could be obtained from existing Societies (Burial Clubs, &c.), as it was well known that their financial position was very far from satisfactory, and moreover it was usual in those Societies to charge the same premium for widely differing ages at entry. The tables finally decided upon were eight in number, six of which were so calculated as to allow the policyholder to withdraw one-half of the premiums paid in after two years had elapsed. The youngest age to be assured was 10 and the oldest 60. The following is a specimen of the first table issued:–

	Age.	Sum Assured.		
		£	s.	d.
	10	11	9	0
	15	9	16	0
	20	8	11	0
Weekly Premium 1d.	25	7	7	0
	30	6	6	0
	35	5	7	0
	40	4	11	0
	45	3	16	0
	50	3	3	0 /

"Full Benefit" was granted in all tables from the date of entry. It was eventually found that the business could not be maintained unless younger ages were admitted, and the minimum was therefore reduced to 7; it was also found impossible to continue those tables which permitted of the premiums being withdrawn. It was not until some time later that the Company decided to issue policies on the lives of infants, and even then it was thought advisable to introduce the table into a few districts only, but the results proving satisfactory, the system was gradually introduced into other districts. The following is a copy of the first table issued:–

TABLE OF SUMS PAYABLE FOR ONE PENNY WEEKLY.

Amount payable if Child should die after the Policy has been issued.

Age of Child at Entry.	Three Months.	1 Year.	2 Years.	3 Years.	4 Years.	5 Years.	6 Years.
	£ s.	£ s.	£ s.	£ s.	£ s.	£ s.	£ s.
Not less than 3 months, and not exceeding 6 months	0 10	1 0	2 0	2 10	3 0	3 10	4 0
1 Year next birthday	0 10	1 0	2 0	2 10	3 0	3 10	4 0
2 Years next birthday	0 15	1 5	2 5	2 15	3 5	3 15	4 5
3 Years next birthday	0 15	1 5	2 5	2 15	3 5	3 15	4 5
4 Years next birthday	0 15	1 5	2 5	2 15	3 5	3 15	4 5
5 Years next birthday	2 10	3 5	4 10	5 10	6 10	7 0	8 0
6 Years next birthday	3 0	4 0	5 5	6 5	7 0	7 15	8 10
7 Years next birthday	4 0	5 0	6 0	6 15	7 10	8 5	9 0
8 Years next birthday	4 15	5 15	6 10	7 5	8 0	8 15	9 10
9 Years next birthday	5 10	6 5	7 0	7 15	8 10	9 5	10 0

If the Child should die within Three months from the date of the Policy no sum will be payable.

The table was shortly afterwards replaced by the following:–

TABLE OF SUMS PAYABLE FOR ONE PENNY WEEKLY. (No HIGHER PREMIUM CAN BE TAKEN

Amount payable if the Child should die after the Policy has been issued fo

Age at Entry.	Three Calendar Mths.	One Year.	Two Years.	Three Years.	Four Years.	Five Years.	Six Years.	Seven Years.	Eight Years.	Nine Years.	T[en] Ye
	£ s.	£ s.	£ s.	£ s.	£ s.	£ s.	£ s.	£ s.	£ s.	£ s.	
1 Year next birthday	1 10	2 0	2 10	3 0	3 15	4 10	5 15	6 15	7 15	9 15	
2 Years next birthday	1 10	2 0	2 15	3 5	4 5	5 10	6 10	7 10	9 10	10 0	
3 Years next birthday	1 10	2 0	3 0	4 0	5 5	6 5	7 5	9 5	10 0		
4 Years next birthday	1 15	2 15	3 15	5 0	6 0	7 0	9 0	10 0			
5 Years next birthday	2 10	3 10	4 15	5 10	6 10	8 15	10 0				
6 Years next birthday	3 0	4 10	5 5	6 5	8 10	10 0					
7 Years next birthday	4 0	5 0	6 0	8 5	10 0						
8 Years next birthday	4 15	5 15	8 0	10 0							
9 Years next birthday	5 10	7 15	10 0								
10 Years next birthday	7 10	10 0									

If the Child should die within Three calendar months from date of Policy no amount will be payable. /

Some of the early difficulties attending Industrial Assurances have already been referred to, but there were many others. To arrange to collect a number of premiums in one district is a fairly simple matter, but it is quite another matter to provide for the policyholder who suddenly removes to some remote rural district and still expects to have someone call upon him regularly every Saturday night to collect a few pennies. The difficulty of building up a great system of agencies was still further increased by the ill-fame of the class of men who had formerly been employed by the Burial Clubs (or dead briefs as they were sometimes called) and kindred Societies. These men were often those who had failed to procure an honest living at other callings, and it certainly cannot be said that they succeeded (so far as honesty is concerned) when acting as collectors. The temptations and difficulties met with by insurance agents are very many, and it is therefore highly essential that they should be in all cases men of some considerable business ability as well as of the highest moral character. The difficulty of their task in the past was considerably increased owing to the unenviable reputation earned for them by their predecessors, but it is a matter for the sincerest congratulation that, notwithstanding the old adage concerning a dog and a bad name, assurance agents of the present day are rapidly outgrowing, if indeed they have not already outgrown, their past reputation, and the mere fact of a man being a valued servant of any large and respected Insurance Company should be a sufficient guarantee that he is also a business-like and honourable man.

In 1864 a Bill was introduced in Parliament with the object of enabling the Government to transact the business of assurance. This Bill was strongly opposed by a large Company and a Burial Society. The Chancellor of the Exchequer (Mr. Gladstone) during the discussion on the Bill made certain speeches in which the solvency of the Insurance Company was made to appear extremely doubtful.[5]

It is needless to say that a statement of this kind made by so high an authority might have been expected to have most prejudicial effects by creating a bad opinion in the minds of those who had no technical knowledge of assurance matters, but the result was exactly the opposite. The absolute solvency of the Company was amply proved, and Mr. Gladstone, in a subsequent speech, considerably toned down his previous statements. The attention of / many people was thus directed to Industrial Assurance who probably would not otherwise have heard of it, and from that time the business of Industrial Assurance has grown in a manner which then would have seemed impossible. The Bill above referred to was duly passed,[6] and from that time the Government has been a competitor for Industrial Assurance business, but it has met with singularly little success. Big Companies have, however, risen up and succeeded in obtaining enormous numbers of policies, until we find by the end of 1900 that 14 Companies are able to report a total number of 18,653,846 Industrial policies in force, insuring a net amount of £181,135,538.

In order to give some idea of the remarkable growth of Industrial Assurance during recent years I have taken some figures from the Board of Trade Returns and drawn diagrams to represent them.[7] Thus in the first diagram I represent the number of Industrial policies in force from 1887 to 1900, the actual figures being as follows:–

Year.	Policies.	Year.	Policies.
1887	9,145,844	1894	13,324,778
1888	9,208,671	1895	14,990,581
1889	9,412,991	1896	15,301,621
1890	9,432,778	1897	15,860,654
1891	9,879,928	1898	17,230,712
1892	12,834,142	1899	17,857,134
1893	13,213,554	1900	18,653,846

In the next diagram I show the total amount insured for the years 1887 to 1900. The figures are as follows:–

Year.	£.	Year.	£.
1887	83,434,487	1894	128,064,110
1888	83,891,620	1895	144,142,569
1889	85,920,639	1896	147,189,925
1890	86,203,873	1897	152,075,807
1891	90,983,761	1898	165,990,481
1892	122,760,631	1899	172,649,457
1893	126,797,704	1900	181,135,538

In the third diagram I show the total assets for 20 years, viz., from 1881 to 1900. It will be noticed that during these 20 years the amount has increased in the ratio of nearly 14 to 1. It will also be noticed by comparing Diagrams 2 and 3 that in 1887 the assets of the Companies represented £6 13s. 2d. per cent. of the sums assured, whereas in 1900 it represented £11 / 17s. 6d. per cent., or nearly double the percentage of 1887. The actual figures are as follows:–

Year.	£.	Year.	£.
1881	1,588,915	1891	9,662,026
1882	2,060,856	1892	10,771,689
1883	2,411,754	1893	11,385,953
1884	3,065,285	1894	12,439,285
1885	3,834,709	1895	13,803,227
1886	4,667,916	1896	15,003,789
1887	5,566,131	1897	16,511,278
1888	6,248,513	1898	18,157,993
1889	7,187,076	1899	19,775,676
1890	8,737,936	1900	21,512,384

It will be noticed that in all three diagrams there is a sudden increase at the end of five years and also at the end of periods of three years; this is owing to the figures being those given in the Board of Trade Returns, which are taken from the periodical valuation returns.

The last diagram represents the amounts paid in claims. Thus the first column represents £697,778, which was the amount paid in 1881. The second column represents £697,778 + £779,985, being the claims paid for the two years 1881 and 1882. The last column represents £39,939,193, being the total amount paid in claims during 20 years. The actual figures for each year are as follows:–

Year.	Claims.	Year.	Claims.
1881	£697,778	1891	£2,184,851
1882	779,985	1892	2,537,261
1883	957,350	1893	2,451,965
1884	1,124,622	1894	2,547,832
1885	1,250,250	1895	2,418,754
1886	1,366,537	1896	2,774,101
1887	1,461,832	1897	2,751,230
1888	1,588,174	1898	2,912,046
1889	1,663,661	1899	3,131,916
1890	1,928,406	1900	3,410,642

The number of Industrial Assurance Companies in the United Kingdom during the 20 years 1881 to 1900 has been as follows:– /

1881	11	1891	12
1882	12	1892	12
1883	13	1893	11
1884	10	1894	11
1885	9	1895	11
1886	9	1896	11
1887	12	1897	11
1888	13	1898	11
1889	11	1899	14
1890	13	1900	14

I may point out that the reason why the first two diagrams only include 14 years, instead of 20 as the last two diagrams do, is that the Board of Trade Returns are not in the requisite form for obtaining the necessary data.

Some of you gentlemen who are present to-night could, I expect, recount many interesting histories of the way in which part of this enormous business was obtained. Industrial canvassing was not always carried on under the same conditions as at present; there may be some here who can remember a certain gentleman who, instead of going round from house to house, used once every week to sit at a table in the open air and register the names of a crowd of intending insurers. Sometimes, whilst still surrounded by anxious customers, he would suddenly close his book and call out "Full up for this week, can't take any more." He himself used to declare that the idea of possibly being too late induced many to come the following week who otherwise would not have done so.

Although the figures represented in the diagram show an enormous rate of increase in Industrial Assurance, they do not, I think, represent the true progress, since a very large amount of the ordinary policies in force would never have existed had it not been for the introduction afforded by the Industrial policy. An Industrial policy for a small amount is taken out, and subsequently the amount assured is increased, then probably it is pointed out by the agent that for a very slightly increased amount per week the sum assured could be increased to £50 by taking out an ordinary policy on which the premiums could be paid quarterly. Very probably the ordinary assurance is increased after some years, and in this way there is a steady march forward. Industrial assurance is an education, and is undoubtedly the direct origin of much of the ordinary assurance. It is quite possible that the rate of increase in the total amount of Industrial assurance will / not in the future be anything like what it has been in the past, but we may safely predict that the small ordinary assurance policy will become more and more popular.

In considering the enormous progress of industrial assurance during the past 20 years it is necessary to notice other features besides the gigantic increase in the number of policies. One of the most important of these features is the increased security afforded to the Industrial policyholder. We have already referred to the very unsatisfactory financial state of the various Burial Clubs, &c., at the time Industrial Assurance was first started. From the very commencement the greatest care was exercised by those Industrial Assurance Companies which are now in existence in order to make the fulfilment of the contract as certain as possible, but it was for many years impossible to offer that absolute security which the large Industrial Companies are now proud to be able to point to. The working man pays his small weekly premium and is able to rest on the absolute certainty that the sum assured will be paid. The directors of large Industrial Assurance Companies, recognizing the necessity for absolute safety, will not be tempted by any high rate of interest; the desirability of unchallengeable security is always foremost in their mind, and hence we find millions and millions of Industrial funds invested only in the highest class trustee securities, although by doing so they (the directors) reject larger profits and lay themselves open to much adverse criticism for what, by some, are considered unnecessary precautions. I think, however, that Englishmen should be proud of the position of Industrial Companies to-day; they are monuments of the people's own unselfish forethought and love of independence; the funds are a great trust which must under all circumstances be strictly guarded and tended, in order that the amounts stated in millions of Industrial policies may be paid immediately they become due.

In the early days of Industrial Assurance it was found advisable to charge higher premiums for various occupations, such as miners and sailors, but for many years past it has been the practice of large Companies to charge one general scale of premiums, thus avoiding a restriction which was always somewhat vexatious. It is of course evident that a concession of this kind is only possible when the number of policies in force is sufficiently large to include a fair proportion of all classes of the population. Another example of a valuable concession which has recently been made to policy-holders / is the dispensing with extra premiums for the risk involved by our soldiers and volunteers in South Africa.[8] It would be difficult to measure the actual loss thus incurred by the Companies, but it may safely be said that it is very much greater than is generally supposed.

Mr. Eady, in a valuable and interesting paper read before the Insurance Institute of Victoria and Melbourne in June last,[9] gives some figures showing the astonishing growth of Industrial Assurance in the United States, thus:–

Year.	Number of Companies.	Number of Policies.	Amount of Assurance in force.
1876	1	2,500	£48,668
1881	3	359,942	6,528,359
1886	3	1,764,158	39,338,975
1891	9	4,302,427	96,212,143
1896	11	7,375,688	177,296,974
1899	14	10,048,943	258,551,208

It will be noticed that the average sum assured is £26, as compared with about £10 in Great Britain. The very much larger average sum assured in the United States is probably owing to the different scale of infantile assurance allowed by statute, and also to some extent to the difference in the classes of assurance which are popular in the two countries.

The maximum amount of assurance on the lives of infants in Great Britain, as allowed under the provisions of the Friendly Societies Act,[10] is, as you know, £6 up to age 5, and £10 for ages between 5 and 10, and even these amounts are higher than those adopted by Assurance Companies, whereas the legal maximum allowed in most of the States is as follows:– /

Between ages	1 and 2 years	30 dollars
Between ages	2 and 3 years	34 dollars
Between ages	3 and 4 years	40 dollars
Between ages	4 and 5 years	48 dollars
Between ages	5 and 6 years	58 dollars
Between ages	6 and 7 years	140 dollars
Between ages	7 and 8 years	168 dollars
Between ages	8 and 9 years	200 dollars
Between ages	9 and 10 years	240 dollars
Between ages	10 and 11 years	300 dollars
Between ages	11 and 12 years	380 dollars
Between ages	12 and 13 years	460 dollars
Between ages	13 and 16 years	520 dollars
Between ages	16 and 17 years	612 dollars
Between ages	17 and 18 years	700 dollars
Between ages	18 and 19 years	784 dollars
Between ages	19 and 20 years	855 dollars
Between ages	20 and 21 years	930 dollars

Mr. Eady also points out that Industrial Assurance is practically unknown outside the British Empire and the United States. The following table is given as showing the comparative amount in the different countries:–

	No. of Policies.	Amount of Assurance.
United Kingdom	18,653,846	£181,135,538
United States	10,048,943	£258,551,208
Australasia	241,000	£5,200,000

In the past there have been many objections raised to infantile assurance on the ground of its being conducive to neglect or even worse, for the purpose of obtaining the assurance money. Without entering into any lengthy argument on the subject, I would like to point out some of the many ways in which the life of the child is safeguarded.

1. The amount of assurance allowed by statute is so small that it is barely sufficient to meet the expenses of burial, &c. 2. More than one assurance on the same life is impossible, owing to the regulation respecting the Registrar's Certificate of Death, viz., that no claim shall be paid without the production of the Registrar's Certificate, stating the amount to be received, and whether it is the first or second certificate issued. By this means it is made impossible to exceed the statutory limit. 3. The leading Assurance Companies will not accept any proposal on the life of an illegitimate child until at least three years of age. 4. In the case of death of any child in which an inquest is held, the first / question usually asked is whether any assurance has been effected. It is obvious that the mere fact of there being an assurance would cause a closer enquiry to be made than would otherwise be deemed necessary. I think if these points are properly considered the weakness of the arguments of opponents to infantile assurance will be evident.

In 1890 a Committee of the House of Lords considered the Children's Life Insurance Bill, which was introduced by the Bishop of Peterborough (afterwards Archbishop of York).[11] Many witnesses were examined, but there was no convincing evidence of any specific cases of child murder by parents for the sake of the insurance money. The Bill was eventually withdrawn.

Perhaps the only really unsatisfactory part of Industrial Assurance at the present time is the lapsing of policies, unsatisfactory to the assured and Assurance Office alike, for it must be remembered that Assurance Companies would always prefer that the assurance should be continued. To the great majority of working people the whole subject of assurance is a mystery. If a policyholder dies after a comparatively short period of assurance the claim is promptly paid, and no question is asked as to where the money comes from: but if a man, after being assured for many years, tires of his contract, he will persist in regarding his assurance as a Penny Bank, and he endeavours to make (or get someone else to make for him) a calculation as to what his pennies would have amounted to had they all been accumulated at 5 per cent. compound interest (everything is 5 per cent. in this sort of calculation). The result is to show that he has been grossly swindled out of a very large sum of money. Once this kind of calculation has been made, it is almost useless to talk to him of a free policy, he discontinues paying his penny or pennies, and spends the money on stamps instead, writing up to the chief office. I well remember one such letter, which ran something like this: "You will, of course, say that I might have died, and so have received the sum assured but this, Sir, is only foolish talk, because you see I am not dead, thank God."

No doubt some of you have frequently had occasion to point out that it is evident, in order to pay the claims which constantly arise, a certain portion of each premium paid must be deducted, and if some persons receive much more as a claim than they have paid in, it is evident that some must pay in more than they receive. And again as to the Penny Bank argument, that it must be / evident that the two transactions are of an entirely different nature. But apart from this the question may well be asked, "Would they have put their penny a week in the bank, even if inclined to do so, and do they really think that the bank manager or his clerk would have called upon them every week for it?" They could of course post it to the bank, but then there would be the cost of postage to deduct as well as envelopes and paper. There would be also the trouble of going to the pillar box (unless there should be one outside their front door). As to the rate of interest obtainable, they could not invest their money in any bank offering the same security as a large Industrial Assurance Company at any higher rate than 2 1/2 per cent., and even that rate may very possibly be reduced in the future. The Company would not be acting fairly if it returned the full reserve value or its equivalent to those who wish to withdraw, because it is well known that on the average those who withdraw are a better class of lives than those who remain, and consequently the greater the number who withdraw the higher will probably be the rate of claim amongst those who remain. If his weekly premiums should be more than a few pence (in which case the argument as to banking would become less obviously absurd) there is nothing to prevent him taking out an Ordinary policy, by which means he will get his assurance at a cheaper rate. Moreover, if the Industrial policy is held in a Company which also transacts ordinary business, special terms can be obtained for any policy transferred. The rates charged for Industrial Assurance must necessarily be much higher than for Ordinary Assurance owing to the cost of collection. Many people who make violent attacks on Industrial Assurance seem to insinuate that the whole amount paid is subject to no deduction for expenses. A person who pays 1d. per week and has a collector call upon him for that amount must be most unreasonable if he complains because he is charged rather more than a farthing out of the penny for the convenience of having it collected. He often buys a box of matches in the street for a penny, but I have never yet seen any calculation as to how much a man would save in his lifetime if he occasionally bought a large quantity at wholesale rates instead of buying them in small quantities as required. I am not, however, going to attempt to supply this calculation, as it is no more likely that people would dispense with the convenience of having a box of matches put into their hands when required in exchange for a penny than it is that / a man would every week go out of his way to pay an Industrial premium.

There are innumerable things constantly purchased by everyone for a few pence without any question as to their actual wholesale value: the object is required in a convenient form, and we are content to pay the vendor a price which will repay him for his trouble of supplying us in small convenient quantities; but I would venture to suggest that the pennyworth of Industrial Assurance is amongst the cheapest of these everyday necessities, and the English people know this fact too well to permit of its withdrawal.

JOSEPH BURN, F.I.A.
Bristol Insurance Institute,
January 31, 1902.

J. F. Williams, *Life Insurance of the Poor: An Illumination of Economic Disadvantage* (1912)

LIFE INSURANCE OF THE POOR.

IT is a commonplace with all who have given attention to economic facts that the poor spend their money to less advantage than the rich. That they do so is in some degree an inevitable result of the fact that they buy in small quantities and so demand an additional process of sub-division in excess of the sub-division required by the rich. But to a far larger degree it is the result of their own financial inexperience and economic weakness – a condition which is perhaps only another name for poverty.

The object of the following notes is to give an illustration of this economic fact by calling attention to the official figures as to life insurance, with the hope and suggestion that if these official figures are more widely known and understood, there are some practical steps which may be taken to remedy the disadvantages of the poor. It is not now my object or intention to enquire into the moral aspects of the matter, nor to suggest that there is anything either morally improper or morally laudable in the actions of those who sell life insurances to the poor. I wish on the present occasion neither to praise nor blame, but simply to state facts.

I may perhaps however barely remind a reader that apart altogether from the purely economic question of the *price* at which life insurance is sold to the poor, there is the general moral or political question of the desirability of industrial assurance, especially that part of it which relates to the insurance of infants, and doubts have occurred to some whether the poorer classes of wage-earners ought to stint themselves of necessaries now, in view of a future they may never reach. This question I do not discuss; I simply call attention to the terms on which the poor insure and the economic waste of money and effort which is involved in their insurances. It will also be seen that I deal only with the simpler aspects of the question and make no claims to technical knowledge.

The insurance of the lives of the poor is a separate branch of the business of life insurance. The main* source from which the poor buy life insurance is the

---

*   The Post Office does about 0.13 per cent. of the business done by the companies. See figures on p. 3. Some life or rather "burial" insurance is also done by the Friendly Societies proper.

group of companies which carry on business as "industrial" assurance companies, the epithet, "industrial" being applied by law to societies which grant assurances "on any one life for a less sum than twenty pounds." (Collecting Societies and Industrial Assurance Companies Act,[1] 1896, s. 1). There are some companies which carry on both industrial insurance and ordinary life insurance, but these form separate funds and charge / separate rates for the two classes of business. The "industrial," *i.e.*, poor people's, branch will sometimes issue policies up to as much as £200 but the average amount insured by an industrial policy is about £10. But the real criterion of "industrial" assurance is not so much the amount assured as the method by which the payments are made. In "industrial" assurance the premiums are not paid by yearly, half yearly, or (generally speaking) quarterly payments but almost invariably by small sums paid weekly or sometimes monthly, a method of payment which in practice involves the intervention of the "Agent" or "Collector."

The main facts as to the insurance of the poor on the one hand and the comfortable and rich classes on the other are to be found in the accounts* under the Assurance Companies Act 1909[2] laid before Parliament by the Board of Trade. The latest return relates for the most part to the year ending 31st December, 1910, but in the cases of some companies the accounts are for the twelve months ending on some date in 1911; the following are the most important summary figures: –

	Ordinary Life Insurance Companies established in the United Kingdom.	Industrial Life Insurance Companies established in the United Kingdom.
Premiums	£28,994,404 (*a*)	£15,707,214
Interest on Investments	£13,166,857	£1,601,393
Claims paid	£21,453,454(*b*)	£6,205,793
Surrenders	£2,265,911(*c*)	£301,917
Bonuses to Assured	£1,274,499	(*e*)
Commission to Agents	£1,545,343 (*d*)	£3,924,722
Expenses of Management	£2,337,270	£3,008,243
Dividends and Bonuses to Shareholders	£487,450	£700,381

(*a*) includes £8,130,084 for business outside the United Kingdom.
(*b*) "   £2,230,632   "   "   "
(*c*) "   £233,450   "   "   "
(*d*) "   £35,757   "   "   "
(*e*) The amounts which appear in the detailed accounts of the Industrial Companies as bonuses are included, in the summary return, under the item "Claims Paid." /

Using these figures we may test the value of poor men's insurance in three ways: –

(1) What proportion of gross income (apart from annuity premiums) do rich men's and poor men's companies return to insurers? (2) What are the ratios of expenses to premiums in the two classes of companies? (3) When the comparison can be made, what do poor men's companies charge for benefits, as compared with the prices at which the same can be had elsewhere?

*   No. 334 of 1912. Return Assurance Companies 1911. Part A.

I take the first test, ratio of income to benefits. For the period under review the total income (premiums and interest) of ordinary life insurance companies was £42,161,261 of which £28,994,404 represented premiums, while the total income (premiums and interest) of industrial insurance companies was £17,308,607 of which £15,707,214 represented premiums,* surely a vast sum to be paid by the wage-earning class. The sum returned to policyholders by way of claims paid, surrender values and bonuses, by ordinary insurance companies was £24,993,864, or roughly rather more than £4 for every £7 of income. The sum similarly returned by industrial insurance companies was £6,507,710, or roughly rather more than £1 for every £3 of income. In other words if the same ratio of return obtained in the case of the poor as of the rich, the poor would have received about £10,000,000 instead of £6,507,710; on this showing the poor have lost about £3,500,000 in a single year.

Now for the second test. Let us look at the expenses of the companies, and see what ratio they bear to premiums. The expenses (including commission) of the ordinary insurance companies are £3,882,613 for £28,994,404 of premiums, an average ratio of 13.5 per cent. for all companies; the expenses (including commission) of industrial insurance companies are £6,932,965 for £15,707,214 of premiums, an average ratio of 44.1 per cent for all companies. If the ratio of expenses was the same in the case of the poor as of the rich, the total amount of the expenses of the industrial companies would be £2,020,474 instead of £6,932,965: on this showing the poor lose about £5,000,000 in a single year as compared with their more fortunate neighbours. The second test works out worse for the poor than the first.

As to both these tests however it may be observed that as the average industrial policy is only for about £10, the amount / of clerical work involved is necessarily larger than in the case of the policies of the rich. A slightly higher ratio of expenses to premiums and of income to returns is therefore a necessity in the case of the poor. But on the other hand, the amount of policies that are allowed to lapse is far higher (the official figures do not enable me to say how far) in the case of the poor than of the rich; consequently there is (in proportion) a larger fund outside the premiums in the case of the poor than of the rich for the payment of expenses.

The third test remains – to compare the premiums charged by an industrial assurance company with those charged for the same benefits by a totally different class of vendor, namely, the Post Office. Unfortunately this method is not of general application to all premiums, for while the industrial insurance companies offer every kind of policy and option, the choice of insurance policies given by the Post Office is comparatively meagre, and it is only in the quite simple

---

* To get the full working class expenditure for life insurance there must be added to their figures a proportion of the Friendly Societies Subscriptions and also the small amount (£20,045 19s. 4d.) paid in premiums to the Post Office. (Government Insurances and Annuities, White Paper 83 of 1912, see also the Post Master General's Report for the year).

form of the direct life insurance policy or life insurance and endowment policy that a non-expert can make a reliable comparison. And he may perhaps suspect that it is just in these simple cases that the industrial insurance company gives the best terms. I take at random two instances from the prospectus of the largest industrial insurance company[3] and from the figures of the Post Office: –

> (1) A premium of 1d. per week (4s. 4d. a year – it must be remembered that the Post Office takes *yearly* premiums) payable by a person aged 25 next birthday, secures a life insurance of £10 in the Post Office and £7 7s. in the industrial insurance company – ratio over 4 to 3 in favour of the Post Office.
>
> (2) A yearly premium of 38s. 6d. (say 9d. a week) payable by a person aged 26 next birthday, secures a life insurance of £100 in the Post Office. The charge for a similar policy in the industrial insurance office is 13d. a week – ratio over 13 to 9 in favour of the Post Office.

In other words, the same premium that produces £4 in the Post Office produces rather less than £3 in the industrial company; on the year's business to which the official figures given above relate, the poor should have received £8 ¾ millions instead of £6 ½ millions – an annual loss of £2 ¼ millions.

The three tests thus give varying estimates of £3,500,000, £5,000,000 and £2,250,000 as the loss to the poor. Even if the two earlier figures be discounted so as to allow a higher ratio of expenses it is safe to say that the poor pay every year £3,000,000 too much / for their insurance. This is more than the yield of the sugar tax!* And it is *all* paid by the poor.†

The waste of the money of the poor which these huge figures represent is so enormous as to be almost incredible.

It is worth while to examine in detail one or two typical "industrial" policies as illustrations of this waste. I have before me two policies issued by the largest company doing industrial business. The first of these is what is called an "endowment and temporary assurance" policy. The assured is a perfectly good life, a domestic servant, aged about 20 at the time of insurance. The weekly premium is 1s. for 15 years. At the end of that period or on death before its expiration (unless indeed the death is a non-accidental death within 3 months when only one fourth, or within 6 months when only one half of the sum assured is payable);‡ the assured or her representatives is entitled to £25 16s. But if she live to the end of the period (and it includes the healthiest years of life) she has paid £39!

---

* The yield of the sugar tax was £2,960,841 in 1911.

† The last figure in the official returns should be noted. For the year to which the official figures relate, ordinary insurance companies yielded to their shareholders dividends of £487,450; the industrial insurance companies paid £700,381; in other words, shareholders for about half the business got £7 out of the poor for every £5 they got out of the rich.

‡ Post Office policies without medical examination are subject to a similar condition.

At rates similar to those obtainable for ordinary insurance policies the £25 16s. should be about £45. In other words the servant girl's £1 buys about the same amount of insurance as the rich man's 12s. 6d. Further, the policy lapses if default is made for three weeks at any time in payment of the premium; it becomes void if the assured attempts to do what the rich frequently do – that is mortgages or charges her policy; an alteration or erasure is also to render the policy void, and it has no surrender value. In fact the commercial advantages of the rich man's policy are non-existent in the case of the poor. The company however as an act of grace, offered in this case to give after payment of five years premiums a "free policy," i.e. a policy maturing at the expiration of the 15 years or earlier death on which no further premiums is payable, for £7 4s. In other words, having received £13, they were willing to undertake to repay £7 4s. at some uncertain date, possibly 10 years after the date of the undertaking.

The second policy is called an "endowment and whole life" assurance policy. It is for a weekly premium of 1s. for 20 years, 28 days of grace are allowed for payment. The assured is again a good young life, about 25 years old, and a domestic servant. Twenty years at 1s. a week makes £52. But at the end of 20 years the assured is entitled to £33 12s. only, and that not unless she is then / alive, while the only amount certainly payable is the sum of £16 16s. on her death. This £16 16s. is additional to the £33 12s. if death occurs after the 20 years, but otherwise it is the only sum secured by the policy. The £16 16s. is not reducible below £16 in the event of death within six months from the date of the policy, this trifling concession resulting from the fact that a previous policy by the same assured had lapsed through non-payment of premiums. In this case the company offered a "free policy" for £9 12s., when 5 years premiums (£13) had been paid, the extra £2 8s. as compared with the other policy being presumably attributable partly to the value of the old policy which had lapsed and partly to the longer period of the policy. The conditions as to mortgaging and so forth were the same in this policy as in the other.

Now, how does it come about that the poor pay away these large sums for so little return? How is a domestic servant persuaded to pay £39 for £25 and even to run a risk that she may pay £51 for £16 16s.?

To this question no one answer can be given based on the assumption that the ordinary poor man or woman who takes out a policy in an industrial company acts on logical grounds. "Industrial" insurance was in its origin mainly regarded as "burial" insurance and not as a means of providing for dependants in case of death, or for the insurer in old age. It often was merely a provision by a parent for the possible expenses of burying a child. Such an insurance is apt to be regarded as a provision rather for a risk that may or may not take effect than for an event the time of which alone is uncertain. The distinction between life insurance, which is a form of saving, and an "insurance" proper – which is an attempt to secure indemnity against a possible but wholly uncertain loss, is overlooked.

In insurance proper the consideration to the insurer is the indemnity enjoyed for a fixed period, and so he usually (i.e., whenever the risk does not take effect) does pay away more than he gets back, but in life "insurance," regarded as a form of investment or of saving, the ordinary commercially competent insurer expects at the least a return without interest of what he pays, and he frequently gets more. The poor woman who looks on her child's death as a contingency involving her in expense, does not distinguish between the insurance which indemnifies her against the expense and the insurance that acts as a savings bank for the child; she does not as a rule add up the premiums that she pays and consider whether they exceed the amount repayable on the policy.

To this confusion of thought must be added the crushing force of the unchecked, uncontrolled and uncontrollable persuasions of the army of agents and collectors employed by the Industrial Assurance / Companies. It is this army which accounts both for the large total of premiums received and for the enormous expenses of the companies. One large company which does about half the total of the industrial assurance business of the U. K. employs 17863 agents to collect £7,426,316 in premiums, at an average remuneration in commission of about £117 per annum each. It is a fair inference that the whole £15,707, 214 industrial premiums are responsible for 35,000 agents. These agents constitute a definite trade or branch of industry; they have a trade union in some form.[4] They constitute a vested interest in the business of industrial life insurance, most formidable from the political point of view. But from the point of view of the community an economist might be inclined to class their activities as parasitic, inasmuch as their living depends on getting their fellow workmen or workwomen to buy insurance at a total cost of about £3,000,000 more than it would cost if bought at the rate at which it is bought by the rich.

These agents carry on their business by house-to-house visits and collections. They are for the most part skilled and intelligent men, and compared to the working-class men and women whom they persuade to take out policies, they are experts. To talk of "freedom of contract" on such a matter as between a labourer's wife or a general servant and an insurance agent, is to use words without meaning. There is no reality of contract where there are not two understanding minds.

The existence of these agents might be cited an example of the strength of habit and custom in business matters. One might have supposed that the poor would have rather have gone to the shop to buy and the rich have had the luxury of being visited at home. Very rich people, I am told, are visited by their tailors and their barbers; ordinary men go and seek out these ministers of covering and comfort. But in the insurance world the rich send their premiums to the office; the poor are waited on at their own homes.

So much for the evil: is there any remedy?

To a visitor from another planet it would seem simple. Why should not the Government, even if the fear of the 35,000 agents will not allow it boldly to claim a monopoly of "industrial" life insurance, issue in connection with the Post Office Savings Bank life policies for small amounts at fair rates? No "industrial" company, it would be thought, could stand against the competition.

The remarkable thing is that the Government does this already. It does issue life policies at reasonable rates. As already mentioned a life assurance policy or a combined life and old age endowment policy for any sum from £5 to £100 can be bought at the Post Office at a much lower rate than that charged by the industrial / insurance company. It is true that the Post Office does not offer so many options and combinations, and in this respect (particularly by offering endowment policies for shorter periods) its business badly needs overhauling.* But it does offer ordinary life and endowment insurance at proper rates and it advertises the fact on every savings bank pass book that it issues. It must be concluded that the agents and the customs of the working classes are too strong for the Post Office and that instructed working class opinion has not yet been brought to bear on the subject. In any case, whatever the cause, the failure of the Post Office to attract the working classes is complete. In the year 1910 it issued in all 372 life policies!†

But we should not despair of the Post Office. In wise hands it has enormous possibilities of growth in all directions. It has long since passed beyond the stage of being merely the monopolist vendor of facilities of communication by letter, telegraph and telephone. It is becoming more and more the organ of the central government which enters into daily civil life; it pays the old age pensions, it receives savings, it will collect some Insurance Act contributions,[5] it is the great organ of official information in many branches of life. Nor need the common objections to Government action dismay us; they have little force when applied to life insurance, which is of all contracts that into which the human element enters least. For the administration of sick or unemployment benefit the personal knowledge of the members of a friendly society may be needed in order to check malingering or shirking, but the mere payment of money after death is a purely mechanical operation. If confirmation of this is wanting, it is surely supplied by the fact that the business of life insurance is the sphere of the com-

---

* An Industrial Assurance Company issues a pamphlet of 56 pages with an attractive figure taken from the window of the chapel of a famous Oxford College on the cover, to explain its policies, with premiums worked out in terms of *weekly* payments (the ordinary reckoning of the poor). The Post Office issue two meagre leaflets, 7 pages in all, dealing with both annuities and policies, the premiums calculated *yearly*. For advertising purposes public management as compared with private energy stirred by the hope of personal gain is at a hopeless disadvantage, and none the less so when the public article is better than the private.

† The whole subject of Post Office Life Insurance was considered by a departmental committee in 1908, see its report No. 311 of 1908; it is not encouraging reading. The system needs both reform from within and support from without, but especially the latter.

mercial "industrial assurance" company rather than of the more human friendly society. Therefore a reasonable individualist need have no objection to letting the facilities for insurance offered by the Post Office becoming more widely known and better adapted to the needs of the poor. In this way the poor may realise that they can derive a real advantage from their citizenship in a rich country, democratically governed; / and when they desire to insure, if private enterprise* cannot furnish them with a good article on fair terms, let them take advantage of the terms that are to be had from the Government.

Another line of action is also open to a Government that is in earnest. The Legislature might be invited to prescribe a standard form of "industrial" insurance policy which should apply compulsorily to all policies of life insurance, whether for whole life or for a term of years, where the sum assured does not exceed £100: any policy not complying with the form should be illegal and any moneys paid under such policy recoverable from the company with interest. The form should be extremely simple, and it should provide that in case of failure to pay further premiums after some liberal delay, the policy should carry some fair surrender value. The Legislature should also prescribe a schedule of maximum premiums designed to give the poor fair value for their money. Precedents for such legislation are not wanting; perhaps the most obvious are the Bills of Sale Acts, 1878 and 1882,[6] the work of a generation far less inclined to interfere with so-called "freedom of contract" than the present. A generation that has seen Money-lenders' Acts and Irish Land Acts and that has fixed the minimum wage for miners should not boggle at the protection of the servant girl and the working man's wife from the wiles of the industrial collector. The legal scale of premiums should approximate to that charged by the better class non-industrial offices, with a fair allowance for the greater expense of insuring small sums, but it should not be high enough to allow the offices to employ the present extravagant force of insurance agents. Such legislation might accompany an extension of the activities of the Post Office.

Things ought not to be left in their present condition. It is not creditable to the common sense of the country that the poor should pay yearly at least three million sterling for a commodity (for life insurance is a commodity) in excess of its market value in a case where the commodity can be supplied to the poor at a proper price. It is difficult to justify the economic waste of a system by which the energies of 35,000 poor men are devoted to making the poor poorer, and the rich (in the shape of the shareholders in the industrial companies) richer. It is surely incumbent on all who have the ear of the working classes – politicians, labour leaders, co-operators, social workers of every kind, to abate this evil.

J.F. WILLIAMS.

---

*   The Co-operative movement[7] offers considerable advantages to insurers. It has organized an ingenious method of collective insurance available for co-operators and also offers the outside public insurance at less than ordinary industrial rates. Its expense ratio is commendably low.

INDUSTRIAL INSURANCE IN AMERICA

John F. Dryden, 'The Social Economy of Industrial Insurance: A Lecture Delivered before the Senior Class of Yale University, 1904', in *Addresses and Papers on Life Insurance and Other Subjects* (Newark, NJ: Prudential Insurance Company of America, 1909), pp. 65–80.

Frederick Hoffman, *Life Insurance of Children* (Newark, NJ: Prudential Insurance Company of America, 1903).

John Dryden (1839–1911), as the Prudential's founder, first secretary and president from 1881 until his death, and Frederick Hoffman (1865–1946), a German immigrant who worked his way up through the company's statistical department between 1892 and 1922, left indelible imprints both on America's largest industrial insurance company and on American insurance, politics and statistics more generally. When Dryden delivered this lecture, he was three years into a term as US senator for New Jersey, filling the vacancy caused by the death of William Sewell. By 1903 Hoffman had made a name for himself among American statisticians with his controversial 'Race Traits and Tendencies of the American Negro' (1896), which sought to demonstrate the uninsurability of African Americans and the superior vitality of white Southerners; he would later contribute important studies of poverty, tuberculosis, cancer and occupational mortality.[1]

Dryden's office shared more than a name with the Prudential Life Assurance Company in London, which had pioneered industrial life insurance in the 1860s. Two years after it formed in 1875 as the Prudential Friendly Society, Dryden changed its name to the Prudential Insurance Company of America, having returned from a tour of the British Prudential's head office with a new business model and revised premium tables. By 1879 Metropolitan Life of New York and the Boston-based John Hancock had also converted to industrial insurance. Like their British counterparts, all three firms would move into the middle-class market by 1900: Prudential's 'ordinary' branch accounted for 37 per cent of its business in 1905, by which time Metropolitan Life and John Hancock were also pursuing all forms of life business.[2] Also as in Britain, industrial insurance was massively profitable to the men who pioneered it. Dryden died worth an estimated $50 million, and John Rogers Hegeman, the president of

Metropolitan Life from 1891 until his death in 1919, left $3.3 million, and had been reputed to be worth much more than that.[3]

Hegeman (1844–1919) was the driving force behind Metropolitan Life, which increased its income from $11.4 million to over $200 million (paid on more than 20 million policies) between the time he joined the firm in 1870 and 1919; by 1918 the Prudential insured 16.1 million policies worth $3.5 billion. Although the John Hancock placed a distant third in this contest, its location in Massachusetts made it an important political ally. All three companies, which were joined by ten smaller industrial firms by 1900, succeeded by closely following the British Prudential's 'block' system, which organized canvassers and collectors by district and carefully monitored their results. As in the case of the middle-class life insurance market, the leading American firms soon far outstripped their British counterparts in volume of sales: the Metropolitan's premium income in 1918 was roughly three times that earned by the British Prudential.[4]

As in Britain, a major lightning rod during the emergence of industrial insurance concerned the insurance of the lives of children. As in Britain, nearly a third of all industrial policies issued in the United States were on children under the age of fifteen; and the public outcry this form of insurance engendered also closely resembled the British case. In defending themselves against such charges, American firms went beyond waging wars of words, which was as common in Britain as it was in Hoffman's pamphlet on child insurance, and pooling their resources to lobby legislators (in their case, spreading this effort across an ever-shifting variety of states). The Prudential also broadcast the benefits of industrial insurance in a full-scale exhibit at the 1904 International Exposition in St Louis, some of which Dryden cribbed for his Yale lecture; and the Metropolitan, through its actuary Louis Dublin, bolstered its public image by promoting public health and social hygiene campaigns, first in New York and later across the country.[5]

Notes

1. Keller, *The Life Insurance Enterprise*, p. 20; Bouk, 'The Science of Difference', pp. 180–3, 253–9; F. L. Hoffman, *The Mortality from Cancer throughout the World* (New York: Prudential Press, 1915).

2. Dennett, *A Sense of Security*, pp. 90–2; Keller, *The Life Insurance Enterprise*, pp. 19–21.

3. *New York Times*, 25 November 1911, 22 April 1919, 28 April 1920.

4. J. N. Ingham, *Biographical Dictionary of American Business Leaders* (Westport, CT: Greenwood Press, 1983), vol. 1, p. 305; vol. 2, p. 565; Keller, *The Life Insurance Enterprise*, p. 14; *Insurance Observer*, 23 (1918), p. 135; *Statements of Assurance Business under the First, Second and Third Schedules of the Assurance Companies Act, 1909, Deposited ... December, 1917* (London: HMSO, 1918), p. 151.

5. Keller, *The Life Insurance Enterprise*, pp. 221–2; F. L. Hoffman, *Handbook and Reference Guide to the Exhibits of the Prudential Insurance Company of America* (Newark, NJ: Prudential, 1904); E. Toon, 'Managing the Conduct of the Individual Life: Public Health Education and American Public Health, 1910 to 1940' (PhD dissertation, University of Pennsylvania, 1998), pp. 200–74.

John F. Dryden, 'The Social Economy of Industrial Insurance: A Lecture Delivered before the Senior Class of Yale University, 1904' (1909)

THE SOCIAL ECONOMY

OF

INDUSTRIAL INSURANCE

INDUSTRIAL insurance is of comparatively modern origin in this country. All forms of life insurance are the result of slow development in theory and practice, but for Industrial insurance it may be claimed that it is the outgrowth of ages of experiments to provide, by an effective and absolutely certain method, for the financial needs of the mass of the population at the hour of bereavement. The mass of the people are confronted by the fact that death means a large expense – often a burdensome debt – to meet the cost of burial, or a heavy draft on slender savings, the result of years of abstinence and foresight, or the alternative of state or private charity. However remote the chance of death may appear at times, it is an ever-present contingency, for which an effective provision has become a necessity in civilized life.

Industrial insurance is so called because the system is primarily designed to meet the needs of wage-earners employed in manufacturing industries, and the weekly premium payments coincide with the weekly payment of wages and salaries. The premiums are from five cents to seventy cents a week.* The system provides for family insurance on a comprehensive plan, and every member of the family at any age from one to seventy, if in good health, is insurable. The weekly premiums for a family of five average about thirty-five or forty cents, being respectively ten cents each for the father and mother and five cents each for the children. The amounts of insurance vary with age, but average about one

---

* Policies with three-cent premiums were issued by The Prudential during the period 1875 to 1892. They were discontinued March 21, 1892, but beginning with January, 1907, this form of Industrial policy has again been issued by The Prudential.

/ hundred and fifteen dollars.* For children under age ten the average is thirty dollars, and for persons over age ten, one hundred and fifty dollars. The system is sufficiently elastic to meet the needs of the most humble laborer, even though advanced in years, as well as the requirements of the more prosperous mechanic or skilled workman, able to pay premiums for enough insurance to provide for more than the immediate needs of his family after his death.

The premiums are collected weekly from the houses of the insured by authorized agents, who are also required to solicit for new insurance. While the collection of weekly premiums necessarily increases the cost of insurance, the difference is relatively small when the great convenience of this method is taken into account. Attempts, especially by the British government, to transact a weekly-payment system of life insurance without collectors have failed. Efforts to transact a life insurance business on the monthly-payment plan have not been successful to any considerable degree. These are the simple elements of a business which has grown to immense proportions during the twenty-eight years since The Prudential Insurance Company of America was organized, in 1875, as the first company to transact this form of life insurance in this country. The total number of Industrial policies in force in the United States on January 1, 1904, was approximately 14,625,000.†

Industrial insurance had its origin in England, and the evolution of the business can be traced backwards by an unbroken record through friendly societies and burial clubs to the trade and craft gilds of the fifteenth century. The development was the inevitable result of economic laws making for a higher degree of efficiency and security in social institutions. This is not the place, however, to go into the / history of these interesting associations for social betterment under different conditions of life. They served their purpose at the time, but they would ill meet the conditions of the present.‡

In 1853 a comprehensive investigation was made by a Parliamentary committee into the practice of life insurance companies in England, and among other conclusions the committee advanced the view that "the ground hitherto occupied by these useful institutions (life assurance associations) has been comparatively limited, and that their application is capable of a great extension, not only in the higher and middle classes of society, but also among the humbler classes, to whom it has recently been very considerably applied."

---

* The average amount of the Industrial policies in force in the United States, December 31, 1908, was $136.

† On January 1, 1909, the number of Industrial policies in force in the United States was 19,687,675.

‡ See article on Gilds, in Walford's Insurance Cyclopedia, vol. V. p. 341 et seq.; also article on Friendly Societies, by the same author, Insurance Cyclopedia, vol. IV, p. 379 et seq.

Acting on this suggestion, the Prudential of London, organized as an Ordinary life insurance company in 1848, made inquiries and ascertained that, almost without exception, the then existing so-called friendly societies and burial clubs were in an unsound financial condition, while many indeed had failed, with disastrous results to the people they were supposed to benefit. A modest attempt had been made by the Industrial and General and by the British Industrial, among other English companies, to transact the business of life insurance for wage-earners on a commercial basis, but the results had not been very encouraging. The Prudential, however, realized the immense opportunity to extend the principles of life insurance to the broad field of workingmen's insurance in general. On the recommendation of the best available actuarial talent, required for the construction of tables and plans, The Prudential, in 1854, commenced the business of Industrial insurance, destined to make it one of the great life insurance companies of the world.

During the fifty years which have passed since the introduction of Industrial insurance the business has been / extended to almost all civilized countries, with more or less success; but the development has been greatest in English-speaking countries, and there are now (January 1, 1904) more than forty millions of Industrial policies in force in the world. Of this number over one-half are in force in the United Kingdom, about four millions in Germany, and not far from half a million in Australia.*

There are now (1904) in force in this country almost fifteen million Industrial policies; or, with five policies to a family, it would appear that about three million families in the United States are insured with Industrial companies for sums which range from $15 to $1,000. When we take into consideration the fact that there are about fifteen million families, we have it that at present about one family out of every five is financially interested in the success and future of this form of life insurance in the United States. When we further consider the fact that the total number of savings banks depositors is only about seven millions† – although we have had savings banks since the beginning of the nineteenth century, and Industrial insurance for only a little more than one-fourth of that period – it will be conceded that Industrial insurance is a social institution of great magnitude.

The *office practice* of Industrial insurance is, in a general way, almost identical with the practice of an Ordinary company, using that term in a technical way; and nearly all of the Industrial companies transact, in fact, an Ordinary business as a complement to their particular system of family insurance on the weekly-premium-payment plan. The essential points of difference arise out of the vast

---

*   A conservative estimate the number of Industrial policies in the world on January 1, 1909, is 58,000,000.

†   On January 1, 1909, there were about 9,000,000 depositors in savings banks in the United States.

number of necessary office transactions resulting from the weekly collection of premiums from the houses of the insured and the character of the class of risks assumed under Industrial policies. It would carry me too far to discuss, even in a general / way, the office and field administration of an Industrial company, and my remarks are, therefore, limited to essential points.

First. The calculation of premium charges for both infantile and adult risks is upon a sound actuarial basis derived from trustworthy mortality tables. The premiums vary with age, but there are practically no restrictions as to occupation or residence. Careful inquiry is made as to the moral character of the risks assumed.

Second. The collection of premiums from the houses of the insured is made by authorized collectors, or agents, who are under a most effective system of supervision, supplemented by an audit system of weekly accounts and debits and credits, by which defalcation, fraud, and intentional errors are made difficult and, generally speaking, impossible. Every policyholder has a premium receipt book in which the weekly payments must be entered by the agent, while at the same time a corresponding entry is required to be made in the agent's collection book. The system has worked so well that during the half-century since Industrial insurance has been in operation no important changes have been made in this branch of office practice.

Third. To every person insured is issued a policy which in all essentials conforms to the contract issued to Ordinary policyholders. The language used is so plain and free from confusing technicalities that it is seldom indeed that there are controversies or misunderstandings between the company and the insured. The contract provides for a definite sum payable in the event of death in return for a definite weekly premium; but, in addition, certain privileges and options are granted to the insured, which provide for a paid-up policy after three years, for additional benefits after five years, for cash dividends after fifteen years, and for a cash surrender value after twenty years.

Fourth. Every policy contains a provision that all / premiums must be paid in advance on the Monday of the week for which they are due. In the event of a policy being more than four weeks in arrears for non-payment of premiums, the agent is required to report the policy for lapse. Most of the lapses of Industrial policies occur during the early weeks of policy duration, when only a few premiums have been paid. Policies can be revived without difficulty provided the arrears do not exceed one year, but it is required that the applicant for revival pass a medical examination or furnish other evidence of being in good health. There are no fines, and every facility is granted to keep the policy in force. If the arrears exceed thirteen weeks the policy may be revived without the payment of arrears, but in place thereof a non-interest bearing lien will be issued, the amount of which is deducted from the face value of the policy when it becomes payable as a claim.

Fifth. In the event of death every effort is made to pay the claim as soon as possible, to carry into effect the general intent of Industrial insurance to provide for the burial expenses of the insured. The proof of death, however, requires to be supplemented by documentary evidence: *a*, claimant's certificate; *b*, certificate of identity; *c*, certificate of the superintendent or assistant superintendent; *d*, certificate of the undertaker; *e*, certificate of the attending physician.

Sixth. The agency system of Industrial companies is in a measure unique and deserving of special mention. A large number of agents are necessarily required to conduct the office and field operations of a company insuring millions of risks, for I may point out in passing that 95 per cent. of the entire Industrial business is carried on by three companies.* The office organization consists of a large number of departments, which cannot very well be dealt with on this occasion. I have elsewhere, in my address on "Life Insurance / as a Career," elaborated upon this part of my subject. The field operations require a superintendent in charge of a district, who is aided by a number of assistant superintendents, under whose direction is an agency force that varies in number according to the size of the territory. On an average an agent makes collections from about five hundred to six hundred policyholders, but his compensation is so adjusted that it is necessary for him, in addition, to solicit for new insurance. By this means it is to his pecuniary interest to prevent the lapsing of policies and to increase as far as possible the number of policies in force. The amount of collectible premiums is called the "debit," and the agent is held responsible for the condition of his accounts. His books and papers are periodically inspected by assistant superintendents who have a thorough knowledge of the business and are personally familiar with all the insured, so that in the event of the resignation or death of the agent there is no interruption or intermission in the collection of the weekly premiums.

With these facts clearly stated we may now consider the place of Industrial insurance in practical economics. President Hadley very properly draws a distinction between public and private wealth, and points out that "the growth of national wealth depends upon causes far deeper and more profound than those that the statesman or legislator can control."† In life insurance we have a species of material wealth representing more than two and a quarter billions of accumulated funds as security for the faithful discharge of promises made and obligations incurred, and, in addition, a vast amount of economic security resulting from the successful elimination of a risk inherent in the uncertainty of human life. We may, therefore, it seems to me, speak of life insurance, and in particular of Industrial insurance, as "public wealth" in the true and complete sense of / President Hadley's definition. He insists upon the supreme impor-

---

* On December 31, 1908, 93.2 per cent. of the Industrial policies in force in the United States were with the three largest companies.

† Economics, by Arthur T. Hadley, New York, 1897, p. 12.

tance of *security* and the institution of *property*, to render possible the progress, social, moral, and economic, of the race, for it is only by accumulated wealth that men are more or less removed from the immediate and destructive pressure of poverty. While, no doubt, much of human poverty is unavoidable and inherent in the very constitution of society, a vast amount of existing misery is preventable by the development of right habits of savings and insurance – by frugality and efficient industry. Abstinence from the immediate use of money as soon as earned is of the utmost importance in the economic development of the people. No other means have yet been discovered to insure the economic security of the masses as effectually as by insurance. President Hadley well says that "great evils arise from trusting too much to Providence and not making a distinct personal effort to meet the contingencies of life," and no method has yet been devised by which the contingency of death, especially of premature death, can be better provided for than by life insurance. Although the sphere of Industrial insurance is limited to the providing of relatively small sums as security against death, they are large indeed when considered from the viewpoint of the masses who consume their weekly wages almost as soon as earned.

The place of life insurance in social economics is, therefore, most important. The accumulation of capital, the struggle of the masses for property and economic independence, the possibility of a more equitable and general distribution of wealth, are all problems which rest fundamentally upon the power and habits of the people to save. But saving habits are acquired only with great difficulty, and the ordinary savings bank is far from being the evidence of workingmen's thrift which it is often assumed to be. Hon. Carroll D. Wright has estimated that not more than one-half of the sum on deposit with savings institutions represents accumulations / of wage-earners, the remainder being the investments of the relatively well-to-do. Industrial insurance serves both an economic and a social purpose. It is the most effective, even though perhaps the most elementary, education in thrift which has yet been developed. The weekly premium payments develop systematic habits of saving and lead to the accumulation of millions which but for this method of insurance would be expended largely for needless and often vicious purposes. The usual method of accumulating savings banks deposits is in marked contrast to Industrial insurance premium payments, in that, as a rule, deposits are made at irregular intervals and not in the small sums which represent true foresight, frugality, and abstinence from needless expenditures.

The weekly premium payments soon become a habit of life, even with the young, who in time learn to pay the five or ten cents a week necessary to meet the expense of their own insurance. The education in thrift, however, does not end here. Systematic habits of saving are developed which have their effect in other directions, and the conclusion is quite in accordance with our experience that general saving habits, accumulations in savings banks, or payments for building loans, *follow* Industrial insurance rather than precede it, and are most widely diffused among the people where Industrial insurance is most general as a mode or method of family protection. For illustration: In this country Philadelphia, Pa., and Dayton, Ohio, are often referred to as cities in which building and loan associations have made most progress, but they are also cities in which Industrial insurance is most general as a method of family insurance. In England, it is claimed on good authority that school savings banks and penny provident funds have been most successful in Manchester, Liverpool, and Birmingham, but these are also the cities in which Industrial insurance is almost universal, so much so that at least four-fifths of the entire population of these cities hold Industrial policies. /

Industrial insurance is not only of great value as an aid to the development of general saving habits and the accumulation of property, but it is a contributory agent of great importance in the progress and public appreciation of other forms of insurance – Ordinary life, fraternal, accident, fire insurance, etc. Industrial insurance has enormously extended the field of other methods of insurance by familiarizing the mass of the population with the elementary principles and beneficial results of a method of life insurance particularly adapted to special needs. Industrial insurance came into existence in the United States at a time when public faith in financial institutions, savings banks, Ordinary life insurance companies, and, especially, so-called workingmen's insurance on the co-operative plan was profoundly shaken by panics and financial depressions and evidences of mismanagement and fraud. Industrial insurance has kept faith with the people, and every promise made has been fully carried out. Security, stability, permanency, have been the watchwords, and no social institution of to-day is established on a more scientific and trustworthy theory of mortality and finance than the vast structure of Industrial insurance with its more than forty millions of policyholders in different parts of the world. It is not going too far to say that this method of life insurance protection forms to-day one of the most effective measures making directly or indirectly for accumulation of property. However small the premium payments and however small in many cases the individual returns, the fact remains that fifty-two times a year payments are made, and these lessons in thrift and accumulation are taught and brought home to an element of the population which is most in need thereof.

We often hear the old complaint that there is no real progress, but only a shifting of wealth, by which the poor are made poorer and the rich grow richer. Relatively this is true, for, by contrast, in a more advanced society the condition / of the very poor becomes more striking and apparently less necessary. Actually, however, our progress during the past half-century has been real and of vast benefit to the mass of our population, who in an ever-increasing proportion are attaining a relatively high degree of economic security and social well-being. The object of all thrift agencies is not only to aid persons to become savers in the first instance and to accumulate a fund for future contingencies, but also "that they may have the consciousness of being removed (by their own efforts) from the burden of relief-receiving."

Industrial insurance provides a sum certain, from $15 to $1,000, at a time when in many households no ready money is otherwise available for the expenses incident to death and the last illness. The problem reduces itself to the necessity: that the burial of the father or the child must be paid for, that it will cost at least from $15 to $100, and that this sum must be provided for either by the convenient method of Industrial insurance or by a draft upon a sum possibly accumulated during years of careful husbandry of slender resources or by the incurrence of a debt with the undertaker and the doctor. With the last as the alternative, it is an open question whether an undertaker can be found who will take the risk, and there will often be no escape from the necessity of an appeal to the public poor fund or for private charitable relief. The poor have their standard of life and customs as thoroughly established as the well-to-do or the rich, and, however humble their station, they prefer the burial of their dead at their own expense in a manner which to them represents the common decencies of life.

Deep at the root of the problem of life insurance for the poor lies their abhorrence of a pauper burial and their willingness to provide out of present savings for a future contingency and the ever-present possibility of premature or unexpected death. As the result of the introduction of / Industrial insurance into the United States there is now returned to policyholders about $25,000,000 per annum in the payment of claims alone, and the relative number of pauper burials has been materially reduced during the past twenty years. On the basis of a conservative estimate there would be 25,000 more pauper burials per annum in American cities if this system were not in almost universal operation. From a moral and sentimental point of view, therefore, the value of Industrial insurance as making for a higher standard of family life cannot be overestimated. It certainly is a matter of considerable importance in the life and struggle of many who are on the very verge of pauperism and dependency to know that at the end of their earthly difficulties they will not be cast away in a potter's field.

But the good effect of Industrial insurance as a direct means of reducing pauperism does not end here. In many instances a sufficient sum remains, after the payment of funeral and doctors' bills, to establish the widow in some kind of business, on a small scale perhaps, but sufficient to provide the necessary means of support for herself and children. As a rule there will be other savings available, for Industrial insurance suggests the advantage and importance of other forms of investment and encourages economy in family expenditures. How far the burden of poor-relief, indoor and out, has been actually diminished cannot be stated with even approximate accuracy, but there are some very significant data for certain States and cities which indicate that, regardless of a large immigration, there has been, during recent years, a relative and substantial decrease in the number of paupers and in the amount paid out for poor-relief.

The indirect results of Industrial insurance are, therefore, of very considerable importance. Just as the vast accumulations in savings banks are to a considerable extent the aggregate of a large number of small deposits, so in Industrial insurance the assets of about $150,000,000, held as / reserve and surplus, represent a vast amount of *capital* as the result of small weekly payments which average about ten cents.* These accumulations do not stand for idle capital, but for public wealth in the complete sense of the term. It is wealth made available for the conduct of general business, of active enterprise, and other social and economic ends. Of the two billions of assets held by American legal reserve life insurance companies 75 per cent. is invested in stocks, bonds, and mortgages, 8 per cent. in real estate, 6 per cent. in loans on policies, and the remainder in other forms of investment and as cash in bank. The absolute necessity for life insurance companies to earn a certain rate of interest on their investments makes it of the highest importance that the assets should be constantly employed in profitable enterprises, thus increasing materially the national prosperity and social security of the people.

I, therefore, do not go too far in holding that the indirect results of this form of insurance, with its encouragement of systematic saving, are at least equally important with the direct results represented by the annual payment of over $25,000,000 in claims, etc., to Industrial beneficiaries. The creation of capital by this method of insurance is indeed of far-reaching importance, even to the laborer or wage-earner, whose economic security and opportunity for employment are enhanced by the real amount of capital made thus available for increased production. There is no more generally accepted postulate in economics than that "in proportion to the increase in capital the share of the annual product falling to capital is augmented absolutely but diminished relatively, while the share falling to labor is increased both absolutely and relatively." Considered from this point of view alone Industrial insurance makes for a more general and equitable distribution of wealth.

The success of Industrial insurance may be summed up / in a remark made by Abraham Lincoln, that "with public sentiment on its side everything succeeds – with public sentiment against it nothing succeeds." The system of family insurance forms an integral part of the domestic economy of the American people. Organized in the State of New Jersey, the progress in local development has been most complete in that State and in the adjoining States of New York and Pennsylvania. In New Jersey there are now about 1,500,000 Industrial policies in force, indicating that about 65 per cent. of the aggregate population is insured.

---

* On December 31, 1908, the aggregate reserve held by the Industrial companies for the protection and benefit of the Industrial policyholders and their beneficiaries was approximately $220,000,000.

In certain sections of Newark, of New York City, of Philadelphia, and of other large cities, the system is so general that from 75 to 95 per cent. of all insurable persons hold Industrial policies.

We have made a number of investigations to ascertain the actual extent of Industrial insurance in various cities, and there is one significant fact which we have learned, especially in and around Newark – that the proportion of population insured on the Industrial plan is somewhat higher among those who own their own homes than among those who do not. Whether as cause or effect, the fact remains that the progress and development of the business have been most satisfactory among the thrifty and stable element of our industrial population. We can go further and say that policyholders are in other respects a superior class. For illustration: We find by our mortality statistics that the death rate of insured children is less than the mortality of children in the general population as determined by the census. Our percentage of deaths from intemperance and alcoholism is less than that expected by the general standard of mortality, and, finally, we find that our ratio of deaths from homicide and suicide is below the average for the country at large. I mention these facts, which are supported by irrefutable evidence, to show that there is a close relation between Industrial insurance and the progress and well-being / of the industrial population, and that the Industrial policyholders represent a more thrifty, more temperate, and more law-abiding element than the uninsured.

It remains for me to speak of the evolution of Industrial insurance and the adaptation of the business to new conditions. When established, in 1875, the financial and industrial conditions were such as to call for an elementary form of life insurance, with absolute security as the first consideration. By slow degrees public confidence in insurance and financial institutions was restored, and as early as 1881 it became necessary to issue a special policy for the round sum of $500, to meet a distinct and increasing demand from the superior element of our industrial population. By 1886 the insurance education of the masses had gone far enough to make it seem advisable, and, in fact, necessary, to establish an Ordinary department. That was less than twenty years ago; but during the intervening period the three Industrial companies which transact 95 per cent. of the business in this country have built up a vast Ordinary business with about 720,000 policies and $800,000,000 of insurance in force.* At least one-half of this sum – and perhaps three-fifths – represents Ordinary insurance on the lives of wage-earners, or persons in positions or situations practically outside of the field of the solicitor for exclusively Ordinary companies. The number of persons insured with Industrial companies for both Industrial and Ordinary is indeed

---

*   On December 31, 1908, the Industrial companies had 1,295,942 Ordinary policies in force, representing $1,317,887,524 of insurance.

quite large and constantly increasing. The Industrial policies are held primarily for the payment of expenses incident to death; the Ordinary for family protection, education of children, and other purposes of social and economic importance. Coincident with the progress and evolution of Industrial insurance there has been a material improvement in the Industrial policy contract, which to-day contains all the essential and important provisions and privileges of the regular Ordinary policy. So / we see how close is the relation between the two forms of insurance and how important is Industrial insurance as an education in general insurance theory and practice, making gradually, but with certainty, for the social and economic security of the people.

If there is any one thing that "social classes owe to each other" it is that all shall aim and work to diminish the needless suffering and unnecessary burdens of those for whose well-being and future protection we are individually or socially responsible. The evidence is conclusive that the mass of our population is engaged in a heroic struggle to escape from dependent poverty to relative economic and social freedom, and whatever contributes toward this much-to-be-desired end is certainly deserving of sympathetic consideration. I believe that in Industrial insurance we have a most valuable aid in this effort for social betterment on a large scale, and the evidence is conclusive that a vast amount of direct and indirect good is accomplished by this elementary, but effective, form of thrift. During the almost thirty years since Industrial insurance has been in active operation in this country, gradual but constant progress has been made toward a higher degree of social efficiency, so that we may hopefully look forward and anticipate a time when this form of insurance will be indeed a social institution of universal utility, in every respect a far-reaching power for good, directly to the people and indirectly to the nation. I believe that the evidence warrants the conclusion that Industrial insurance makes first for private wealth and second for public wealth, as well as directly and indirectly for the all-important end of a higher degree of security for the industrial population of this land.

Frederick Hoffman, *Life Insurance of Children* (1903)

The Life Insurance of Children.

INTRODUCTION.

Institutions for savings and insurance are the bulwark of our civilization and a guarantee of the continuance of the American standard of life. Ordinary life insurance is now so well understood that attempts to cast discredit upon this form of family protection, because of occasional instances of abuses or crimes, would meet with no response from an intelligent public, or call for legislative interference. Time was, not many years ago, when serious religious and social objections were urged against the practice of thus providing for the uncertainties of the future. The insurance of women, especially of wives, and of persons above the age of fifty was once looked upon as prejudicial to public policy, and it required time and experience to demonstrate that such anticipations were as groundless as they were opposed to any rational view of public morality. Fire and marine insurance also passed through a period of agitation and opposition, although with more foundation in fact, since it is even now officially admitted that over six per cent. of all the fires in the United States are of incendiary origin, with a corresponding immense destruction of property and the sacrifice of many human lives.

Industrial insurance, the most modern form of life insurance protection for the wage-earning masses, is occasionally made the subject of attacks, because of certain features or elements, alleged to be against the best interests of the general public. But the opposition is especially directed against that feature of the system by which small insurances are granted on the lives of children, at ages over one, and as members of the family. It is asserted by those who are opposed to this form of insurance that from time to time serious abuses, and even crimes, have occurred in connection with this form of thrift, but to those who are thoroughly familiar with the practice and results of Industrial insurance in this and other countries, this part of the system / seems to require no defence. From a moral, social and economic point of view, Industrial insurance forms now an integral part of the family life of the people of the United States, whose demand for a simple, effective and absolutely secure form of insurance brought it into existence, as the logical and inevitable evolution of the ancient burial regulations of Gilds and the more modern Funeral Briefs and Burial Societies.

THE ORIGIN AND PRESENT EXTENT OF INDUSTRIAL INSURANCE.

Industrial insurance was established on a practical working basis by the Prudential Assurance Company of England in 1854. Twenty-one years later the business was introduced into this country by Mr. John F. Dryden, who organized The Prudential Insurance Company of America, and after some twenty-six years of business operations this form of life insurance for the masses has been so widely diffused that the total number of policies in the United States exceeds 13,000,000, while in the entire world there are now over 35,000,000 Industrial policies in force. The rapid growth of the business is illustrated by the following table, which shows the totals for each of the years 1882, 1892 and 1902. The complete returns for 1903 are not yet available.

INDUSTRIAL INSURANCE IN THE UNITED STATES. 1882–1902.

January 1st	No. of Companies	No. of Policies	Amount of Insurance	Premium Income	Losses Paid
1882	3	360,000	$33,000,000	$1,609,000	$542,000
1892	9	4,302,000	481,000,000	20,655,000	7,725,000
1902	15	12,333,000	1,640,000,000	74,660,000	22,003,000

INDUSTRIAL INSURANCE DEFINED.

Although this form of life insurance has now been in operation in the United States for more than a quarter of a century, many erroneous conceptions prevail as to its principles, practice and business results. Thus, for example, a well-known government / expert on questions of economics and sociology made the statement before the Industrial Commission in 1898 that, "Industrial insurance means the insurance of children by their parents, so that in case of death they shall have a sufficient amount of money for a decent and respectable burial. That is what is meant by 'Industrial insurance.'" While it is true that Industrial insurance companies accept risks on the lives of children, it is entirely erroneous to define the business in this manner. Industrial insurance, briefly stated, is *life insurance for the masses on the plan of family insurance*, and every member of the family in good health, ages one to seventy, is insurable. There are no "Child Insurance" companies, and "Child Insurance," as such, has no existence.

AGES OF INSURED CHILDREN.

It is readily possible to support this statement by the experience of The Prudential, which shows that of the total number of policies in force at the present time 30.4 per cent. are at ages under fifteen, while the normal proportion of population, according to the last census, is 31.0 per cent. At the younger ages the proportion of children insured in The Prudential is, therefore, somewhat *less* than in the entire population. The facts are set forth in more detail in the following table [...]. It is conclusively shown that there is no adverse selection against the Company in a disproportionate number of risks on the lives of children at young ages.

COMPARATIVE AGE DISTRIBUTION OF INDUSTRIAL
POLICY-HOLDERS AND OF THE TOTAL AMERICAN
POPULATION.

AGES	American Population Census of 1900 Per Cent.	Industrial Policy-holders Prudential 1903 Per Cent.
Two to three	2.5	1.9
Three to four	2.5	2.2
Four to five	2.5	2.3
Five to nine	12.3	12.1
Ten to fourteen	11.2	11.9
Total under fifteen	31.0	30.4
Over fifteen	69.0	69.6
All ages	100.0	100.0 /

On the basis of a conservative estimate the number of Industrial policies in force in the United States at ages under twelve is, approximately, 3,000,000, out of a total of 12,500,000 at all ages, or 24 per cent., which compares with 24.5 per cent. of children at ages one to twelve in the total population. Children under one are not insured, because the amounts payable at death for a five or ten-cent weekly premium at this early age would, on account of the very high death-rate, be too small to prove a sufficient contribution to the burial expenses.

FUNDAMENTAL PRINCIPLES OF INDUSTRIAL INSURANCE.

There are four fundamental principles of Industrial insurance: the *first* is that the premiums are payable weekly; the *second*, that the amounts of insurance are adjusted to a premium / unit of five cents or multiples thereof; the *third*, that the premiums are collected from the houses of the insured; the *fourth*, that every member of the family is insurable if in sound health, at ages from one to seventy inclusive. In other words, Industrial insurance is *family insurance*, of which the insurance of children forms an integral part. The customary method is to insure the father and mother for a weekly premium of ten cents each, while each of the children is insured for a weekly premium of five cents. In this manner the average weekly payment per family is from twenty-five to fifty cents.* In virtue of these principles life insurance has become available to the masses, and today no other form of insurance or savings approaches Industrial insurance in popularity. While the number of Industrial policies in force in the United States in 1901 was about 12,500,000, the number of savings-bank depositors was 6,700,000, of Ordinary policy-holders 4,000,000, of fraternal insurance certificates 4,000,000, and of building and loan certificates 1,500,000.

THE PRIMARY OBJECT OF INDUSTRIAL INSURANCE.

The principal object of Industrial insurance is to provide for the burial expenses of the insured on the ground of common decency and self-respect as a safeguard against the possibility of a pauper burial. The high death-rate in infancy makes it desirable that a small insurance should be placed on the lives of children, and accordingly tables have been constructed, under which such policies for small amounts are issued at ages over one year. The premiums for which children can be insured are limited to ten cents, and the amounts of insurance at different ages are almost equivalent to the funeral expenses and the cost of the last illness. /

THE OFFICE PRACTICE OF INSURING CHILDREN'S LIVES.

In view of the fact that the mortality-rate of children decreases rapidly from birth to age ten or twelve, the amounts of insurance on the lives of children rapidly increase with advancing age although the premium remains the same. Thus, if a child is insured for a ten-cent premium at age two next birthday, should death occur after a policy has been in force one year, $34 would be payable ; should death occur during the first three months, however, only $16 would be paid; after six months, $24 ; and after nine months, $30. Should death occur after the policy has been in force eight years, $240 would be payable, *which is the maximum amount for which a child at age ten next birthday can be insured.* In other words, should death occur during the early period of child life the amounts due under the policy are about sufficient to meet the burial expenses, but if the child

---

*   According to a report of the United States Department of Labor, the average expenditure for life insurance in workingmen's families in the United States is from 2.5 per cent. to 3.5 per cent. of the total family income. The average annual expenditure for life insurance is $21.00 per family, against $31.00 for liquor and tobacco. In other words, out of a weekly family income of $10.00 on the average, from twenty-five to thirty-five cents is paid for life insurance. These statistics are confirmed by the investigations of the Economic Club of London, published under the title "Family Budgets," showing an average expenditure for life insurance of 4.6 per cent. of the weekly family income. For other data see B. S. Rowntree's book on "Poverty,"[1] published in 1901, by Macmillan & Co., London and New York.

survives, which, of course, in the large majority of cases is the fact, the amounts payable at death in later life are the largest obtainable for the premium paid. If death occurs at any time after age ten next birthday, the amount payable for a ten-cent weekly premium is always $240, subject, however, to additional benefits and cash dividends. After twenty years the policy has a cash surrender value. The following table will show the amounts for which children are insured at any age below ten next birthday for a ten-cent weekly premium.

INDUSTRIAL INFANTILE RATE TABLE. – WEEKLY PREMIUM, TEN CENTS.

BENEFIT PAYABLE IF POLICY HAS BEEN IN FORCE FOR	AGE NEXT BIRTHDAY WHEN POLICY IS ISSUED.							
	2	3	4	5	6	7	8	9
Less than three months	$16 00	$18 00	$20 00	$22 00	$24 00	$28 00	$32 00	$40 00
Over three but less than six	20 00	22 00	26 00	28 00	32 00	38 00	44 00	56 00
Over six but less than nine	24 00	28 00	32 00	36 00	44 00	52 00	70 00	100 00
Over nine mos. but less than one year	30 00	34 00	40 00	48 00	58 00	70 00	110 00	150 00
One year	34 00	40 00	48 00	58 00	78 00	110 00	160 00	240 00
Two years	40 00	48 00	58 00	86 00	120 00	170 00	240 00	
Three years	48 00	58 00	94 00	130 00	180 00	240 00		
Four years	58 00	102 00	140 00	190 00	240 00			
Five years	110 00	150 00	200 00	240 00				
Six years	160 00	200 00	240 00					
Seven years	200 00	240 00						
Eight years	240 00							

The *maximum* amounts for which children can be insured, under the New York law of 1892, paragraph 55, are as follows:

Between ages one and two	$30 00
Between ages two and three	34 00
Between ages three and four	40 00
Between ages four and five	48 00
Between ages five and six	58 00
Between ages six and seven	140 00
Between ages seven and eight	168 00
Between ages eight and nine	200 00
Between ages nine and ten	240 00

To this law the practice of the Industrial companies has been adjusted and children can not be insured for higher amounts with either one company or more. In the event of this having been done under a misapprehension, the excess premiums paid are returned to the beneficiary.

AVERAGE INFANTILE CLAIM PAYMENTS.

While children *can* be insured for the amounts given in the table, as a general rule the policies issued are only for a weekly premium of five cents. The average premium in actual experience is only a trifle over five cents, and the average claim payment at different ages, according to the Prudential experience for 1901, has been as follows:

AVERAGE AMOUNTS PAID IN CLAIMS AT AGES
UNDER TEN YEARS. PRUDENTIAL
INDUSTRIAL EXPERIENCE – 1901.

AGE AT DEATH.	AMOUNT OF CLAIM.
2	$12 84
3	21 13
4	25 58
5	29 78
6	35 27
7	50 73
8	76 29
9	96 55
Average, ages one to nine, inclusive	30 00

It is shown by this table that at age two next birthday the average claim payment is a trifle less than $13. At ages under ten the amounts paid are, therefore, very small, and only in part meet the actual burial expenses and the cost of the last illness. There / is absolutely no speculative element in this form of insurance, and there is no opportunity for gain when the actual expenses incurred in the bringing up of the child and the actual cost of insurance are taken into account.

CLAIM PAYMENTS AND FUNERAL EXPENSES.

As has been stated, the primary object of Industrial insurance is to provide for the possible contingency of burial expenses. Industrial insurance is not, primarily, an attempt at investment, and the so-called "investment feature" of modern life insurance is of secondary importance in this form of insurance protection for the masses. It is therefore of importance to learn how far the actual experience supports the theoretical conception, and it is [...] / possible to make accurate answer to this question by the available facts derived from the experience of The Prudential: The accompanying table [...] show the average funeral expenses for children and adults, as determined by correspondence with responsible undertakers in the principal cities, and the average amounts paid in claims on children and adults, according to the Prudential mortality experience during 1901.

FUNERAL EXPENSES AND CLAIM PAYMENTS.

	Funeral Expenses.	Average Claim.
Children, ages one to nine	$40 00	$30 00
Adults, ages over ten	74 00	154 00

According to this table the average funeral expenses at ages under ten are $40, while the average amount paid in claims at this period of life, in the Prudential experience, has been only $30. There is, therefore, a deficiency of $10 to meet the average funeral expenses, and it is evident that there is no opportunity for speculation, since there is not even a sufficient amount to provide in full for the decent interment of the child. At adult ages the case is reversed and the average claim payments quite considerably exceed the average amounts paid out for burial purposes. This is due to the fact that the average premiums are higher, and there is, of recent years especially, a distinctive attempt to provide for more than the burial expenses, that is, the immediate support and protection of the family. This point is now so well recognized by well-informed writers like Mr. Charles Booth,[2] that he takes occasion to point out in his book on "Pauperism and the Endowment of Old Age"[3] that "provision in this way against death has become very general in recent years; and I am told that the amounts insured with such companies as The Prudential tend continually to increase, showing that something beyond mere funeral expenses is thought of." The evidence is therefore conclusive that in the actual experience of Industrial companies the practice of insuring the lives of children is in harmony with the theoretical conception that the object and aim of such insurance is to provide for the respectable burial of a child. Since the large majority of policies do not terminate by death during early years, but continue in force after infancy, the / secondary result of this form of insurance is its educational value in teaching the child habits of prudence, forethought and thrift at an early age when such lessons are most likely to be enduring. Having early in life become familiar with life insurance methods, the policy is continued in later years and supplemented by other forms of insurance on the Industrial, Fraternal or Ordinary plan. Habits of systematic saving are thus inculcated in the mind at a very early period, and good results in other directions follow. The majority of Industrial policy-holders are savings-bank depositors, holders of building and loan certificates and investors in other forms of saving and accumulation.

CHARGES OF CHILD MURDER FOR INSURANCE MONEY.

However improbable as a fact of civilized life, and however opposed to any fair-minded conception of human nature as it is, the charge of child murder has from time to time been made against this form of insurance during the past sixty years. It is charged that children are insured, and subsequently murdered for the sake of gain through the proceeds of the policy, even though the amounts receivable are exceedingly small and, in the large majority of cases, insufficient to meet the total burial expenses. The charges had their origin in a case which occurred in England about 1840, but in which the evidence was inconclusive to connect the probable crime of murder with the method of burial societies in granting small sums of money at the death of a child. During the early forties, however, a considerable *class* agitation on the subject resulted in the passage, in 1846, of an act prohibiting the insurance of children as members of Friendly Societies, which act remained in force until 1855, when, on the basis of an exhaustive investigation by a Parliamentary Committee appointed for the purpose, a new act was passed, under which it was made lawful to insure children for limited amounts at all ages. The limitations were, 6£ at ages under five years and 10£ at ages five to ten. Giving due consideration to differences in local conditions, the amounts are fairly sufficient for the general requirements of the industrial / population of the United Kingdom. Although a considerable number of acts have been passed in the meantime, regulating the business of Friendly Societies and Industrial Assurance Companies, the provisions of the act of 1855 regarding the insurance of children and the limitations of amounts have remained the same.* The subject has been carefully inquired into from time to time, by a special Royal Commission during the early seventies, and subsequently by special committees of the House of Lords and the House of Commons, but no conclusive evidence has been presented to the point that this form of insurance has been productive of crime, or in other words, the cause of child murder for insurance money.†

THE PRESENT STATUS OF PUBLIC OPINION IN ENGLAND.

The subject has continued to attract attention, but the opposition to the insurance of children in England is now almost entirely limited to a few individuals, in particular to the secretary of the National Society for the Prevention of Cruelty to Children. From time to time the earlier charges are reiterated and the attempt is made to support such charges by isolated cases of child neglect. Of the large number of children which come under the supervision of the society, only a small proportion, according to the official record, are found to be insured; while on the basis of a trustworthy estimate, over eighty per cent. of the children of English wage-earners are insured on the weekly-payment plan with either Industrial insurance companies or with Collecting Friendly Societies. The total number of Industrial policies in force in England exceeds 20,000,000, or about

---

*　By an act passed in 1850, the law of 1846 was modified, and permission was granted to pay on the death of children the actual funeral expenses, if not in excess of 3£, but the money was to be paid to the undertaker or person by whom the burial was conducted. In practice the law proved a failure in that the burial expenses usually exceeded the 3£ limit, while the payment to the undertaker proved a burdensome restriction to people accustomed to the management of their own affairs.

†　For an exceptionally valuable discussion of Industrial insurance as an economic factor in the life of the people, see the works of Thomas Mackay, in particular "The English Poor," London, 1889, "Working Class Insurance," London, 1890, and "Insurance and Savings," London, 1892. Mr. Mackay is the recognized authority on English Poor Law history and administration.

two-thirds of the entire / population.* In cities like Liverpool practically the entire population of wage-earners and their families are insured in this manner, and it may not be out of place to quote the opinion of one of the foremost public health authorities in England, Dr. E. W. Hope, the Medical Officer of Health of Liverpool, who, under date of July 20, 1898, expressed his views as follows:

> I have to say that the subject is one to which I have given very careful attention for a good number of years. I have formed a very strong opinion that the insurance in the great bulk of cases is effected entirely for prudential reasons. No single instance has ever come under my notice in which I could say that the child had been maltreated for the sake of the burial money.

Another English medical authority, Dr. T. N. Kelynack, in a paper read before the Third International Congress for the Welfare and Protection of Children, held in London, July 15–18, 1902, concluded his remarks regarding the insurance of children as follows:

> One word must be said respecting infant insurance. The belief still exists that infant insurance is a fruitful source of criminal neglect. This view I am inclined to think is not well founded. As far as I can gather, the restrictions are such that at the present time there is but little encouragement to insure an infant from criminal motives. I do not think that insurance and infant mortality can be associated to any extent as cause and effect.

THE AGITATION AGAINST THE INSURANCE OF CHILDREN IN THE UNITED STATES.

Leaving out of consideration fragmentary references to the English agitation in American newspapers previous to 1884, the / first official suggestion to prohibit, by legislative enactment, the issue of policies for small amounts on the lives of children, was made in that year in an address by Governor Benjamin Butler, of Massachusetts. General Butler evidently had no clear conception of the point

---

*   According to the report of the National Society for the Prevention of Cruelty to Children in England, of the total number of children considered by the Society during 1901, only 24.3 per cent, were found to be insured. It is not stated whether the insurance was actually in force, or had been in force at some time previous to the children being taken in charge by the Society, nor is it stated whether the child was actually in benefit so that the parents would have been entitled to at least part of the insurance in case of its death. According to the last annual report of the S. P. C. C. of New York, the proportion found to be insured of the total number taken in charge during the year was 24.1 per cent., or almost identical with the English ratio. In contrast, it may be pointed out that the proportion of insured children of wage-earners in London and New York is between sixty and eighty per cent., so that the returns of the two Societies rather prove that the companies have only the better class of children insured.

at issue and assumed that children were insured for very large amounts and by irresponsible companies or societies. The subject was revived in 1889 by Governor Beaver, of Pennsylvania, who made an attack upon the system in his message to the legislature. The Governor based his views upon a child-murder case which had occurred in Philadelphia the year previous and which attracted wide-spread attention.* The evidence was conclusive that the woman was insane, and that she murdered not only her children but also her husband, who was the breadwinner of the family. The subject was thoroughly inquired into by the legislature and the conclusions were adverse to the passage of restrictive legislation. In the following year the Insurance Committee of the Assembly of the State of New York inquired carefully into certain features of Industrial insurance in due consideration of a bill introduced to prohibit the insurance of children under the age of ten years. The evidence presented was so overwhelmingly in favor of the system that it was not considered necessary to pass restrictive legislation. By an act passed in 1892, a table of maximum amounts for which children can be insured was incorporated in the laws of New York, which is in force at the present time and to which the practice of Industrial insurance companies has been adjusted. (See page 9.)

In 1893 a bill was introduced into the Colorado legislature prohibiting the insurance of children under the age of ten years, and the bill subsequently became a law. The bill was passed under a misapprehension on the part of members from the rural and mining counties, where the business was unknown, and the law has remained in force to the present time. The demand for the repeal of the law assumed considerable proportions by 1899, / and a measure to that effect introduced into the house passed that body by a considerable majority, and would have passed the Senate but for the obstructive tactics of a single member. Colorado is the only State where the insurance of children is prohibited by law.†

An attempt was made in Massachusetts in 1895, and another in 1896, to prohibit the insurance of children, but after a very thorough investigation the

---

*   There is at present a similar case pending in the Philadelphia courts, but the trial has been postponed from time to time, no doubt on account of insufficient evidence. Such facts as have been made public would make it appear that, while a crime may possibly have been committed, the insurance on the lives of the children could not possibly have been a motive. The amounts insured for were used for the legitimate purpose of providing a respectable burial, the cost of mourning, the purchase of a cemetery-plot, etc.

†   The following is one of many letters of protest against the law of 1893, made by representatives of the clergy and others interested in social problems in different parts of Colorado. The Rev. Edward Pearsons Newton, of Pueblo, Col., president of the Associated Charities, wrote under date of February 16, 1899: "For years my interests have led me to read much upon social and charitable lines. I believe Industrial insurance makes for thrift and independence and these are both good things to be fostered among the poor. I heartily desire its introduction among the wage-earners of Pueblo."

General Court decided, by a vote of twenty-three for and one hundred and forty-nine against the measure, that adverse legislation was not required.*

An attempt was made in Ohio in 1900 to pass a law prohibiting the insurance of children, but after a careful investigation and hearing before the senate committee on insurance, the bill was defeated by a vote of twenty-four against the measure, and only one vote, by the author of the bill, in its favor.

This brief review of legislative measures and investigations proves conclusively that the more carefully the subject is inquired into the more favorable the opinion as to the value of this form of life insurance for the masses from the standpoint of public policy. During the past twenty years some seventy attempts have been made to pass laws of this kind, always on the ground of sentimental consideration, but, with the exception noted, all the propositions have been voted down. It is difficult to look upon these attempts in any other manner than persecution of a legitimate business interest, in view of its public approval by the millions of policyholders of Industrial companies, assuming in some States and cities a proportion of from fifty to eighty per cent. of the entire wage-earning population. /

THE CHARGE OF CHILD NEGLECT AND FUNERAL EXTRAVAGANCE.

Following the earlier attacks, the charge of child murder for insurance money has been repeated in recent times, invariably, however, without the necessary support of trustworthy evidence of actual instances of crime. There are no cases on record, nor is there record of a conviction by a jury, that the murder of a child *has been induced* by the small insurance on the life of the child. Murder cases of insured children occasionally reported by the newspapers, prove, on investigation, that the murder was induced by other considerations than the insurance, and in such cases the money realized barely covered the burial expenses of the child, so that there was no financial gain.

When the enormous extent of the operations of Industrial companies is taken into account, it would not be remarkable if such cases had actually occurred, but the experience of the companies is to the contrary, and their records fail to show that evil results have followed. The opposition to this form of insurance, finding it impossible to maintain the charge of child murder, has changed its views to the more subtle charge of child neglect, and in recent years to the economic ground of wasteful extravagance.

---

* The following is an extract from a letter of Edward Frothingham, general manager of the Boston Provident Association, issued to the public during the Massachusetts agitation against the life insurance of children. "The advantages of life insurance of children of worthy parents cannot be ignored. In one sense Industrial insurance is philanthropic, for it encourages parents to thrift. With twenty years of experience with poverty-stricken families, I have never met with a case of cruelty to children because of their lives being insured."

Thus, quoting from a newspaper article relative to the attempt to prohibit the insurance of children in Massachusetts by the present legislature, the secretary of the Children's Aid Society is quoted to the effect that "he did not think that the insurance led to child murder." Mr. Frank B. Fay, who, in 1895, led the attack upon the companies, is quoted to the effect that "I do not say that it leads to child murder, because I could not prove that it does." Miss Jane Addams, the well-known founder of Hull House, Chicago, is quoted in the Chicago *Tribune* of January 4th to the effect that "it is hardly probable that the small amount of insurance in such cases would prove enough to incite to the murder." She, however, for other reasons, is opposed to the system, largely on the ground that Industrial insurance is too expensive a form of life insurance for the masses to prove / desirable from an economic point of view.* Since this point does not form the basis of the legislative measures attempting to prohibit the insurance of children, it might properly be ignored, but a brief consideration may not be out of place.

The Committee made the following report: "Your Committee is not aware of any facts tending to show that Industrial insurance ever produces crime in this country."

THE COST OF LIFE INSURANCE AT RETAIL.

It is not possible to make an exact comparison of the cost of life insurance of children on the Industrial plan, since the only corresponding method on the Ordinary plan is that of "Child's Endowments," which is, in fact, pure endowment, with premiums returnable if death occurs before the end of the endowment period. A fairly accurate comparison, however, can be made of adult policies, and at age forty a policy of $1,000 would cost $52 per annum if paid for by weekly premiums. Since Industrial policies are sold to the general wage-earning population, a class of people are thus insured who are not, as a general rule, solicited by Ordinary companies on account of a much higher mortality-rate. The men are often employed in unhealthful or dangerous occupations, which in the practice of all Ordinary companies are charged an extra premium, often as high as the original whole-life premium, and a considerable proportion are absolutely declined.†

---

* An exhaustive investigation of the subject was made by the Social Reform Club of New York City in 1898. Among those employed in connection with the investigation was Miss Jane E. Robbins, of the University Settlement. Her views are expressed in the following communication:

"This system of insurance is well-nigh universal in tenement houses. It appeals to the natural horror of not being able to bury one's dead properly. The money in most cases entirely used for the funeral expenses. I have never seen anything to suggest an abuse of the system in the case of the insurance of young children. Sickness and death take on a new horror when abject poverty is added, and I do not wonder that people make sacrifices to have their children's lives insured."

† The problem involved in the calculation of Industrial premium-rates is the larger problem of the comparative mortality of the rich and poor. It is a well-known fact that the

This class of risks, however, is readily insured / by Industrial companies on the Ordinary plan under what is known as "Intermediate" policies, where the rates are somewhat higher and adjusted to the peculiar necessities of the case. Keeping in mind the fact that under the Industrial plan the premiums are collected from the houses of the insured during fifty-two weeks, and that on the Ordinary plan the premiums must be sent to the office of the company, we have fifty-two transactions to consider under the one plan which find no place in the other. At age forty an Intermediate policy, payable quarterly, would cost $42 per $1,000 per annum. The excess of retail over wholesale cost is, in this case, represented by 24 per cent.

If we now make a rough comparison of the differences in wholesale and retail costs of certain necessaries of life, as, for example, the cost of coal or of railroad transportation, we find that coal purchased by the pail at twelve cents would cost $10.80 per ton against $6.50 if purchased by the whole ton, with a still further reduction if purchased in larger quantities. The excess in cost to the retail purchaser is represented by 66 per cent. over the wholesale cost. A single railway ticket on the Lackawanna railroad for a fifty-mile ride costs $1.40; if a fifty-trip ticket is purchased, the cost is reduced to one-half, showing a difference between the retail and wholesale costs of 100 per cent. Numerous other illustrations could be furnished, to show that the difference between retail and wholesale cost in life insurance is less than in the retail and wholesale cost of important necessaries of life. At the same time, the additional labor involved in a multitude of business transactions is very much greater in / Industrial life insurance than in the sale of commodities. Giving due consideration to the special accommodation granted, the patrons of Industrial companies have never objected to the price paid for the goods purchased.

---

city wards, inhabited by wage-earners and their families, have a much higher death-rate than the wards containing the more prosperous element of the population. Accurate data for European cities show that, approximately, the mortality of the poor is twice as high as the mortality of the well-to-do. Rowntree, in his book on "Poverty," being a study of town life in the city of York, shows that the mortality in the poor section is twenty-eight, in the medium section twenty-one, and in the best section fourteen per 1,000 of population of all ages. The death-rates of children under five are given as fourteen per 1,000 population of all ages for the poorest, eleven for the medium and six for the best parts of the city. Extending this comparison a little further, the following table from the United States census of 1900 shows the comparative mortality in professional occupations and of laborers, servants, etc., representing the wage-earning element.

COMPARATIVE MORTALITY RATE OF MALES.
UNITED STATES CENSUS, 1900.

OCCUPATIONS	AGES AT DEATH.			
	15–24	25–44	45–64	65+
Professional occupations	4.8	7.6	20.7	105.6
Laborers, servants	7.7	13.9	31.9	126.6

THE COLLECTIVE EVIDENCE OF INSURANCE COMMISSIONERS.

In view of the agitation on the subject, steps were taken to ascertain the views held by insurance commissioners in charge of the insurance interests in the different States, as to essential points involved in what may properly be termed a controversy between a small group of individuals only indirectly interested in the subject, and the millions of policy-holders of Industrial companies directly and vitally interested in what, to them, forms a convenient and entirely satisfactory mode of thrift. A letter of inquiry was sent out to each State Department of Insurance and the replies received were as follows:

In answer to the question, "Do the records of your Department show an undue number of complaints against Industrial insurance companies?" the Insurance Commissioners of thirty States replied, without exception, "No."

In answer to the question, "If frequent complaints have been made, can you conveniently favor us with a statement of the nature of such complaints and your action in reference to the same?" of the thirty Insurance Commissioners the large majority replied to the effect that there had been no complaints whatsoever, while some replied that such complaints as had been made had been for trivial reasons of no public interest.

In answer to the question, "Has your Department official knowledge of any abuses connected with this form of insurance, especially with reference to the murder of adults for insurance money, the murder of children for insurance money, negligence or cruelty to children for insurance money?" thirty Insurance Commissioners replied, without exception, "No."

In reply to the question, "Has your Department on record specific complaints against the practice of Industrial insurance, with special reference to the insurance of children, made by the / officers of charitable or relief associations, by the officers of children's protective societies, or by individuals who are not policy-holders in such companies?" the thirty Insurance Commissioners replied, without exception, "No."

It may not be out of place here to quote an extract from a letter from the Insurance Commissioner of New Jersey, dated January 31, 1899, to the Insurance Commissioner of Colorado, expressing the official opinion of the Department, of particular value in view of the almost universal extent of Industrial insurance in that State.

> As you are doubtless aware, Industrial insurance, on the lives of both adults and infants, has been prosecuted in this State for many years, and has attained a volume as large perhaps, if not larger, in proportion to population, than any other State in the Union, and *this Department has yet to receive the first charge or complaint that the insurance of children under ten years of age was productive of infanticide.* I have long since rejected the assertion as entirely unfounded and unjustifiable. The beneficence and value of this kind of insurance has been demonstrated beyond question."

We have here conclusive evidence, first, that no abuses, cases of cruelty, or of the murder of children for insurance money, have been officially recorded or reported to the Insurance Commissioners; second, that in not a single instance has a complaint of this nature been made to the Insurance Departments by an official in charge of children's interests, or by a private individual interested in the protection and welfare of children. These replies prove conclusively that the proper authorities supervising the methods of Industrial insurance companies have no knowledge of any serious abuses resulting from the practice of Industrial insurance, or of any evidence tending to prove the insurance of children to be detrimental to public policy.

THE MORTALITY OF INSURED CHILDREN.

As has been previously stated, although the companies have transacted this form of insurance for some twenty-six years, no conclusive evidence of the murder of a child for insurance money has ever become a matter of record or of official opinion returned as a jury verdict. If such abuses existed or had occurred, the evidence, no doubt, would be found in the comparative mortality of / [...] / insured children and of the general population. Such investigations as have been made have proven, without exception, that the mortality of children insured with Industrial companies is less than the mortality of children in the general population.

The following table [...] show, for ages one to nine, the mortality experience of The Prudential during 1897–1901 and the expected mortality per one thousand living at each age by the United States census of 1900.*

COMPARATIVE MORTALITY OF INSURED CHILDREN AND THE GENERAL POPULATION OF THE UNITED STATES. (RATES PER 1,000.)

Ages	United States Census of 1900	Prudential Experience 1897–1901	Actual Deaths to every 1,000 Expected
One to two	46.6	31.6	678
Two to three	20.5	14.6	712
Three to four	13.2	10.2	772
Four to five	9.4	8.0	851
Five to nine	5.2	4.4	846

It is shown by this table that at all ages the mortality of insured children has been below the standard mortality of the United States. This conclusion, based on the Company's experience, is further supported by a mass of statistical evidence relating to the general mortality of children in the United States, all tending to

---

*   The mortality experience of the Prudential Assurance Company of London corresponds very closely to the observed experience of the American Prudential. A comparative table of the mortality of insured children and the general population will be found on page 144 of the Report of the Select Committee of the House of Lords (No. 225) of the Session of 1890. The London Prudential on January 1, 1903, had 14,770,865 Industrial policies in force on the lives of the people of the United Kingdom. Of this number about four million are policies on the lives of children under twelve years of age.

prove that the death-rate of such children has very materially decreased within the last twenty-five years. Taking, for the purpose of illustration, the results of the last census, in which comparison is made with the facts ascertained in 1890, it appears that there has been a material decrease in child mortality during the decade under observation. /

COMPARATIVE MORTALITY OF CHILDREN
IN THE UNITED STATES. (REGISTRATION
AREA 1890–1900.)

AGES	Rates per 1,000 1890	Rates per 1,000 1900	Decrease per 1,000
One to two	84.9	46.6	38.3
Two to three	23.8	20.5	3.3
Three to four	16.8	13.2	3.6
Four to five	13.0	9.4	3.6
Five to nine	7.3	5.2	2.1
Ten to fourteen	3.8	3.3	0.5

There has been a similar reduction in the child mortality of large cities and the decrease has been especially marked during the past five years, as set forth in graphic form in the diagram below, derived from official returns for the period 1892–1901.

REDUCTION IN CHILD MORTALITY, AGES ONE TO NINE.

[...]

These comparisons are entirely trustworthy, being limited to the Registration Area, or that part of the United States in which vital statistics are kept with the accuracy common to European countries. It is shown that at ages one to two, for example, the mortality has decreased from 84.9 per one thousand to 46.6 per one thousand. It is safe to assume that such exceptional results could not have been experienced had there been at work insidious influences tending to lower the health and physical well-being of the children of the insured population, for it is in the Registration Area that the Industrial insurance companies transact almost their entire business, and the conclusions apply to not less than one-third of the entire child population of these cities. In Newark, N. J., where the Industrial companies have about eighty per cent. of the entire population insured, there has been a similar and pronounced decrease in the mortality of children since the introduction of the business in 1875. /

The mortality of children from homicide has also decreased since the introduction of Industrial insurance into the different States. Quoting, for illustration, the official data for Massachusetts, there have been twenty-five deaths from homicide of children, ages one to fourteen inclusive, during the period 1887–1893, against twenty-three deaths from this cause during the period 1894–1900. If allowance is made for the increase of population, the homicide-rate per million of children at this age period was 6.5 during the first seven years, against 5.3 during the last. During the same period the proportion of insured children in Massachusetts has very largely increased.

REDUCTION IN PAUPER BURIALS.

On the outset it was pointed out that the primary object of Industrial insurance is family protection against the contingency of a pauper burial. The business, in fact, was established in Newark in 1875, with the assistance of a number of wealthy manufacturers and large employers of labor, to check the increasing demands upon public charity for assistance in the burial of the poor. It is therefore of importance to note how far this form of life insurance for the masses has operated to effect a reduction in the pauper burial-rate of American cities. As the result of a careful investigation it is possible to state that the rate has been reduced from 17.4 per ten thousand of population during 1881-85 to 11.8 per ten thousand of population during the period 1897-1901. A careful estimate for all American cities on the basis of data supplied by city officials shows that if the earlier pauper burial-rate prevailed at the present time there would be about twenty thousand more pauper burials per annum than is actually the case. Since the average cost of a pauper burial is about $7, the annual saving to American cities represents approximately $150,000.* This, of course, is only a fraction of the actual / saving to the State resulting from this form of family protection and the actual diminution of public burdens.†

[...]

---

* According to the official reports of the State Board of Charities of Massachusetts, the rate of burials of State paupers per 1,000 of population has decreased from 0.6 during the four years 1880–1883 to 0.3 per 1,000, exactly one-half, during the four years 1899–1902. The difference in the number of paupers who would have to be buried at State expense if the earlier rate prevailed at the present time is about 700 per annum.

† It may be of interest to quote an extract from a letter addressed to Mr. John F. Dryden, president of The Prudential, by Robert MacClermont, of 2,012 South Gratz street, Philadelphia, which reads as follows: "I was very much pleased at your promptness in settling my claim; as I was in need of money to bury my wife, and *without that assistance the county would have had to bury her*, as I have been out of employment for months, and I can assure you that I consider your institution as the real 'Savings Bank' of the poor people." (History of The Prudential Insurance Company, p. 264.)

GENERAL CONSIDERATIONS.

During the past decade Industrial insurance in the United States has increased, in round figures, from four million policy-holders to twelve. No other form of savings or insurance has made a corresponding progress, nor is any other form of thrift so universal at the present time among the wage-earning population. In the words of Mr. Charles Booth: "We have here a natural and active growth of thrift which it will be wise to leave alone, except in so far as its action can be facilitated, or its benefits be made more secure." The business has been developed entirely on the basis of contract and the merits of the proposition. Its advantages and cost are fully understood by those who make use of this form of insurance to provide with security against one of the contingencies of human life. Quoting the words of Lord Hobhouse,[4] from Mackay's "State and Charity":[5] "If in any practical matter we lose sight of the maxim that we must offer to the people the thing they want and not the thing they do not want; that the users of an article are in the long run (longer or shorter, according to the simplicity of the article) the only available judges of its value; and that the exertions of / mankind must be stimulated by their interest, we shall come to disaster."

No business proposition is more simple, or more readily understood, than the Industrial policy. The premium payments are weekly in recognition of the truth, so ably pointed out by Helen Bosanquet,[6] that "The majority of wage-earners can only manage their income on a weekly basis." To this fact the business of life insurance on the weekly-payment plan has been carefully adjusted, and practically the whole family is included in its operations. To question the motives and the judgment of Industrial policy-holders is an indictment of the general intelligence; and the broad charges of neglect and crime, for a possible paltry gain, are an assault on the public conscience and the moral status of the American people.

It is well to keep in mind, in considering the underlying purpose of Industrial insurance, that "the important matter for man is less what he does than the spirit he does it in,"[7] and only a cruelly wrong conception of human nature can impute criminal motives to the millions of parents who, in return for a small weekly payment, provide for the possible necessity of the decent burial expenses of their children. "Of all human qualities," observes Helen Bosanquet, in her admirable work on the "Strength of the People," "the instinctive love of the mother is the last to fail; women who have sinned against every other law of man and nature will still cling to the infant, whose helplessness they can defend; and as long as this is so, any intervention between them is sacrilege."* To the mass of people Industrial insurance represents a satisfactory and exceedingly convenient form of savings and family protection, and of this system of family insurance, the insurance of children forms an integral and inseparable part.

---

*   Macmillan & Co., New York, 1902, p. 187.

CONCLUSIONS.

The preceding summary of general facts and data is sufficient evidence that, *first*, the aggregate experience of Industrial insurance companies in the United States has not produced a single authenticated case of the murder or abuse of a / child for insurance money; *second*, that the united opinion of thirty Insurance Commissioners in the different States of this country is emphatically in favor of the system and of the conclusion that no evil results have followed the practice; *third*, that the evidence of mortality data proves conclusively a superior longevity on the part of insured children and a decreasing death-rate at young ages since the introduction of this system of insurance into the United States; *fourth*, that the office practice has been devised with exceptional care and due regard for the best interests of the child's well-being, and that the sums to be insured for have been so adjusted, and are so small, that speculation on the life of the child is a practical impossibility; *fifth*, that the average amounts paid in claims on the lives of children are somewhat below the average burial expenses and considerably below the combined expenses of burial and the cost of the last illness; *sixth*, that the relative frequency of pauper burials has been materially decreased through the extension of Industrial insurance among the wage-earning population.

[PELICAN LIFE INSURANCE COMPANY], 'LIFE INSURANCE. TO PARENTS, GUARDIANS, AND OTHERS, DESIROUS OF SECURING A PROVISION AGAINST SUDDEN DEATH', *NEW-YORK EVENING POST* (1808)

'Life Insurance. To Parents, Guardians, and Others, Desirous of Securing a Provision against Sudden Death', *New-York Evening Post*, 13 July 1808, p. 3.

The Pelican Life Assurance Company had been in existence less than ten years when it established an agency in New York in 1806, part of an aggressive export strategy that also included Hamburg, Sweden, and the Maritime colonies in Canada. The company shared agents in New York and Philadelphia with its sister fire office, the Phoenix, and these men were by most accounts the first life insurance salesmen to actively solicit risks in the United States.[1] In stark contrast to the Phoenix, which thrived into the twentieth century, the Pelican's success in the American market was brief – a pattern that paralleled the more general fate of British life insurance in the United States. Although many companies, including the North British, Royal, and London & Liverpool & Globe, were major players in the US fire insurance market throughout the nineteenth century, British life insurance offices seldom rose to prominence during this period.

After the Pelican pulled out of the United States in the 1820s, no British firms returned until 1844, when a dozen offices set up agencies; their market share fell from a high point of 7 per cent in 1855 to 2 per cent in 1865, and continued to decline thereafter. Unlike fire insurance, where reinsurance treaties with American firms enabled British offices to assess risk more effectively, establishing effective gatekeeping mechanisms was a more serious challenge for British firms selling life insurance in the United States. An even bigger hurdle, once American firms began sharing their profits with customers, was that British firms lacked the access to higher-yielding American investments that 'native' life offices possessed.[2]

Notes
1. Trebilcock, *Phoenix Assurance and the Development of British Insurance*, vol. 1, pp. 320, 561–2.
2. Alborn, *Regulating Lives*, p. 30.

[Pelican Life Insurance Company], 'Life Insurance. To Parents, Guardians, and Others, Desirous of Securing a Provision against Sudden Death', *New-York Evening Post* (1808)

LIFE INSURANCE.

*To Parents, Guardians, and others, desirous of securing
a provision against Sudden Death.*

THE utility of Institutions to enable the various classes of a Mercantile Company to provide for their families and dependants, in case of premature or unexpected death, is too obvious to require an enlarged exposition. In the pursuits of life a principal anxiety with every one is to secure, either by frugality or foresight, the means of independence and comfort to his family; but the most laudable and industrious exertions to accumulate a small fund, for such purposes, are frequently defeated by the sudden death of the individual, and poverty and destitution as often fall upon those who depended upon him. All income arising from talents and personal exertion must be liable to prove inadequate to such objects, unless some security is at the same time provided to prevent a disappointment from its failure. The means, however, of rendering the attainment of such views certain, are easily supplied by Life Insurance; and it is accordingly in Europe generally resorted to by persons who, possessing life incomes only, are solicitous to bequeath to their families the means of a decent and independent subsistence.

The PELICAN LIFE INSURANCE OFFICE of London is one of the most solid and respectable foundations of the kind, and is the first that ever offered to the inhabitants of America a facility of making insurances upon moderate and equitable terms.

To persons unacquainted with the subject the principle of such insurances may be easily explained. – It is that of paying a certain annual sum to the Office, for which it engages, in return, to pay to the heirs, assigns, or legatees of the assured an equivalent amount at death. Thus, for instance, a person whose age does not exceed twenty-one, by paying annually, during life, £38 7 6 may secure, beyond the power of contingency, the sum of £1,000 sterling, which he may leave to his widow, or any other relation or person, or appropriate it, in the hands of trustees, for the education of his children; or, in short, dispose of it in as absolute a manner as any other property. It will be obvious, therefore, that this mode of accumulating the savings of an income is preferable, in many cases, to any other, inasmuch as it enables a person to secure a fixed sum, subject to no chance of casualty. Persons who borrow money on personal loan, Supercargoes, or Captains of Ships, will in many instances, find conveniences in having recourse to such policies as they furnish good collateral security for debts. In many other ways Life Insurance contribute greatly to the conveniences of the public. The Premiums charged for such insurances are calculated according to the age of the party, and other circumstances which affect the value of the risk.

The terms generally, as well as other particulars on the subject, may be learnt of the under-signed, who will be happy to transect any business of this kind which may be proposed to him.

THOMAS W. SATTERTHWAITE,
26 Wall-st. opposite Merchants' Bank.
July 13

THE 'AMERICAN INVASION'

'The Equitable Life Assurance Society of the United States', front-page advertisement, *Insurance Record*, 23 January 1874.[1]

Joseph Allen,[2] *There is Dust in John's Eyes; or, American and British Life Insurance Offices Contrasted*, 2nd edn (London: H. J. Smart, 1882).

Book review of *There is Dust in John's Eyes, Post Magazine* (1882), pp. 356–7.

'The Mutual's English Business', *Independent*, 17 May 1906, p. 1179.

When the Equitable of New York established a branch office in London in 1869, it had already established itself, along with the Mutual of New York and New York Life, as one of the largest life insurance offices in the world – and earned more than twice as much premium income, from a thriving home business and agencies in more than twenty countries, as the leading British firm at the time. New York Life followed close on its heels, setting up a London branch in 1870, while the Mutual of New York waited until 1886 to enter the British market. By that time the claim of the 'big three' to world domination was undisputed: in 1887 the Equitable alone generated nearly as much new business (£23.2 million) as all British insurers combined (£28.5 million).[3] In Britain, as elsewhere, these three firms relentlessly promoted their 'deferred dividend' or tontine policies, which promised to pay policyholders much higher bonuses, and they masterfully influenced public opinion with expert marketing campaigns. An early example of one such effort was the Equitable's solicitation in 1873 of testimonials on its behalf by three leading British actuaries.

Such efforts did not go unchallenged by British life offices and their defenders. In addition to brokers like Joseph Allen, who fired shots at the American invaders on behalf of British insurance writ large, specific company representatives also joined in the fray. Foremost among these was James Watson, the manager of the Scottish Provident, which (not coincidentally) boasted a bonus scheme that was the closest thing going in Britain to tontine insurance.[4] The final, and by far most effective, backlash against American interlopers came in the wake of the revelation of financial scandals that led to the Armstrong hearings in New York during 1905–6. This time the impetus came from customers, with the formation of an International Policy Holders' Protection Committee in 1905, followed by a large-scale exodus by Mutual of New York policyholders to the Edinburgh-based North British and Mercantile office – which pilfered the Mutual's London manager, D. C. Haldeman, in the process. Although the Mutual persisted as the largest American insurer in Britain for another decade, with £7 million in sums insured in 1914, after 1906 none of the 'big three' ever fully recovered their former standing in Britain.[5]

In terms of market share, the American presence in Britain was never especially significant, either within the broader US export market or in competition with British firms. At their height at the beginning of the twentieth century, the 'big three' earned around £2 million in premium income in the UK, less than 4 per cent of their total business and around 5 per cent of the British market. When state legislatures restricted the amount of new business life insurers could pursue after 1906, all three made the deepest cuts in their foreign business, and by 1914 American earnings in Britain had dropped below £1 million.[6] Contemporaries and subsequent commentators agreed, however, that during the two decades after 1885 (in the words of one historian) they produced 'pressure for change' through their 'brash advertising and high pressure salesmanship on a level out of character with the methods used by British firms'. New business practices in Britain that can be traced, at least in part, to pressure from American firms included bonus schemes that more closely resembled 'tontine' policies, more liberal surrender values and protection of beneficiaries from creditors.[7]

Notes

1. This full-page advertisement appeared on the front page of the weekly *Insurance Record*, one of the two leading insurance trade journals in London, from 23 January through 6 February 1874, and on the back page from 13 February through 13 March.

2. Joseph Allen was elected Fellow of the Royal Statistical Society in 1877 and acted as an insurance broker in Halifax through the 1880s; in 1877 he published an insurance guide, *Where Shall I Get the Most for my Money* (from which this pamphlet was adapted), which went through nineteen editions by 1908. He should not be confused with Joseph Allen (1833–88), who was Gresham Life's secretary during the same period.

3. Buley, *The Equitable Life Assurance Society of the United States*, vol. 1, pp. 114, 265–6; Hudnut, *Semi-Centennial History of the New-York Life Insurance Company*, pp. 144–5; Clough, *A Century of American Life Insurance*, p. 162; *Statist*, 19 March 1887, p. 312. Another early American entrant into the British market was the Continental, which established a branch office in London before winding up in 1874.

4. See e.g. James Watson, *American Life Offices in Great Britain* (Edinburgh: Bell and Bradfute, 1884).

5. *Report from the Select Committee of the House of Lords on Life Assurance Companies* (London: HMSO, 1906), question 731.

6. Ibid., questions 78–80, 249–50; Keller, *The Life Insurance Enterprise*, p. 276; Supple, *Royal Exchange Assurance*, p. 276.

7. R. Ryan, 'A History of the Norwich Union Fire and Life Assurance Societies from 1797 to 1914' (PhD dissertation, University of East Anglia, 1983), p. 255; Alborn, *Regulated Lives*, pp. 161–2, 179, 209.

'The Equitable Life Assurance Society of the United States', advertisement, *Insurance Record* (1874)

THE EQUITABLE LIFE ASSURANCE SOCIETY
OF THE UNITED STATES,
(ESTABLISHED IN 1859.)
HAS ACCUMULATED ASSETS EXCEEDING
**FOUR MILLION, FIVE HUNDRED THOUSAND
POUNDS STERLING,**

Invested only in *First-Class Convertible Securities,* as restricted by the Insurance Laws of the State of New York. Such investments are beyond the reach of MONETARY DISTURBANCE, and complete protection to Policyholders is thus assured.

THE WHOLE OF THE PROFITS
ARE RESERVED FOR THE ASSURED.

The business of this Society is carefully distributed over the Continent of North America and the British Isles; *an additional and exceptional safety* is consequently guaranteed to the insured by a broad basis of operations.

The greater earning power of money in the United States enables THE EQUITABLE of New York to offer to its patrons

UNEQUALLED ADVANTAGES.

A popular scheme of Life Insurance, on
THE TONTINE PLAN,
Has originated with and is granted by THE EQUITABLE, which, upon a principle of deferred bonus, adds very considerably to the proportionate profit of those holding these Polices.

THE EQUITABLE LIFE ASSURANCE SOCIETY of New York has received an unqualified indorsement from leading Actuaries in London,[1] expressing opinions of the soundness of the Institution, of its good management, and of its full title to confidence, in an

IMPORTANT DOCUMENT,

Which ought to be read by every person desiring a life insurance, as it shows that THE EQUITABLE furnishes, on the most favourable terms, a perfect security for the future, which is of great importance to those depending upon their insurance policies for the ultimate support of their families. This document has been recently published by the Society, and can be had on application at the London Office, or of any of the Society's Agents in Great Britain and Ireland.

ALEXANDER MUNKITTRICK,[2] Manager for Great Britain,
No. 1, PRINCES STREET, BANK, LONDON.

Joseph Allen, *There is Dust in John's Eyes; or, American and British Life Insurance Offices Contrasted* (1882)

CHAPTER I.
INTRODUCTORY.

THE technicalities of Life Insurance are not understood by the great bulk of persons who take out Policies, and it is not likely that they ever will be. Consequently companies of very inferior grade will always be able to obtain business; the only requisite agency for the purpose being a staff of canvassers, gifted with sufficient "talk," enforcing upon the public the moral duty of making provision for their families. The science of Life Insurance is of so subtle and abstruse a nature that few insurers will tax their minds to the extent necessary for an understanding of the subject.

We have no hope of being of much service to the reader of this pamphlet unless he will prepare himself for a slight mental effort while we endeavour to explain shortly a few of the technicalities connected with Life Insurance. We will promise to adhere as nearly as possible to ordinary commercial language, and to discard certain professional niceties, the observance of which would only harass the mind of the plain man of business.

Principles of Life Insurance.

In the first place, it is necessary to understand *the normal bases* from which a Life Company starts its operations. These are,

(1) A Table of Mortality;
(2) An assumed Rate of Interest;
(3) A per-centage of "Loading" on the net Premiums. /

Let us suppose a case where a Company adopts the English Life Table No. 2 as the foundation of its business, This Table shews that, assuming the money to be received from insurers will be improved at 3 per cent. interest, the *net* annual premium to insure £1,000 on a Life aged 35, without allowing anything for the expenses of working the business, is £23 10 0

Something must of course be added to meet the Expenses, &c.,

say 20 per cent. (technically called "Loading")	4 14 0
Gross Premium	£28 4 0

The Company would therefore collect from the Insured £28 4s. 0d. per annum, and would hold itself in duty bound (and as a crucial test of solvency) to invest and keep sacred £23 10s. out of each year's premium as a contribution towards a fund (accumulating at compound interest), for providing the money wherewith to pay the sum insured at the death of the Life.

Now look at another company adopting the same table of mortality, and charging the same Premiums for insurances, but assuming 4 per cent. interest in its calculations. In this company the *net* premium, for a similar Insurance would be set down in the books of the office at £21 7 6

The "Loading" at	6 16 6
Gross Premium	£28 4 0

This Company is content to assert its solvency by the investing and keeping sacred of *no more* than £21 7s. 6d. per annum, out of the £28 4s. 0d. received from the Insured, whereas as we have seen, the 3 per cent. company insists that the investment of *no less* than £23 10s. out of each year's Premium will satisfy their notions of solvency. /

If we now look for a moment at the other point we mentioned, viz.,

The "Loading,"

we observe that the 3 per cent. Company obstinately insists that under no circumstances must more than £4 14s. 0d. per annum out of the £28 4s. 0d. be used for Expenses, &c., whereas the 4 per cent. Company asserts, with the utmost complacency, that £6 16s. 6d. of the amount may be expended each year with perfect safety.

Thus matters go on during long series of years, until *Millions of Money* are accumulated by both Offices; the 4 per cent. Company however always asserts that £850,000 is a sufficient amount to have in hand to cover risks which the 3 per cent. Company declares cannot safely be covered by a less sum than £1,000,000, *i.e.*, when the same table of mortality has been adopted.

CHAPTER II.
AMERICAN AND BRITISH LIFE OFFICES CONTRASTED.

THE foregoing observations have been made in order to enable the reader to understand something of the fundamental principles upon which Life Offices carry on their business, and also to show what radically different lines of finance prevail amongst them.

We may inform the reader that there are only two American Life Offices[1] doing business in this country, we are therefore only concerned to discuss the merits of these two particular Offices anent those of British Companies. /

Now both the American Offices in question base their calculations on the assumption of 4 1/2 per cent. interest, which is a higher rate than any British Office assumes; the effect of this is

(1) That the American Offices treat a much larger proportion of the Premiums received as "Loading," and therefore as being available for Expenses, than do the British Offices. This gives a larger licence for

Extravagant Management Expenses

than would be allowed if a lower rate of interest were assumed.

(2) It places a company in the position of being handicapped with regard to making Profit out of Interest on its Investments, because it is only the *excess* of Interest actually realised beyond the amount assumed which is Profit.

If these American Offices had no larger Funds than the Reserves shewn as being required by a Valuation of their existing business at 4 1/2 per cent. we should say at once (considering the high ratio of Expenses to the Premium income) that they were in a very weak financial position; we must however state that in the amounts set down in column 3 of the annexed Table, there are included the surplus Reserve Funds of those companies, the possession of which Funds – in addition to the Reserves brought out by the valuations – places the solvency of the companies beyond question.

We are now in a position to consider the advantages offered to Insurers by both British and American Offices, and in doing so we shall proceed from the standpoint of the familiar question.

"Where shall I get the Most for my Money?"

The figures in the accompanying Table will enable us to deduce an answer to the question which will be both / sound and conclusive, because these figures lay bare and expose to view in the most prominent manner, the hidden resources possessed by each Company for producing Profit to Policy-holders, and as there is not much difference in the rates of premiums charged by these several Offices, the solution of the problem turns on the question of "PROFIT TO POLICY-HOLDERS."

We give the figures of four British Companies,[2] and those of the two American Companies.*[3]

If the reader will kindly refer to the Table, whilst we make a few observations upon its contents, we have no doubt that he will be able to see the true bearing of the figures.

The first point which strikes us as being noticeable is that the *largest* companies come last in order, and show the *smallest* per-centage of Profit to Policy-holders. Many people are led astray in the selection of Life Offices by the dazzling effect of an array of figures, showing an enormous amount of business done; they infer (reasoning from experience in ordinary commercial matters) that where there is

An immense turn-over

a much better Profit will be produced than will be the case where the turn-over is small, even although the *per-centage* of Profit in the former case be smaller than in the latter – as in a trading concern; a net profit of 5 per cent., on a turnover of £1,000,000 gives the proprietor £50,000, whereas a net profit of 7 1/2 per cent. on a turn-over of £500,000 would only give him £37,500. The difference between a case like this and that of a Life Office, is that whilst in the trading concern the aggregate amount of Profit made goes / to one individual, the proprietor; in a Life Office the number of partners, (*i.e.*, Policyholders) who have to share in the Profits increases as the business increases. If, therefore, the means adopted for the purpose of increasing the business of a Life Company have the effect of reducing the *per-centage* of Profit to the Policyholders, the increase is not an advantage, but a decided disadvantage. The *size* of a company is a matter of trifling consequence to an Insurer – what we are concerned to know with regard to a Life Office is

(1) Whether the liabilities of the Society are assessed upon sound principles.

(2) What is the ratio of Profit to the Insured after those liabilities have been thus provided for.

A sound and economically managed company, doing but a very small new business, will pay its Claims, and distribute much larger Bonuses than will a large company which is accumulating enormous liabilities, and in doing so is squandering the policyholders' money at an excessive rate.

---

*   The author will be glad to furnish inquirers with any further particulars which may be desired respecting these or any other Offices. All communications to be addressed to Mr. Joseph Allen, F.S.S., Halifax, or 5, London House Yard, London, E.C.

The main Sources of Profit

in a Life Office are

(1) The *unspent* portion of the "Loadings" charged on the premiums received from policyholders.

(2) The *excess* of Interest actually realised on the Invested Funds beyond the amount assumed in the Office calculations.*

Under the first head, the Profit is *saved*, there being no profit, unless less money is spent than has been charged for "Loadings."

Under the second head the Profit is *earned*, there being / no profit unless a higher rate of Interest is obtained on the Investments than the rate assumed in the Office calculations.

---

*   There is also a considerable amount of Profit made when the mortality actually experienced proves less than has been estimated. There are no data available for making a comparison with regard to this, but inasmuch as there is very little variation in the mortality experienced by different Offices where Lives are carefully selected, our argument will not be affected by the omission to deal with this element of profit.

STATEMENT

Prepared from the Parliamentary Returns respecting the several Life Insurance Offices, at the date in each case, when the last Valuation of the business was made.

N.B. – THE VALUATION YEARS ARE THE ONLY OCCASIONS WHEN THE COMPLETE FIGURES NECESSARY TO MAKE THE COMPARISONS ARE GIVEN.

OFFICES.	*Figures relating to "Loadings."*			*Figures relating to Interest.*			*The Participating Premiums and the Profit divisible amongst them.*				
	1 ANNUAL PREMIUMS RECEIVED.	AMOUNT THEREOF TREATED AS "LOADINGS." — per cent. of Premiums.	2 ANNUAL OUTGO FOR EXPENSES, &c., AND AS PROFIT TO SHAREHOLDERS. — per cent. of Premiums.	3 ACCUMULATED FUND.	4 RATE PER CENT. OF INTEREST ASSUMED. £ s. d.	5 RATE PER CENT. OF INTEREST OBTAINED. £ s. d.	6 ANNUAL PREMIUMS "WITH PROFITS."	7 PROFIT PER ANNUM TO PARTICIPATING POLICYHOLDERS. — OUT OF LOADINGS ON TOTAL PREMIUMS.	OUT OF INTEREST ON INVESTMENTS.	TOTAL.	per cent. of the Participating Premiums.
Office No. 1 (British)	£129,083	£27,094 = 20.99	£18,081 = 14.0	£1,550,716	3 0 0	4 19 11	£98,038	£9,013	£30,952	£39,965 being 40.7	40.7
" No. 2 (British)	74,858	14,193 = 18.96	12,517 = 16.72	841,044	3 0 0	4 17 8	48,991	1,676	15,836	17,512	35.7
" No. 3 (British)	246,210	60,887 = 24.73	29,555 = 12	2,838,081	3 0 0	4 12 8	239,208	31,332	46,345	77,677	32.4
" No. 4 (British)	247,785	68,735 = 27.74	38,302 = 15.45	4,369,532	3 10 0	4 6 2	228,457	30,433	35,305	65,738	28.7
"No. 5 (American)	1,128,420	372,378 = 33	250,613 = 22.2	8,752,064	4 10 0	5 9 0	853,406	121,765	83,144	204,909	24
"No. 6 (American)	1,368,022	451,447 = 33	301,797 = 22.06	8,136,093	4 10 0	4 18 6	1,127,995	149,650	34,578	184,228	16.3

All the above Companies have been established upwards of Twenty-three Years.

This Table is Copyright. Joseph Allen. /

Our Table is in three sections.: –
The first Section contains the figures required to enable us to ascertain

How much each Company saves

per annum out of the money received from policyholders, under the designation of "Loadings on the Premiums."

The Second Section contains the figures which will enable us to ascertain how much Profit each company *earns* per annum from the excess of Interest realised on the Invested Funds, beyond the amount anticipated in the Office calculations.

The Third Section contains a summary of the Profit from the two sources, and shews its distribution amongst the participating-policyholders.

We will offer a few observations on each Section of the Table: –

FIRST SECTION. – The figures here presented are dissected in a form altogether novel, but exceedingly interesting and instructive. For example: it is both interesting and instructive to know that when two gentlemen have each paid a Premium of £100 for an Insurance, the one to Office No. 2, and the other to Office No. 6, the money received is dealt with in the books of the Companies in the following manner: –

	In Office No. 2.	In Office No. 6.
	£ s. d.	£ s. d.
Amount received for "Net Premium," which must be kept intact, and invested for paying Claims	81 0 9	67 0 0
Amount received for "Loading" available for Expenses, &c.	18 19 3	33 0 0
	£100 0 0	£100 0 0 /

This illustration conveys its own moral! Comment is therefore unnecessary.

Column No. 2 shews us how much of the Premiums is paid away per annum for Expenses &c., and as Profit to Shareholders. In making up these figures, every item of Outgo* on current account has been included in order that we may ascertain precisely

---

* It is more convenient for our purpose to dispose of all the items of Outgo here, although we are quite aware that a proportion of the management expenses is properly chargeable against Interest on the Accumulated Fund. The method we are adopting, however, keeps the Table within smaller limits, and seeing that we carry forward from the Second Section the whole of the Profit made out of Interest, we get precisely the same result in the last column of the Table as we should get if we shewed the Outgo in Sub-divisions, leaving a *larger* amount of money saved out of Loadings, and a *smaller* amount earned out of Interest. Moreover, there are no such Sub-divisions in the Parliamentary Returns, and we prefer not to quote any figures which we cannot substantiate from these Returns.

How much clear Money

there is left between the Total Annual Outgo and the proportion of the Premiums treated as Loadings. With regard to the Profit taken by Shareholders, we have included the whole amount taken less the amount which the Paid-up Capital* yields at the rate of interest stated in Column 5. We now *deduct* the amount of the "Annual Outgo" from the amount of the "Loadings" and carry the difference to the first Sub-division of Column 7, to be there dealt with as Profit to Policyholders.

SECOND SECTION. – Column 3 shews the amount of each Company's Accumulated Fund *i.e.* the amount to which the Policy-holders' Premiums have accumulated (after paying Claims) since the starting of the Company, up to the date of last Valuation. /

Column 4 shews the Rate of Interest assumed by each Company in fixing its "Net Premiums" and in making its Valuation – or in "taking Stock." The *modus operandi* in making these Valuations is mysteriously technical, but we may illustrate the effect of

Valuing at a high or low rate of Interest

by making a comparison with Stock-taking in an ordinary trading concern. If in taking stock, a trader sets down the Stock and other assets at a liberal Valuation, the credit side of the balance-sheet will come out more favorably than it would do if the assets were dealt with severely, and discounted to provide against future fluctuations in prices and losses by bad debts &c.; but any trader knows that his financial position is stronger if his concern shews a Surplus after going through the ordeal of *a severe Valuation* than it would be if the same Surplus had been arrived at by means of a liberal Valuation. It is exactly the same with regard to the Valuations of Life Companies – the severer the principles employed in making the Valuation, and the stronger is the financial position of the Company, and the more legitimately may it be said that any Surplus shewn is a true and real Surplus.

Column 5 shows the rate of Interest at which the Accumulated Fund of each company was invested at the date of the last Valuation. We have calculated the annual amount of Interest obtained on the Accumulated Fund *in excess* of the amount assumed in the valuation of the business of each company, and carried it forward to the second sub-division of column 7.

---

*   We have purposely omitted from the Table the figures shewing the amounts of Share-Capital. We are confining ourselves exclusively to *Policy-holders'* money – shewing what amount is received from them and what becomes of it.

A large quantity of Dust

has been thrown into the eyes of John Bull with regard to the ENORMOUS
PROFITS SAID TO BE MADE BY THE AMERICAN OFFICES OUT OF INTEREST
ON THEIR INVESTMENTS, and the notion has got abroad to a considerable / extent
that the *gross* amount of Interest obtained is PROFIT. Here we have an example
showing how deeply Life Insurance is involved in technicalities, and to what a serious extent non-professional men are liable to be misled with regard to the most
vital points of the subject. The reader must understand distinctly and unmistake-
ably that up to the point "the rate of Interest assumed by the Office," there is

No Profit whatever;

all the money which this rate will yield is anticipated by the actuary in his calculations, and there is a corresponding liability standing against it on the debit side
of the account – it is only the amount of Interest received *beyond* the assumed
rate which is genuine Profit. Exactly as in the case of property which is mortgaged; the only income to the owner of the property is the amount which is left
out of the rents after the interest due to the mortgagee has been paid.

THIRD SECTION. – Column 6 shows the Annual Premiums payable by the
Participating-Policyholders remaining on the books at the date of last Valuation.

Profit coming to Policyholders.

Column 7 shows *the total Amount of clear Profit per annum* out of LOADINGS
and INTEREST which remains after every charge in connection with working
the business and remunerating the shareholders has been disposed of; this clear
money falls to be divided amongst the Participating-Policyholders (Col. 6); and
we now show, lastly, what is the PER-CENTAGE OF PROFIT ON THE PREMIUMS
OF THE PARTICIPATING-POLICYHOLDERS IN EACH COMPANY. This con-
cludes our task, and gives the answer to our enquiry, "Where shall I get the most
for my Money?" /
    The reader will have gathered from our observations upon the Table, that it
is indispensably necessary for the producing of a high rate of Profit to insurers
that there must be

A wide Margin between the normal bases upon which the business of a company is founded and the actual results of working. Any company which presumes
to distribute Bonuses when its figures do not show any "margin," such as we have
indicated, must be viewed with grave suspicion, as it is almost certain to turn out

on strict scrutiny, that the Society in thus distributing "surplus" is destroying its own vitality by reducing its resources below their normal strength.

CHAPTER III.
THE GAME OF TONTINE.[4]

STOP, my friend! not so fast; the comparison you "have instituted is an 'all round' comparison, and does not thoroughly settle the question, for you must know that by means of the 'Tontine Policies,' issued by the American Companies, much higher Profits can be obtained than can be got from British Offices."

Now although we know full well that the comparison we have given does *thoroughly and completely* settle the question, we feel under the necessity of making a few observations on the subject of these

Tontine Policies,

because a goodly number of them have been taken out in this country.

The first remark we have to make is that if the American Companies had had no such feature, but had come here to / compete for ordinary Life Policies, they would have taken very little of John Bull's money. We have no doubt our friends across the Atlantic were pretty well assured with regard to this, and therefore with characteristic inventive genius they have produced this wonderful Tontine contrivance which has filled the soul of many an easy-going Briton with bewildering delight. Not a finer field is there in the wide world for the successful exercise of the science of 'cuteness than Life Insurance. As we said at the outset, the public don't, and it is not likely that they ever will understand it,* and John Bull would much rather *pay* some one to solve a problem for him than tax his own brains to work it out.

Now what is a Tontine?

Let 20 boys have each a Shilling, and let each boy pay his shilling into a dice-box; all the boys now stand in a group whilst a friend tosses the coins into the air above the boys' heads. There is a scramble for the money, and four of the boys get two shillings each, twelve get one shilling each, but there are four of the boys who get nothing; these four last-named "go out" of the Tontine, and all the coins are replaced in the box. In scramble No. 2, three other boys get nothing and go out. In the third scramble three other boys get nothing, and go out. This completes the Tontine, leaving ten boys surviving. All the money is now handed to the Treasurer, and counted, when it is discovered that there are positively suf-

---

*   There are of course exceptions, but these only serve to prove the rule.

ficient Funds in hand to repay to each survivor in the Tontine *the whole of the money he invested, and 100 per cent. Profit added!*

Prodigious!! Now this is the Tontine system pure and simple. What a sweet principle to apply to Life Insurance! /

The reader may inquire what useful purpose can the Tontine system serve in Life Insurance? We will see.

Policyholders frantic to play the Game.

Suppose a Company is making an annual Cash Profit to its Participating-Policy-holders equal to 24 per cent. of their Premiums. The Policyholders are dissatisfied because they find that their neighbours in another Office are getting 40 per cent, and they appeal to the Directors to produce a better result. After consideration, the Directors give this reply: – "If you will allow us to put your Policies on the 'Tontine system' we will guarantee to increase your Profits to 40 per cent., or even higher, in a very few years." The Insured reply, with lamb-like innocence – Oh certainly, do whatever you please so that we get the 40 per cent.!"

The Tontine system then comes into operation. Every Policyholder who fails to keep up his annual payments

Forfeits the "Surrender-value"

of his Policy, and this forfeited money goes to help up the Profits on the Policies remaining. Each year numbers of Policyholders "go out" of the Tontine, until at length the Profits to the Survivors actually reach and even exceed the veritable 40 per cent. predicted! Now when these people agreed to have their Policies put on the Tontine system was the value of those Policies by that act improved in the smallest degree? Certainly not: the Profit was 24 per cent. per annum, *and no matter how this 24 per cent. might be manipulated,* whether by lot-drawing, or any other form of metamorphosis, it remained 24 per cent., *i.e.,* of the original amount, and that is the standpoint from which the merest novice at finance will look at it; and yet we are asked to pass by Companies which are making 35 and 40 per cent Profit for their Policyholders, and select in preference / others which are making only 16 and 24 per cent., because the "advantages" of the Tontine system are attached to the Policies of those Companies.

The Game in full Swing.

We are asked to believe that 1000 men, each having 40 sovereigns in his pocket, will be in a better financial position if they FLING AWAY 16 SOVEREIGNS APIECE AND COMMENCE PLAYING TONTINE WITH THE REMAINING 24! It must be supposed that John Bull is a very stupid idiot!

It will be of service if we here interpose parenthetically a remark on the subject of

"Surrender-Value."

The expression is a technical one which conveys but a misty and indefinite idea to the minds of many people. The reader will be aware that every Life Office possesses, or ought to possess, an Accumulated Fund. This Fund is *entirely distinct* from Shareholders' Capital, it being formed out of Premiums paid by the *Policyholders*, year by year, and Interest received from the Investment thereof. This Fund has to provide the money wherewith to pay Claims arising under Policies. Very well; after all *immediate* Claims have been discharged, the "Accumulated Fund" belongs

Literally and exclusively to the Policyholders,

i.e., while they are still living. True, the Sums insured are only payable in the event of Death, or other maturing of the Policies; but supposing (for the sake of illustration) that a Society should agree to dissolve, without waiting for any further deaths, *the entire Accumulated Fund would have to be divided amongst the Insured,* and the Share of the money to which each person would be entitled would be determined by the proportion of Premiums which he had / contributed to the Funds in hand; these "SHARES IN THE ACCUMULATED FUND" are designated in actuarial language by the euphonious term "SURRENDER-VALUES."

If the reader will kindly refer to the figures of Office No. 4, he will see that the Accumulated Fund of that Company is equal to seventeen times the amount of the Annual Premiums, thus shewing that the surrender-value of a Policy in that Company, the Annual Premium on which is £100, would average about £1,700.

It will thus be seen that the Surrender-Value of a Policy is

No Visionary Phantasm,

but an actual *bona fide* share in the enormous hoards of wealth accumulated by our Insurance Companies, and a Policyholder's share of this money is (subject to the rules of the Society) as certainly and indefeasibly *his own property* as if it were standing to his credit in the ledger of a bank, and he can claim it any day he may think proper to apply for it.

To bring matters fairly home we may inform the reader that in the game of Insurance Tontine,

The Stake

which each Policyholder lays, is "his Share of the Accumulated Fund," against "the Share of every other Policyholder." Each person who fails in the Tontine has to submit to the confiscation of this good money for the benefit of the survivors. Of course, all who enter feel confident that they will be strong enough to hold out to the end of their Tontine-periods, but this feeling does not help matters in the least, because by the law of average, a proportion of Insurers will unquestionably come to grief, and inasmuch as all are strong at the outset, one is as likely to break down as another. /

If in the American Offices the Tontine principle was merely applied to operate upon the "Surplus" or "Profits" made by the Companies, it could not do much serious damage, but it is appalling to find that the "ACCUMULATED FUND" of a Company which constitutes its very backbone and core, is to be operated upon and dismembered by this cruel and heartless system. It is sickening to know that whilst the facade of a Company's Offices presents the appearance of the purest respectability, and is emblazoned with emblems of "the shield of the widow" and other devices idealistic of philanthropy,

The Backdoor

is utilized for the purpose of handing over to favoured individuals the Shares of the Funds contributed by, and until recently standing to the credit of other members, whose families are now in distressed circumstances.

As we have before demonstrated, this "privilege" of playing Tontine with the Accumulated Fund of a Company does not give the slightest additional value to an Insurance, and seeing that British Insurers cannot join in the game without entering Companies making *considerably less Profit* than their own home Offices, it is quite as absurd to do so as it would be for the lads in the Shilling Tontine to pay sixpence a-piece premium to the boxholder for the privilege of taking a chance with their shillings!

Enjoying the Fun.

The American actuaries are laughing and chuckling at a pretty rate at the sight of simple-minded John Bull, meekly placing his bullion into the magic cabinet, and – and –*/

The reader must not suppose that we are treating the subject with levity. The illustrations we have employed for the purpose of explaining the Tontine System give nothing more than a vivid and correct view of its working. Now if we claim

---

*   You know the rest; it is there, and you may perhaps get it out again; or – or – well; some one else may save you the trouble.

to be men of business, with any pretensions to mental capacity or financial skill, we shall be no longer blinded with this Tontine nonsense;

Companies of an exceedingly Skeleton-like Type, who are making very trifling Profits, can easily distort those Profits to apparently high proportions, if the Insured will only be the simpletons to have their numbers decimated *à la Tontine*! and what are we to think of the "financiers" who delude themselves with the notion that the Profits are thereby really increased?

We advocate that all changes or improvements in Life Insurance should go in the direction of *ridding the system of every possible contingency*, so that a Policy may prove an inalienable provision for widows and orphans: the Tontine idea is, however, an iniquitous retrograde movement; the essence of the system being the confiscation of the property of persons overtaken by misfortune, and the transformation of our Insurance Offices into gambling institutions.

CHAPTER IV.
THE INTERNATIONAL DIFFICULTY.

IN the foregoing chapters we have discussed the relative merits of the British and American Companies. There is however, a most important additional point which an intending Insurer requires to take into consideration; we refer to the *legal aspect* of the question. We are so thoroughly satisfied that International Law presents /

An unsurmountable Barrier

against the effecting of Life Insurances in Foreign Companies on a satisfactory basis, that had we dealt with this phase of the subject at the outset, we could not, with any logical consistency, have proceeded to discuss details as we have done.

Life Insurance ought to be freed from every contingency which it is possible to guard against, so that whatever events may transpire in the world, a Life Policy shall be found remaining inviolate, until the latest point of time.

Now in the event of a War breaking out between this country and the United States, what will become of all the Policies in American Offices, held by our countrymen? They will, unquestionably, along with all other commercial transactions, become

"Illegal and void."

We are not now giving our opinion, or the opinion of any one else; we are stating what is the Law on the question, and if the reader cares to take the trouble to refer to *Woolsey's International Law*, 4th edition (1874), he will there find the law laid down very clearly, as follows: –

"All commerce between the subjects of the Belligerents is unlawful, unless expressly licensed, or necessary for the War itself. Hence partnerships with an enemy are dissolved, and all power of prosecuting claims through the Courts of the enemy is suspended during the War; *and all commercial transactions with the subjects, or in the territory of the enemy, of whatever kind,* except ransom contracts, whether direct or indirect, as through an agent or partner, who is a neutral, *become illegal and void.*"[5]

In a previous pamphlet we stated briefly what was our opinion on the legal aspect of this question, and as an /

Answer to our Objections

one of the American Offices has now introduced into its Policies the following clause: –

"That in the event of a war between the United Kingdom of Great Britain and Ireland and the United States of America, this Policy shall not be avoided or defeated if the payment of premiums is rendered illegal by such war, but it shall be competent for the assured within three months after the declaration of peace, to pay to the Society the amount of premiums accrued during the war, with interest thereon, at the rate of 7 per cent. per annum, and thereupon the policy shall be of full force. And that in the event of the sums assured becoming payable during the war, the amount thereof shall be payable on due proof of death, within three months after the declaration of peace, with interest at the rate of 7 per cent. per annum, from the time when but for the war the same would have been payable, until actual payment, but subject to set-off or deduction in respect of premiums not paid by reason of the war, with interest thereon, at the rate aforesaid, during such time as such premiums, though payable, are not actually paid.

"It is, however, hereby declared that if through any treaty or convention or otherwise, the payment of premiums or sums assured should be lawful and practicable, notwithstanding the war, the above clause shall not operate."[6]

We have not the least doubt that this clause has been drawn by one or more eminent counsel, American or English (possibly both) as the very best way of meeting the difficulty in question, but what does it amount to? simply this, that one additional clause has been added to the contract – it, of course, forms *a part* of the contract – / but it must be remembered that when from any cause whatever the contract becomes "VOID" *this particular clause will become void also* along with all the others. Truly we are a simple people!

What a glorious Tontine there would be for the Americans if the whole of the British policy-holders were declared "OUT" at a stroke! and in the event of a war this would unquestionably be the case. To venture on the assertion that they would be kept "out" is a very safe prediction, because any single policyholder in the United States could obtain

An Injunction

from the Courts in that country, restraining the Directors from paying a single cent on account of any Policies which had thus become void.

The interests involved in Life Insurance are of so serious a character that it really will not do to take out any Policies which cannot be *sued upon* in the ordinary process of Law, and we are satisfied that this International difficulty is (as we stated at the commencement of this chapter) an unsurmountable barrier against effecting Life Insurances in Foreign Companies.

Even if we had found that the American Offices were *de facto* superior institutions to the British Companies, we could not in the face of this difficulty have advised our countrymen to effect Insurances in them. We have, however shewn, that these American Companies rank very much below some of the British Offices.

Book review of *There is Dust in John's Eyes*, *Post Magazine* (1882)

AMERICAN LIFE OFFICES
'THERE IS DUST IN JOHN'S EYES,'
by Joseph Allen, F.S.S. (H. J. Smart, Paternoster Row).

The contents of this pamphlet are symbolized on the cover by a wood cut, representing John Bull, holding in his hand a paper inscribed "American Life Insurance;" with a curious winged apparition, – not angelic – presumably the author, blowing the dust into his eyes with a tube or pea-shooter. Inside, after describing mortality tables, loading, &c. – which the author erroneously calls 'principles of life assurance,' – a table is given of some figures from the accounts of 6 selected life offices, all established upwards of 23 years, 4 being British, and 2, American offices located in England. Choosing his own tests, and using them in his own way, the author arrives at his own (prescribed?) conclusions, favorable to the 4, as against the 2. In a precisely similar way, the whole 6 might be easily made out to be preferable to 60, and *one* out of the 4 superior to the other 3; so that, by a process of unnatural selection, the insurance fair might be ultimately reduced to a single booth, and the would-be policy holder treated to 'Hobson's choice.' No such consummation is possible, even if it were desirable. The comparison of offices by mere figures cannot be made in this off-hand kind of way, and there are many and important differential conditions that cannot be expressed by figures at all. What is best for the community is a healthy competition favoring development, and a market open to all who comply with the law. We must keep Chouvinism out of Life Insurance. The tontine policy is attacked, apparently on the principle of making abuse serve for argument. An endowment without surrender value is not exactly life insurance certainly, but it may suit some persons, and it is honestly stated, and quite optional. If such a policy, moreover, has no office value it may be worth buying by an outsider, as is very frequently done with ordinary life policies, and to / the advantage of the vendor. With the war argument, which is pushed in an unfair and disingenious manner in this pamphlet, we have no patience. The question, as usual, is begged, with quite feminine logic and disregard of facts, and the inuendo is a libel on the governments, the conscience, and the religion, of two great end enlightened nations, who have set the world an example in arbitrating a quarrel, which involved much less of moral considerations than would be raised in any proposal to confiscate the provision made for the widow and the orphan.[1] We have no interest or motive to defend the American companies in particular; they can take care of themselves; but we are concerned to repudiate, on behalf of the British Insurance interest, a one-sided and inhospitable critical attitude, which contrasts so unfavorably with the courteous and friendly reception accorded to many of our own large institutions, on the other side of the Atlantic.

'The Mutual's English Business', *Independent* (1906)

IT is evident that the British public is inclined to skepticism in regard to American insurance matters. This fact is emphasized by very recent happenings in London in which the Mutual Life Insurance Company, of this city, is vitally interested. Incidentally, it may be stated that the Mutual has done, in the past, a very considerable English business. The company was formerly represented and managed in London by D. C. Haldeman.[1] The developments regarding the management of the Mutual and the expenditures of Andrew C. Fields and certain other extravagances and gross abuses created a feeling of distrust on the part of the English policyholders in the Mutual, which has not been allayed by the present reform management. The result has been the withdrawal of Mr. Haldeman as London manager, and of his affiliation with the North British and Mercantile Insurance Company, of London, which company now seeks to take over the Mutual's English business. Cables to *The New York Times* indicate that the so called process of "twisting" is meeting with much success and there appears to be a considerable number of persons now holding policies with the Mutual who are now and will be eager to avail themselves of the North British and Mercantile Insurance Company's offer to reinsure them. The text of the circular[2] issued under the inspiration of Mr. Haldeman, as printed in the *Times* (New York) is given below:

"Each policyholder is to surrender his policy in the Mutual to the North British and Mercantile Insurance Company, and in exchange, upon payment of the same premium as provided in his Mutual policy, is to receive without medical examination and free of all expense, a policy on the same lines as his Mutual policy, but with the usual liberal privileges and conditions relating to the North British and Mercantile Insurance Company's policy, provided a sufficient number of policyholders assent at once to this arrangement, so as to avoid selection against the office.

"Under participating policies issued since 1898, with fifteen or twenty years' distribution periods, the North British and Mercantile Insurance Company will provide assurance of the same amount as at present and for the same premium, with immediate participation in profits, under the following tables:

"Ordinary whole life premiums during life; ordinary whole life premiums limited to twenty payments, if there are five or more still to pay; endowment assurances for ten, fifteen, twenty, twenty-five, and thirty years.

"In other classes and under all ten year distribution policies, in order to give full face value from the commencement, it will be necessary to defer participation in the profits for an equivalent period, unless the policyholder prefers to pay a slightly increased premium carrying immediate participation.

"Regarding any policies not embraced in the above or those which have no surrender value, a fair and liberal proposal will be made."

The Mutual Life Insurance Company, thru Harrison Hogge, its new London manager, has issued a circular letter warning its policyholders against "the folly of allowing themselves to be carried away by the specious offer" of the English company.

EDITORIAL NOTES

Morgan, *Familiar Observations on Life Insurance*

1. *3 per cents*: Consolidated annuities, issued by the British government to service its national debt, yielded 3 per cent interest between 1757 and 1888; these were commonly referred to as 'consols'.
2. *Mr. Simpson*: Thomas Simpson (1710–61); in fact, the lectures were delivered by James Dodson (in 1756), not Simpson: see Ogborn, *Equitable Assurances*, pp. 257–8.
3. *none ... should thereafter ... the society*: meeting of the General Court of the Equitable Life Assurance Society, 24 April 1800; quoted in Ogborn, *Equitable Assurances*, p. 125.
4. Ils leurs ... continuer leur train: 'They are allowed to speak ill of the King and the government – to point out their errors and criticize their actions – but also, when they have the chance, they feel free to mock them and continue on their way!' The apparent source of this quotation is Gaspar Grimani, *Calepin ou Grammaire philosophique* (Bath, 1792).
5. *The Asylum*: The Asylum Foreign and Domestic Life Assurance Company formed in 1824 and continued to specialize in insuring under-average lives until the London Assurance absorbed its business in 1858.
6. *The West of England*: The West of England Life Assurance Company, based in Exeter, lowered its premiums to approximate the Norwich Union's rates in 1818 – these were around 10 per cent lower than the Equitable's.
7. *Mr. Milne*: Joshua Milne (1776–1851) worked for Sun Life from 1810 through 1843. The premium scale referred to was based on Milne's Carlisle mortality table, which became the industry standard by the 1840s.

Jencks, 'Life Insurance in the United States, Number I'

1. *a charter was obtained by some public spirited gentlemen of Boston*: The author is most likely referring to the New England Mutual Life Insurance Company, which was chartered in 1835 but did not begin selling policies until 1844.

Jencks, 'Life Insurance in the United States, Number II'

1. *Mr. Babbage*: Charles Babbage (1791–1871) was a famous British mathematician and author of *A Comparative View of Various Institutions for the Assurance of Lives* (London, 1826).

2. *Chancellor Kent*: James Kent (1763–1847) was the first professor of law at Columbia College (1793–8) before becoming a justice of the New York Supreme Court (1798–1814), where he served as chief justice from 1804. He then became chancellor of the New York State Court of Chancery (1814–23), and he was the author of the four-volume *Commentaries on American Law* (New York, 1826–30). He was also an incorporator and member of the board of trustees for the New York Life Insurance and Trust Company.

Frend, *Rock Life Assurance Company*

1. *the Society may pay a greater sum than the sum assured*: The Rock's first division of its profits to policyholders came in 1819, when it added two-thirds of its declared surplus of £303,450 to its customers' policies.

Proposals and Rates of the Standard Life Assurance Company

1. *W.S.*: *writer to the signet* (shortened as *writer* below), a branch of the legal profession in Scotland.
2. *WILLIAM WALLACE*: Wallace (1768–1843) taught mathematics at Edinburgh University between 1819 and 1838. As auditor of Standard Life's rates, he was effectively the company's actuary between 1825 and 1837, when it bestowed that title on James Cheyne and appointed William Thomson as manager.
3. *JAMES A. CHEYNE*: Cheyne (1795–1853) managed Standard Life between 1831 and 1837, and remained with the firm as its actuary into the 1840s.
4. *ARCHIBALD BORTHWICK*: Borthwick acted as secretary for Standard Life from 1832 through 1834, when he resigned to return to his accounting practice. Either he or Cheyne was the likely author of this prospectus.
5. *but for the burden of government duty*: Between 1782 and 1869 the British government imposed a duty of 3 shillings per £100 insured on all fire policies, roughly doubling their price.
6. *ampler jointures to their wives*: A jointure is a prenuptial settlement of property effected by a husband for the benefit of his wife.
7. *an heir of entail or liferenter*: An heir of entail, typically the eldest male offspring in the nineteenth century, is someone who stands to inherit his father's entire estate; a liferenter, under Scottish law, is anyone who can receive rent on land during the course of his or her life but cannot dispose of the property. Tenants on either form of property were at risk of losing their lease if the property changed hands at the owner's death.
8. *The Capital ... Pounds Sterling*: Of this capital (issued in 10,000 shares of £50 each), only £10,000 was paid up.

Life Insurance: Its Principles, Operations and Benefits

1. *Foreign Companies*: 'Foreign' usually refers to out-of-state companies, but in this case the author is referring to non-southern companies.
2. *dust thou art ... shalt return*: Genesis 3:19.
3. *Mr. Morgan*: William Morgan (1750–1833) was actuary of the Equitable Society of London from 1774 to 1830.
4. *during the war*: the Napoleonic Wars from 1803 to 1815.

5. *it shall be lawful ... his creditors*: These rules mirror the 1840 New York law granting women the right to take out life policies on their husbands without needing to demonstrate insurable interest and free from the claims of creditors. Firms (like North Carolina Mutual) that were domiciled in states without this law often included its provisions in their company rules, which were legally upheld in several court cases of the period.

Freestone, *Where to Insure*

1. *one of the schedules*: Under the Life Assurance Companies Act of 1870 (33 & 34 Vict., ch. 61), most companies submitted detailed returns every five years.
2. *unprecedented rate of £2 10s*: In December 1889 the Atlas became the first British life insurance company to use 2.5 per cent (£2 10s. per £100) in valuing its liabilities: see *Post Magazine*, 51 (1890), p. 658.
3. *This is the reverse of Division A (increasing scale)*: In the tables corresponding to this section (pp. 20–3 in the guide, not included in this excerpt), Freestone lists forty-two offices that pay bonuses on an 'ascending' scale, twenty on a uniform scale and nine on a 'descending' scale.

'Life Insurance'

1. Vt. Chron.: The *Vermont Chronicle* was a weekly newspaper published from 1826 to 1898 out of Bellows Falls, Windsor, and Montpelier, Vermont.

'Life Insurance – A Scruple'

1. *There is no counsel or might against the Lord*: most likely quoting John Dick, 'On God', in *Lectures on Theology*, 2 vols (Philadelphia, PA: F. W. Greenough, 1840), vol. 1, pp. 158–284, on p. 238. Dick was a Glasgow minister who belonged to the Free Church of Scotland.
2. *he had 'not where to lay his head'*: Matthew 8:20, 'And Jesus saith unto him, The foxes have holes, and the birds of the air have nests; but the Son of man hath not where to lay his head'. See also Luke 9:58.

'Life Insurance of Ministers'

1. *That all savings ... on previous savings*: Thomas Rowe Edmonds, *Life Tables, Founded upon the Discovery of a Numerical Law Regulating the Existence of Every Human Being* (London: James Duncan, 1832), p. xl.
2. *Prof. Caspar of Berlin made extensive researches*: Johann Ludwig Casper, *Die Wahrscheinliche Lebensdauer des Menschen, in den Verschiedenen Bürgerlichen und Geselligen Verhältnissen* (Berlin: Dümmler, 1835).
3. *Dr. Nott of Franklin*: Samuel Nott (1754–1852) served as Congregational minister in Franklin, Connecticut, between 1780 and 1850.
4. *what prodigious sums ... solid gold*: adapted from Richard Price, *Observations on Reversionary Payments*, 5th edn (London: T. Cadell, 1792), vol. 1, p. lii.

'Prospectus of the Dissenters' and General Life and Fire Assurance Company'

1. *the Congregational Library*: established in Blomfield Street, Central London, in 1831.
2. *Most of them... of their station*: This and the subsequent quotation are from a circular issued by the Dissenters' and General, signed by four directors (Thomas Challis, Joseph Fletcher, Thomas Piper and Thomas Wilson); it was reprinted in full, accompanied by a letter from Thomas Price, in the *Baptist Magazine*, 30 (1838), pp. 307–8.
3. *of the Congregational ... Connexion*: The Congregational Union of England and Wales was founded in 1831; the Baptist Union was founded in 1813 among Particular Baptists, and included General Baptists after 1833; Lady Huntingdon's Connexion was an informal network of dissenting chapels that originally gathered around Selina, Countess of Huntingdon, in the last third of the eighteenth century.

'Life Insurance'

1. Weekly Messenger: probably the *Georgia Messenger*, which was published in Ft Hawkins, Georgia, starting in 1823, and merged with the *Georgia Journal* to form the *Georgia Journal and Messenger* in 1847.

Neal, 'Life Assurance'

1. *the law allows ... dollars a year*: He is referring to the 1840 New York law permitting women to take out insurance policies on the lives of their husbands to the amount of $300 in premiums, free from the claims of their husbands' creditors.

Scratchley, *Observations on Life Assurance Societies, and Savings Banks*

1. *to sit on the margin of the grave*: This may be a reference to the Wesleyan hymn 'On Recovering from Sickness', which opens with the line 'When on the margin of the grave, / Why did I doubt my Saviour's art?'
2. *all men think all men mortal but themselves*: Edward Young, *The Complaint: or, Night Thoughts on Life, Death, and Immortality* (London: R. Dodsley, 1742), p. 28.
3. *the proud man's contumely*: William Shakespeare, *Hamlet*, Act III, scene i (from the 'To be or not to be' soliloquy).
4. *Table 1, page 51*: This refers to a premium table printed in a different section of the book, which reflects the rates charged by the Western Life Assurance Society.
5. *although in the great number ... courier of death*: This quotation, which was also used in G. E. Sargent's short story 'History of a Life Insurance' (1854), is credited there to 'an address issued by the British Empire Mutual Life Assurance Company'.

Reade, 'Before the Wedding Ring'

1. *He that provideth ... an infidel*: 1 Timothy 5:8.
2. *the late George Dawson ... insurance policy*: George Dawson, *A Lecture on Life Insurance ... Delivered at Birmingham, England, in Aid of the Queen's Hospital* (Boston, MA: Nathan

Sawyer and Son, 1876), p. 11: 'If I were a despot, no man should marry without he was insured'. Dawson (1821–76) was a dissenting minister and lecturer on literature; much of Reade's story is cribbed from this lecture.

Benefit Societies versus Saving Banks and Insurance Companies

1. *novel scheme of* Saving Banks: The Tory MP George Rose (1744–1818) was a leading proponent of the 1793 Friendly Societies Act (33 Geo. 3, c. 54), which required all such societies to submit rules to their local justices of the peace. In 1816 he turned his attention to savings banks, publishing a pamphlet on their behalf that year and introducing legislation in 1817 (57 Geo. 3, c. 105 and 130) that enabled savings banks in England, Wales and Ireland to deposit their funds with the National Debt Office at generous interest rates.
2. *in July, 1819, a further Act was made*: Besides the rules mentioned here, this law (59 Geo. 3, c. 128) also required actuaries or 'persons skilled in calculation' to approve new societies' premiums; it also extended to registered friendly societies the privilege of investing their funds with the National Debt Office at the same rate as savings banks.
3. *an Institution was about to be formed*: This (and the discussion that follows) is most likely in reference to the London-based General Benefit Insurance Company, which was the only British insurance company to form between 1819 and 1820 that focused on working-class customers, and which offered all the products mentioned in this pamphlet; it lasted from 1820 until 1854. A similar firm, the Mutual Assurance Benefit Institution, formed in London in 1822.
4. *for which he has to pay a* stamp duty: Under a later law in 1829 (10 Geo. 4, c. 56), companies such as the General Benefit that registered as friendly societies were exempted from the stamp duty.

Johnson, 'The Relative Merits of Life Insurance and Savings Banks'

1. *Bavarian government ... victuals*: A Bavarian poor relief law of 1816, which remained in force until 1869, ruled that 'the free exercise of benevolence between man and man ... must not be allowed to interfere with the general obligations incumbent upon all towards the Poor Law institutions ... nor to contravene the policy of the enactments relating to begging': A. Emminghaus (ed.), *Poor Relief in Different Parts of Europe* (London: Edward Stanford, 1873), p. 23.
2. *conflagrations of San Francisco*: A massive fire on 14 June 1850 destroyed much of San Francisco.
3. *a man in London ... his wife*: This is most likely a reference to Thomas Griffiths Wainwright, who in 1829 allegedly poisoned his sister-in-law Frances Phoebe Abercrombie, whose life he had insured for £18,000. He fled to France before charges could be filed; upon his return to London in 1837, he was sentenced to transportation for forging Bank of England notes.
4. *Girard's and Astor's lives*: Stephen Girard (1750–1831) and John Jacob Astor (1763–1848) were two of the wealthiest Americans during the early Republic.
5. *The poverty of the poor is their destruction*: Proverbs 10:15. The full quotation reads, 'The rich man's wealth is his strong city: the destruction of the poor is their poverty'.
6. *Men's judgments ... all alike*: *Antony and Cleopatra*, Act III, scene xiii.
7. *If a man come ... are ye not partial*: James 2:2–4. The full quotation reads, 'For if there come unto your assembly a man with a gold ring, in goodly apparel, and there come in also a poor

man in vile raiment; and ye have respect to him that weareth the gay clothing, and say unto him, Sit thou here in a good place; and say to the poor, Stand thou there, or sit here under my footstool: are ye not then partial in yourselves, and are become judges of evil thoughts?'

8. *Astor House*: a famous luxury hotel in New York City, on Broadway between Vesey and Barclay Streets, which opened in 1836.

9. *banks are required by their charters*: see e.g. An Act to Incorporate the Albany Savings Bank, passed 24 March 1820: 'it shall be the duty of the trustees of the said bank to regulate the rate of interest to be allowed to the depositors, so that they shall receive a rateable proportion of all the profits of the said bank, after deducting therefrom all necessary expenses authorised by this act to be incurred': *Laws of the State of New York, passed the Forty-Third Session of the Legislature* (Albany, NY: J. Buel, 1820).

Collins, 'Life Insurance'

1. *directors reject notes ... in the street*: Prior to the Civil War, bank notes in the United States were issued by individual banks which promised to redeem them at face value for specie when presented at the originating institution. However, when used in payment for goods or services, or in the payment of debts, these bills often traded at a discount off of their face value (known as shaving); the amount of the discount or shave depended on the reputation of the issuing bank and the distance the bill was trading from that institution. Although technically illegal, banks during this period also often temporarily refused to redeem their bank notes for specie or placed restrictions on this redemption, forcing the bearer to assume the risk of holding the bill or take the penalty of a discount by placing the bill back into circulation.

'Insurance amongst the Working Classes'

1. *three Annual Reports*: These reports were produced by John Tidd Pratt (1797–1870), who was Registrar of Friendly Societies from the inception of the office in 1852 until his death. He had been involved in certifying friendly society rules since 1829.

2. *The Registrar states in one of his Reports*: Report of the Registrar of Friendly Societies in England (London: HMSO, 1857), p. 6.

3. *accounts received from continental countries*: ibid., pp. 23–63.

4. *has taken root ... no other nation*: Unlike the author of this article, who neglects to mention the United States (an obvious point of comparison), Tidd Pratt did refer to American friendly societies in his report – only to complain that the US Secretary of the Interior informed him that 'it was not in his power to furnish information of the character required': ibid., p. 63.

Scudamore, *Life Insurance by Small Payments*

1. *a little tract ... concerning them*: Frank Ives Scudamore, *Post Office Savings' Banks: A Few Plain Words Concerning Them* (London: Emily Faithfull & Co., 1861).

2. *the advantages of the scheme have been appreciated*: Under this plan, life insurance companies charged postal workers up to 20 per cent less than their usual annual rates. The Treasury Office discontinued it in 1871.

Meyer, 'Fraternal Beneficiary Societies in the United States'

1. *Ethical Subcommittee of the Committee of Fifty*: The Committee of Fifty was a group of businessmen and scholars who advocated moderate alcohol consumption in opposition to the ultraist stance of the prohibition movement. They met from 1893 to 1905 with the purpose of investigating and publishing factual information regarding drinking in the United States. The Ethical Subcommittee, charged with investigating the reasons for the popularity of saloons, published in 1901 its *Substitutes for the Saloon*, in which it advocated, among other things, the encouragement of fraternal organizations to provide wholesome activities as alternatives to saloon attendance.

2. *National Fraternal Congress*: Formed in 1896, the National Fraternal Congress was a trade organization for fraternal benefit societies. It was renamed the American Fraternal Alliance in 2011.

3. *abduction of Morgan*: William Morgan was a stonemason who had joined the highly secretive yet extremely well-connected and influential Masonic Lodge in Rochester, New York. Upon later moving to Batavia, New York, and being refused admittance to the local lodge, he decided to write a tell-all book about the secrets of the Masons. In 1826, as word spread that he had found a publisher, he was repeatedly harassed by local law enforcement before being kidnapped and never seen again; it was widely believed by both contemporaries and historians that Morgan was murdered to prevent publication of the book. Yet the officials, sheriffs, lawyers, judges and jurors charged with investigating the case – most of whom were connected to the Masons – did everything in their power to impede the investigation. In response, a highly organized Anti-Masonic Movement quickly emerged to counter the power and influence of the Masons. The Anti-Masons would become a major force in the party politics of the late 1820s, tainting the reputation of not only Masons but all secret fraternal societies of the period.

Nott, 'Statistics of Southern Slave Population'

1. *Dr. G. Emerson*: Gouverneur Emerson (1795–1874) was a prominent Philadelphia physician and founding member of the American Medical Association in 1847.

2. *Dr. Shattuck*: Lemuel Shattuck (1793–1859) helped to found the American Statistical Association in 1839 and published *The Vital Statistics of Boston* two years later. He directed the 1845 Boston census, and would later draft the questionnaires and enumerators' instructions for the 1850 federal census.

3. *on a former occasion, in the Southern Quarterly Review*: Josiah C. Nott, MD, 'Two Lectures on the Natural History of the Caucasian and Negro Races', *Southern Quarterly Review* (April 1845), pp. 372–448; 'Dr. Nott's Reply to "C"', *Southern Quarterly Review* (July 1845), pp. 148–90; and 'Unity of the Human Race – A Letter Addressed to the Editor, on the Unity of the Human Race', *Southern Quarterly Review* (January 1846), pp. 1–57.

4. *Champollion, Young, Vyse, Birch*: Jean-Françoise Champollion (1790–1832), Thomas Young (1773–1829), Richard William Howard Vyse (1784–1853) and Samuel Birch (1813–85) were all Egyptologists.

5. *Baron Bunsen and Lepsius*: Karl Richard Lepsius (1810–84) was a Prussian Egyptologist who led a major expedition to Egypt in 1842–6; his findings would later be published in the twelve-volume *Monuments from Egypt and Ethiopia* (1849–58). Christian Karl Josias von Bunsen (1791–1860), a Prussian nobleman and ambassador to the British monarchy, was a major promoter of the Lepsius expedition.

6. *The good old Bishop of Blois (H. Gregoire)*: In addition to being a French revolutionary leader, Henri Grégoire (1750–1831), bishop of Blois, was an abolitionist and advocate of equality for blacks and Jews. In 1808 he published *De la littérature des nègres, ou Recherches sur leurs facultés intellectuelles, leurs qualités morales et leur littérature* (*An Enquiry Concerning the Intellectual and Moral Faculties, and Literature of Negroes: Followed with an Account of the Life and Works of Fifteen Negroes and Mulattoes, Distinguished in Science, Literature, and Arts*), in which he argued that racial differences were the result of historical circumstances and not due to innate characteristics.

7. *Rankin, in his 'Visit to Sierra Leone'*: F. Harrison Rankin, *The White Man's Grave: A Visit to Sierra Leone, in 1834* (London: R. Bentley, 1836).

8. *Dr. Niles*: In 1827 Dr Nathaniel Niles published *Medical Statistics, or a Comparative View of the Mortality in New York, Philadelphia, Baltimore, and Boston, for a Series of Years: Including Comparisons of the Mortality of Whites and Blacks in the Two Former Cities: and of Whites, Free Blacks, and Slaves in Baltimore.*

9. *Mr. Lyell*: Sir Charles Lyell (1769–1849) was a British geologist who wrote about his visits to the United States in *Travels in North America* (1841–2) and *Second Visit to the United States* (published posthumously in 1855). During his travels in the South, he concluded that blacks could only become civilized through contact with and the influence of whites.

10. Colored Home: The Colored Home and Hospital (later renamed the Lincoln Home and Hospital) was established in 1839 on 65th Street (near First Street) to care for the sick and poor black residents of New York City.

11. *Dr. S. G. Morton*: Dr Samuel George Morton (1799–1851) was a professor of anatomy at Pennsylvania College (now Gettysburg College) and a prominent phrenologist. He published *Crania Americana, or, a Comparative View of the Skulls of Various Aboriginal Nations of North and South America* (1839) and then *Crania Aegyptiaca, or, Observations on Egyptian Ethnography, Derived from Anatomy, History, and the Monuments* (1844), in which he divided humans into races with characteristics based on their cranial measurements.

12. *Richards' physical history of man*: This probably refers to James Cowles Prichard's (1786–1848) *Researches into the Physical History of Man* (1813) – republished in two volumes as *Researches into the Physical History of Mankind* (1826) and then again in five volumes (1836–47) – which offered a racial theory of heredity.

13. *Lawrence*: Sir William Lawrence (1783–1867) was a prominent surgeon who specialized in the diseases of the eye. Beginning in 1815 he gave a series of controversial lectures that were published in 1819 as *Lectures on Physiology, Zoology, and the Natural History of Man*.

14. *Many are consequently attacked by pleurisy*: Pleurisy is an inflammation of the chest cavity around the lungs, which causes pain when breathing.

15. *the wandering Circassians*: The Circassians were the indigenous inhabitants of the Caucasus region, located between the Black Sea and Caspian Sea. From 1817 to 1864 the Russian Empire invaded this region, annexing much of the northwestern part of the Caucasus. Large portions of the Circassian people either fled or were deported during this period, with the vast majority crossing the Black Sea and settling in the Ottoman Empire.

16. *Baron Larrey*: Baron Dominique Jean Larrey (1766–1842) was a French military surgeon during the Napoleonic Wars. He wrote about the peoples of the Caucasus in *Mémoires de Chirurgie Militaire, et Campagnes* (*Memoirs of Military Surgery, and Campaigns of the French Armies*), published in five volumes in 1812–17.

Du Bois (ed.), *Some Efforts of American Negroes for their Own Social Betterment*

1. *Laidlaw, 2nd Sociological Canvass, 1897*: Walter Laidlaw, *Second Sociological Canvass (Report B)* (New York: G. F. Nesbitt and Co., 1897); commissioned by the New York Federation of Churches.
2. *DuBois, The Philadelphia Negro*: W. E. B. DuBois, *The Philadelphia Negro: A Social Study* (Philadelphia, PA: University of Pennsylvania Press, 1899); apparently still in press when this document was published.
3. *James M. Colson*: James M. Colson, Jr (*c.* 1858–1912), the son of a Virginia free black, graduated from Dartmouth College in 1881 and taught at the Virginia Normal and Collegiate Institute in the 1890s; he later served as principal of the Dinwiddie Normal School, also in Virginia.

Tarn, 'Some Notes on Life Assurance in Greater Britain'

1. *Canada Life … Society*: Based in Hamilton, Ontario, the Canada Life Assurance Company was founded by the banker Hugh C. Baker, who served as president, actuary and general manager until his death in 1859; the Australian Mutual Provident, based in Sydney, flourished under its actuary Morris Alexander Black, who took over in 1867.
2. *Colonial Life Assurance Company*: This company formed after Standard Life's actuary, William Thomson, discovered that his firm was overcharging its colonial customers. He convinced two of his directors, George Patton and David Smith, along with Smith's legal partner James Kinnear, to promote a new firm, with premiums based on colonial mortality data that Thomson had privately collected.
3. *J.I.A., xxiv, 373*: This citation is incorrect; the first published mortality statistics from the Barbados Mutual were by George F. Hardy and Howard J. Rothery, 'On the Mortality of Assured Lives in the West Indies (Chiefly Barbados)', *Journal of the Institute of Actuaries*, 27 (1888), pp. 161–95, which is referred to in the second citation.
4. *Colonel Templeton, C.M.G.*: John Montgomery Templeton (1840–1908).
5. *Mr. J. H. Richardson*: See Richardson, 'State Insurance in New Zealand', *Transactions of the Second International Congress of Actuaries* (1899), pp. 195–219.
6. *interview by a leading American insurance paper*: This interview appeared in the *Spectator*, 22 June 1893.

Burn, 'Industrial Life Assurance'

1. *We have had … or annually*: This excerpt from the *Liverpool Chronicle* was reprinted for an American audience by *Hunt's Merchants' Magazine*, 24 (1851), p. 521, suggesting that the date of publication was 1851 and not 1849. The brochure cited has not been located, but its author was possibly Joseph Bancroft Reade (not Beade) (1801–70), a Buckinghamshire vicar and amateur scientist; *Hunt's* identifies him as 'M.A., F.R.S.', which matches Reade's credentials.
2. *Clothing life assurance … better classes*: British Industry Life Assurance Company and Family Friendly Society, prospectus. Cornelius Walford claimed that the company was 'understood to have been founded by some of the men foremost in the management of the late Fergus O'Connor's land scheme': C. Walford, *Insurance Cyclppaedia* (London: Layton, 1871–80), vol. 1 (1871), p. 380. It transferred its business to the Prudential in 1860.

3. *a tea meeting at the Town Hall of Birmingham*: See the report of the meeting in *Reynolds's Newspaper*, 9 October 1853, and a reply by the British Industry's secretary, Michael O'Grady, in the 16 October issue; *Reynolds's* continued to run reports on the British Industry through the following February.

4. *an ordinary Assurance Company*: Burn is referring to the Prudential, which started business in 1848 as the Prudential Investment, Loan and Assurance Association.

5. *In 1864 ... extremely doubtful*: See e.g. *Hansard's Parliamentary Debates*, 3rd ser., 173 (1864), cols 1565–81. The debate is discussed in Dennett, *A Sense of Security*, pp. 58–68. The burial society referred to is most likely the Royal Liver, which also came under attack from Gladstone.

6. *The Bill above referred to was duly passed*: the Government Annuities Act of 1864 (27 & 28 Vict c. 43).

7. *diagrams to represent them*: These 'diagrams' (not included here) were bar graphs, with years along the horizontal axes and number of policies, amount insured, assets and claims along the vertical axes. In the final graph, claims paid are aggregated annually, as described in the text.

8. *our soldiers and volunteers in South Africa*: See the review of Frederick Schooling and Edward A. Rusher, *The Mortality Experience of the Imperial Forces during the War in South Africa*, in Volume 3 of this collection.

9. *Mr. Eady ... in June last*: Arthur M. Eedy, *Industrial Life Assurance* (Sydney: Insurance Institute of Victoria, 1901). Eedy was General Secretary of the Citizens' Life Assurance Company in Sydney.

10. *maximum amount ... Friendly Societies Act*: In Britain, the Friendly Societies Act of 1850 (13 and 14 Vict. c. 115) limited coverage on children to the cost of the funeral; this was increased to £6 and £10 (as discussed by Burns) by the Friendly Societies Act of 1875 (38 and 39 Vict. c. 60, sect. 28), which remained in force until further legislation in 1923 raised the limit to £15 for children over the age of three.

11. *In 1890 ... Archbishop of York*: *Report from the Select Committee of the House of Lords on Children's Life Insurance Bill ...* (London: Herbert Hansard and Son, 1890). The Bill was introduced into the House of Lords by William Connor Magee (1821–91). Born in Cork, Magee was consecrated as bishop of Peterborough on Benjamin Disraeli's recommendation in 1868, and appointed archbishop of York in January 1891, four months before his death.

Williams, *Life Insurance of the Poor*

1. *Collecting Societies and Industrial Assurance Companies Act*: 59 and 60 Vict. c. 26.

2. *Assurance Companies Act 1909*: 9 Edw. VII c. 49.

3. *largest industrial insurance company*: i.e. the Prudential Life Assurance Company.

4. *they have a trade union in some form*: The National Union of Life Assurance Agents formed in 1884 to represent the interests of agents who worked for collecting societies and industrial insurance companies other than the Prudential; the National Association of Prudential Assurance Agents formed in 1893. Both were still in existence in 1912, but qualified as 'weak' unions, with memberships between 10 and 20 per cent of the total number of agents.

5. *it will collect some Insurance Act contributions*: The Post Office acted as the default option for those beneficiaries under the 1911 National Insurance Act (1 and 2 Geo. V c. 55)

who did not sign up for benefits administered by insurance companies, friendly societies or trade unions; this comprised less than 3 per cent of the total in 1912.

6. *Bills of Sale Acts, 1878 and 1882*: The Bills of Sale Acts of 1878 and 1882 (41 and 42 Vict. c. 31; 45 and 46 Vict. c. 43) reinforced an earlier law from 1854; all were designed to protect consumers against fraudulent contracts, typically involving credit.

7. *The Co-operative movement*: The Co-operative Insurance Society formed in Rochdale in 1867 to provide fire and accident coverage for members' property; it added a life insurance branch in 1886. After a slow start, this branch experienced rapid growth in membership after 1910.

Hoffman, *Life Insurance of Children*

1. *B. S. Rowntree's book on 'Poverty'*: Benjamin Seebohm Rowntree (1871–1954) was a businessman in York, England. His *Poverty, A Study of Town Life* was an investigation of the causes and effects of poverty in his hometown.

2. *Mr. Charles Booth*: Booth (1840–1916) was a philanthropist and businessman most widely known for his investigation of urban poverty, published in seventeen volumes between 1889 and 1903 as *Life and Labour of the People in London*.

3. *Pauperism and the Endowment of Old Age*: The full title of this work is *Pauperism: a Picture, and the Endowment of Old Age: an Argument* (London and New York: MacMillan and Co., 1892); the quotation is on p. 156.

4. *Quoting the words of Lord Hobhouse*: Sir Arthur Hobhouse, *The Dead Hand, Addresses on the Subject of Endowments and Settlements of Property* (London: Chatto and Windus, 1880).

5. *Mackay's 'State and Charity'*: Thomas Mackay, *The State and Charity* (London: Macmillan and Co., 1898), p. 44.

6. *Helen Bosanquet*: Bosanquet was a social reformer and a leader of the Charity Organisation Society in London. The following quote is from *The Strength of the People: A Study in Social Economics* (1902), p. 263.

7. *the important matter ... does it in*: Bosanquet, *The Strength of the People*, p. 50.

'The Equitable Life Assurance Society of the United States', advertisement

1. *leading Actuaries in London*: The three actuaries who 'endorsed' the Equitable were A. H. Bailey (London Assurance), T. B. Sprague (Scottish Equitable) and Robert Tucker (Pelican). They responded to questions posed by Alexander Munkittrick, which he framed in consultation with the British actuary R. P. Hardy: Equitable Life Assurance Society of the United States, *A Statement and Opinions Thereon by Leading Actuaries* (London: C. and E. Layton, 1873).

2. *ALEXANDER MUNKITTRICK*: Munkittrick (1809–92) served as Equitable Life's London manager from 1870 until his retirement in 1881. He had previously been President of the Guardian Fire Insurance Company of New York; he then worked for the Equitable for one year as its agent in Manchester before moving to London.

Allen, *There is Dust in John's Eyes*

1. *two American Life Offices*: These were the Equitable Life Assurance Society of New York, which started conducting business in England in 1867 and opened a London branch in 1869, and New York Life, which set up a general agency in London in 1870.

2. *four British Companies*: These are, in order of appearance in the table, the Equity and Law (est. 1844), London and Provincial Law (est. 1845), United Kingdom Temperance (est. 1840) and Law Life (est. 1823): cf. *Statements and Abstracts of Reports Deposited with Board of Trade under Life Assurance Companies Act* (London: HMSO, 1882), pp. 378–86; ibid. (1881), pp. 135, 170. Three of the four were 'legal' offices, which tended to have higher yields and lower expense rates (and correspondingly higher bonuses) than most other British firms, since their shareholders, mostly lawyers, attracted business without needing to go through agents and had access to better investment opportunities. The United Kingdom Temperance also paid higher than average bonuses owing to its high proportion of policyholders who were abstainers.

3. *two American Companies*: 'Office No. 5' in the table is New York Life and 'Office No. 6' is Equitable of New York, and the figures are for the year ending 1878: cf. *Eleventh Annual Report of the Insurance Commissioner of the State of California* (Sacramento, CA: F. P. Thompson, 1879), p. 98.

4. *THE GAME OF TONTINE*: See the discussion of tontine insurance in Volume 2 of this collection.

5. Woolsey's International Law ... illegal and void: Theodore D. Woolsey, *Introduction to the Study of International Law: Designed as an Aid in Teaching, and in Historical Studies*, 3rd edn (New York: Charles Scribner & Co., 1871), pp. 199–200 (emphasis added by Allen).

6. *It is, however ... shall not operate*: This clause is from an Equitable of New York policy: see *Insurance Times*, 15 (1882), p. 344.

Book review of *There is Dust in John's Eyes*

1. *arbitrating a quarrel ... the orphan*: This is most likely a reference to the successful resolution in 1872 of the 'Alabama claims', whereby the United States received compensation from Britain for damages caused by British warships used by the Confederacy in the Civil War.

'The Mutual's English Business'

1. *D. C. Haldeman*: Donald Carmichael Haldeman (1859–1930) was born in Pennsylvania and moved to London in 1880 to work for the Equitable of New York's branch there, then took over as general manager of the Mutual of New York's London office in 1886. In 1906 he became life manager for the North British and Mercantile Insurance Company (which did succeed in absorbing much of the Mutual's British business), where he remained until his retirement in 1920.

2. *The text of the circular*: 'Mutual Policy Holders Rush to North British: Eager to be Reinsured by the English Company', *New York Times*, 15 May 1906.

LIST OF SOURCES

Text	Source
Richard Morgan, *Familiar Observations on Life Insurance* (1841), Chapter 4	University of Edinburgh Library, shelfmark Fact: Pamphlet file, vol. 67.
Life Insurance Offices, New and Speculative, with a Table of the Inducements Held Out by Each of the Existing Offices (1846), excerpt	Baker Library, Harvard Business School, Goldsmiths'-Kress Library of Economic Literature microfilm series, no. 34685.
'Securitas', 'Life Insurance', *Connecticut Courant* (1833)	26 August 1833, p. 2.
T. R. Jencks, 'Life Insurance in the United States, Number I', *Hunt's Merchants' Magazine and Commercial Review* (1843)	(February 1843), pp. 109–31.
T. R. Jencks, 'Life Insurance in the United States, Number II', *Hunt's Merchants' Magazine and Commercial Review* (1843)	(March 1843), pp. 227–40.
William Frend, *Rock Life Assurance Company* (1809)	Baker Library, Harvard Business School, Goldsmiths'-Kress Library of Economic Literature microfilm series, no. 21539
An Address from the President and Directors of the Pennsylvania Company for Insurances on Lives and Granting Annuities to the Inhabitants of the United States, upon the Subject of the Beneficial Objects of that Institution (1814)	*Early American Imprints* digital collection; Readex, a division of NewsBank, Inc.
Proposals and Rates of the Standard Life Assurance Company (1833)	Baker Library, Harvard Business School, Goldsmiths'-Kress Library of Economic Literature microfilm series, no. 28064.
William Bard, *A Letter to David E. Evans, Esquire, of Batavia, on Life Insurance* (1832)	Heidelberg University, Beeghly Library, shelfmark HG8773 .B24.
Life Insurance: Its Principles, Operations and Benefits, as Presented by the North Carolina Mutual Life Insurance Company (1849)	Duke University, Rubenstein Library, shelfmark 15939 c.1.
John Freestone, *Where to Insure: An Impartial and Independent Guide* (1890), excerpt	British Library, shelfmark 8228.bb.23.

Text	Source
Charter of the Corporation for the Relief of the Widows and Children of Clergymen (1769), excerpt	*Early American Imprints* digital collection; Readex, a division of NewsBank, Inc.
'Life Insurance', *Religious Intelligencer* (1835)	18 July 1835, p. 103.
'Life Insurance – Ministers', *Christian Secretary* (1847)	26 February 1847, p. 2.
'Life Insurance – A Scruple', *Christian Secretary* (1847)	12 March 1847, p. 2.
'Life Insurance of Ministers', *Christian Secretary* (1847)	23 April 1847, p. 2.
'Prospectus of the Dissenters' and General Life and Fire Assurance Company', *Eclectic Review* (1839), excerpts	University of Michigan Libraries, shelfmark AP4 .E19.
'Life Insurance', *Macon Weekly Telegraph* (1838)	8 January 1838, p. 3.
John Neal, 'Life Assurance', *Columbian Lady's and Gentleman's Magazine* (1846)	(January 1846), pp. 8–12.
Arthur Scratchley, *Observations on Life Assurance Societies, and Savings Banks* (1851), excerpt	University of Oxford, Bodleian Library, shelfmark 232.a.148.
Arthur Reade, 'Before the Wedding Ring', *Policyholder: An Insurance Journal* (1885)	16 (September 1885), pp. 297–8.
Benefit Societies versus Saving Banks and Insurance Companies: An Address to the Members of Benefit Societies and the Public in General (1822)	Baker Library, Harvard Business School, Goldsmiths'-Kress Library of Economic Literature microfilm series, no. 23585.4.
A. B. Johnson, 'The Relative Merits of Life Insurance and Savings Banks', *Hunt's Merchants' Magazine and Commercial Review* (1851)	(January 1851), pp. 670–7.
Joseph B. Collins, 'Life Insurance', *Hunt's Merchants' Magazine and Commercial Review* (1852)	(February 1852), pp. 196–8.
'Insurance amongst the Working Classes', *Economist* (1858)	2 October 1858, pp. 1090–1.
Frank Ives Scudamore, *Life Insurance by Small Payments: A Few Plain Words Concerning It* (1861)	University of Edinburgh Library, shelfmark Fact: Pamplet file, vol. 35.
George D. Eldridge, 'Assessment Life Insurance', *North American Review* (1890)	(October 1890), pp. 507–10.
B. H. Meyer, 'Fraternal Beneficiary Societies in the United States', *American Journal of Sociology* (1901)	6 (1901), pp. 646–61.
Josiah C. Nott, 'Statistics of Southern Slave Population, with Especial Reference to Life Insurance', *DeBow's Commercial Review* (1847)	University of California Libraries, shelfmark HF1 .D2.
W. E. Burghardt Du Bois (ed.), *Some Efforts of American Negroes for their Own Social Betterment* (1898), excerpts	Stanford University Libraries, shelfmark 325.26 .A881 NO.3.

Text	Source
Arthur Wyndham Tarn, 'Some Notes on Life Assurance in Greater Britain', *Journal of the Institute of Actuaries* (1899), excerpt	Stanford University Libraries, shelfmark 368.06 .I59.
Joseph Burn, 'Industrial Life Assurance', *Journal of Federated Insurance Institutes* (1902)	University of Michigan Libraries, shelfmark HG 8016 .C49.
J. F. Williams, *Life Insurance of the Poor: An Illumination of Economic Disadvantage* (1912)	British Library, shelfmark 08225.h.58.(8).
John F. Dryden, 'The Social Economy of Industrial Insurance: A Lecture Delivered before the Senior Class of Yale University, 1904' (1909)	University of Michigan Libraries, shelfmark HG 8769 .D8.
Frederick Hoffman, *Life Insurance of Children* (1903)	Smith College Libraries, shelfmark 368.973 H675.
[Pelican Life Insurance Company], 'Life Insurance. To Parents, Guardians, and Others, Desirous of Securing a Provision against Sudden Death', *New-York Evening Post* (1808)	13 July 1808, p. 3.
'The Equitable Life Assurance Society of the United States', advertisement, *Insurance Record* (1874)	British Library, shelfmark 1874 LON 182 [1874] NPL.
Joseph Allen, *There is Dust in John's Eyes; or, American and British Life Insurance Offices Contrasted* (1882)	British Library, shelfmark 8229.d.28. (3.).
Book review of *There is Dust in John's Eyes*, *Post Magazine* (1882)	St John's University, Kathryn and Shelby Cullom Davies Library, shelfmark Insurance Periodicals.
'The Mutual's English Business', *Independent* (1906)	17 May 1906, p. 1179.

For Product Safety Concerns and Information please contact our EU
representative GPSR@taylorandfrancis.com Taylor & Francis Verlag GmbH,
Kaufingerstraße 24, 80331 München, Germany

Printed and bound by CPI Group (UK) Ltd, Croydon, CR0 4YY
08/05/2025
01864484-0003